Three Consuls

For two generations after independence, Americans viewed the Mediterranean as the new commercial frontier. From common sailors to wealthy merchants, hundreds of Americans flocked to live and work there. Documenting the eventful lives of three American consuls and their families at the ports of Tangier, Livorno, and Alicante, Lawrence A. Peskin portrays the rise and fall of America's Mediterranean community from 1776 to 1840. We learn how three ordinary merchants became American consuls; how they created flourishing communities; built social and business networks; and interacted with Jews, Muslims, and Catholics. When the bubble burst during the Napoleonic Wars and the War of 1812, American communities across the Mediterranean rapidly declined, resulting in the demise of the consuls' fortunes and health. A unique look into early American diplomacy, *Three Consuls* provides a much needed overview of early consular service that highlights the importance of US activities in the Mediterranean region.

LAWRENCE A. PESKIN is Professor of History at Morgan State University. He is a leading scholar of the early national United States in international context, with a focus on the Mediterranean world. He is the author of *Captives and Countrymen: Barbary Slavery and the American Public, 1785–1816* and co-author of *America and the World: Culture, Commerce, Conflict.*

Three Consuls

Capitalism, Empire, and the Rise and Fall of America's Mediterranean Community, 1776–1840

LAWRENCE A. PESKIN

Morgan State University

CAMBRIDGE
UNIVERSITY PRESS

CAMBRIDGE
UNIVERSITY PRESS

Shaftesbury Road, Cambridge CB2 8EA, United Kingdom

One Liberty Plaza, 20th Floor, New York, NY 10006, USA

477 Williamstown Road, Port Melbourne, VIC 3207, Australia

314–321, 3rd Floor, Plot 3, Splendor Forum, Jasola District Centre,
New Delhi – 110025, India

103 Penang Road, #05–06/07, Visioncrest Commercial, Singapore 238467

Cambridge University Press is part of Cambridge University Press & Assessment,
a department of the University of Cambridge.

We share the University's mission to contribute to society through the pursuit of
education, learning and research at the highest international levels of excellence.

www.cambridge.org
Information on this title: www.cambridge.org/9781009444620

DOI: 10.1017/9781009444606

When citing this work, please include a reference to the DOI 10.1017/9781009444606

First published 2024

Printed in the United Kingdom by TJ Books Limited, Padstow Cornwall

A catalogue record for this publication is available from the British Library.

Library of Congress Cataloging-in-Publication Data
NAMES: Peskin, Lawrence A., 1966– author.
TITLE: Three consuls : capitalism, empire, and the rise and fall of America's
Mediterranean community, 1776–1840 / Lawrence A Peskin, Morgan State University.
DESCRIPTION: Cambridge, United Kingdom ; New Yok, NY : Cambridge University
Press, 2024. | Includes bibliographical references and index.
IDENTIFIERS: LCCN 2024010715 | ISBN 9781009444620 (hardback) | ISBN
9781009444590 (paperback) | ISBN 9781009444606 (ebook)
SUBJECTS: LCSH: Consuls – United States – Biography. | Americans – Mediterranean
Region – History. | Mediterranean Region – Foreign relations – United States. | United
States – Foreign relations – Mediterranean Region. | Mediterranean Region – Foreign
relations. | United States – Foreign relations – To 1865.
CLASSIFICATION: LCC DE96.5 .P47 2024 | DDC 327.73009–dc23/eng/20240605
LC record available at https://lccn.loc.gov/2024010715

ISBN 978-1-009-44462-0 Hardback

Contents

Figures

Maps

Tables

Acknowledgments

As befits its focus on long-serving cosmopolitan consuls, this book has taken more than a decade to research and write and has depended on the generosity and helpfulness of institutions, scholars, and others on six continents. It may be a cliché to say so, but it gives me great pleasure to acknowledge their helpfulness after all this time and, as is not only customary but true, to absolve them of any errors of fact or interpretation found herein.

Institutional support came mainly in the form of time and money. Morgan State University, besides providing a congenial home base, generously granted me a sabbatical, course reductions, travel grant, and a research grant through the Benjamin Quarles Foundation. A National Humanities Endowment Award for Faculty at Historically Black Colleges and Universities was instrumental in providing time and funding to do research in Spain. A Visiting Fellowship from the Australian National University provided more time and allowed me to present ideas in their early stages to helpful audiences. A Mayers Fellowship from the Huntington Museum and Library allowed me access to the papers of William Eaton. The American Institute for Maghrib Studies' TALIM Fellowship funded research in Tangier and Gibraltar. Finally, I am grateful to the Université Côte d'Azur for supporting my travel to Nice.

Archivists and librarians have offered crucial assistance with remarkable patience. Certainly, this project would not have even begun without assistance from the archivists and staff at the National Archives in College Park, MD. I also benefitted from the assistance and good cheer of James Greene and Connie King at the Library Company of Philadelphia, help from Jennifer Ballantine Perera and Christopher Tavares at the Garrison

Library in Gibraltar, Maria del Olmo Ibáñez of the Archivo Histórico Provincial de Alicante and Susana Llorens Ortuño of the Archivo Municipal de Alicante.

I would not have been able to begin my research in Alicante without the generous assistance and hospitality of Rafael Zurita of the University of Alicante. I am also grateful to him for introducing me to Dr. Antonio J. Piqueres Diez whose incredible skill and dedication as a research assistant allowed me access to a wealth of data hidden in obscure notarial notebooks and other records in Alicante's archives. At the American Legation in Tangier John Davidson and Yhtimiad Bouziane provided welcome assistance. Also in Tangier, I am grateful to Elena Prentice for inviting me to her home and spending a fruitful afternoon discussing the old American community. Karim Bejjit graciously hosted me at Abdelmalek Essaadi University in Tétouan and offered assistance on all things Moroccan. At Morgan State, I benefitted from research assistance conducted by Candace Jackson Gray, Emeka Anaedozie, and Damon J. Turner.

The often-serendipitous generosity of individuals who shared information they had come across regarding the three consuls is enough to restore faith in the academy and humanity. Among those generous souls I must acknowledge Tamara P. Thornton of the University of Buffalo; Luis R. Dunoyer of Cartagena, Colombia Diego Hernandez of Bethesda, Maryland; Christine Heyrman of the University of Delaware; Brett Goodin of Shanghai Tech University; Emil Kaukonen of Åbo Akademi University in Turku, Finland; Silvia Marzagalli of the Université Côte d'Azur; Guadalupe Carrasco-Gonzalez of the University of Cádiz; and Salvador García Castañeda of the Ohio State University. I am also grateful to Silvia and Guadelupe for their hospitality and assistance in, respectively, Nice and Madrid and to Professor García Castañeda for putting me in touch with helpful individuals in Alicante. A number of people also offered useful criticism of early drafts including Cathy Matson, Holly Brewer, Rick Bell, Matt Mulcahy, Matthew Hale, Kelly Gray, and Christine Heyrman. I am also indebted to the anonymous readers for the Cambridge University Press and, most importantly, Cecelia Cancellaro, who showed much faith in this book and shepherded it efficiently from messy manuscript to finished project. I wrote this book in Baltimore, Cleveland, and McHenry, MD, and I am grateful to friends and family in all those places who offered support and assistance in all sorts of non-academic matters.

MAP O.I The Mediterranean, from William Jowett, *Christian Researches in the Mediterranean, from MDCCCXV to MDCCCXXI* (London: R. Watts, 1824). (Map redrawn by David McCutcheon FBCart.S, www.dvdmaps.co.uk)

Introduction

This book tells the story of the birth, growth, and decline of the early American community in the Mediterranean world. Despite recent interest in American history outside of US borders, this is a subject that has received very little attention. The only monograph to address it, James A. Field's *America and the Mediterranean World, 1776–1882,* was written nearly sixty years ago and focused primarily on issues of diplomacy. While some recent work has dealt with specific topics in the Mediterranean world such as naval activity, trading networks, missionaries, and above all the Barbary Wars and the interaction with Islam, these authors have not conceptualized their topics as particularly Mediterranean. In fact, the most authoritative recent study of the Barbary Wars is subtitled "American Independence *in the Atlantic World*"![1]

---

[1] James A. Field, *America and the Mediterranean World, 1776–1882* (Princeton University Press, 1969); Frank Lambert, *The Barbary Wars: American Independence in the Atlantic World* (New York: Hill and Wang, 2005). A number of essays and essay collections have touched on the topic without evaluating it as a whole. See Silvia Marzagalli, James R. Sofka, and John J. McCusker, *Rough Waters: American Involvement with the Mediterranean in the Eighteenth and Nineteenth Centuries* (Newfoundland: International Maritime Economic History Association, 2010). For work discussing aspects of the American experience in the Mediterranean, see Luca Codignola, *Blurred Nationalities Across the Atlantic: Traders, Priests, and Their Kin Travelling between North America and the Italian Peninsula, 1763–1846* (University of Toronto Press, 2019); Axel Korner, *America in Italy: The United States in the Political Thought and Imagination of the Risorgimento, 1763–1865* (Princeton University Press, 2017); Brett Goodin, *From Captives to Consuls: Three Sailors in Barbary and Their Self-Making across the Early American Republic, 1770–1840* (Baltimore: Johns Hopkins University Press, 2020); Priscilla H. and Richard S. Roberts, *Thomas Barclay (1728–1793): Consul in France, Diplomat in Barbary* (Bethlehem, PA: Lehigh University Press,

Yet surely since Fernand Braudel, at least, historians can agree that the Mediterranean littoral has a coherent and distinctive culture that is easily differentiated from that of the Atlantic world. These features include its unique geography, agriculture, and human culture. For the purposes of this study some of the important aspects of Mediterranean-ness include a diverse non-Protestant population, relative lack of British domination, and, perhaps most importantly, well-defined trading networks consisting largely of fish, flour, wine, and West Indian exports. As this book demonstrates, a distinct network of Americans developed in the Mediterranean, or actually in what Braudel defines as the western section of the Mediterranean, forming a ring from Gibraltar through Morocco, Algiers, western Italy, eastern Spain, and back to Gibraltar. Americans in this region formed a social and business community. They became tightly linked through trade, correspondence, and family and social connections.

***

Perhaps the most important thing about the Mediterranean world for Americans was that it was not the Atlantic, which had been defined by restrictive British mercantilism and continued to be controlled by a British government that was hostile to the United States. After the American Revolution, the path to creating a new polity had been relatively straightforward, beginning with the Declaration of Independence and concluding with the ratification of the new Constitution roughly thirteen years later. But the path toward an independent national economy was less clear. The colonies had long been prosperous, so much so that Benjamin Franklin famously joked (probably with a straight face) that the colonial economy would eventually surpass that of the mother country and the relationship of dependency would be reversed.[2] Nevertheless, at the time of the

2008); Lawrence Peskin, *Captives and Countrymen: Barbary Slavery and the American Public, 1785–1816* (Baltimore: Johns Hopkins University Press, 2009); Christine Leigh Heyrman, *American Apostles: When Evangelicals Entered the World of Islam* (New York: Hill and Wang, 2015); Iván Jaksić, *The Hispanic World and American Intellectual Life, 1820–1880* (New York: Palgrave McMillan, 2007); Richard Kagan, ed., *Spain in the United States: The Origins of Hispanism in the United States* (Urbana: University of Illinois Press, 2002); Richard L. Kagan, *The Spanish Craze: America's Fascination with the Hispanic World* (Lincoln: University of Nebraska Press, 2019); James G. Lydon, *Fish and Flour for Gold, 1600–1800: Southern Europe in the Colonial Balance of Payments* (Philadelphia: Library Company of Philadelphia e-publication, 2008).

[2] Leonard W. Labaree, ed., *The Papers of Benjamin Franklin* (New Haven: Yale University Press, 1960) II: 182.

Revolution the colonial economy was far from independent of the mother country. Years of colonial dependency resulted in a stunted manufacturing sector, so that Americans imported a large proportion of necessary finished goods from Britain. Americans celebrated their nation's agricultural fecundity, but settlement did not extend much to the west of the Atlantic plain, and despite the victory in the Revolution, western expansion faced stiff opposition from Native Americans and potentially from European powers as well. American merchants had sailed around the globe with little difficulty under the protection of the British flag, but that was no longer possible after the Revolution, and, in fact, Britain consciously sought to limit American navigation.

The question Americans faced in 1776 was one with which they would grapple for many decades: What would be the structure of the new national economy? Two basic possibilities would emerge. One was the development of a continental territorial nation that would seek so far as possible to provide for itself through exploitation of abundant agricultural lands and the development of a viable manufacturing sector and which might be considered a precursor of industrial capitalism. The second possibility was a cosmopolitan trading nation modeled on the Dutch or British that would seek so far as possible to expand into overseas markets, to trade for profit and subsistence and which might be considered merchant capitalism. In theory these models were not mutually exclusive, and both models assumed state support for what might today be considered private ventures. In supporting merchant capitalism, the new nation, despite having revolted against mercantilistic measures such as customs duties and admiralty courts, would replicate many of the structures of the British Empire, including the consular service.

Although Americans, as part of the British Empire, had long been active in overseas trade (unlike domestic manufacturing), after the Revolution the United States needed to do a great deal in order to restructure its commercial sector. The new nation could boast a large number of active merchant trading houses, both within the United States and in overseas ports. American ships and captains had long sailed routes connecting these places. But this trade had always depended on British capital and, more importantly, protection offered by the British Navy and mercantile restrictions. After the Revolution, the apparatus of the British system no longer supported American commerce and, in fact, at times appeared to be set on destroying it. In addition to countering any active interference from Great Britain, the new nation now needed to provide the basic support to commerce that was customary among nations. This infrastructure included at a minimum a system of flags, customs houses, official documents, and officials such as consuls and ministers that could protect American ships and sailors from ordinary problems such as disease, captivity, lost cargo, and commercial disputes that mariners and traders from all nations constantly faced. Additionally, it usually included a navy to protect the nation's ships from hostile navies or pirates. It was also clear that with the postrevolutionary hindrances to the old trading routes that went through Great Britain and its colonial possessions, the United States needed to develop new trading networks that would provide access to commodities and capital. Considering the new alliance with France, the proximity of the Iberian Peninsula and nearby points, and the general prosperity of southern European trade, development of Mediterranean networks was the obvious course to pursue.

This book traces the development of these networks within the framework of a developing American identity, economy, and state. These networks were multinucleated structures centering on American consuls in the various Mediterranean ports and ultimately encompassing hundreds if not thousands of Americans ranging from common sailors through captains, merchants, travelers, consuls, and ministers (ambassadors). Historians of the early republic have generally taken two approaches toward American identity in this era. On the one hand, they have viewed it through the lens of Benedict Anderson's work, which basically sees shared stories and beliefs as crucial in creating national identity. This is a view that works particularly well for the United States, which from the start emphasized the narrative of the American Revolution and its founding documents. Recently, other historians have viewed experiences overseas as being crucial to identity formation, including definitions of territorial citizenship that were necessary to differentiate American sailors and merchants from other nationalities, especially the British.[3] It does not appear to me that, in the Mediterranean at least, either approach is entirely sufficient, although it is certainly true that shared political ideology and notions of national citizenship both played a part in determining American identity there. What proved most important,

---

[3] Benedict Anderson, *Imagined Communities: Reflections on the Origins and Spread of Nationalism* (New York: Verso, 1983); Nathan Perl-Rosenthal, *Citizen Sailors: Becoming American in the Age of Revolution* (Cambridge: Harvard University Press, 2015); Matthew Taylor Raffety, *The Republic Afloat: Law, Honor, and Citizenship in Maritime America* (University of Chicago Press, 2013); Brian Rouleau. *With Sails Whitening Every Sea: Mariners and the Making of an American Maritime Empire* (Ithaca: Cornell University Press, 2015).

however, was the creation of the very networks described in this book. Individuals who were tied to the American community through commercial or social bonds often shared a republican political ideology and were often official citizens of the United States, but not all of them necessarily shared these traits. What they all did share was a strong connection to the new nation and to each other due to their role within the American Mediterranean community; and, in developing this community, they also developed a new sense of American identity within the region. In short, the Mediterranean networks discussed here were not only defined by identity with America, but they also determined American identity in the region.

***

Almost without debate, Americans moved toward an increased state and commercial presence in the Mediterranean world after 1776. Protecting and building American trade in the region was an important objective of Washington's first administration. In his second annual address, the president directed Congress's attention to "that particular branch of our trade which belongs to the Mediterranean." He urged Congress not to "think any deliberations misemployed, which may lead to its relief and protection." This advice led the secretary of state, and future president Thomas Jefferson to compile a "Report on American Trade in the Mediterranean." In his eighth annual address, President Washington again called for protection of "our trade in the Mediterranean." Here he alluded to protecting the emerging Mediterranean trading networks from attacks by corsairs from Algiers who could potentially shut down American shipping and had nearly done so in 1785 and 1793 when they held a number of American ships and sailors captive while threatening to catch many others if the new nation refused to pay them an annual tribute. These concerns led to the creation of the US Navy as a means to control the threat in the Mediterranean. In 1801, the United States sent its first squadron to the Mediterranean and that region would remain the center of American naval operations for some time.[4]

---

[4] George Washington, "Second Annual Message to Congress" (Dec. 8, 1790) and "Eighth Annual Message to Congress" (Dec. 7, 1796); "Report on American Trade in the Mediterranean, 28 Dec. 1790," Founders Online, https://founders.archives.gov/documents/Jefferson/01-18-02-0139-0004. On the debate over and early implementation of the Navy, see Marshall Smelser, *The Congress Founds the Navy, 1787–1798* (South Bend: University of Notre Dame Press, 1959); Craig L. Symonds, *Navalists and Antinavalists: The Naval Policy Debate in the United States, 1785–1827* (Newark: University of

Just as the Mediterranean region was the major beneficiary of the creation of the Navy, it also was the primary beneficiary of the development of the consular service. When the State Department finally began to organize in earnest in the 1790s, roughly one in three consular appointments were made for Mediterranean ports, despite the fact that in many of these places in 1790, there were no resident American merchants and in some you could go most or all of the year without seeing an American flag. Among the ports with US consuls but few or no Americans initially were Málaga and Cartagena in Spain; Naples, Genoa, and Venice in Italy; Trieste in Austria (now Italy); and all of the Barbary ports. As a result, roughly half of all consular appointments in the region before 1815 were not American citizens. Clearly many of these were aspirational appointments, made in the hope and expectation that merchant capitalism would soon follow the consular infrastructure.[5]

For a time, all these preparations and expenditures seemed to pay off spectacularly. After 1795 or so, when the threat of the Barbary corsairs was minimized and the Napoleonic Wars created new opportunities for lucrative neutral trade, US merchants began to make enormous profits in the Mediterranean and, to many, it must have looked as though that would be the future of the new national economy. In that pre-statistical era, it is hard to define the extent of US trade in the region with certainty, but all indications are that it grew enormously. Figures provided by consuls on the scene showed a rapid increase in shipping. In 1803, one of the peak years, 111 American ships landed in Gibraltar, the entrance to the Mediterranean and a spot where captains typically rested and restocked on their way into the region. Doubtless, a good many more ships entered the Mediterranean without stopping. Even the spotty national statistics pointed to real gains in Mediterranean trade. The fish trade to the Mediterranean grew during the first decade of the nineteenth century so that, at its peak in 1806, the United States was shipping roughly 291,000 quintals of dried fish to ports in Italy, Spain, and France. This was

Delaware Press, 1980); Peskin, *Captives and Countrymen*, 110–33; Kenneth J. Hagan, *This People's Navy* (New York: The Free Press, 1991) 21–90.
[5] I calculated the number of appointments from Lists of US Consular Officers, 1789–1939, M587 RG59, NARA. From 1790 to 1799, of 107 appointments, 8 (7%) were to Asia, 3 (3%) to African islands, 7 (6.5%) to mainland America, 1 (1%) to Eastern Europe, 33 (31%) to the Mediterranean, 36 (34%) to Northwest Europe, and 19 (18%) to the West Indies. Even in Ireland, where there were much tighter initial connections to the United States, many early consuls were not US citizens. See Bernadette Whelan, *American Government in Ireland, 1790–1913: A History of the US Consular Service* (Manchester University Press, 2010) 1–11ff.

just over half of the total of US fish exports, and when the numerous exports to French and Spanish colonies in the West Indies are included, Mediterranean countries and their colonies received over three-quarters of American fish. The Mediterranean also played an outsized role in the lucrative reexport trade, which largely involved shipping valuable West Indian goods to Europe. For example, in 1807, 47% of brown sugar reexported by US ships went to the Mediterranean as did 38% of reexported coffee.[6]

As a result, until 1815 or so, the cosmopolitan trading nation model remained vigorous if not dominant. Merchants, and probably others as well, expected the new nation to continue to extend its trade into new Mediterranean ports and to expand its presence in those it had already entered. For them, national destiny was tied to this impressive mercantile expansion. In practice what this meant was that a vigorous community of American traders sprung up in Mediterranean ports. Consuls and other merchants were at the center of this community, which became a stable group of interconnected individuals, merchant houses, and families, many of whom remained in the same place for decades. In many ways this group was similar to earlier communities of foreigners trading in far-off lands, such as Sephardic Jews, the Portuguese "trading nation," and Genoese and Armenian colonies of the seventeenth century. However, there were differences as well. By the late eighteenth century, with the emergence of the nation-state, foreign traders expected certain protections that the non–state-affiliated traders of earlier centuries did not have. Consuls, as representatives of the nation-state, most frequently were the conduits to these protections. In this sense, the American trading nation might be seen as more similar to British traders, such as the London associates described by David Hancock, who benefitted from the protections offered by British mercantilism. However, as will become clear, the relative weakness of American military power meant that, in actuality, they did not always enjoy such benefits.[7]

Unfortunately for the American community in the Mediterranean, the bubble burst by 1815 due to a number of factors. First was the advent of

---

[6] Timothy Pitkin, *A Statistical View of the Commerce of the United States of America* (Hartford: Charles Hosmer, 1816) 76, 139–41. Numbers for Gibraltar are calculated from the shipping news in the *Gibraltar Chronicle* newspaper which, so far as I know, is only available at the Garrison Library in Gibraltar.

[7] Daviken Studnicki-Gizbert, *A Nation Upon the Ocean Sea: Portugal's Atlantic Diaspora and the Spanish Empire, 1492–1640* (New York: Oxford University Press, 2007); Francesca Trivellato, *The Familiarity of Strangers: The Sephardic Diaspora, Livorno, and*

the Peninsular War in 1807 and the general devastation to much of the Mediterranean trade that followed in its wake. After that, the end of the Napoleonic Wars limited the profitability of neutral trade in the portions of the Mediterranean not devastated by war, as British and French ships rushed back into markets where Americans had thrived during the war years. Domestically, the Louisiana Purchase of 1803 and the successful conclusion of the War of 1812 provided the new nation with the territory and confidence to undertake one of the largest and most rapid agricultural expansions in human history. This land acquisition coupled with the development of the cotton gin would transform American overseas commerce, crowning cotton as king and reorienting American ships toward Great Britain, whose emerging textile industry created an insatiable demand for cotton. As a result of all these factors, America's economic future no longer appeared to be in the Mediterranean, and the newer model of territorial growth and industrial capitalism began to replace the merchant capitalism that undergirded the trading nation.

Paradoxically, though, the relative decline of the Mediterranean trade and the trading nation model coincided with an upswing in American confidence and nationalism. Surviving the War of 1812 was interpreted as a victory over Great Britain and evidence of America's ability to join the ranks of the great powers. Americans viewed their rout of the North African Barbary States in 1815 similarly. The Louisiana Purchase of 1803 and the development of new modes of cotton production converged to open the door to a vast and lucrative empire of cotton in what was then the southwestern portion of the new nation, and increasing industrialization combined with new modes of transportation brought new wealth to the North and Northwest. The Monroe Doctrine of 1823 also impressed Americans at home and abroad as evidence of the new nation's arrival. Thus, after 1815, the United States as a whole had entered a period of rapid growth and growing influence, but Americans in the Mediterranean were no longer at the center of national development.

***

Cross-Cultural Trade in the Early Modern Period (New Haven: Yale University Press, 2012); David Hancock, *Citizens of the World: London Merchants and the Integration of the Atlantic Community, 1735–1785* (Cambridge University Press, 1997); Sebouh Aslanian, *From the Indian Ocean to the Mediterranean: The Global Network of Armenian Merchants from New Julfa* (Berkeley: University of California Press, 2014).

The chapters that follow examine the American community in the Mediterranean through the careers of three long-serving American consuls: James Simpson of Gibraltar (1794–96) and Tangier (1796–1820), Robert Montgomery of Alicante (1793–1823), and Thomas Appleton of Livorno (1798–1840). While their individual stories are all quite interesting, my method has been to move beyond their personal biographies to study their family, business, and professional networks and the people within them. In doing so I am trying to get at the broader social and cultural history of the American community of which they were a part in addition to addressing the diplomatic and commercial concerns within the early American Mediterranean.

I have chosen these particular consuls because of their geographic spread and their longevity. The former helps to make the study more representative of the Mediterranean as a whole, with characters situated in Muslim North Africa, a mid-level port in what is today known as the Spanish Costa Blanca, and an Italian port receiving more American ships than virtually any other in the region. The latter aspect arguably limits the subjects' representativeness since few consuls served as long as they did (although a number did serve nearly as long, or even longer).[8] Nevertheless, the typical consul was neither as long-serving nor successful as these three. Still, following the lives of these long-term consuls serves two important purposes. First, it allows us to follow the long arc of the history of the American Mediterranean and, second, it allows for a rich documentary base including long runs of State Department documents, foreign records, a good number of private letters, and even some published accounts. Considering their relative historical obscurity, these three men left extraordinary archives that frequently allow detailed reconstructions of their lives and experiences.

As consuls, Simpson, Montgomery, and Appleton were representatives of the state generally and the State Department specifically. Consuls were arguably the largest and most visible segment of the early national State Department. By 1800 there were perhaps seventy consuls in American consulates around the world, and they in turn employed many translators, secretaries, vice-consuls, and others, so that more than likely 200 or 300

---

[8] John Gavino served in Gibraltar eighteen years (1797–1815); William Kirkpatrick, in Málaga seventeen years (1800–1817); Stephen Cathalan, in Marseille twenty-nine years (1790–1819); Sylvanus Bourn, in Amsterdam for twenty-one years (1794–1817); Thomas Aspinwall, in London thirty-eight years (1815–53); Alexander Hammit, in Naples fifty-two years (1809–61).

individuals worked within the consular service alone at that time. Yet, American consuls and the consular service have received astonishingly little attention from historians. The few classic institutional histories of the State Department hardly mention them, and diplomatic historians have only recently begun making use of the voluminous State Department records documenting their stories. Although not an institutional history, one contribution that this study attempts to make is to give some outline of the consular service and its importance to the early republic.

Consuls and the consular service were intertwined with the new nation's first efforts to project an image abroad and to develop a foreign policy mechanism. This was at best a haphazard, underfunded undertaking, much to the frustration of consuls who hoped to build trade throughout the Mediterranean. The disorganization of the consular service reflected the relative weakness of the new nation compared to most Mediterranean powers. Consuls did not and could not realistically have much interest in the territorial expansion associated with late nineteenth-century imperialism. They did, however, uniformly push for a stronger navy, not so much as an expansionist measure but as a means to protect American ships from continual interference from European and North African captors. Personally, they were frequently able to benefit from the disorganization within the State Department that allowed them essentially to volunteer for positions that they wanted and to carve out powerful roles within the port cities and the developing American trading nation.

While the evolution of the consular service is an important element, it is only one aspect of the story of the Mediterranean community and of the experience of Americans abroad during an era of rapid globalization. The consuls' job was to facilitate networks of trade and communication that would link Americans within the Mediterranean to their compatriots within the borders of the United States. Despite the rapid increase in American traffic to the Mediterranean and fast-growing profits, the new trade network faced serious threats, most notably from Barbary corsairs and the warring European powers, which frequently interdicted American ships, captured crews, and held them captive whether in North African *bagnos* or European prize courts. To a lesser extent, these networks were also threatened by epidemic disease which disrupted lives and often led to quarantines that, by design, cut off communications and trade.

From 1793 to 1807, the period covered by Part I of this book, the consuls' efforts to deal with these disruptions helped to solidify the developing American community. They played an important role in maintaining the flow of goods and communications between the new nation, the Mediterranean, and points between. At the same time, this crucial role put consuls at the center of American affairs. The undeveloped State Department and the pressing need for dealing with ship captures gave them a diplomatic role beyond the traditional consular function of assisting ships. With only two American ambassadors (or ministers) in the Mediterranean through most of this period, and both in inland capitals of Paris and Madrid, consuls became the face of the new nation in their ports and often beyond. All of these developments brought the consuls into close contact with other Americans, both in the new nation and in the Mediterranean and tied the developing trading nation more tightly together over time. By 1807, consuls had established strong networks among each other and among the Americans trading in the region. Additionally, with the rise of the Navy and its attendant support system, including a number of naval agents in European ports, a good deal more American officials could be found in the region. Finally, the rapid increase in the neutral trade brought in many more captains, crew members, and resident American merchants. The new trading nation seemed to be taking shape as a community.

Part II of this book examines various aspects of that community. The American experience throughout the Mediterranean was almost always centered on making money. The three consuls in this book were no exceptions. Each in his own way viewed a consular post as a helpful means to profit as well as a way of serving the new nation. The very vision of the trading nation, which consisted of the assumption that expanding mercantile activity was in the national interest as well as that of individual merchants, allowed them to justify efforts to increase the scope of their own trade (within legal limits) as in the national interest. But economic activity was rarely their sole pursuit. As long-time residents in the Mediterranean, most consuls formed family units, a difficult task in a region with few Americans and few Protestants. Even those who did not have families engaged in social networks which often were dominated by their fellow Americans and non-Americans connected to the trading nation. Finally, consuls and other Americans in the region had to come to terms with groups of people with whom they had little previous contact and for whom they had little affinity, most notably Catholics, Jews, and Muslims. Encounters with these groups sometimes encouraged nascent imperialist views among Americans in the region, though as yet there was little possibility for actual imperialism.

Part III traces the collapse of this Mediterranean community. The first generation of consuls by now had grown old. They faced health problems, diminished capacity, and in many cases deep frustration due to a lack of recognition from Washington. These problems were greatly exacerbated by the end of the neutral trade and the devastation of the Peninsular War. While many hoped that their children would stay on and prosper in the Mediterranean, for most the situation was not tenable. Additionally, with increasing emphasis at home on territorial expansion and the growth of the cotton kingdom, and with presidential administrations less concerned with serving merchants trading overseas and more interested in rewarding political allegiance at home, merchant influence within the consular service began to wane. These trends would culminate in the 1840s and 1850s with the professionalization of the consular service and the Mexican War, which ushered in an even more intense focus on continental expansion and domination. As a result of all these factors, the American Mediterranean community was much diminished at the time of the deaths of these three consuls, and American energy clearly was no longer being exerted to the same extent toward the Mediterranean trade. Furthermore, the very notion of the trading nation was now eclipsed by the rise of the continental territorial nation.

The children and grandchildren of the Mediterranean consuls, therefore, were left to find new lives for themselves, most frequently in new places. An epilogue traces their divergent paths from Latin America to New Zealand. Many completely lost what were already tenuous American identities. But, more broadly, the old sense of a cosmopolitan trading nation that had tied together a diverse group of individuals into something broadly viewed as an American community was now overshadowed by the idea of a territorial nation based on domestic production and defined by habitation within the rapidly expanding boundaries of the American republic.

PART I

RISE OF THE MEDITERRANEAN COMMUNITY

I

Becoming American (and) Consuls

Why and how would anyone become an American consul in the Mediterranean or elsewhere after the Revolution? Those are the crucial questions to understand the early days of the American consular system, but in order to answer them it is important to comprehend the purpose and evolution of the consular system itself. Trade never just happens on its own, certainly not in the eighteenth and early nineteenth centuries, when relatively slow transit and communications made long-distance commerce more complicated and risky than it is today, with instantaneous communications and fast shipping. Merchants provided transit when they built or purchased ships and financial support when they issued and redeemed bills of exchange to move money around the world. They also provided crucial information through the letters and price currents (literally lists of current prices for goods bought and sold in their ports) that they disseminated to their correspondents. But they were largely incapable of protecting commerce from interference. This could come in many forms, from unforeseen quarantines to hostile local officials, to capture by privateers or Barbary corsairs. To deal with these contingencies and a host of others, ship captains and merchants needed somebody on hand with power who could represent their interests. That is where consuls stepped in. Because they were state officials, local authorities had to take them seriously or risk the possibility of an international incident.

The institution of consulship predated the modern state. In the early days, consuls benefitted from what scholars call full extraterritoriality. Merchants who lived abroad formed small communities that were exempted from local laws (extraterritoriality) and granted various economic, judicial, and political privileges. These included the ability to elect their own representatives, known as consuls, who served not only as political representatives to the surrounding polity but also as quasi-judicial officials empowered to settle disputes within the merchant community. By the time of the American Revolution and French Revolution, which ushered in the modern nation-state, the institution of consulship was in transition in the United States and other Western powers. Merchant communities residing within nation-states were becoming less autonomous at the same time that the nation-states which they represented began to take over some of the functions that merchant communities once controlled, most notably the appointment of the consuls themselves.[1]

Consuls, then, became an important device for the early nation-state in promoting merchant capitalism. The relatively large number of consuls appointed by the United States early on, particularly in the Mediterranean, can provide a sense that supporting overseas trade was an urgent priority of the new government. Yet, from the perspective of Mediterranean traders and, especially, the consuls themselves, the new US government seemingly evinced as little interest in consuls as subsequent scholars have shown. The causes were both institutional and structural. At the institutional level, the early State Department, and indeed the entire US government, was disorganized and underfunded. As late as 1800 the State Department employed only eight clerks to handle correspondence relating to consuls, ministers, envoys, private citizens, and others throughout the globe, including as many as seventy-nine consuls.[2] The utter lack

---

[1] Nicholas Barreyre and Claire Lemercier, "The Unexceptional State: Rethinking the State in the Nineteenth Century (France, United States)," *The American Historical Review* 126 (June 2021) 481–503; Ferry de Goey, *Consuls and the Institutions of Global Capitalism, 1783–1914* (London: Taylor and Francis, 2014) 1–13; Nicole M. Phelps, *US–Habsburg Relations from 1815 to the Paris Peace Conference* (Cambridge University Press, 2013) 13–38; Charles Stuart Kennedy, *The American Consul: A History of the United States Consular Service, 1776–1914* (New York: Greenwood Press, 1990) 1–4.

[2] I found 113 appointments by 1800 based on my examination of the List of US Diplomatic Officers, 1789–1839, M587 RG 59, NARA, which show official appointments for consuls and a few vice-consuls. From that list I find as many as seventy-nine consuls serving in 1800 (by eliminating those who had left before 1800 and those whom I know never served). I counted a few vice-consuls with official appointments. There were undoubtedly other vice-consuls who did not receive official appointments, but there were probably also a good number of appointees whom I counted who never showed up to their posts. William Barnes, *The Foreign Service of the United States: Origins, Developments, and Functions* (Washington DC: US Department of State, 1961) 63, found only fifty-two sitting consuls in 1800. He notes that his source was "a compilation prepared from original records by the Historical Office of the [State] Department" (350).

of responsiveness of those clerks to consuls' frequent requests for information was a direct result of the clerk–official ratio. Crucially, the federal government approved salaries for only four of those consuls, which meant that all the rest, by necessity, had to spend most of their time on private rather than public duties if they hoped to sustain themselves.

This apparent neglect was not accidental or transient. It was baked into the very structure of the early consular service which reflected early Americans' distrust of government and the Federalists' efforts to align the moneyed interests with the new nation. Rather than rely on government to build capitalist infrastructure, early Americans generally used state power to encourage private industry. Domestically, this meant that they granted monopolies and other forms of encouragement to corporations willing to construct bridges, waterworks, and other infrastructure, or they issued bonds that would provide investment vehicles for capitalists while tying them closer to the state. Alexander Hamilton exemplified these tendencies when he created a funding system that relied not on mass taxation but on investment in a national "sinking fund" by moneyed merchants who would thereby find support of the new government to be in their interest so long as they could profit from treasury bonds. By essentially forcing consuls to fund their own activities by depriving them of salaries, the new government followed much the same policy as on domestic infrastructure; that is, providing overseas infrastructure for the activities of merchants at minimal cost to them and to taxpayers. Thus, while the state supported commercial endeavors of all stripes, it was designed most often to do so indirectly and with few actual expenditures, and in this regard the consular system fit logically with contemporary conceptions of the role of the state within the development of American capitalism.[3]

***

So, once again, given the lack of salaries in all but the four "Barbary" posts and lack of interest on the part of the State Department, why would anyone want to be a consul? The short answer is prestige and connections. Successful merchants needed to be easily recognized by potential clients and to be perceived as trustworthy and respectable. Newcomers to a port

---

[3] Brian Murphy, *Building the Empire State: Political Economy in the Early Republic* (Philadelphia: University of Pennsylvania Press, 2015); Andrew Schocket, *Founding Corporate Power in Early National Philadelphia* (Northern Illinois University Press, 2007).

might spend years attempting to build that sort of reputation. A consular appointment allowed merchant-consuls to bypass much of the hard work necessary in reputation-building as their position immediately provided them with name recognition and respectability. At a minimum they would certainly seem more trustworthy than someone whose name was completely unknown to Americans. As representatives of a nation-state, even a second-tier power, consuls were also usually treated respectfully by foreign governments. The remnants of extraterritoriality still protected their persons, their houses, and their employees from interference from the state in which they were posted except in extreme circumstances.

Their appointments also provided consuls with superior access to information and connections compared to most other merchants. In theory, at least, all American ships reported to them upon arriving in port to provide information about their cargos, points of origins, and destinations. Advice from the State Department (though rare) and other American and non-American consuls also gave them information on changing market conditions that was not accessible or at least not as readily or quickly accessible to most other merchants. As the American community grew, consuls also were able to draw on each other and on other Americans in their circles for capital and valuable advice and support not readily available to less-connected merchants. Finally, though consular positions were unsalaried, merchant-consuls were able to augment their income with fees paid to them by Americans for services such as notarizing documents, issuing passports, handling the property of deceased citizens, and so forth.[4] In short, while a consular appointment certainly did not guarantee success (plenty of consuls failed and returned home), it gave consuls a significant advantage over other merchants in the region. Not surprisingly, then, many of the men who applied to be consuls were individuals who calculated that a consular position would make the difference between success and failure in establishing a merchant house in a new port.

Some of these advantages might appear to be uncomfortably close to corruption or insider trading by modern standards. Contemporaries did occasionally raise concerns, and no doubt some consuls used their offices for personal profit in unsavory ways. Yet consuls themselves mostly believed that their personal interests were generally aligned with national interests. By protecting American ships and allowing American trade to

---

[4] For a full description of consular duties see J. Sidney Henshaw, *A Manual for United States Consuls* (New York: J. C. Riker, 1849).

expand, they believed they served their country and themselves. This formulation worked better in the early days of Mediterranean trade when the commercial tide was rapidly rising. The relationship between personal profit and national service was, suffice it to say, a complicated one which will receive more discussion in Chapter 6.

The question of *how* one became a consul is actually more complicated than the "why" as is clear from the stories of the three consuls at the center of this book. In the beginning, the State Department had a hard time finding qualified applicants. It had essentially three options. First, it could choose from the vast number of young American men who, in the midst of postwar depression, would be happy to be sent abroad to earn a fortune or at least a competency. There were two problems with this approach. On the one hand, being an effective consul required specialized linguistic, business, and administrative skills that most young men did not possess. On the other hand, even those who possessed the requisite qualifications would have difficulty supporting themselves in most posts due to the inability or unwillingness of the new government to provide them with salaries and resources. A second approach was to appoint foreigners, which was relatively common, particularly for the smaller, less powerful countries. The problem with this option was obvious: non-Americans might have little knowledge of the country they represented and less incentive to represent it well. Third, the government might try to appoint Americans already living abroad. This approach had merits, but it was impossible at the many ports where American ships landed (or merchants hoped to land) but no Americans had settled permanently. Ultimately the first national governments made use of all of these options, each of which is represented by one of our three consuls.

At first, the vast majority of consuls were either non-Americans or Americans who were already living abroad. Only half of the consuls appointed during the Washington administration were listed as American citizens by the State Department.[5] In the Mediterranean region, only three of the eighteen Washington administration appointees were recorded as citizens. This low number reflects the perceived potential utility of Mediterranean ports to the numerous American traders who were already sending goods there or who aspired to do so. Since few Americans were

---

[5] Names of consular appointees are from List of Diplomatic Officers, 1789–1939, M596 RG59, NARA, which notes birthplaces and citizenships of appointees. As will be discussed below, State Department records are not entirely to be relied on here, due to clerical vagaries and to the difficulty in defining citizenship at this early stage.

living in these strategically important commercial locations, appointing foreigners seemed the only way to begin creating a commercial infrastructure there. Over the entire 1788–1830 period, the Mediterranean would continue to have a high number of noncitizen consuls compared to other areas. Of the citizen-consuls appointed worldwide by the Washington administration for whom we have relevant information, roughly equal numbers were appointed in the United States and sent out to their posts or already resident where they were appointed. To put it differently, only 20 percent of all Washington's consular appointments were Americans who were sent out to their posts from the United States.[6] In the Mediterranean, however, State Department records show only noncitizens and citizens who were sent out from the United States, and not a single resident American appointee until the Adams administration. There was, however, at least one error in these records since Robert Montgomery, one of our three consuls, was in fact a citizen residing in Alicante though not listed as such.

***

James Simpson of Gibraltar and Tangier, the first of the three consuls, was an example of a foreigner appointed to represent the United States. Overall, the best estimate is that 23 percent of all American consuls appointed by President Washington were non-Americans like Simpson.[7] Simpson was a Scotsman who appears never to have visited America or to have had any connections there, although his wife's family had been there during the Revolution. An ambitious, but not particularly successful merchant residing in Gibraltar, Simpson clearly was considering ways of making contacts outside of Britain's trading empire in the 1790s. He turned first to Russia, which had a bourgeoning trade with the Mediterranean region in this

---

[6] Or at least only 20% were definitely indicated to be such by the consular recommendations. I doubt, however, whether there were many more since this is the group that is best documented by the recommendation letters as they were most in need of formal appointments, unlike citizens and non-citizens already living abroad who often just volunteered to be consuls at first without any formal appointment or letters of recommendation. These documents are found in Letters of Application and Recommendation during the Administrations of John Adams, Thomas Jefferson, James Madison, James Monroe, John Quincy Adams, and Andrew Jackson, M406, M418, M438, M439, M531, M639 RG59, NARA. They are organized alphabetically within administrations.

[7] Based on List of US Consular officers, 1789–1839, M587 RG 59, NARA. The appointments only list whether appointees' "allegiance" is US or not. Where I have more information on citizenship and appointments I have used it. For the Washington administration I could only label thirty-one of the total of sixty-four appointments with certainty. They broke down into thirteen (42%) Americans appointed in the US; eleven (35%) Americans appointed abroad; and seven (23%) foreigners.

period and was expected to negotiate favorable treaties with the Barbary powers, becoming their consul in Gibraltar by the early 1790s.[8] It is not surprising that he also sought connections with the United States, another rising power with its eyes on the Mediterranean trade.

Because of his location in Gibraltar, Simpson was well connected to British military and other imperial officials who shared a cosmopolitan outlook. He was also part of the broad British Mediterranean network that was heavily populated with Irish, Scots, and Scots-Irish due in large part to the importance of the fish trade. With a North Atlantic location and, frequently, Catholic connections, Irish and Scots-Irish merchants were well positioned to act as brokers between fishermen in Canada, New England, and the Catholic Mediterranean, which had long consumed Atlantic cod due to religious dictates and the convenience of heavily salted cod, known as *bacalao* in the Portuguese and Spanish Mediterranean. This trade connected the Atlantic world to the Mediterranean for centuries.[9] As a Gibraltar merchant, partnered with a Scotsman and with connections in Britain and Lisbon, it would have been Simpson's specialty. A number of other early foreign-born American consuls circulated within the same Anglo-Spanish trading networks as Simpson, including Michael Morphy at Cartagena, William Kirkpatrick at Málaga, and Joseph Ysnardi at Cádiz, a Spaniard who had served for some time in a British mercantile firm.[10] Robert Montgomery of Alicante, although born in the United States, also traded in these circles and in many ways, as we shall see below, was quite similar to Simpson despite being an American citizen.

While Simpson had no apparent connection to the United States, his wife, Harriet Mawby was born there while her father served with the 18th Royal Irish Regiment.[11] The regiment traveled extensively, from

---

[8] Thomas Barclay to Thomas Jefferson, Dec. 31, 1791; May 10, 1792, both in Gibraltar Despatches; F. L. Humphreys, *Life and Times of David Humphreys* (New York: Putnam, 1917) II: 205.

[9] On the cod trade, see James G. Lydon, *Fish and Flour for Gold, 1600–1800: Southern Europe in the Colonial Balance of Payments* (Philadelphia: Library Company of Philadelphia e-Publication, 2008); Christopher P. Magra, *The Fisherman's Cause: Atlantic Commerce and Maritime Dimensions of the American Revolution* (New York: Cambridge University Press, 2009); Mark Kurlansky, *Cod* (New York: Penguin Books, 1997).

[10] Although not appointed to the Málaga consulship until 1801, Kirkpatrick had been recommended for the position as early as 1791.

[11] There is some confusion about Harriet's father's date of birth because his father, perhaps facetiously, enlisted him as a "volunteer" as a very young child. As a result, Steven M. Baule, *Protecting the Empire's Frontier* (Athens: Ohio University Press, 2014) 74, suggests he may have been born as early as 1760, but his obituary unequivocally states that he was 80 when he died in 1851.

Philadelphia to Illinois, and through the Mississippi valley back to Florida during the Revolution. Though the Mawbys would not have taken part in all these peregrinations, Harriet's father and probably she and her siblings as well, would have seen a good deal of the continent before she returned to England in 1775 at roughly 5 years of age.[12] There is no evidence that she ever sought to return to America or maintained any connections there. It is possible, though, that her recollections piqued her husband's interest in the new republic. This theory is bolstered by the fact that Simpson once specifically requested that David Humphreys, the American minister to Madrid and Lisbon, send him a copy of *Travels through the Interior Parts of America 1776–1781*, written by Thomas Anburey, an officer in the 47th Regiment of Foot during the American Revolution, who could very well have been an acquaintance of the Mawbys.

Simpson's first personal interaction with the United States appears to have been in the early 1790s when he acted as an intermediary between the Washington administration and Francis Chiappi, the Italian who served as the American agent in Barbary. Simpson shipped packets from Chiappi to President Washington. He also sent Washington information on American prisoners held captive in Algiers and would later correspond with their de facto leader, Captain Richard O'Brien.[13] It was no surprise, therefore, that Simpson made a point of meeting the Irish-American consul and diplomat Thomas Barclay when he arrived in Gibraltar in December 1791, en route to Morocco to negotiate a peace treaty. Much to Barclay's dismay, he was forced to spend more than a year in that claustrophobic setting waiting for permission to enter Morocco.[14] During this uncertain and frustrating interlude, the Scottish Russian consul to Gibraltar and the Irish-American consul to France struck up a close and occasionally ribald friendship. When Barclay finally departed Gibraltar for Lisbon in January 1793, he left his personal goods and a great deal of American property intended as presents for the Moroccan emperor at Simpson's country house. Simpson insisted that on his return Barclay should stay in one of his extra bedrooms rather than an inn.[15] In the

---

[12] *Ibid.*, 1–26, 210–13, 189–91.

[13] James Simpson to George Washington, Apr. 13, 1791; n.d.; Aug. 25, 1791; to Sec. State, Jan. 3, 1794, all in Gibraltar Despatches.

[14] Priscilla H. Roberts and Richard S. Roberts, *Thomas Barclay (1728–1793): Consul in France, Diplomat in Barbary* (Bethlehem, PA: Lehigh University Press, 2008) 260–65.

[15] Barclay to Jefferson, Dec. 31, 1791; Simpson to Barclay, Oct. 18, 1792; Nov. 12, 1792, all in Gibraltar Despatches.

meantime, Simpson essentially served as Barclay's vice-consul, keeping him apprised of events in Gibraltar and handling American business.

Unfortunately, Barclay never returned. He died on January 19, 1793, just two days after arriving in Lisbon. Simpson was shocked to learn the news from David Humphreys. Simpson and Humphreys were now faced with the unpleasant task of opening Barclay's boxes, cataloguing the contents, and going over his accounts. Simpson took charge of these goods, eventually auctioning off some and saving others for use in future negotiations. Disposing of the property of nationals who died in foreign ports was traditionally the job of a consul. As consuls typically did, Simpson also pocketed a fee for his services, $86.50 in this case, and he received nearly $1,700 as a reimbursement for purchasing goods and providing services to Barclay.[16]

Simpson was not a US official of any sort at this time, but like other consuls-to-be, including Robert Montgomery, he essentially took on consular duties without invitation or appointment. He wrote Secretary of State Thomas Jefferson, "I am highly disposed to do whatever may be in my power to promote the interests of the United States and ... I will be extremely careful to give you regular advice of whatever may happen in this part of the world [or] can in any way affect it, until a successor to Mr. Barclay shall answer here." Simpson made good on this promise, sending back frequent reports and handling a number of delicate tasks, including ship captures and a possible plot against American shipping. He also sent a list of American ships landing in Gibraltar and their cargo to the State Department. All of these activities were traditionally performed by consuls. As Russian consul to Gibraltar, Simpson would have been aware of consular duties, and it seems likely he performed them in part to prove his suitability for the position. He increasingly became more explicit about his aspirations, opening a full-scale campaign for nomination in December when he expressed his interest in the position to both Jefferson and David Humphreys.[17] Simpson finally learned he had been appointed US consul in September 1794. Not satisfied with achieving this goal, he immediately pressed Jefferson to appoint him to succeed Barclay in the

---

[16] "Acct. Sales and Net Proceeds of Sundry Articles Sold at Public Auction by order of Mr. James Simpson, Gibraltar 2nd Oct. 1793"; Simpson to Jefferson, Aug. 23, 1793; Feb. 15, 1793, all in Gibraltar Despatches; Roberts and Roberts, *Thomas Barclay (1728–1793)*, 264.

[17] Simpson to Jefferson, Dec. 18, 1793, "A Return of American Vessels in Gibraltar Bay the 21st Oct. 1793," in Gibraltar Despatches; Simpson to David Humphreys, Dec. 23, 1793; Jan. 16, 1793, both in Simpson Letterbook.

Barbary negotiations. Receiving no word from Jefferson, he soon took it on himself to initiate negotiations on behalf of the United States with Muley Solimon the Moroccan emperor, eventually receiving approval from David Humphreys. He wasted little time in informing Jefferson of his availability for the salaried consulate in Morocco.[18]

Clearly Simpson sought the US consulate both for its ability to provide more contacts and also for the potential of the salaried Morocco position. But what of Simpson's utility to the United States? What he offered was primarily his extensive network of correspondents. Long before arriving in Tangier, he knew most of the Moroccan consuls. "They are all my old acquaintances," he wrote, adding, "I have the satisfaction of being in habits of strict friendship with most of these gentlemen and intimately acquainted with the whole." In recommending Simpson, David Humphreys also commented on his connections, observing that "He has also, a considerable correspondence in Barbary and knowledge of the affairs in that country."[19] Simpson's consular correspondence in Gibraltar alone included ten other consuls. His most frequent and closest correspondent was Peter Wyk, the Swedish consul in Morocco, with whom he was in contact at least eight times between 1792 and 1796, and probably much more frequently. Wyk served as a conduit between Simpson and the Moroccan sultan, even helping Simpson translate his outgoing letters into Arabic.[20] Simpson's other consular correspondents, discussed in more detail in Chapter 2, included Englishmen, a Frenchman, Danes, a Portuguese, and a Spaniard. His ties with these individuals were often quite strong and personal.[21]

The story was quite similar in Livorno, which, like Alicante, was an important node in the transatlantic fish trade and had attracted a good deal of American shipping in the 1770s. The first American consul to Livorno and predecessor to Thomas Appleton, Philip Felicchi, was, like

---

[18] Simpson to Sec. State, Oct. 20, 1794; Sept. 27, 1794; Sept. 24, 1794; Nov. 1, 1794; Nov. 12, 1794; Feb. 12, 1795; June 22, 1795; July 15, 1795; Aug. 18, 1795; Oct. 29, 1796, all in Gibraltar Despatches; Roberts and Roberts, *Thomas Barclay (1728–1793)*, 266–67. The modern transliteration of the emperor's name is Mawlay Sulaymon. Muley Solimon was typically used by Simpson and his correspondents at the time and I have kept it to avoid anachronism.

[19] Humphreys, *Life and Times of David Humphreys*, II: 205; James Simpson to Sec. State, Dec. 16, 1797, Tangier Despatches.

[20] "Extracts of Letters from Barbary," Nov. 15, 1792; Simpson to Barclay, Nov. 15, 1792; Dec. 13, 1792; Dec. 17, 1792; to Sec. State, Oct. 20, 1794; Nov. 1, 1794; Feb. 10, 1795; Feb. 17, 1795, all in Gibraltar Despatches.

[21] Simpson to Sec. State, Dec. 10, 1797, Tangier Despatches.

Simpson, a resident non-American merchant although, unlike Simpson he had visited the United States twice and had extensive interests there. Although they were not citizens by a long stretch, Felicchi's family was well connected to the American trading network. His father Nicola, who had been a pioneer in the American trade, sent young Philippi to Livorno from his native Umbria in the early 1780s as a representative of the family firm. From there, Phillip embarked on two voyages to America, the first from 1785 to 1788 and the second in 1789 during which he met important merchants from New York, Baltimore, Philadelphia, and Boston as well as his future wife, whom he married in New York, probably in 1789.[22]

Felicchi was first recommended for a consular post in 1791, but, as with most of the early recommendations, nothing came of it due to the general neglect of the consular service. In the meantime – like Simpson, Montgomery, and others – Felicchi took it on himself to act as the de facto American consul. In the fall of 1793 the British Navy, which held a very powerful position in Livorno, threatened to impress American sailors aboard the New York ship *Minerva* under Captain Joseph Ingraham. The British commander argued that the oaths of allegiance taken by the Minervans were not sufficient to prove that they were American rather than English. This was a typical problem for American sailors at the time (some of whom actually did seem to change their national allegiance when it benefitted them) and identifying who was or was not American was a typical consular function.[23]

Felicchi took the matter to both the Italian and British officials, ultimately succeeding in convincing the British to keep their hands off the Americans and allowing the ship to sail on. Felicchi kept the state department informed of the situation and of his successes, sometimes by writing directly to George Washington and sometimes through his American patron, William Seton, who shared his letters with the State Department. Like Simpson and others, he also lobbied for an official appointment. Felicchi made a not-so-subtle hint of his suitability for

[22] Luca Codignola, "Relations between North America and the Italian Peninsula, 1763–1799: Tuscany, Genoa and Naples," in S. Marzagalli, J. R. Sofka, and J. J. McCusker, eds., *Rough Waters: American Involvement with the Mediterranean in the Eighteenth and Nineteenth Centuries* (Newfoundland: International Maritime Economic History Association, 2010) 26–33; Maria Argiero and Algerina Neri, *Bostoniani a Livorno: il Console Thomas Appleton e I suoi conterranei* (Pisa University Press, 2012) 21–22; J. Vinesy to [George Washington], Mar. 1, 1791, Washington Papers.

[23] Matthew Taylor Raffety, *The Republic Afloat: Law Honor and Citizenship in Maritime America* (University of Chicago Press, 2013) 147–96.

a consular position when he wrote Seton, "I think the President of the United States will be pleased to find that the Court of Tuscany has been so solicitous to afford every protection to the American vessel, *tho the United States have nobody here authorized to support the interest of the people of America*." Unfortunately, after Felicchi succeeded at freeing the Americans, Algerian cruisers promptly captured the *Minerva* and imprisoned Captain Ingraham and his crew along with ten other American ships and their crews, keeping some of them in captivity for more than two years, a fate they would have avoided if they had been sailing under the British flag.[24]

The role of American merchants in Felicchi's appointment and that of many others reflects the transitional nature of the consular position in the first days of the nation-state. During the earlier period, when extraterritoriality was complete, merchants had traditionally appointed consuls to represent themselves. In the modern nation-state that role has been taken up by the state. But in the early national period, while consuls were government-appointed, merchants still played an important part in nominating and lobbying for consuls who would represent them abroad. In America, William Seton spearheaded the campaign to get Felicchi appointed. As a frequent trader to Livorno, owner of the *Minerva*, and intimate with Felicchi, Seton saw the need for an American consul there and stood to benefit from Felicchi's appointment. Because Felicchi was not an American, Seton took pains to emphasize his connections to the trading nation. He described his "constant" trade with the United States, the value of his cargoes, and the duties that he paid on them. He also stressed Felicchi's service to the United States during the *Minerva* incident, and his American connections, including his wife. Finally, he emphasized the ideological dimension, noting that Felicchi was "from principle every way attached to America." Apparently, these arguments were convincing. Congress approved the appointment in late 1794 and Felicchi acknowledged receiving it in April 1795, when he pledged to "pay the strictest attention to fulfill the duties incumbent on me and to promote the American interest on all occasions."[25]

---

[24] Vinesy to [Washington], Mar. 1, 1791, Washington Papers; Philip Felicchi to George Washington, Oct. 29, 1793; to William Seton, both in Leghorn Despatches. Quote from Oct. 29, 1793, emphasis added. On the *Minerva*, see Richard O'Brien to David Humphreys, Dec. 6, 1793, Despatches of US Ministers to Portugal.

[25] William Seton to Edmund Randolph, Mar. 29, 1794, Washington Papers; Felicchi to Sec. State, Apr. 21, 1795, Leghorn Despatches.

Seton's campaign for Felicchi's appointment was not unusual. While some foreigners, like Simpson, merely stepped in out of necessity and were later confirmed without recommendations, others were supported by Americans in the region they represented or by Americans at home who were involved in trade at the consul's location. Some, like Joseph Ysnardi of Cádiz, also visited America to solicit appointments. Still others, like Simpson and Michael Morphy of Málaga, had already served the United States as "voluntary agents," to quote one of Morphy's recommendations.[26] But, at this early juncture, when the American trading nation was still inchoate, many potential consuls could only claim mercantile competence and a desire to serve the new nation. John Church of Cork submitted a petition signed by representatives of fourteen local merchant houses and certified by the mayor testifying to his fitness to "represent any kingdom or state whatever as consul." James Holmes of Belfast submitted a similar petition as well as a recommendation from an American mercantile acquaintance. Occasionally, foreign-born applicants also asserted their support of American ideals, as did Hans Rudolph Saabye of Copenhagen who wished that the United States would enjoy the reward of "that dear brought liberty, which with the protection of so wise a government, must become an inexhaustible source of universal bliss throughout all our territories."[27] Frances Coffyn, who sought to replace his foreign-born father as a foreign-born consul to Dunkirk, went so far as to argue that he should actually be considered an American citizen because of his family's service to the United States. He wrote, "We have ever since that country thought of recovering her independence, been attached to her cause, acting in her service, sacrificed all considerations of personal interest; and finally fell victim of our courage in defending the interest of American citizens, when at the tyrannical time of Robespierre, all principles of justice and virtue seem'd to be banished and persecuted."[28] What united nearly all of these foreign applicants was their effort to show that, while not native born, they were tied to the American nations by cords of commerce and affection.

***

[26] Joseph Ignat to Thomas Jefferson, Feb. 25, 1793, Morphy File, Washington Recs; Nathaniel Cutting to Jefferson Jan. 30, 1792, Yznardi File, Washington Recs.

[27] Hans R. Saabey to George Washington and the Deputies of the United States of N. America, Aug. 5, 1789, Washington Recs.

[28] Frances Coffyn to James Monroe, June 2, 1795, Nantes Despatches.

Robert Montgomery, the second of the three consuls, was one of many Americans who were already living abroad at the time of their appointment. Perhaps 35 percent of the consuls appointed by Washington were Americans living abroad. The fact that Montgomery had been in Spain since the middle years of the American Revolution meant that his experiences had been quite different from Americans at home. He had not suffered the ravages of the Revolution. In fact, he benefitted from them. His allegiance also could easily be called into question, and certainly some American consuls in the same position, like Thomas Bulkeley of Lisbon, had in fact become expatriates because they did not support independence. Even though Montgomery was undoubtedly an American citizen, the State Department described him as "of Spain" rather than as an American on his initial appointment, a designation that would come to haunt Montgomery in later years. Such confusion over citizenship status appears to have been very common in the first years of the republic. A good number of consuls who, like Montgomery, were identified as noncitizens in their appointments apparently were actually citizens, or at least were described as such in letters recommending them.[29] While poor record-keeping seems to have been part of the problem, especially for Montgomery, his situation also reflects the larger confusion over the nature of citizenship and the status of cosmopolitan merchants at a time when the idea of the territorial nation-state was still very new.

Born in the northern Ireland town of Newry, probably in 1754, Montgomery spent fewer than ten years of his long life in North America.[30] Like Simpson, his Protestant Scots-Irish family was imbedded in the trading network that connected Ireland to the Mediterranean and North America through cargos of fish, grain, wine, and other products.[31] His Philadelphia relatives had connections to the Mediterranean. One was born near Lisbon. Another traveled to the Mediterranean for his health and died in Gibraltar. By the late 1740s, a John Montgomery had established himself in Lisbon, where he formed a partnership with John Parminter, a flour merchant. It is unclear how or if this Montgomery was connected to Robert Montgomery, but their Lisbon firm was one of

[29] These include Joseph Donaldson, Philip Marck (Merck), William McCarty, John Culnan, and John Street.
[30] Thomas Harrison Montgomery, *A Genealogical History of the Family of Montgomery* (Philadelphia: Printed for Private Circulation, 1863) 149.
[31] On the fish trade, see Christopher P. Magra, *The Fisherman's Cause: Atlantic Commerce and Maritime Dimensions of the American Revolution* (New York: Cambridge University Press, 2009) in addition to Lydon, *Fish and Flour for Gold, 1600–1800*.

the important consignees of American fish in Lisbon during the 1760s, making the connection more likely. This possible connection would also help to explain why Robert's brother John would have settled in Boston, which was a major entrepôt of the Mediterranean fish trade.[32]

Robert and his brother James left Ireland as young teens and both arrived in Philadelphia about 1766, when Robert was 12 years of age. They joined the family of their merchant uncle Thomas Montgomery, who had resided in the Delaware Bay region for at least three decades. Robert "received the early parts of his education and a knowledge of commerce in Philadelphia" under Uncle Thomas, before the uncle's untimely death.[33] Young Robert did not stay in Philadelphia long. While still in his teens he joined the crew of the *Elizabeth*, which was owned by Thomas Montgomery. Robert later remembered taking this step "in imitation of his brother James," who at that time (the late 1760s or early 1770s) was master of another of Thomas's vessels. Robert made several voyages on the *Elizabeth* to Cádiz and other Mediterranean ports. By the time he was 19 he was master of the 250-ton brig *Charlotte*, another of the Montgomery family's vessels.[34] Having gained some experience and, presumably, capital, he then purchased the *Charlotte* with James. In addition to a 1773 voyage to Ireland, he captained the *Charlotte* to Cádiz, Málaga, and Alicante, where, he later recalled, he "encreased his capital and formed good connexions." During the Revolution he traded aggressively, forming a partnership with William Bingham to purchase the brig *Betsy*, which he sailed to Málaga and Alicante.[35] Bingham was one of Philadelphia's leading and best-connected merchants, part of a very influential group including Robert Morris and Thomas Willing. Bingham's impressive fortune would be built on the profits made during the Revolution.[36] Montgomery soon sold the *Betsy* and returned to Philadelphia, where he established himself as a merchant and

---

[32] John Montgomery to Sec. State, July 20, 1807, Alicante Despatches; Lydon, *Fish and Flour for Gold, 1600–1800*, 152–54; Harrison, *A Genealogical History of the Family of Montgomery*, 151–52.

[33] It is possible that some of this education occurred before Robert emigrated or at sea, as one source has Thomas dying the same year Robert arrived in Philadelphia. Harrison, *A Genealogical History of the Family of Montgomery*, 149–51; "Memorial of Robert Montgomery" [1793] in Alicante Despatches.

[34] *Belfast Newsletter*, Feb. 19, 1773, Irish Emigration Database, http://ied.dippam.ac.uk/records/38858.

[35] "Memorial of Robert Montgomery" [1819], Alicante Despatches.

[36] Thomas M. Doerflinger, *A Vigorous Spirit of Enterprise: Merchants and Economic Development in Revolutionary Philadelphia* (Chapel Hill: University of North Carolina Press, 1980) 237.

contracted with two other Philadelphians to have the *Juliana* built in New York. He made several more voyages to Europe during the Revolution in this 500-ton ship. Eventually, due to ill health, he decided to settle in Alicante in 1777.[37]

Montgomery supported the United States from the start. He and his brother James converted the brig *Charlotte* into an American privateer in the early days of the war. With James as captain, the *Charlotte* captured a number of valuable British prizes and brought them into Philadelphia. From his first arrival in Alicante, Robert registered as an American in the annual survey of foreign merchants. Concerned that he might, nevertheless, be classified as an English national, he wrote to Benjamin Franklin in April 1778 requesting a certificate proving his American nationality. In July he traveled to Paris to see Franklin and the other American commissioners in person. On September 16 they administered an oath of allegiance to the United States to Montgomery and issued him a document certifying his allegiance. Montgomery was among the first three Americans to get one of these certificates. The commissioners wrote of a "multitude" of Americans scattered about the various parts of Europe, who needed certificates in order to ensure that American or French ships would not capture them on suspicion of being British. The idea of issuing certificates originated with the commissioners, rather than Congress, and as the commissioners noted, they were not really legally valid, although Montgomery's certainly proved useful to him. Recognizing the need to support as well as to define Americans abroad, the commissioners also requested that Congress consider appointing American consuls to overseas ports.[38]

Nevertheless, Montgomery ran into trouble back in Alicante. There, authorities were preparing to ban British traders from Spain's ports as a result of the Spanish alliance with France against Britain. This is certainly the reason why Montgomery was anxious to receive his certificate, since once the British and Irish Catholics were expelled, he would be one of the

---

[37] Memorial of Robert Montgomery [1819], Alicante Despatches. This memorial suggests he was already established in Alicante in 1778, while an 1816 memorial suggests he first settled there in 1778. However, Montgomery claims to have been there "nearly seventeen years" in a 1793 petition, suggesting a 1777 arrival. The best evidence for this date is his 1778 letter to Franklin, in which he claims to have been in Alicante about twelve months.

[38] Memorial of Robert Montgomery [1819], Alicante Despatches; Robert Montgomery to Benjamin Franklin, Apr. 5, 1778; July 6, 1779, both in Papers of Benjamin Franklin, http://franklinpapers.org; Commissioners to the President of the Congress, Sept. 17, 1778, Papers of John Adams, vol. 7, in C. James Taylor, ed., *Founding Families: Digital Editions of the Papers of the Winthrops and the Adamses* (Boston: Massachusetts Historical Society, 2007).

few remaining merchants in the region with access to the Anglo-Irish Mediterranean trading network. When the Spaniards arrested the British traders in June 1779, they included Montgomery in their sweep. Although it is likely that Alicante's governor was well aware that Montgomery was American, and his identity will get more scrutiny in Chapter 3, this episode suggests that the difference between American citizen Montgomery and Scottish Gibraltarian Simpson should not be exaggerated. Neither seemed entirely American in Europe or America. At a time when both the United States and the notion of citizenship in a nation-state were entirely new, to insist on stark differences between citizen consuls and noncitizens may be a bit anachronistic. There was as yet no real American network in Spain and little conception of the United States or Americanness. The development of both would depend on consuls like Montgomery.

Like Simpson and others, Montgomery more or less appointed himself as de facto consul long before receiving an official appointment. In January 1783, even before the Treaty of Paris officially ended the Revolution, and apparently without contacting any American officials, he tried to initiate negotiations for a peace treaty between the United States and the emperor of Morocco, who threatened to capture American ships if the United States did not treat with him. Montgomery promised the Moroccan emperor that the United States would soon appoint a negotiator in Paris, prompting the emperor to send his agent, Giacomo Francisco Crocco, to Europe. Benjamin Franklin was blindsided and dumbfounded when he learned of these developments from Crocco.[39] Demonstrating a striking lack of self-awareness, Montgomery then tried to leverage his rogue operation into a consular appointment. In April 1783, he wrote to Robert Livingston, the first secretary of foreign affairs under the Continental Congress, requesting the Alicante consulate. Despite receiving no encouragement, he continued to pursue the position, writing to Livingston's successor and his old acquaintance, John Jay, in August 1786. Montgomery obliquely referred to his earlier efforts to gain peace with Morocco and promised his "continued zeal and best exertions for the advancement of our commerce and promoting the interests of our country." Jay promised to discuss Montgomery's appointment with Congress, but nothing came of it. Montgomery's failure may not have reflected on him personally so much as

---

[39] Giacomo Francisco Crocco to Franklin, July 15, 1783; Nov. 25, 1783; Franklin to Crocco, Dec. 15, 1783; Crocco to the Committee for Foreign Affairs, Nov. 16, 1794, all in Papers of Benjamin Franklin, http://franklinpapers.org; Roberts and Roberts, *Thomas Barclay (1728–1793)*, 128, 200.

on the Continental Congress's hesitation to appoint any consuls, since they only named two during their entire existence.[40]

Montgomery continued to assist the United States with some success and to request the consulship with no success over the next six years. After Algerians captured two American ships and their crews in 1785, he offered his services as an intermediary between the United States and his influential contacts there. He promised John Jay that his services would "be of the greatest utility to our trade in the Mediterranean evident from our present inability to supply this coast with [goods] from America in our own vessels in this season of scarcity exclusive of the constant supply of dry fish that might be sent hither from the northern states." Of course, such an improvement would also greatly benefit Montgomery, who, along with his brother, was deeply involved in the fish trade. When Thomas Jefferson was appointed secretary of state under the new constitution, Montgomery renewed his proposal to mediate with Algiers and repeated his request to be appointed consul. Increasingly, like Simpson, he acted as a de facto consul, providing information to the State Department and, in 1793 taking charge of the United States' efforts to provide the captives in Algiers (now increased by nearly a hundred souls due to further ship captures) with clothing and a small allowance. Finally, just before receiving his formal commission as consul to Alicante later in 1793, he petitioned Jefferson to be appointed consul to Algiers while continuing to reside in Alicante. Algiers was one of the four salaried posts, so holding it at the same time as the Alicante consulate would have given Montgomery the best of both words – lucrative trading profits in Spain and a secure salary in North Africa. In making this request he followed the same strategy taken by Simpson, who at one time hoped to hold both the busy Gibraltar consulate and the salaried Morocco post simultaneously. While the Algiers position never came through, Montgomery would continue to serve the United States in Alicante for the next three decades.[41]

***

[40] Robert Montgomery to Robert Livingston, Apr. 2, 1783; to John Jay, Aug. 8, 1786, both in Papers of John Jay, www.app.cc.columbia.edu; Kennedy, *The American Consul*, 16, counted two consuls, one vice-consul and "some foreign consuls operating on an interim arrangement with the United States."

[41] Montgomery to John Jay, Aug. 5, 1788; to Thomas Jefferson, Aug. 21, 1790; July 24, 1791; July 26, 1791; Dec. 17, 1793; Receipt for money and goods from David Humphreys, Dec. 9, 1793; Invoice of merchandise notarized by David Humphreys and Nathaniel Cutting, Dec. 17, 1793; Memorial of Robert Montgomery [1793], all in Alicante Despatches.

Thomas Appleton, our third consul, exemplifies the third mode of appointment: sending consuls out from the United States. The smallest proportion, approximately 11 percent, of Washington's appointments fit into this category. It is no coincidence that Appleton was the latest appointment of the three consuls – 1798 – since initially it was very hard to find any qualified American citizens ready to head out to a European post. The small number was not due to lack of interest. In the lean years following the hardships of the Revolution, plenty of American men were desperate for government office. Beyond pecuniary considerations, the fires of patriotism kindled by the war persisted for many applicants who expressed the desire to continue serving their country. The problem was that consulships required a fair outlay of money while (other than the four salaried posts) bringing in only a small income from fees collected for routine tasks, making it impossible for nonmerchants to take on the job. As a result, nearly all the applicants appointed from the United States either had spent a great deal of time abroad and were temporarily back home (making them not that different from those appointed while already abroad) or they planned to establish themselves as overseas merchants and hoped a consulship would help them to succeed.

Sylvanus Bourn, son of an important Massachusetts mercantile family is a good earlier example even if he was not in the Mediterranean. Bourn began his campaign for a job with the new government just before President Washington's first inauguration. He was a 28-year-old Harvard graduate who had planned to study law, but he was forced to go into business in a merchant house when his father died. Bourn hoped to set up shop in Europe or the West Indies, to recoup some of the family's considerable wartime losses.[42] He was one of a number of applicants with similar hopes and concerns at this time, all of whom calculated that a consular position would make their mercantile efforts more successful.[43] Like others, Bourn stressed his allegiance to Revolutionary

---

[42] Sheayashat Bourne to [Washington], Jan. 20, 1792; Sylvanus Bourn to Washington, May 22, 1789; B. Lincoln to Washington, Apr. 15, 1789; Sylvanus Bourn to Washington, Dec. 10, 1791, all in Washington Papers.

[43] William Vans to Washington, Dec. 24, 1790; Edward Church to Washington, May 11, 1789; Sept. 30, 1789, all in Washington Papers. Edward Church wrote to the president that he was "one of the unfortunate number whom the late revolution has precipitated from a state of decent competence, and reduced to the necessity of joining the class of your most humble and needy petitioners." As a wholesale merchant, he made efforts before and

ideals, writing that "being born in a land where ideas of liberty and the rights of mankind have ever been early indoctrinated [he] soon felt that laudable zeal which animated my country" and was determined to "devote my future life to my country's call."[44] While Jefferson and other cosmopolitan Republicans may have hoped that the American Revolution and its Atlantic counterparts would create a brotherhood that transcended national boundaries, in practice putative and actual consuls, as American representatives, had to reinforce the notion of citizenship and allegiance for themselves and others participating in the trading nation by repeating nationalistic tropes[45]

Bourn's patriotic motives did not go so far as to prompt him to ask for a consulship that might be unprofitable. Cádiz, Lisbon, Hispaniola, Martinique, and Guadelope, all rich ports and major destinations for American trade, topped his list. All were places where a well-connected American merchant could hope to make a substantial income.[46] This consideration was important even when applicants may have expected that positions would be salaried, but it became particularly crucial after 1790, when it began to become clear that Congress would not grant salaries for consular posts. That June, Bourn learned of his appointment to Cape François, St. Domingue, the crown jewel of the French Empire and a wealthy West Indian port teeming with American traffic.

---

after the war to recover his fortune abroad. He requested a consulship in Holland or the post of Collector of Imports for the Port of Savannah before receiving consular appointments to Bilboa and Lisbon. William Vans, consul to Morlaix, France claimed to need a position after suffering severe setbacks due to investments in American funds during the Revolution.

[44] Sylvanus Bourn to Washington, May 22, 1789; July 13, 1789, Washington Papers. To further demonstrate his attachment to and concern for the United States, Bourn had been working on a statistical table of America's overseas trade which he hoped to share with some future department of the new government that might be charged with regulating trade. Frederick Folger to Thomas Jefferson, May 8, 1792; Thomas and Zubdiel Rogers and Samuel Woodbridge to Hon. Benjamin Huntington Esq., May 13, 1790, both in Washington Papers. Bourn was not the only candidate to pepper his solicitation for office with patriotic appeals. Frederick Folger wrote of himself that "few citizens were actuated by a more enthusiastic zeal for the prosperity of the United States during their late struggle for independence," and Samuel Snow was described as having "spent the prime of life in the service of our common country in the military line with much reputation and little pay." Folger to Jefferson, May 8, 1792; Rogers, Rogers, and Woodbridge to Huntington, May 13, 1790, both in Washington Papers.

[45] Armin Mattes, *Citizens of a Common Intellectual Homeland: The Transatlantic Origins of American Democracy and Nationhood* (Charlottesville: University of Virginia Press, 2015) 141–83.

[46] He also flirted with the idea of a salaried domestic office.

Unfortunately for Bourn, all his careful strategizing came to nothing. Less than a year after his arrival in Cape François the Haitian Revolution broke out, described by Bourn as "[a] new and alarming catastrophe." For Bourn the revolution brought "accumulated expences, disappointment and chagrin." Without prospects, having "expended considerable money and received no income under these disagreeable circumstances," he was forced to return home.[47] Finally, after many applications, including one to return to Cape François, Bourn got himself appointed to the lucrative and relatively safe consulate at Amsterdam in 1794, where he would serve until his death in 1817.[48]

Bourn's personal situation may have improved with his Amsterdam appointment, but the lack of consular salaries continued to hinder recruitment for consular posts and frustrate existing consuls. In 1794 when Thomas Jefferson sent around a circular requesting input from consuls on plans to improve the consular system, recipients bemoaned their lack of salary and the general weakness of their office. Bourn complained that many posts continued to be occupied by foreigners because "the poverty of the existing consular establishment ... in regard to compensation or emoluments forbids that any one could accept of a consular appointment ... ." Bourn added that the previous year he had to spend over $1,500 of his own money on consular expenses (not including housing or transportation) and had taken in only $183 in fees. In Bristol, Elias Vanderhorst agreed that "the want of salaries adequate to the dignity of the office" was the chief impediment to a successful consular system.[49]

Like Bourn, Thomas Appleton sought a consulship in a lucrative port as a means of advancing his mercantile career. He was born into a well-connected Boston family in 1763. His grandfather was the chaplain at Harvard College. His father, Nathaniel Appleton, was a Harvard graduate, and a member of the Sons of Liberty during the Revolution. After the war Nathaniel held a number of political offices, including a seat in the General Court and a long term as state commissioner of loans. As a prosperous officeholder and candle manufacturer he was not quite

---

[47] Sylvanus Bourn to [Jefferson] Sept. 8, 1791; to [Washington] [Dec. 10, 1791], both in Washington Papers. Fulwar Skipwith faced a similar setback after arriving as consul to Martinique.

[48] Sylvanus Bourn to [Washington], Jan. 20, 1792; Jeremiah Smith to Washington, Mar. 29, 1792; Bourn to Jefferson, Jan. 9, 1793; to [Jefferson], June 17, 1793, all in Washington Papers.

[49] Elias Vanderhorst to Sec. State, July 31, 1795, Bristol Despatches. Sylvanus Bourn to Sec. State, Aug. 6, 1795, Amsterdam Despatches.

among the commercial elite, but his daughters (Thomas's sisters) both married elite merchants: Thomas Perkins and Samuel Emery. Perkins, in particular, was at the top of the heap of Boston traders. Unlike his father and grandfather, young Appleton did not attend Harvard but was instead "educated in the mercantile line," meaning that he served as a clerk in a merchant house in Boston. At about 24 years of age, he sailed to France, where he worked as a merchant for more than a decade during which he became familiar with all things French, including the language.[50]

On returning to the United States in 1797, Appleton opened up a campaign to land a consular position in Paris, a post he learned Fulwar Skipwith had recently quit. This position would have been very desirable despite the lack of salary as, in addition to getting him back to France, the heavy mercantile traffic would have produced a good income in consular fees and a multitude of commercial connections among the many American traders and officials who would have felt obliged to visit the American consul in Paris. Like most successful consular applicants in the Adams administration, Appleton had the support of powerful patrons. His politically connected father led the charge and probably enlisted the support of Benjamin Lincoln, an influential Boston political operative; John Lowell, progenitor of the famous Boston family; and longtime Rhode Island governor, Arthur Fenner. Appleton's lengthy absence from the United States caused a bit of concern that he might have lost his sense of American identity. Lincoln stressed that despite his experience in France, Appleton was "an American and not a Frenchman," while Fenner stressed the applicant's "attachment to the Constitution" and pointedly added how fortunate it was that "the United States has rais'd up from her own bosom such characters as are able to fill and discharge the several duties connected to their public stations . . . ."[51]

Like many successful applicants, Appleton also submitted petitions supporting his application signed by merchants and officials familiar with his commercial reputation. Often these were submitted by merchants specifically connected to the post where the applicant hoped to be assigned, although in Appleton's case there is no evidence that his supporters were chosen due to their connections to France. The fifty-three

---

[50] Argiero and Neri, *Bostoniani a Livorno*, 29–34; Benjamin Lincoln to the President, Oct. 12, 1797; N. Appleton to the President, Oct. 16, 1797, both in Adams Recs.

[51] Appleton to the President, Oct. 16, 1797; to Timothy Pickering, Oct. 16, 1797; John Lowell to Pickering, Oct. 18, 1797; A. Fenner to the President, Oct. 19, 1797, all in Adams Recs.

signers consisted of the topmost merchants in both Boston and Providence, including members of the Lowell, Sargent, and Amory families of Boston; the Browns of Providence; and Appleton's in-laws, the Perkins.[52] Support from merchants was particularly important because consuls were still seen as merchants' representatives in foreign ports, a relic from the days of full extraterritoriality, when consuls were appointed directly by the merchants they served. Therefore, it was crucial that consuls understood their patrons' interests and that merchants be comfortable with the men appointed to these positions.[53]

All of this support failed to land Appleton a position in France, but it did lead to an interview with President Adams who suggested he might qualify for a position in Dunkirk or Ostend. Appleton rejected these posts as lacking the requisite volume of American commerce. He countered with an offer to go to Livorno. For Appleton, Livorno would have seemed a suitable position due to the relatively heavy and persistent volume of American trade. Appleton also had information that some Americans had lodged complaints against Felicchi, who was still the consul there. If Appleton's information was true, it may have reflected American merchants' uneasiness with a non-American consul during the French occupation, when American ships and goods were subject to confiscation on the suspicion that they were English. It was not uncommon for American citizens to angle to replace foreign appointees in lucrative ports.[54] In light of these concerns, Appleton would have doubtless seemed an excellent choice as an American citizen, knowledgeable merchant, and fluent francophone who appeared ideally suited to deal with French authorities.[55]

***

By 1800 thirty-five American consuls had been appointed to the Mediterranean, including Appleton, Montgomery, and Simpson. These new consular appointees and their colleagues formed the nucleus of the American community in the region. When one considers that most of these

---

[52] Petitions in support of Thomas Appleton dated Boston, Apr. 4, 1797 and Providence, Oct. 19, 1797, Adams Recs.

[53] For other successful applicants who conducted similar petition drives, see the files of Thomas Bulkeley and George Knox in Adams Recs. Bulkeley in particular, who was under suspicion as a Loyalist, submitted identical petitions from multiple cities.

[54] See, for example, Daniel Sargent and others to Pickering, Feb. 23, 1797, in support of Thomas Bulkeley, Adams Recs.

[55] Appleton to the President, Dec. 7, 1797; to [the President?], Jan. 22, 1798, both in Adams Recs.

appointees also employed a number of clerks and others in their merchant houses and had family members, too, the number of people in their collective households would have been well over a hundred. The growing American community would have also included other nonconsular merchants and their families as well as seamen and others passing through the region regularly.

Yet to consider this group of perhaps several hundred people an American community from the start would be a stretch. Since the majority of consuls were either noncitizens or men who had not lived in the United States for some time, their American-ness was certainly open to question. And, considering their disparate origins and lack of connection in many cases to America, the idea of a community may also seem questionable. What really forged these individuals into an American community was their mercantile and consular function. The period between 1785 and 1808 was one of great promise in the Mediterranean, and increasingly these merchant-consuls worked together to promote and benefit from American trade in the region. But these years were also a time of continual threat to the Mediterranean trade. The danger came from two directions. First, beginning in 1785 "Barbary pirates," more accurately state-supported North African cruisers, posed a danger to American vessels in the region. Next, French and English ships also threatened American commerce during the course of the warfare beginning in the mid-1790s. Consuls were on the first line of defense. They were in a good position to learn of early indications of possible captures, and they were expected to spread this news throughout the American community. As a result, American consuls were in frequent contact with each other as part of this warning system, and they were also in frequent contact with American captains and State Department officials. These official contacts often led to mercantile contacts as well, since merchant-consuls needed reliable trading partners in nearby ports. As a result of all these developments, this group of individuals became much more American and much more of a community over the coming decades.

2

James Simpson

Isolation and Diplomacy in Gibraltar and Tangier

Nineteenth-century writers sometimes portrayed consuls as do-nothing sinecured officials who spent more time in local barrooms than in meeting or assisting their countrymen.[1] This stereotype could not have been further from the truth for James Simpson. In particular, the fear of North African corsairs, whether originating in Morocco or any of the ports to its east, made him into a key figure in the new nation's foreign policy, thrusting him into frequent communication and cooperation with Americans in the region and at the State Department. Rather than a low-level official in a backwater post, he was actually one of the most important diplomats in the entire region due, in large part, to the lack of higher-level State Department officials in the Mediterranean. He spent an inordinate amount of effort attempting to prevent conflict with North African states and anything that might impede American commerce in the wider Mediterranean. Not only did this activity diverge from later stereotypes, it also diverged from the role of most American consuls in the Mediterranean and strikingly from those in the north where the State Department had a larger footprint and a few high-level American diplomats to handle the sort of delicate treaty negotiations that fell into Simpson's lap.[2]

---

[1] Examples include Mark Twain, *The Innocents Abroad* (New York: Harper Bros, 1911, reprint of the 1869 edition) which has derogatory comments on US consuls throughout, most memorably the Tangier Consul (79); George Washington Montgomery, *Narrative of a Journey to Guatemala in Central America in 1838* (New York: Wiley and Putnam, 1839) 100–101; Malcolm Lowry, *Under The Volcano* (New York: Reynal and Hichcock, 1947) may be the most famous modern example.

[2] In Ireland, by way of contrast, consuls appear to have spent most of their time trying to certify citizenship of Americans (in part due to impressment issues), helping needy seamen,

Much of Simpson's importance derived from the location of his appointments. Though on opposite sides of the Mediterranean, and, to different degrees, isolated from the center of European power, both were crucial for American efforts to penetrate the Mediterranean. At Gibraltar, his first position, Simpson was in near constant contact with Americans and other Europeans. Every single American ship that entered the Mediterranean passed through the Strait of Gibraltar. On the left side of that narrow channel (as little as 9 miles wide at its tightest) the Rock of Gibraltar juts out of the sea, forming the region's most notable landmark with its unmistakable rocky cap. To the right loom the less recognizable but much larger mountains of Morocco and the relatively flatter port of Tangier, Simpson's second post. Gibraltar, Simpson's home since at least the 1770s, was a tiny piece of the British Empire surrounded by hostile Spain. It was, perhaps, the closest thing to a perfect natural fortification. Separated from the Spanish mainland by miles of sand and protected on that side by a massive vertical cliff rising roughly 1,300 feet, it was impregnable to land forces, while the side facing the sea was protected by the world's greatest navy in addition to natural cliffs.

Gibraltar was first and foremost a garrison, designed to allow the British Empire to control access into and out of the Mediterranean. It also offered some opportunities to the merchants among its heterogeneous population of roughly 3,000 Catholics, Protestants, Jews, and Muslims. With its banking connections to London, it served as a financial node where merchants could easily purchase pounds sterling and find good access to credit. As a free port, it also served as a good transshipment point both for cargos legally entering and exiting the Mediterranean and for those whose provenance was murky. Even in the best of times, however, Gibraltar could not support a great deal of trade considering that it had absolutely no hinterland of its own and that it was surrounded by hostile Spaniards. The only real trade that occurred there was the import of provisions for the garrison from across the Strait in Morocco and Algiers. Gibraltar merchants, including Simpson, brought in cattle, poultry, barley, and other items to feed the troops under the watchful eye of the Rock's British governor, who spent a good proportion of his time monitoring this trade.[3]

---

and working on emigration issues rather than engaging in treaty negotiations. See Bernadette Whelan, *American Government in Ireland, 1790–1813: A History of the US Consular Service* (Manchester University Press, 2010). As will be evident below, neither Montgomery nor Appleton spent nearly as much time on diplomacy.

[3] On Gibraltar generally, see L. A. Sawchuk, S. G. Benady, and S. D. A. Burke, *Passing through the Fever: Anatomy of an Epidemic* (Toronto: Diva Media, 2005); Diane Sloma, "Gibraltar Fortress and Colony in Strategy, Economics and War 1918 to 1947," PhD

But the years during and after the American Revolution were not good times at all for Gibraltarians like Simpson. While Britain had been engaged in a losing and costly effort to retain its American colonies, Spain had taken advantage of the situation to attempt to regain Gibraltar, which had been a sore spot since the British captured it in 1704. The ensuing siege of Gibraltar (1779–83) was the European end-game for the conflict between Britain, France, and Spain which had begun with the American Revolution. It was a trying time for Simpson and his neighbors, to put it mildly. Most were forced to flee towards the top of the Rock in order to escape the Spanish bombs. There they created temporary shelters in Gibraltar's stony cliffs, and, because the North African trade was cut off, they faced malnourishment and the real possibility of starvation. Britain's ultimate victory in 1783 partially redeemed the loss of the colonies and confirmed the impregnability of Gibraltar. Nevertheless, the years following the siege were uncertain ones for the Rock. The population had declined drastically, as anyone who was able to had escaped. Continual bombardment had destroyed much of the low-lying town. Simpson and other Gibraltarians would have had real doubts about the long-term viability of commerce there, and the population failed to reach its pre-siege level until at least the early 1790s.[4]

It is not clear when or why he arrived in Gibraltar, but Simpson was certainly there as early as the Great Siege when he was in his early thirties. He worked as a merchant in partnership with Robert Anderson for some time. Anderson, who was recorded by authorities as having been born in "north Britain" (most likely Scotland given his name) arrived in Gibraltar in 1756 as a young teenager. Four years older than Simpson, he would have been the senior partner in their Scottish-influenced firm.[5] In addition to Anderson, Simpson likely had a dense social network in Gibraltar. He may well have been drawn there by the presence of other family members. There certainly was an unusually large number of Simpsons in the small British community. Stephen Simpson, a sailmaker, arrived before 1777. Another Stephen Simpson, possibly his son, was working as a watchmaker by the early 1790s. Two other Simpsons, Alexander and William, worked as merchants. If, as seems likely, James was related to one or more of these

---

dissertation (Anglia Ruskin University, Cambridge, 2000). While focused on later periods, both offer some discussion of earlier decades, for which there is still very little literature other than military history.

[4] Sloma, "Gibralter Fortress and Colony in Strategy, Economics and War 1918 to 1947," 32–33.

[5] Gibraltar Inhabitants 1704–1914; *Scots Magazine*, Mar. 10, 1820, 95.

Simpsons, he would have had a comfortable social circle. Additionally, Simpson socialized regularly with the British officers stationed at Gibraltar, including General George Whitmore and Major John Vignoles, with whom he was particularly close during the Siege of Gibraltar, and whose grandson would later become governor of New Zealand.[6]

Much later, Simpson's son wrote that the consul left a successful mercantile business when he departed Gibraltar. But, in all probability, Simpson struggled after the siege. He was able to resume the provisioning trade, but that does not seem to have been enough. He unsuccessfully sought government permission to try to trade new items over the Strait.[7] It was at this time, too that he became Russian consul to Gibraltar, a position that would offer a small but fairly steady stream of additional income. Increasingly it must have become clear to him that his greatest capital was the numerous contacts he had cultivated with influential figures in southern Europe and across the Strait, contacts made possible by his location in Gibraltar. These contacts served him in the provisioning trade and probably also with the Russians, who were interested in expanding their Mediterranean trade at this time. Simpson was ultimately able to use them to convince the United States to appoint him consul to Tangier.

Simpson's days in Gibraltar ended when, in October 1796, he received news of the long-coveted appointment to Morocco. Before leaving, he successfully lobbied the State Department to appoint his "particular friend" John Gavino as his replacement. Gavino was a native of Cartagena, Spain, who had recently settled in Gibraltar. His brother had been the Dutch consul for Gibraltar and his partners in Cartagena had English surnames, suggesting he had long been involved in the Anglo-Spanish trade to which Simpson and so many Americans in Spain were also connected.[8] Having taken care of his public and private affairs, Simpson finally left Gibraltar behind in December 1797, arriving in Tangier on December 7 where he and his family were greeted by the "usual complementary salute of 11 guns" and received by the governor

---

[6] Gibraltar Inhabitants 1704–1914; *Scots Magazine*, Apr. 1, 1795, 275; Helen Ann Wilson to Donald McLean, Jan. 22, 1863; May 19, 1863, both in McLean Letters; John Drinkwater, *A History of the Late Siege of Gibraltar* (London: T. Spilsbury, 1786) XI; "Whitmore, George Stoddart" in *Te Ara: The Encyclopedia of New Zealand*, www .teara.govt.NZ.

[7] Governor to Messrs. J. Ross and James Simpson, Nov. 2, 1789; to James Matra, Oct. 23, 1789; Governor's Secretary to Simpson, May 9, 1797, all in Governor's Letterbook 1795–1801, Gibraltar National Archives.

[8] James Simpson to Sec. State, Oct. 29, 1796, Gibraltar Despatches.

as American consul "with marks of cordial friendship." He would live the rest of his life in Tangier, removed from his former home and the nearest anglophone community by approximately 36 miles of often stormy sea which could be crossed in about six hours in the best of weather and could be extremely treacherous in the worst.

Tangier had a long, fraught relationship with the Europeans who lived across the Mediterranean. It was occupied by the Portuguese from 1471 until 1661, when Charles II of England acquired it from his Portuguese bride, Catherine of Braganza. For a time, the English hoped that this extremely strategic port at the entrance to the Mediterranean would become the crown jewel of their empire, and they invested large sums into fortifications and an impressive mole, all of which the British destroyed before abandoning it to the Moroccans in 1684.[9] By the time Simpson arrived, Tangier's chief importance was as a diplomatic link between the Moroccan emperors and Europe.

Foreign consuls had previously been housed about 40 miles to the southeast in Tétouan, a place that Simpson's fellow Gibraltarian and likely acquaintance Dr. William Lemprière found "far preferable to Tangier as well on account of the inhabitants being more civilized, as the beauty of the adjacent country." Lemprière wrote that the consuls were expelled and moved to the "distant and uncivilized" port of Tangier due to a Christian consul's trespassing on a sacred path and accidently shooting a local woman. More likely it was part of Emperor Sidi Muhammed's policy of expanding his contact with Europe while simultaneously seeking to "pick and choose how and when to engage with the political and commercial representatives of foreign powers." By keeping European officials at arm's length from the center of power, Moroccan officials hoped to avoid the growing dependence on Europe experienced by the Barbary regencies of Tripoli, Tunis, and Algiers to the east.[10]

Tangier remained a crucial diplomatic hub and a cosmopolitan city where Islamic, Jewish, and occasional European residents lived in close proximity and relative harmony, although Europeans generally had disdain for it (and often still do today). European travelers estimated its population at anywhere from 6,000 to 15,000. Dr. Lemprière observed,

---

[9] Linda Colley, *Captives: Britain, Empire, and the World, 1600–1850* (New York: Anchor Books, 2002) 23–32.

[10] William Lemprière, *A Tour from Gibraltar to Tangier . . .* (London: J. Walter, 1793) 7–9; James A. O. C. Brown, *Crossing the Strait: Morocco, Gibraltar and Great Britain in the 18th and 19th Centuries* (Leiden: Brill, 2012) 33–54.

"The houses are in general mean and ill furnished, the roofs are quite flat, and both these and the walls are entirely whitened over." James Curtis, another British medical man from Gibraltar wrote that, while "delightfully situated," Tangier, "like all Moorish towns" was "dirty and disagreeable; the streets are so narrow that a person cannot traverse them without difficulty, and the indolence of the people surpasses any thing of the kind which may be found in the southern climates of Europe." James Grey Jackson, yet another British traveler in the early nineteenth century, noted that Tangier was "favourable to Moorish piracy" and would "never be a commercial town, having but few productions in its vicinage." The walled city with its distinctive whitewashed houses, was surrounded by a narrow agricultural belt "laid out into vineyards, orchards, and cornfields, beyond which are tracts of sand, with lofty and barren hills." Europeans found this suburban area more to their taste. "Every part of the country in the environs of Tangiers is beautiful, and interspersed with villages and gardens," Curtis wrote. Here Simpson and other European consuls would establish their country estates.[11] (See Maps 2.1 and 2.2.)

In Simpson's day, Tangier, and Morocco generally, offered few trading prospects to American merchants. Another English doctor who visited Tangier in 1806 wrote that "excepting a few small vessels, fitted out for piracy, there is no shipping in the harbor." Consequently, during his first decade in Morocco, Simpson had little reason to be optimistic about trade. Commerce did grow a bit, beginning around 1802, but that modest boom was short lived.[12] From January 1804 until December 1805 only one American merchant vessel arrived in Morocco, and conditions never improved much during the rest of Simpson's tenure. Even during a relatively robust period in 1804 Simpson concluded that, "[A]t all

[11] Lemprière, *A Tour from Gibraltar to Tangier*, 10. Colley, *Captives*, 23–37; James Curtis, *A Journal of Travels in Barbary, in the Year 1801* (London: T. N. Longman and O. Rees, 1803) 6–13, quotes from 6 and 12; James Grey Jackson, *An Account of the Empire of Morocco and the District of Suse* (London: W. Bulmer and Co., 1809) 87, 93–95, quote from 94. Yet another British doctor, John Buffa, made similar observations in 1810. See John Buffa MD, *Travels Through the Empire of Morocco* (London: J. J. Stockdale, 1810).

[12] Simpson reported a total of thirteen US vessels arriving in all of Morocco for the year of 1802, mostly at Mogadore. In the eighteen months from January 1802 to July 1803 approximately $126,000 in US imports arrived at Mogadore, including about $55,000 in specie. Americans paid roughly $29,000 in import and export duties during this period Buffa, *Travels Through the Empire of Morocco*, 23; "General Report of the Arrival and Departure of Vessles of the USA … during the year 1802; James Simpson to Sec. State, Jan. 31, 1803; July 28, 1803, all in Tangier Despatches. By comparison the average single US cargo arriving in Livorno during this period was worth $100,000 as detailed in Chapter 3 below.

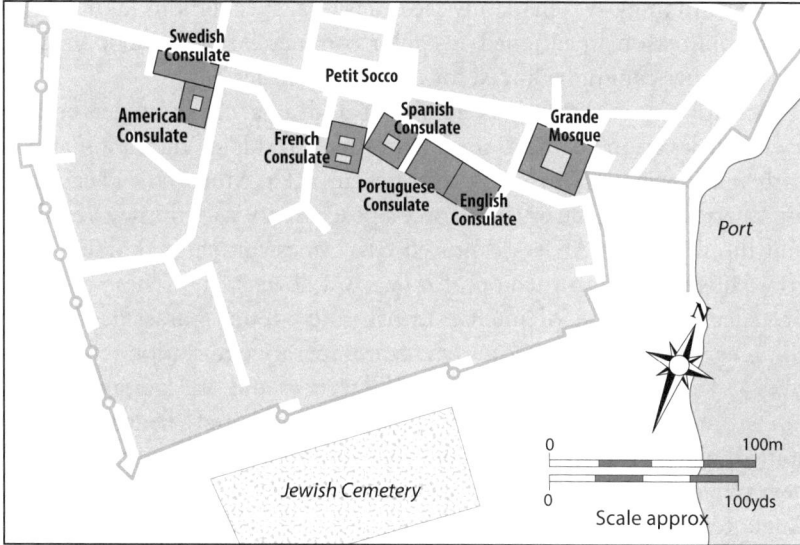

MAP 2.1 Details from an 1808 map of central Tangier showing the locations of consular houses. (The American consulate is shown attached to the much larger Swedish consulate at upper left.) (Map redrawn by David McCutcheon FBCart.S, www.dvdmaps.co.uk)

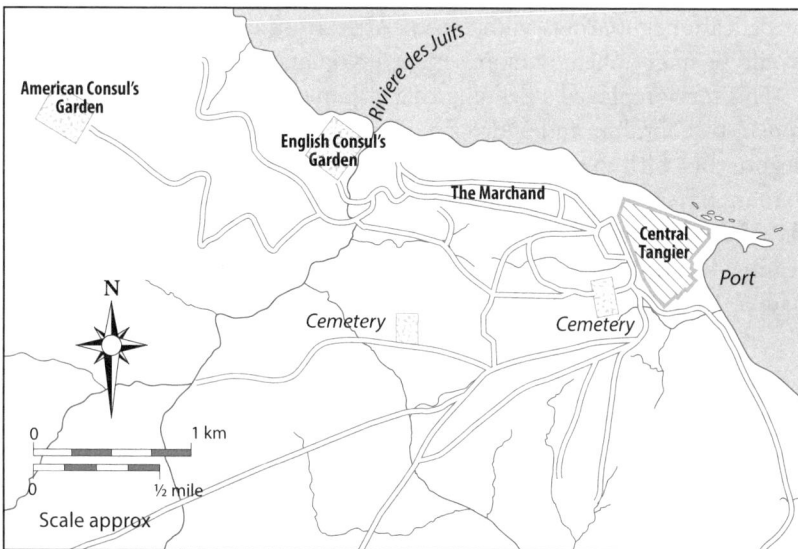

MAP 2.2 Details from an 1808 map showing the environs of Tangier. (The British consul's country estate is at top center near the coast and James Simpson's country estate is at far left.) (Map redrawn by David McCutcheon FBCart.S, www.dvdmaps.co.uk)

times (I still think) we shall only see occasional speculations taking place, as for the reasons mentioned a regular commercial intercourse between the countries cannot be hoped for on a grand scale."[13]

Despite any shortcomings as a port and as a city, Tangier became a crucial location to the United States as a result of the new nation's early tensions with North African states. In 1784, Morocco had captured an American ship in an effort to force a peace treaty with the new republic, and the next year Algiers captured two American ships, holding their crews hostage, as it turned out, for nearly a dozen years. These incidents preceded the period of intense British and French harassment of US shipping by about a decade and made it imperative to station representatives at Tangier and Algiers. A second, larger round of Algerian captures in 1794 and then the first Barbary War, 1801–5, created a near-permanent state of alert on the part of US shipping in the Mediterranean during the next two decades and more, eventually merging with US–French and US–Anglo tensions during the Napoleonic Wars. Ship captures and sporadic warfare had the potential to paralyze America's Mediterranean commerce just when it was at its most lucrative and important. At the same time, there were no senior American diplomats whatsoever on the southern side of the Mediterranean, and none south of Madrid for most of the period. As a result, the Barbary consuls, all of whom were salaried, gained outsized diplomatic importance as they frequently embarked in the sort of delicate negotiations with North African officials that in later years would be undertaken by more senior diplomats.

This tension played a defining role in James Simpson's life, because, as consul to Gibraltar and Morocco, he was one of the primary American negotiators with the North Africans. This might seem like an inordinate amount of responsibility for a Scottish merchant who had never set foot in the United States, although it was hardly exceptional at the time. In reality, hiring foreigners as agents where no nationals were available had a long history in the Mediterranean and elsewhere. Simpson's

---

[13] In 1806 conditions improved slightly, with the arrival of eight American ships – five in Tangier, two in Mogadore, and one in Tétouan. One of these vessels was hauled in by privateers and two were unable to trade because they had come in quest of mules which the emperor would not allow to be exported. Two others arrived with only ballast, while the others carried a mix of tobacco, reexports, and miscellaneous goods. The most common cargos for outward journeys included waxes, animal skins, and oils. Fear of cruisers, the Barbary Wars, and the emperor's commercial policies clearly did not help US–Moroccan trade. Simpson to Sec. State, Mar. 2, 1804; July 13, 1805; Feb. 12, 1806; Jan. 17, 1807, all in Tangier Despatches.

predecessors as American agents in Morocco, the Chiappi brothers, had even less connection to the United States and questionable English to boot.[14] What Simpson brought to the table was his familiarity with the region and the players in it, a result of his long career as a merchant at the connecting hinge between North Africa and southern Europe. In time, despite not being a citizen and being posted in an isolated port where he rarely met an American face-to-face, his consular activities integrated him into the American community in the Mediterranean region, and he increasingly spent his time corresponding with other members of that community. He was not only a member of this community; he also became, despite his lack of citizenship, one of its founders and leaders. In Tangier itself he was the physical embodiment of the new nation. And, through his key position, he was instrumental in binding together disparate actors into an American community, even though, like him, a good number were not citizens. Whether citizens or not, though, all of them shared the business and political interests that brought them together.

***

In Gibraltar, well connected as he may have been in the Mediterranean, at first Simpson had few to no contacts in the United States. Nevertheless, Simpson was interested enough in the new republic to begin acting as an intermediary between the Chiappi brothers, who were serving as American agents in Morocco, and the State Department. Simpson also took it on himself to gather information on Algerian officials' plans for ransoming American captives, which he forwarded to George Washington.[15] Probably he sniffed out possibilities for new contacts and various means of profit. Simpson's friendship with Thomas Barclay in Gibraltar helped to graft him on to the American networks, a process that continued with Barclay's unexpected death in Lisbon before he could return to Morocco.[16]

[14] The American seaman Judah Paddock needed a translator to speak to Joseph (Guiseppi) Chiappi, and Simpson's only existing letter to him is in Spanish. See Simpson to Joseph Chiappi, July 13, 1799, Gibraltar Despatches; Simpson to Sec. State, June 7, 1800, Tangier Despatches.

[15] David Humphreys to George Washington, Feb. 3, 1794, in F. L. Humphreys, *Life and Times of David Humphreys* (New York: Putnam, 1917) II: 205; Simpson to George Washington, Aug. 25, 1794; July 9, 1791; Apr. 13, 1791; n.d. [1791], all in Gibraltar Despatches.

[16] Simpson to Thomas Jefferson, Feb. 12, 1793; Feb. 19, 1793; Oct. 21, 1793, all in Gibraltar Despatches.

Barclay's death brought Simpson into contact with more of the American community, beginning with David Humphreys. The US minister to Madrid and Lisbon would eventually become Simpson's closest American confidant. Simpson also worked with two Lisbon merchant houses – those of Bulkeley and Harrison – to settle Barclay's estate. Both were key figures in American affairs and Bulkeley would also become a close acquaintance. Simpson also worked closely with Humphreys' secretary, Nathaniel Cutting, a Massachusetts merchant who would soon be appointed American consul to Le Havre. Finally, Simpson would have had to contact Robert Montgomery to tell him to expect the arrival of fifteen cases of Barclay's merchandise in Alicante, where Humphreys planned to pick them up on his way to negotiate with the Dey of Algiers.[17] As a result, Simpson began to be integrated into the American community in the Mediterranean region and, increasingly, spent his time corresponding with other members of that community.

Simpson kept careful records in Gibraltar, including a book with copies of letters he sent as he pursued American business from 1793 to 1797. This is an unusual document, as all that survives for most consuls during this period is their correspondence with the State Department which typically, other than the occasional enclosure, consists entirely of official despatches addressed to the secretary of state. When his letterbook is combined with information from the despatches sent to the secretary of state, which were retained by the State Department as official records, we can gain an unusually full view of Simpson's correspondence network and consular activities, at least so far as they pertain to American concerns, since letters pertaining to his personal or non-American business do not appear to have survived.

The roughly 325 letters Simpson wrote to fifty-eight correspondents in the course of conducting American business during this period give a good sense of the geographic limits of his world and of its increasing American-ness.[18] The vast majority of Simpson's correspondents (79 percent) lived in Spain, Portugal, Morocco, and Algiers. Most of these lived on the

---

[17] "Thomas Barclay his Account Current with the USA, Oct. 1793"; "The USA in Account Current with James Simpson of Gibraltar, 12 Oct. 1793"; "Invoice of Sundry Merchandize, the Property of the USA, deposited in the charge of James Simpson of Gibraltar Oct. 1793," all in Gibraltar Despatches.

[18] These figures are computed from both despatches and letterbooks and include some letters/correspondents extracted or referred to for which full copies do not exist. Totals are inexact because some letters may have been referred to twice in the two sources.

TABLE 2.1 *James Simpson correspondents 1793–97*[1]

Region	# of correspondents	# of letters
Algiers	3	3
France	1	1
Gibraltar	11	21
Morocco	13	43[2]
Portugal	5	75[3]
Spain	15	89
Great Britain	3	9
United States	8	70[4]
TOTALS	59	311

[1] Combining Gibraltar despatches and Letterbook entries for these dates.
[2] Minimum estimate. I have subtracted some apparent overlap between the sources.
[3] All in Lisbon, including 46 to David Humphreys.
[4] Only counting letters to Jefferson from Letterbook due to overlap with despatches.

northern shore of the Mediterranean and its vicinity from Lisbon to Alicante, and on the southern shore from Tangier to Algiers. Simpson also had the occasional correspondent to the north, particularly in Madrid and Great Britain, as well as a few in the United States, all of whom were government officials. (See Table 2.1.)

Simpson's correspondents on the African shores of the Mediterranean, sometimes referred to by him as "the other side," broke almost exactly into two categories. The first group consisted of Moroccan officials, particularly Emperor Muley Solimon and his son Muley Taib. Simpson's niche was his Barbary connections, so naturally he would have been expected to be able to communicate with these crucial officials. He likely had come into contact with them during the course of his business as a merchant moving provisions between Morocco and Gibraltar in a market that was regulated by government on both ends. He also wrote Humphreys that somewhat earlier in his career he had "extensive trans-actions in business" with the official who later became the Dey of Algiers, suggesting he may have also dealt with shipments to or from Algiers. He may also have dealt with North African officials in his capacity as Russian consul to Gibraltar. When Barclay was in Gibraltar he reported Russia would "shortly attempt to make treaties with all the Barbary powers," information he almost certainly received from his friend Simpson.[19]

Simpson's knowledge of these officials benefitted the United States during the turbulent period after the death of Sidi Muhammed (Muhammed b. Abdulla) in 1790, with whom Barclay had negotiated the first US–Moroccan treaty in 1787. After a tumultuous period in which Sidi Muhammed's sons vied for power from 1790 to 1792, it became apparent that Muley Solimon had gained control.[20] Consequently, it became necessary to renegotiate the US treaty with the new Moroccan administration. Simpson started to lay the groundwork for these negotiations on his own initiative in 1794. Humphreys and State Department officials in Philadelphia were aware of his actions and apparently approved, though it is unclear whether he ever actually obtained an official appointment to continue. Whatever his official status, he traveled to Tangier in June 1795, where he began negotiations with the emperor and his brother, Secretary of State Muley Taib. The party moved to Rabat and continued negotiations throughout the summer, finally reaching an agreement in September that renewed the old treaty. The treaty renewal assured that American ships in the Atlantic and Mediterranean would be safe from Moroccan interference for the time being. In a letter translated by Simpson, the emperor assured President Washington, "we are at peace tranquility and friendship with you in the same manner, as you were with our Father who is in Glory."[21]

The second group of North Africans with whom Simpson corresponded was European consuls. Consuls were among the only Europeans (other than captives) who were able to spend much time in Barbary and gain access to powerful officials there. They tended to be a tight little group with virtually no one to socialize with other than themselves. Consequently, they often ignored differences in nationality. Simpson was particularly close to consuls from Sweden and Denmark which, like the United States, were both neutral nations in the European wars. He wrote at least twelve letters to the Swedish consul, Peter Wyk, during the period considered here, and probably many more were not preserved. Other letters contain frequent references to information provided by Wyk

---

[19] Simpson to David Humphreys, May 13, 1795, Simpson Letterbook; Thomas Barclay to Jefferson, May 10, 1792, Gibraltar Despatches.

[20] J. M. Abun-Nasr, *A History of the Maghrib* (Cambridge University Press, 1971) 241–42.

[21] Simpson to Sec. State, June 22, 1795; July 15, 1795; July 8, 1795; Aug. 18, 1795; Aug. 22, 1795; to Edward Church, Aug. 18, 1795, all in Gibraltar Despatches.

during negotiations with Morocco and of Wyk delivering important documents to him. Simpson singled out Wyk for his help, at one point making the unusual request that the US formally acknowledge the Swede's assistance.[22] Simpson also corresponded frequently with Michael Classen, the Danish general consul to Morocco and met with him when he was in Gibraltar. Classen also appears to have been friendly with Barclay.[23]

Simpson corresponded with a number of other consuls and European officials in North Africa. He appears to have received news from two successive British consuls to Algiers: Charles Logie and Charles Mace. Logie had been consul to Morocco in the 1770s, so he would have presumably continued to have contacts there. In Morocco, Simpson frequently received information from the Chiappi brothers – Geronimo, Guiseppe, and Francisco – who had represented American interests before the consular system was set up, and who also represented Venice and Genoa.[24] He had good relations with James M. Matra, the American-born British consul to Morocco. Educated in Britain, Matra was scion of a loyalist family that lost their wealth during the Revolution. He apparently corresponded regularly with Simpson and when in Gibraltar shared information with him in person. He once described Simpson as his "friend."[25] Finally, Simpson was on good terms with French officials, including M. Mure, the consul at Sallee and Jean Baptiste Du Rocher, the

[22] Simpson to Barclay, Dec. 13, 1792; Dec. 17, 1792, both in Gibraltar Despatches. Simpson to Sec. State, Nov. 1, 1794; Nov. 17, 1794; Feb. 16, 1795; Feb. 17, 1795, all in Gibraltar Despatches. Simpson to Humphreys, May 13, 1795; Sept. 7, 1795; Dec. 14, 1795, all in Simpson Letterbook.

[23] Simpson to Barclay, Oct. 18, 1792; Oct. 25, 1792; to Jefferson, Feb. 19, 1793, all in Gibraltar Despatches. Simpson to Humphreys, Aug. 11, 1794; Oct. 30, 1794; Apr. 27, 1795, all in Simpson Letterbook.

[24] Simpson to Guiseppe Chiappe, Sept. 11, 1795; to Humphreys, July 17, 1794; Sept. 25, 1794; to Geronimo Chiappe, Oct. 10, 1794, all in Simpson Letterbook. Simpson to Sec. State, Sept. 24, 1795; to Washington, Aug. 25, [1791]; Apr. 13, 1791, all in Gibraltar Despatches. On the Chiappes, see the annotation to George Washington to Giuseppe Chiappe, July 18, 1789, Washington Papers. For Logie and Mace, see Simpson to Humphreys, July 7, 1794, Simpson Letterbook; Simpson to Sec. State, Jan. 20, 1794, Gibraltar Despatches; R. Lambert Playfair et al., *Royal Geographical Society. Supplementary Papers*, III(3): *A Bibliography of Morocco from the Earliest Times to 1891* (London: John Murray, 1892) 436.

[25] Simpson to Joseph Ysnardi, Feb. 10, 1795; to Humphreys, June 11, 1795, both in Simpson Letterbook. Alan Frost, "Matra, James Mario," in *Australian Dictionary of Biography*, Supplemental Volume (Melbourne University Press, 2005). James Matra to Governor of Tangier, Sept. 10, 1803, Consular Correspondence, 1780–1830, Box 1, Gibraltar National Archives.

TABLE 2.2 *Simpson's correspondents by position*

Position	# of correspondents	# of letters
Captains	8	11
US consuls[1]	6	77
Other consuls	10	24
Merchants	9	19
Barbary officials	5	15
US officials	13	148
Other officials	3	6
TOTALS	54	303

[1] Includes vice-consuls

consul general for Morocco whom Simpson described as "a most worthy man" and who had also been friendly with Barclay.[26] (See Table 2.2.)

At first when Simpson pursued American business on the northern shore of the Mediterranean he relied primarily on British officials and merchants that he presumably knew before becoming involved with the United States. A good number also had connections with Humphreys and Barclay. The latter, as a newcomer to the region and a close friend and associate of Simpson may have met them through Simpson. For example, when in the fall of 1793, a Portuguese–Algerian truce exposed American ships to capture, Simpson wrote repeatedly to John Lemprière Jr., the British consul at Faro, Portugal, with requests that he forward the news on to Lisbon. Simpson may have known Lemprière through his mercantile business or through John's brother, William Lemprière who was a doctor in the British garrison at Gibraltar and had spent some time as the Moroccan emperor's personal physician. Barclay also corresponded with William during the period when he and Simpson were working together in Gibraltar.[27] Additionally, Simpson received information on

[26] Simpson to M. Mure, June 25, 1796; to Humphreys, May 13, 1795, both in Simpson Letterbook. Priscilla H. Roberts and Richard S. Roberts, *Thomas Barclay (1728–1793): Consul in France, Diplomat in Barbary* (Bethlehem, PA: Lehigh University Press, 2008) 206–7, 213.

[27] Simpson to John Lemprière Jr., Oct. 6, 1793; Oct. 8, 1793, both in Simpson Letterbook; William Lemprière to Barclay, Sept. 19, 1792, Gibraltar Despatches; Lemprière, *A Tour from Gibraltar to Tangier*; "William Lemprière" entry in the Dictionary of National Biography, https://en.wikisource.org/wiki/Dictionary_of_National_Biography,_1885-19 00/Lempri%C3%A8re,_William.

North African cruisers from James Duff, the British consul at Cádiz and a former consul to Morocco.[28]

In these early years Simpson also relied on a number of merchants in southern Spain and Portugal who, like him, were developing ties to the United States despite not being citizens or having received any sort of appointment. Many of these had entered American circles through contact with Humphreys or Barclay. For example, during the 1793 Algerian crisis when he wrote Lemprière he also enlisted two Anglo-Irish merchant houses in Cádiz for assistance. The first, Thomas and Henry Lynch, had Gibraltar connections, had done business with Barclay, and were friendly with both David Humphreys and William Lemprière.[29] The other, Dominick Terry, was a member of a prominent, noble Irish family and one of the most important foreign merchants in Cádiz. Terry also corresponded with two of the American captains captured by the Algerians. His son, Anthony, later served as American vice-consul, and father and son were both friendly with Humphreys.[30]

Additionally, Simpson relied on two Iberian merchants who would later become American consuls. The first was John Bulkeley and Sons in Lisbon who were American Loyalist expatriates and probably the most influential merchants dealing with the US trade in Lisbon. Thomas Bulkeley would eventually become US consul in 1797. Humphreys knew them well and would eventually marry into the family. Simpson had Lisbon connections before becoming US consul, which he used to get access to the Algerian captives, so he certainly would have known the Bulkeleys, most likely for some time. Perhaps they originally connected him to Humphreys. Whatever the case, Simpson corresponded with them frequently to share information and also to have them convey messages to

---

[28] Simpson to Jefferson, Oct. 21, 1793, Gibraltar Despatches; Playfair et al., *Royal Geographical Society*, 437. Like Simpson, Duff was of Scottish descent.

[29] Simpson to Henry Lynch, Oct. 6, 1793; Feb. 8, 1794, both in Simpson Letterbook; Roberts and Roberts, *Thomas Barclay (1728–1793)*, 219. The Lynches were subscribers to books written by Humphreys and Lemprière. See Lemprière, *A Tour from Gibraltar . . .*, viii; Humphreys, *Miscellaneous Works*, "Subscribers Names" (New York: T. and J. Swords, 1804) [n.p.]. Governor to Henry Lynch, May 12, 1797, Governor's Letterbook, Gibraltar National Archives.

[30] Simpson to D. Terry and Co., Oct. 8, 1793, Simpson Letterbook; Lawrence Peskin, *Captives and Countrymen: Barbary Slavery and the American Public, 1785–1816* (Baltimore: Johns Hopkins University Press, 2009) 217; Beatriz García-Alvarez de la Villa and Kevin Terry, "Terrys in Spain and Latin America: Exile and Rise of An Irish Merchant Family," *Estudios Irelandeses* 11 (2016) 75–77; Humphreys, *Miscellaneous Works*, "Subscribers Names."

Humphreys and others.[31] Simpson also corresponded frequently with Joseph Ysnardi, an influential Spanish merchant who was appointed American consul to Cádiz in 1793. Simpson first wrote to Ysnardi at Humphreys's behest to inform him of the Algerian–Portuguese truce of 1793 and ask him to warn Americans of the danger to their shipping. It is unclear whether Ysnardi or Simpson were yet aware of Ysnardi's US appointment, which had already been issued but would typically have taken months to reach the Mediterranean. Simpson wrote to him first in Spanish, suggesting he did not know whether Ysnardi understood English and also that the two probably had not corresponded before. He explained to Ysnardi that Humphreys was the American minister plenipotentiary in the Portuguese court, suggesting that Ysnardi and Humphreys also were not yet acquainted. Over the years, Simpson and Ysnardi's relationship would deepen until Ysnardi became Simpson's most frequent correspondent on American business in the Mediterranean after Humphreys.[32]

As Simpson and his circle became more deeply imbedded in the American trading nation and as the consular service began to take shape, his correspondence increasingly involved other US consuls, some of whom would become close contacts. In his first letter to Edward Church, the American consul to Lisbon, Simpson warned that Algerians had captured two American ships. Hinting at a business as well as a professional connection, he closed his note by writing, "I beg you will command me on every occasion I can be useful to you or your friends." He began corresponding with William Short, recently appointed American minister to Madrid, on the advice of Michael Morphy, the US consul (and British vice-consul) to Málaga, with whom Simpson had been acquainted for some time, also to provide information on Algerian cruisers. Short wrote back almost immediately, sending Simpson information about American negotiations with Britain and requesting information on Moroccan affairs. Short, too, would become one of Simpson's most important American correspondents over the years.[33] (See Table 2.3.)

[31] Barclay to Jefferson, Dec. 31, 1791, Gibraltar Despatches; Simpson to J. Bulkeley and Sons, Feb. 8, 1794; Entry for Aug. 9, 1794; Simpson to Edward Church, Nov. 17, 1794; to J. Bulkeley and Sons, Mar. 12, 1795, all in Simpson Letterbook.

[32] Guadalupe Carrasco-Gonzalez, "La Delegacion Consular de Los Estados Unidas en España: La Oficina Consular de Cádiz a Principio del Siglo XIX," https://rodin.uca.es/bitstream/han dle/10498/16397/LA%20DELEGACION%20CONSULAR%20DE%20CADIZ%5B1%5 D.pdf?sequence=2, 5–6; Simpson to Ysnardi, Oct. 6, 1793, Simpson Letterbook.

[33] Simpson to Church, Oct. 28, 1793; Sept. 1, 1794; to William Short, Oct. 23, 1794; Nov. 13, 1794, all in Simpson Letterbook. Governor to Vice-Consul Morphy, June 7, 1787, Governor's Letterbook, Gibraltar National Archives.

TABLE 2.3 *Simpson's most frequent*
correspondents 1793–97

Name	Number of known letters
David Humphreys	46
Joseph Ysnardi	35
Thomas Jefferson	33
Secretary of State	27
Michael Morphy	19
William Short	15
Edward Church	14
Peter Wyk	12
Joseph Bulkeley	9

In his early months on the job, Simpson drew on his fellow consuls for information which was sorely lacking from the State Department's infrequent communications. As soon as he heard of his appointment, he wrote Church and Ysnardi to find out what consulage fees they were able to charge American vessels, a vital question as this would be an important source of income to an unpaid consul. These fees never appear to have been spelled out in detail by the State Department, so it is no surprise that Simpson was still baffled by the finer points and sought clarification from Church weeks later so as "to act in such a manner as may meet the approbation of the President and ministers and also perfectly consistent with what my brother consuls do."[34]

Lack of information from Philadelphia led him to consult with other consuls on a good number of other issues. Even before Simpson learned of his appointment, Ysnardi apparently had read of it in a newspaper and conveyed the news to Simpson. After his appointment he also asked Ysnardi for a copy of the laws of the United States, and as he mulled over the need to renew the US–Moroccan treaty of 1787 that Barclay had negotiated, he wrote to Morphy and Ysnardi in search of copies. Finally, Simpson made some efforts to keep abreast of events in the United States, particularly negotiations with Britain and the outcome of the Whiskey Rebellion in Pennsylvania.[35]

---

[34] Simpson to Michael Morphy, Aug. 28, 1794; to Ysnardi, Aug. 28, 1794; to Church, Sept. 18, 1794, all in Simpson Letterbook.

[35] Simpson to Short, Dec. 18, 1794; Dec. 25, 1794; to Ysnardi, Sept. 1, 1794; Oct. 9, 1794; to Morphy, Oct. 3, 1794; to Church, Nov. 17, 1794, all in Simpson Letterbook.

But Simpson most frequently contacted his fellow consuls to warn them of danger from North African cruisers. Early in his tenure at Gibraltar, he heard from a trusted Moroccan in Gibraltar who was "in correspondence with some people on the other side" that Moroccan cruisers had orders to detain American vessels. He wrote to Michael Morphy in Málaga and someone in Cádiz, possibly Ysnardi, though the letter is lost, to warn them. He also requested that the Spanish captain who had agreed to convoy American ships warn them of the danger.[36] About the time he was officially appointed to his position, Simpson was still unclear of the identity of more distant American consuls. At one point when he feared Moroccan cruisers were attacking Americans, he had to write Thomas Pinckney, the American minister to Great Britain to warn the consuls in "Holland, Hamburgh and other places to the North" whom Simpson explained he had "not yet been in correspondence with … nor do I know their names."[37] European ships could also prompt concerns, as in 1796 when he warned US consuls in London, Dublin, Alicante, Málaga, Amsterdam, London, and Madeira that French privateers were capturing American vessels off Gibraltar.[38]

At times Simpson was both a recipient and initiator of these warnings. In December 1795 he heard from Joseph Donaldson, who was an old friend, frequent correspondent, and the American agent negotiating a treaty with Algiers, that cruisers from Tripoli and Tunis now posed a greater threat to the United States due to a US–Algerian treaty which would bring more American ships into the Mediterranean. Simpson passed this warming on to Ysnardi at Cádiz, an American captain named William Billings, and probably others.[39] At the same time Simpson was very concerned about reports he was receiving that American ships were trying to trade at the Moroccan ports of Safi and Mazagan (El Jadida). These towns were in a region that was revolting against Muley Solimon, who was attempting to consolidate his control over Morocco and had essentially declared a blockade against them. In Simpson's view, avaricious American captains were putting their private hopes of making big profits before the national interest by running the

---

[36] Simpson to Sec. State, Apr. 25, 1794, Gibraltar Despatches; Simpson to Capt. James Scarnichia, Sept. 26, 1794; to Morphy, Sept. 26, 1794; to Ysnardi, Sept. 29, 1794, all in Simpson Letterbook.

[37] Simpson to Thomas Pinckney, Feb. 12, 1794, Simpson Letterbook.

[38] Circular letter dated Sept. 26, 1796, Simpson Letterbook.

[39] Simpson to Humphreys, Feb. 22, 1796; to Capt. William Billings, Mar. 1796, both in Simpson Letterbook.

blockade. As a result, Simpson sent repeated letters to the consul and vice-consul in Lisbon and to Ysnardi in Cádiz informing them of the danger, presumably with the expectation that they would warn American captains in those busy ports.[40]

***

It might seem as though the lack of American trade and American faces in Tangier would isolate Simpson further from the United States, particularly considering his Scottish origins. Nevertheless, Simpson's move to Tangier arguably drew him still closer to Americans. This was due to the importance of Morocco's location and the lack of higher-level diplomats in the region. Even though there was little American trade coming into Moroccan ports, Morocco's position at the entrance to the Mediterranean made it crucial to the free flow of American commerce into and out of the region. Consequently, Simpson had to work very hard to protect American shipping, a task that made him a very important figure within the American community and kept him in constant contact with Americans despite the remoteness of his post.

Part of his job now was to maintain the peace treaties that he and Barclay had negotiated in the 1780s and 1790s, the most successful and least expensive negotiated by the United States with the Barbary powers. Such treaties demanded annual payments and North African rulers also expected a steady stream of "gifts" as a goodwill offering to maintain peace. In 1801, Simpson promised to help the emperor obtain 100 gun carriages through the assistance of his old friends, the Bulkeleys of Lisbon, who, as discussed above, were crucial players in the American trading nation.[41] This promise should be seen as a typical effort to maintain peace and prevent the possibility of future ship captures. As with just about everything in North Africa, the apparently simple gesture led to unforeseen difficulties. Bulkeley was unable to procure any carriages, leading Simpson to attempt to find other sources, a task made more difficult by the disruptions in Europe and demand for armaments caused by the Barbary and Napoleonic wars. By 1802 he had received assurances from the State Department that the United States could send out carriages to Morocco, but one year later Washington

---

[40] Simpson to Ysnardi, Oct. 29, 1795; to Humphreys, Mar. 7, 1796; to William Porter East, May 5, 1796; to Humphreys, June 23, 1796; Feb. 11, 1796; to East, Dec. 14, 1795, all in Simpson Letterbook. On the Moroccan conflict and embargo see Brown, *Crossing the Strait*, 62ff.

[41] Simpson to Emperor of Morocco, July 31, 1802, Tangier Despatches.

suggested he draw on a fund in London to procure them in Europe instead. In the meantime, Simpson feared the emperor was becoming increasingly agitated by this long unfulfilled promise. It was not until 1804, three years after Simpson first broached the topic of the gun carriages that they finally arrived, marking, according to the emperor, "fresh proof of your diligence and the friendship of your nation . . . ."[42]

Another potential disruption to trade was the threat of epidemics, which was a problem throughout the Mediterranean. For Simpson the issue was the plague, which broke out in 1799, less than two years after his arrival (although one European observer thought it was more akin to yellow fever).[43] Beyond the human toll, the plague could wreak havoc by shutting down ports and isolating residents from the rest of the world for long periods of time. In Tangier, due to the general lack of commerce, this was less of a threat than in busier places, but nonetheless, Simpson and the Americans in the region faced real problems during this outbreak.

Physically, Simpson was not in immediate danger after being evacuated to Tarifa, Spain shortly after the first news of the outbreak in June 1799. Tarifa was an island located in the Strait of Gibraltar 24 miles to the North of Tangier and suitably isolated from the mainland (though today it is attached to the mainland and is considered Europe's southernmost point). Simpson took a ship across the Strait with his wife and daughter, arriving in Tarifa on June 12. The evacuation had been arranged by the Spanish ambassador to Morocco with the permission of the king of Spain. The majority of the consuls in Tangier and their families, totaling 129 people, took advantage of the offer and also benefitted from the expertise of twelve health officers on the island. Simpson stayed there approximately two-and-a-half months before returning to Tangier in late August, when the plague appeared to be abating. Nonetheless, he stayed in his Mount Washington villa, far from the crowded city. This proved a good decision when the plague resumed the next spring. The siege did not abate until the following November. Simpson and the other consuls calculated that 1,783 Tangier residents had died since the first outbreak. Fatalities were much higher in southern Morocco.[44]

---

[42] Simpson to Sec. State, June 17, 1802; Aug. 3, 1802; to Emperor of Morocco, July 31, 1802; to Sec. State, Dec. 24, 1802; June 8, 1803; July 9, 1803; Feb. 28, 1804; Emperor of Morocco to Simpson, Apr. 7, 1804, all in Tangier Despatches.

[43] Jackson, *An Account of the Empire of Morocco and the District of Suse*, 269–76.

[44] Simpson to David Humphreys, June 22, 1799; to Sec. State, June 24, 1799; July 30, 1799, all in Gibraltar Despatches; Translation of letter written His Imperial Majesty Muley Solimon, Aug. 28, 1799; Simpson to Right Honorable Lord Keith, Oct. 11, 1800; to Sec. State, Nov. 14, 1800, all in Tangier Despatches.

Even if there was little trade to disrupt in Tangier, the plague did cause disruptions. Trade at Mogadore, always more voluminous than in Tangier, ceased entirely as European merchants isolated themselves in their houses amongst very high death tolls. It was at this time that information from consuls was crucial to prevent American ships from sailing into plague zones where, in addition to losing a good deal of money, they would expose their crews and potentially other Americans to the epidemic. Just as with the threat of ship captures, the spread of the plague pushed Americans, and particularly consuls, to work together to try to avoid the worst dangers. Simpson tried very hard to get news of the situation to the State Department in his despatches and also tried to provide updates to others in the American community, including Robert Montgomery. During the evacuation, he left his secretary, John Tosh, in Tangier to deal with any issues that might arise there.

Unfortunately, the isolating nature of the epidemic worked against Simpson while he was stuck on Tarifa. Shipping in the region was disrupted. And Europeans, well aware that disease could be transmitted through letters written by sick people, took precautions with written materials ranging from dipping them into vinegar, which, while relatively benign, could make them nearly impossible to read, to simply avoiding delivery of these materials altogether. Simpson complained that he had virtually no connection to Gibraltar, which was located only 24 miles up the Spanish coast from Tarifa and was usually the easiest route through which to connect to America. Gibraltarians, Simpson wrote, "will not even receive letters." The difficulty in communicating with Gibraltar continued even after Simpson returned to Tangier, though he was able to send mail to Tarifa twice a month. Even so, he feared that the Portuguese and Spanish would not forward these letters on due to the spread of the plague. While the plague was very isolating and disruptive in this regard, at the same time it no doubt also reinforced Simpson's identification with his fellow Western consuls considering their shared odyssey to Tarifa and back to Tangier.[45]

Simpson's biggest problem in this first decade at Tangier, however, was the First Barbary War, which the United States waged with Tripoli from 1801 to 1805. This war (and the subsequent Barbary War of 1815) was possible because the United States had begun to create a navy in 1794 after

---

[45] James Simpson to David Humphreys, June 22, 1799; Aug. 7, 1799; to Thomas Bulkeley, Aug. 10, 1799; to Miss Montgomery, Aug. 10, 1799; to Sec. State, May 19, 1800; to Bulkeley, Aug. 31, 1800; to Hugh Cahill, Sept. 5, 1800, all in Simpson NARA.

Algerian corsairs captured eleven American ships. The Quasi-War of
1798 with France had spurred further naval construction. Without this
navy, there would really have been no defense against ship captures when
Tripoli declared war on the United States in March 1801. Typically, such
a declaration by the North African states signaled that they would capture
the enemy's ships until a peace was reached, usually with a one-time fee
and a continuing schedule of annual payments. In this case, Tripoli
demanded a $225,000 tribute payment plus $25,000 annually. President
Jefferson was now able to send a small squadron of three frigates and
a schooner into the Mediterranean to signal to Tripoli and the other North
African powers that the United States would not tolerate such ship captures nor provide tribute.[46] Like all American consuls in the region,
Simpson had hoped for the arrival of naval power in the region for
many years. On the arrival of the squadron he wrote, "I have often since
summer of 1795 had the honor of stating in my dispatches, there is not any
thing has such weight, as showing the Moor that a naval force is at hand,
to act in case of need." Secretary of State Madison acknowledged the role
of consuls in pushing for a navy when he wrote the Tunisian consul, "The
policy of exhibiting a naval force on the coast of Barbary has long been
urged by yourself and other consuls."[47]

   While the arrival of the squadron did indeed solve some of Simpson's
problems, it also exacerbated others. The United States' blockade of
Tripoli, the first in North Africa for many years, created a good deal of
confusion and disruption.[48] Moroccan ships needed passports to avoid
capture by American patrollers, creating more work for Simpson and the
other consuls who had to be careful to differentiate legitimate from
illegitimate requests. The 1786 treaty, as Simpson well knew, stipulated
that the two nations would issue passes to each other's vessels so that they
could recognize each other and therefore avoid mistakenly detaining or
capturing ships. One of Simpson's first orders of business as consul had
been to familiarize himself with these passes so that he could judge their
authenticity and issue them himself when necessary. With the outbreak of
war, this became a flash point. Moroccans were desirous of sending
supplies, particularly wheat, to Tripoli either for profit or to support

---

[46] Frank Lambert, *The Barbary Wars: American Independence in the Atlantic World*
    (New York: Hill and Wang, 2005) 123–26; Peskin, *Captives and Countrymen*, 110–33,
    Marshall Smelser, *The Congress Founds the Navy, 1797–1798* (South Bend: University of
    Notre Dame Press, 1959).
[47] Simpson to Sec. State, July 3, 1802, Tangier Despatches; Lambert, *The Barbary Wars*, 126.
[48] Lambert, *The Barbary Wars*, 133–34.

their co-religionists. In 1802, the emperor demanded that Simpson and other consuls issue passports to allow wheat shipments directly to Tripoli with the threat that Simpson would be forced to leave Morocco should he refuse and, presumably, the emperor would declare war on the United States.[49]

Simpson's hesitation to issue passports exacerbated tensions with the emperor. Morocco and other Islamic states sympathized with Tripoli, or at least its citizens, and made efforts to bypass the blockade to bring in food. When the US Navy captured Moroccans running the blockade, tensions between the two nations further intensified and the threat to American shipping and commerce also grew. Additionally, Morocco's emperor, Muley Solimon, had for some time been attempting to isolate Morocco further from the Western powers. Restricting consuls to Tangier was part of that strategy as was a general lack of interest in expanding trade with Europe much beyond the Gibraltar provisioning trade. At this time, too, he was toying with the idea of expanding Morocco's force of cruisers to extort "tribute" from the more vulnerable Western powers, including the United States.[50]

Simpson was inclined to allow the wheat shipments, which were supposed to be distributed to the poor in Tripoli. He realized that he would be expelled, his property seized, and war declared against the United States should he refuse. A declaration of war would also annul the peace treaties he and Barclay had worked so hard to sustain. However, Commodore Richard Morris, of the Mediterranean squadron, disagreed and forbade Simpson from issuing the passes, a decision which Simpson found "extremely distressing, as I saw great cause to dread the consequences." Simpson tried to delay by suggesting to the Moroccans that the imminent arrival of the frigate USS *Adams* would bring good news, presumably of the anticipated gun carriages. That tactic failed and, on June 16, "soldiers arrived with the Emperor's second orders for my quitting the country immediately *in a state of war.*"[51]

Before departing for Gibraltar, Simpson sent out twenty-six circular letters warning American consuls and agents from St. Petersburg to

---

[49] Treaty of Peace and Friendship between the United States and Morocco (1786), https://avalon.law.yale.edu/; Simpson to Sec. State, Dec. 16, 1797; June 17, 1802, both in Tangier Despatches.

[50] Mohamed El Mansour, *Morocco in the Reign of Mawlay Sulayman* (Outwell: MENAS Press, 1990) 67–71, 109–10.

[51] Simpson to Sec. State, June 17, 1802; June 26, 1802, both in Tangier Despatches. Original emphasis.

Algiers that Morocco had declared war and would likely try to capture American ships. He worked to evacuate American merchants from Mogadore and asked the Spanish consul to Tangier to look after his own property at Mount Washington. Once in Gibraltar Simpson hoped the United States would send a show of naval force to help him negotiate with the Moroccans. Eventually Morris sent the USS *Adams* and the schooner USS *Enterprise* to bring Simpson back to Tangier. The Moroccans agreed to withdraw the order to capture American ships if Simpson would issue their cruisers passports. Simpson refused to do so until the emperor would make a "positive proclamation of his being at peace as heretofore with the United States," which implied adherence to the old treaties. After long negotiations, the Moroccans agreed in early August 1802. Simpson congratulated himself on his hard-nosed negotiating but admitted, "[H]ad there not been a naval force at hand to keep their cruisers in port, I very much doubt if all I could have done, would have been attended with that success I now so much hope for."[52]

With the status quo reestablished, he sent twenty-two circulars to American consuls in Europe advising them that peace had been attained. By the end of August, he was back in the American consulate, where he once again raised the US flag and issued passports for a Moroccan frigate and schooner. The insistence of some Moroccan officials, that, despite the 1786 treaty the United States must provide tribute and the emperor's irritation at the delay of the gun carriages weighed on his mind, but for now the danger of war with Morocco had receded.[53]

Soon the emperor resumed pressure on Simpson to issue questionable passports. In particular, he wanted Simpson and the other consuls to give passes for the *Meshouda*, a Tripolitan ship that was docked at Gibraltar. The emperor wanted the passports to certify that the ship was his personal property. This was pretty evidently a device that would somehow allow the Moroccans to support Tripoli. Neither Simpson nor the other consuls wanted to issue the passes, but they also could not very well call a head of state a liar by pointing out that he was not the owner of the *Meshouda*. As Simpson wrote, "[I]f the Emperor announces to the body of consuls that the ship is his, and demands passports accordingly, merely to go to sea and navigate as his, I really do not see how I can continue to contest the matter

---

[52] Simpson to Sec. State, June 26, 1802; July 3, 1802; July 16, 1802; July 27, 1802; Aug. 3, 1802, all in Tangier Despatches.
[53] Simpson to Sec. State, Aug. 12, 1802; Emperor to Simpson, Aug. 6, 1802; Simpson to Soy Mohammed Ben Absalem Selawy, Sept. 1, 1802, all in Tangier Despatches.

or ... express doubts on what is stated by the sovereign of the country as fact, without running a good risqué of drawing serious resentment on the commerce of the U.S. ... ." The demand, according to Simpson, was "contemptible," and he hoped US naval ships would stay on guard to make sure the Moroccans did not take advantage. But in the end he issued the passport certifying the *Meshouda* as a Moroccan vessel able to "pass very freely and unmolested" with the clear exemption that it was forbidden "entrance into blockaded ports."[54] This exemption was crucial, since it forbade assistance to Tripoli.

Simpson's fears were realized in June 1803 when the US Navy caught the *Meshouda* attempting to run the blockade of Tripoli. Simpson suspected that the ship's captain had acted without the emperor's knowledge in disobeying the provisions of the US passport. He therefore hoped the Navy could release the ship (which was not in very good shape) to Morocco in order to maintain good relations with Muley Solimon. At the same time, he hoped the Naval command would move US ships toward Morocco in order to dissuade the emperor from retaliating for the capture. It took a very long time for Commodore Morris to respond. In the meantime, the United States caught a Moroccan ship, the *Mirboha*, red-handed attempting to capture Americans. On board they also found and captured Rais Ibrahim Lubarez, the naval officer in charge of reviving the Moroccan cruisers. In apparent retaliation, the Moroccans captured an American merchant ship, the *Hanna*, in Mogadore. It is also possible that this capture was less a response to the *Meshouda* and *Mirboha* captures than it was a tentative foray into implementing the emperor's policy of resuming cruises against the weaker Western powers.[55]

With no response from Morris, the Moroccan authorities were very angry and Tangier's governor, Abd al-Rahman Hashash, met Simpson twice with "unceasing" complaints about the *Meshouda* capture. At this juncture an unpleasant war between the United States and Morocco seemed very likely. Such an event, besides posing great danger to Simpson and any other Americans who might be captured by the

---

[54] Simpson to Sec. State, Sept. 3, 1802; Sept. 24, 1802; Translation of Passport Order, Sept. 27, 1802, all in Tangier Despatches.

[55] For detailed discussion of these events see Christopher McKee, *Edward Preble: A Naval Biography 1761–1807* (Annapolis: Naval Institute Press, 1996) 139–72; Richard B. Parker, *Uncle Sam in Barbary: A Diplomatic History* (Gainesville: University Press of Florida, 2004), 156–57. Spellings and even names of the Moroccan ships vary in the literature. Simpson's own despatches are inconclusive. I have followed McKee's spellings. On Lubarez, see El Mansour, *Morocco in the Reign of Mawlay Sulayman*, 109–10.

Moroccans, would also create an unwelcome distraction to the US Navy which was already fighting Tripoli. At this point, instead of immediately informing Muley Solimon of the precise reasons why the United States had seized the *Meshouda* and that they would consider returning it if the captain had run the blockade on his own volition rather than having been ordered to do so, Simpson made "a most unaccountable blunder," according to British consul James Matra. At the apparent urging of Governor Hashash, he agreed to postpone discussion until the United States brought the ship back to Gibraltar. Matra called this agreement "a fit of lunacy" on Simpson's part. It allowed Governor Hashash, described as a "malicious whelp" by Matra, to report to the emperor first and presumably to omit mention that the United States would consider returning the *Meshouda*. Whether that omission led to the capture of the *Hanna* and the intensification of hostilities was unclear to Matra and remains unclear today, but Simpson's inaction seems at a minimum to have allowed Hashash to feed the emperor's anger against the United States and make the crisis more dire.[56]

More immediately, Simpson put himself in danger with his unwise trust of Hashash. On the evening of September 5, the governor invited Simpson to his house to discuss the matter further, which, despite the late hour, was a not uncommon occurrence. But Simpson wrote that, on his arrival at the Casbah, "to my great astonishment the door was immediately shut and I was informed by a relation of the governor's that it was his orders I should be detained." Simpson was not freed until the next day when his "brother consuls came in a body" to demand his freedom "on the principle of the person of a consul in this country as representative of his nation being exempt from all arrest." Unbeknownst to anyone in Tangier, on that very day the United States had captured a second Moroccan cruiser, the *Maimona* off the coast of Portugal, a circumstance, which, combined with the earlier US captures, would be helpful to Simpson and the United States.[57]

After receiving the consular protests, the Moroccan authorities released Simpson. One week later, Commodore Edward Preble arrived in Tangier aboard the USS *Constitution* to confer with Simpson on the crisis.

[56] James Matra to Governor O'Hara, Sept. 10, 1803, Consular Correspondence, 1780–1830, Box 1, Gibraltar National Archives; McKee, *Edward Preble*, 139–45; Simpson to Sec. State, Sept. 5, 1803, Tangier Despatches.
[57] Simpson to Richard Morris, Jr., June 20, 1803; to Sec. State, July 9, 1803; Aug. 15, 1803; Sept. 5, 1803, all in Tangier Despatches; McKee, *Edward Preble*, 139–40.

When Simpson did not raise the US flag and did not respond, Preble assumed Morocco had declared war on the United States. Preble returned to Gibraltar where, with the help of Simpson's subsequent reports, he formulated a hardline approach against the emperor, who was on his way to Tangier. By the time Preble returned to Tangier with two frigates and a schooner, the emperor welcomed them and "ordered ten head of cattle, twenty head of sheep and some fowls to be sent in his name" to the Americans. Simpson and Preble were granted a rare face-to-face meeting with the emperor on the Casbah steps. At Simpson's recommendation, Preble and Commodore John Rodgers agreed to release the *Meshouda* and the two other captured Moroccan ships, in return for which the emperor agreed to release any American vessels and cargo his ships had captured. The Moroccans also agreed to renew the 1786 treaty, thereby restoring the peaceful status quo between the United States and Morocco. Simpson breathed a sigh of relief that the Navy's show of force at Tangier and their capturing of the Moroccan ships had allowed the issue to be settled without the emperor being able to capture more Americans or demand a further subsidy from the United States.[58]

Not everyone celebrated Simpson's handling of the situation. William Eaton, the American consul to Tunis, was appalled that Simpson had given *Meshouda* a passport in the first place and that the American consul in Algiers had apparently issued a passport to another ship to bring wheat to Tripoli from Turkey. Eaton wrote to Secretary of State James Madison in disgust, "[W]hat kind of a blockade is this, where the intended enemy is furnished with arms and ammunition and provisions under the quarantine of the passports of our ministerial agents!" He charged that, "If these concessions be voluntary they are treasonable . . . ." Privately he was even less circumspect, writing in the margins of his letterbook, "Downright treachery or consummate weakness! Is not Simpson's treasure in Morocco? . . . In the name of God what avails integrity and firmness, where a balance of influence is in the hands of corruption or cowardice!"[59]

Eaton was a notorious hothead in the throes of a sort of paranoid meltdown due to events in Barbary, so his criticism should be taken with a grain of salt. His suggestions that Simpson might somehow be profiting from his position seem absurd in the face of Simpson's financial anxieties,

---

[58] Simpson to Sec. State, Sept. 26, 1803; Oct. 8, 1803; Oct. 15, 1803, all in Tangier Despatches.

[59] William Eaton to James Madison, Jan. 21, 1803, Eaton Letterbook 1802–3, 113–14, Eaton Papers.

and there is no hint of corruption in Simpson's affairs. However, another of Eaton's criticisms, that having consuls in Barbary without ensuring their personal safety would lead to them making decisions inimical to the United States in order to avoid personal danger, seems plausible. In Simpson's case, though, if Matra's analysis was correct, he could have insured his safety and that of US ships by making clear to the emperor immediately that the *Meshouda* would be returned if it was found to be acting contrary to orders. Thus, Simpson's failure came less from corruption than it did from his inability to see that the governor and possibly the emperor were using him as a pawn in a larger game. There is irony here, considering that Simpson's chief strength as a consul had always been his knowledge and understanding of the key players in North Africa.

In general, Eaton rejected the sort of inside game that Simpson and others played in favor of the use of force. "It is pretended that these submissions are the preservative of peace!," he wrote. However, "The calculation is erroneous. They tend to precipitate a war, because they show that we dread it … ."[60] Although intemperate, Eaton's criticism was not illogical. He rightly viewed Simpson as the consummate Mediterranean insider deeply imbedded in American trading and diplomatic networks, and well known within the international North African diplomatic community. Although, like all American consuls, Simpson welcomed the muscular assistance of the US Navy, his principal goal was to maintain peace in order to allow American trade in the Mediterranean to continue flowing. Eaton, by contrast, wanted peace in the long run, but in the short term he was more concerned about demonstrating American power. His plan to win the war in Tripoli was to support the ruling Bashaw's brother, Hamet Karamanli as an American puppet. Eaton brilliantly led Hamet's supporters on a daring march through the desert to the city of Derna, where they met with the US Navy to conquer the city and essentially win the war. He was devastated when instead of putting Hamet on the throne, the United States settled with his brother, Yosuf. Eaton saw the move as deceitful and corrupt, much as he had criticized Simpson's efforts in the *Meshouda* incident. Eaton was the prototypical outsider. As an Army officer who had only served in North America and apparently never crossed the Atlantic before arriving in Tunis, he had no connections and little understanding of the American trading nation and its cosmopolitan orientation, which seemed potentially treasonous to him.

[60] *Ibid.*

The fact that Simpson could not resolve the Moroccan situation without the assistance of Preble and the Navy underscores Eaton's position. The *Meshouda* incident and its aftermath has been described as the "first use of gunboat diplomacy" by the United States and, by implication, the predecessor to aggressive actions in Asia and Latin America later in the nineteenth century.[61] In some ways it is true that the gunboats in Morocco and Eaton's approach in Tripoli foreshadowed a day when military power rather than international trade would become the crux of US policy in the Mediterranean and the rest of the world. But for the most part, that more aggressive approach still lay well in the future. Simpson retained his position for nearly two more decades and during that time he, rather than Eaton, was far closer to the norm for American consuls. While the growing US military presence in the Mediterranean and the world augured change, for the time being the old concerns and methods still held sway, as demonstrated by the American settlement with Tripoli that Eaton detested and by Simpson's continuing influence in Morocco.

[61] Parker, *Uncle Sam in Barbary*, 157.

3

Robert Montgomery

Multiple Identities in Alicante

Located on the eastern coast of Spain 400 miles northeast of Tangier, Alicante provided a very different situation for American consuls. Tangier was a salaried position with virtually no commerce and an intense focus on Barbary negotiations. Alicante, where Robert Montgomery was stationed, offered no salary but increasingly lucrative trade with fewer diplomatic duties. The two ports were similar in that few Americans found their way to either before the first decade of the nineteenth century. Like Simpson, Montgomery became gradually more integrated into the American community over time and due to the need to coordinate with other American officials, particularly during the Barbary Wars.

Despite the initial paucity of Americans, Alicante was one of the key ports in eastern Spain along with Barcelona and Valencia, its neighbors to the north. It was situated at the terminus of the most important road connecting Madrid to the sea. Due to this location and the presence of large salt deposits nearby, it was an important node in the fish trade which was so important to British and American merchants in the Mediterranean. It served as an entrepôt for traders wishing to distribute fish into the interior and for ship captains wishing to trade cod and return to the fisheries with specie, various Mediterranean products, and salt to preserve the next shipment.[1] (See Figure 3.1.)

---

[1] Enrique Giménez López, *Alicante en el Siglo XVIII: Economice de una Cuidad Portuaria en el antiguo régimen* (Valencia: Institución Alfonso el Magnánimo, 1981) 367–75, 381–84; James G. Lydon, *Fish and Flour for Gold, 1600–1800: Southern Europe in the Colonial Balance of Payments* (Philadelphia: Library Company of Philadelphia e-publication, 2008) 19, 67, 202.

FIGURE 3.1 Alicante harbor today (author's photo)

Alicante's population had nearly tripled over the course of the eighteenth century, exceeding 20,000 people by the start of the nineteenth. Those residents lived in buildings perched between wide Mediterranean beaches to the east and steep mountains to the west. The narrow streets of the dense town center were overshadowed by a large hill topped by a Moorish fort. Fertile farms in the area known as the Huerta in the flatlands to the north and west benefitted from artificial irrigation dating back to Roman and Moorish times. Farmers in this region produced a number of goods for export including barilla or saltwort (used for soda ash), brandy, wine, fruits, almonds, barley, and saffron.[2]

Shipping to Alicante was largely dominated by the French and British, although Spanish, Dutch, Portuguese, and Italian merchants also played significant roles. Consequently, trading volume was heavily affected by the Anglo-French wars of the late eighteenth and early nineteenth centuries. Commerce was devastated by the Seven Years War but then reached an all-time peak in tonnage in 1766 after peace

[2] Giménez López, *Alicante en el Siglo XVIII*, 35–55, 390–99; *Almanack Mercantil o Guía de Comerciantes Para el ano de 1797* (Madrid: Ramón Ruiz, 1797) 393.

resumed. Similarly, shipping volume crashed during the American Revolution, when Spain was allied with France against Britain, before slowly returning to prewar highs after the peace of 1783. The 1796 Treaty of San Ildefonso which allied Spain with France in the war against Britain briefly cut the number of entering ships by nearly 50 percent, but volume again recovered in 1803 after the Treaty of Amiens created a respite from the conflict, and Alicante merchants saw record high numbers of entering ships (though not in tonnage) in 1803 and 1804. The major imports were cereals and salted fish, particularly *bacalao* (salted cod). The largest quantities and best-quality *bacalao* came from the rich Newfoundland fisheries hugging the coasts of the Canadian maritime provinces and New England and were carried primarily by British ships which typically arrived in Alicante in the fall and early winter after a busy spring and summer of fishing and salting. Consequently, the trade in fish was hit particularly hard by Spain's wartime ruptures with Britain.[3]

United States shipping to Alicante appears to have been minimal until 1796 when the Treaty of San Ildefonso and the end of the Algerian captivity crisis created an opening for American merchants. Thereafter, the fragmentary data suggests that American shipping gained traction and then took off in the period after the Treaty of Amiens, when shipping to Alicante in general was booming, particularly for neutral traders. In each of the four years from 1803 to 1806, the number of American ships annually entering the port of Alicante ranged from twenty-nine to more than forty until a yellow fever quarantine in the second half of 1806 drastically reduced it.[4] (See Table 3.1.)

Only a little more than a third of American ships arriving in Alicante before 1806 came directly from the United States. The vast majority of those vessels brought salt fish from ports in Massachusetts, with a small number of others bringing cereals or other items from ports to the south. Another third of incoming US ships arrived from other Spanish ports, with

---

[3] Giménez López, *Alicante en el Siglo XVIII*, 342–75. On the fish trade see Lydon, *Fish and Flour for Gold*; Christopher P. Magra, *The Fisherman's Cause: Atlantic Commerce and Maritime Dimensions of the American Revolution* (New York: Cambridge University Press, 2009).

[4] Data on American shipping unless otherwise stipulated, comes from Mesadas de Sanidad, Arm. 14, Archivos Municipales, Alicante Spain. These were records kept of incoming ships by local health officials. They are described in more detail in Giménez López, *Alicante en el Siglo XVIII*, 338–39. Giménez's figures on American shipping differ slightly from those presented here. The author is grateful to Antonio Piqueres Diez for collecting data and constructing the database from which shipping figures in this chapter are drawn.

TABLE 3.1 *Number of US ships arriving in Alicante*[1]

Year	American ships
1781	1
1788	5
1789	6
1795	1
1796	11
1803	43
1804	29
1805	32
1806	>40

[1] 1787–1805 data based on Mesadas de Sanidad. Missing years are those for which *mesadas* do not exist. 1806 figure is from Robert Montgomery to Sec. State, March 4, 1806, in Alicante Despatches.

a final third coming from further afield in Europe or North Africa. The largest number of ships not coming directly from the US sailed into Alicante in ballast, suggesting that they sold their goods elsewhere and were looking for products for the return trip. The next largest number carried fish. A good number of these carried other goods as well, suggesting that they had begun their journey with North American fish and had traded part of it for other products before landing in Alicante. The rest carried a wide variety of goods, with no other item exceeding 10 percent of the shipments. (See Tables 3.2 and 3.3.)

Qualitative and quantitative evidence strongly suggests that the typical American ship arriving into Alicante started its voyage in Massachusetts with North Atlantic cod and made at least one intermediate stop in Europe to trade fish for various products. Montgomery attempted to prod more merchants to bring flour, which, despite low prices in Portugal during these years, generally was in demand in Alicante. His efforts were not successful, as only 11 percent of American ships brought cereals or flour of any kind.[5] After anchoring in Alicante and attempting

[5] Robert Montgomery to Sec. State, Sept. 26, 1803; July 30, 1804; Mar. 6, 1806, all in Alicante Despatches.

TABLE 3.2 *Cargo and origin of US ships arriving in Alicante 1787–1805*[1]

Cargo	Ships arriving directly from US (n=46)	US Ships arriving from other ports (n=81)
Brandy/wine	1 (2%)	6 (7%)
Cereals	6 (13%)	18 (22%)
Fish	36 (78%)	17 (21%)
Manufactures	0	2 (2%)
Meats	0	3 (4%)
Naval stores	1 (2%)	6 (7%)
Oils	0	2 (2%)
Other	2 (4%)	1 (1%)
Ballast	0	35 (43%)

[1] Based on Mesadas de Sanidad covering the years 1787–89, 1795–96, 1803–5. For ships carrying multiple items, the table reflects what appears to be the dominant item. Cargo categories include: Fish – bacalao, salmón, sardina; Cereals – Harina, maiz, trigo; Brandy/wine – aguardiente, vino, corcho; Naval stores – arboles, resina, aros de madeira, duelas; Manufactures – seda, mantas, botas, lenceria, pliegos; Oils – aciete, monteca, jabon; Other – arroz, tabaca, pimiento, hierro, café, géneros, queso.

TABLE 3.3 *Location of port from which US ships arriving in Alicante departed previously*

Previous port	1780s n=12	1790s n=12	1800s n=104	Total n=128
Europe (not Spain)	1 (8%)	2 (17%)	26 (25%)	29 (23%)
North Africa	0	3 (25%)	0	3 (2%)
Spain	5 (42%)	6 (50%)	37 (36%)	48 (38%)
United States	6 (50%)	1 (8%)	39 (38%)	46 (36%)
Unknown	0	0	1 (1%)	1 (1%)

to sell what remained of their cargo, Americans most likely would purchase locally produced wines or brandy for the return trip. The voyage of the *Astrea* provides a clearly documented example. The well-traveled 320-ton ship left Salem in 1798 under Captain Henry Prince, evading a number of privateers before landing in Cádiz. There, they were unable to find wine for their return cargo, forcing them to continue to Alicante where Prince wrote, "the only thing that will answer … from America is fish." He suggested that "a voyage from America to Alicante and from thence down to Havana with a load of their red wines" would turn a good profit.

That seems to have been the general wisdom. A few years later, an American merchant resident in Alicante wrote that he was expecting a brig from Cádiz to load a considerable shipment of brandy for its return voyage, presumably for the US or West Indian market. Montgomery also recommended such return shipments, noting that in Alicante "the vineyards in general promise well [and] brandy and wine cost low."[6]

Like most Spanish ports, Alicante sported a large community of resident foreign merchants who engaged in long-distance trade. In 1797 there were consuls representing eleven nations, ten French merchants, four "English" (including Irish), and five from other countries in addition to thirty-seven Spanish merchants. While the numbers of foreign merchants remained relatively steady, the absence of English after the 1790s was remarkable. In 1802, there were no English merchants, eleven French merchants, five Irish, and five of other nationalities in addition to fifty-one Spanish merchants. There was no British consul throughout the first decade of the 1800s, and merchants listed in the commercial almanac as English in 1797 were either gone or considered Irish afterward, presumably in deference to Spain's alliance with France.[7]

For a long time, the two Montgomerys – Robert and John – were the only Americans living in Alicante, and John spent part of the 1790s in Boston. But, as the British presence diminished and American shipping boomed, the nucleus of a small American community started to form. In 1802 John H. Rogers of Newton, Massachusetts arrived in Alicante and set up the second American merchant house there. By 1804, his business was booming. He reported receiving twelve commissioned ships by that summer and was desperately trying to find clerks to assist him. By 1807, eight Americans were registered as foreign residents in Alicante, most of them associated with the houses of Montgomery and Rogers. There also appears to have been a third, short-lived American house, headed by Montgomery's kinsman George Clark, who would soon move 30 miles down the coast to Torrevieja. Because women and children were not

---

[6] [Henry Prince], Log, *Astrea* 1798–99, Phillips-Peabody-Essex Institute, Salem, MA; Tamara Plakins Thornton, *Nathaniel Bowditch and the Power of Numbers* (Chapel Hill: University of North Carolina Press, 2017) 50–51; John H. Rogers to John Rogers, Jr., Oct. 29, 1803, Rogers-Bridges Family Collection; Montgomery to Sec. State, July 30, 1804, Alicante Despatches. The author is grateful to Tamara Thornton for providing him with a copy of a portion of the *Astrea* log.

[7] *Almanack Mercantil ... de 1797; de 1800* (Madrid: D. Joaquín Ibarra); *de 1802* (Madrid: Vega y Compañia); *de 1803* (Madrid: Calle de Capellanes); *de 1808* (Madrid: Vega y Compañia).

listed, the number of Americans living in Alicante at this time was probably closer to fifteen or twenty, which would have been the peak for at
least the first few decades of the century.[8]

***

In a way, Montgomery resembled the cubist portraits made by a painter
born down the coast from Alicante a century later – a figure facing in
multiple directions depending on the perspective of the viewer. When the
people of Alicante looked at Montgomery, they did not always recognize
him as an American. Sometimes they saw him as "British" because he was
a Protestant who was connected to the Anglo-Irish fish trade. Sometimes
they saw him as almost one of their own because he was a respected
property owner and part of Alicante's elite. At other times they saw him
as an American. Over the course of his residency and his early consulship
he became more recognizably American to his neighbors, and his work
tied him more into American networks, but the multiplicity of identities,
and the problems and opportunities stemming from it, continued for his
entire life.

Although Montgomery, unlike Simpson, was an American, he, too,
was isolated from other Americans when he arrived in Alicante in 1777.
His status as the lone American in the region allowed him to profit from
the expulsion of British merchants during the American Revolution, and
he continued to do well there for many decades. His very success, and the
lack of any sort of American community for most of his time in Alicante
tended, in some ways, to weaken his American identity, despite the fact
that he represented the United States and would, over the next five
decades, do more than anyone to encourage American trade with the fast-
growing region. But, the Irish-born Montgomery would never again set
foot in America after arriving in Alicante, and, with the exception of his
family, the only Americans he would see for decades were the sailors who
arrived at port, and occasional state department or naval officials. Because
of his location, he was, at least initially, far more removed from fellow
Americans than Simpson had been in busy Gibraltar. This was due both to
the initial lack of American traffic in Alicante and the fact that the nearest
Americans at this time were probably no closer than Valencia or

---

[8] John H. Rogers to John Rogers, Jr., Mar. 25, 1802; Jan. 24, 1804, both in Rogers-Bridges
  Family Collection; "Lista de los Individuos Americanos residentes en esta Plaza" [1807],
  Matriculó de Extranjeros, Legajo 96, Numero 94, Municipal Archive, Alicante.

Barcelona, located 100 and 300 miles away respectively, and not many were in those places either.

As discussed above, Montgomery registered as an American from the start and was one of the first Americans abroad to gain official recognition of his American citizenship. Nevertheless, confusion over Montgomery's status continued, exacerbated, Montgomery wrote, by "the exact similarity between us and the English (except in sentiment)." His certificate of allegiance from Franklin did not protect Montgomery from being labeled British or from being imprisoned when Spain allied with the French during the American Revolution. Eventually, Montgomery convinced the Spaniards to release him and let him return to business in Alicante. However, after Montgomery indiscreetly teased the local governor that "it was something extraordinary he could mistake the House of a friend for the ships of an enemy," the governor retaliated by rearresting Montgomery, who had to plead with Franklin for further assistance.[9] Franklin's intercession saved Montgomery and allowed him to make enormous profits while his British rivals were out of the picture during the war.

In commenting on the similarities between Americans and the English, Montgomery was implying that he may have been lumped into the category of English by some Spaniards because he spoke English and appeared English. Additionally, the fact that he was Protestant would have differentiated him from the large and influential population of Irish Catholics in the region, thereby consigning him to Englishness by default. English in Alicante were buried in a tiny, "British Cemetery" separated from the larger Catholic cemetery. Irish Catholics were not segregated in this way and had, in fact, been well integrated into Spanish society for centuries. Shortly after Montgomery's arrest, Alicante's governor claimed Montgomery had never been to America and that his papers were fake. The governor, who knew Montgomery well, probably made these charges as a way of gaining revenge against Montgomery, but while the governor most likely knew the truth about Montgomery, these charges suggest that the idea that Montgomery was English rather than American would have been credible to some.[10]

By at least one measure, however, Montgomery's American identity was strengthened by his arrests. While none of Montgomery's letterbooks from

<hr />

[9] Robert Montgomery to Benjamin Franklin, Apr. 5, 1778; June 26, 1778; July 6, 1779; Aug. 12, 1779; between Oct. 1 and Oct. 12, 1779; Nov. 20, 1779; Quotation from Nov. 20, 1779, all in Papers of Benjamin Franklin, http://franklinpapers.org.

[10] Montgomery to Franklin, Aug. 12, 1779, Papers of Benjamin Franklin, http://franklinpapers.org.

this or any period survive, there is a wealth of documentation about him in the well-preserved volumes of the authorities who notarized legal documents for Montgomery and others. Before his arrest, in February 1779, Montgomery had one transaction notarized. In the document he was identified only as "négociant por major" – an overseas merchant. In the two years after the arrest, he was identified as "négociant *Americano*" in six of eight documents produced by four notaries. All of these documents were produced during the period when British merchants and British ships were essentially prohibited form Alicante, so stressing Montgomery's American identity would be important in clarifying the legality of his activities.[11]

After 1781, however, Montgomery would only be identified once as an American in the notarial records and would instead be generally referred to as a merchant (*commercio* or *négociant*) and occasionally as a "*vecino*" (neighbor) which technically implied something akin to modern citizenship, with access to communal rights and sometimes to local offices as well as the duty to submit to local authorities.[12] This latter label suggests that Montgomery was imbedded in the community, and the suggestion is further buttressed by Montgomery's comment to Benjamin Franklin that he had "always supported the highest reputation as a merchant here and also been honored with an intimacy with the governour, lieutenant General Dn George Dunant, with General Mace, and the first Spanish families in this city."[13]

Other evidence of Montgomery's integration into the community includes his frequent business deals with local merchants. He repeatedly posted bonds for his neighbors and, when he was arrested in 1779, a local resident posted bail for him.[14] Finally, Montgomery was at least occasionally a landowner. In 1781, he purchased a little more than two acres of land and a house from Francisco Morales in the region of St. Juan, a few miles to the northeast of Alicante in the fertile Huerta region. He sold the land three years later to Francisco Blanes. Montgomery reentered the land market in 1804, purchasing several parcels of land near St. Juan known

---

[11] July 22, 1779; July 23, 1779; Aug. 21, 1779, Protocolo Notarial de Pedro Fuentes; Feb. 8, 1780, Protocolo de Notarial de Francisco Aracil; Feb. 11, 1781, Pastor y Castellanos; Sept. 21, 1781, PN (Note: "Protocolo de Notariales" (notarial notebooks) are identified by name of the notary and date in the archives and throughout this chapter).

[12] Tamar Herzog, *Defining Nations: Immigrants and Citizens in Early Modern Spain and Spanish America* (New Haven: Yale University Press, 2003) 5–6.

[13] Montgomery to Franklin, Aug. 24, 1779, Papers of Benjamin Franklin, http://franklinpa pers.org.

[14] Feb. 27, 1779, Juan Perez Cuevas, PN.

as Esperanza Cañizarez in Fabrequer. Land purchases in the Huerta region also brought the owners' rights to water distributed by the ancient municipal irrigation system, and Montgomery was duly entered in the Book of La Giradora (i.e., book of drawing water) as a landowner entitled to the flow of water. From the perspective of the local archives, then, and quite probably from the perspective of his neighbors, Montgomery appeared to be becoming less of an American and less of a foreigner and increasingly integrated into the higher echelons of Alicante's society.[15]

From another perspective, Montgomery looked very much like a fairly typical member of the group of Irish, Scottish and, occasionally, English merchants that had become important in the functioning of Spain's overseas trade during this period. After the war, when English merchants returned, he formed a commercial partnership with the British consul to Alicante, Daniel Budd despite the tense Anglo-American relations at the time. This move gave Montgomery access to English trading partners and, presumably, English capital at the same time that it gave Budd access to American markets. During the period of this partnership, Montgomery maintained close ties to England. He conducted business with English traders, traveled to Liverpool to conduct business in person, and sent his children to English schools. It is not hard to see how, despite his certificate of allegiance, his American identity could continue to be questioned.

Early on, Montgomery created a vice-consular network around himself that was clearly part of the larger Anglo-Irish trading network. His first action on becoming American consul was to appoint vice-consuls to Barcelona, Cartagena, and Valencia. After the initial three appointments, Montgomery also appointed vice-consuls to Benicarló and Santander. Over the course of his consular career, he would appoint at least fourteen vice-consuls, an unusually large number. (See Table 3.4.) The role of vice-consul does not appear to have been spelled out by Congress or the State Department, but British consuls traditionally appointed them, and most likely Montgomery, who was business partner to the British consul to Alicante, Daniel Budd, from 1789 until his consular appointment in 1793, learned from that example. Vice-consuls generally could serve either as assistants to consuls in their home ports, or as representatives in other, usually nearby ports. Montgomery appointed the latter.

The appointment process, like the job description, appears to have been more-or-less improvised. Montgomery received at least one application,

---

[15] Nov. 3, 1781; Feb. 17, 1784, Pedro Fuentes; Giradora Libro 2, Feb. 23, 1804, 2, 59, 149, 469, 775, Municipal Archives, Alicante. On the Huerta, see www.huertadealicante.es.

TABLE 3.4 *Montgomery's vice-consular appointees*[1]

Date	Name	Port
1793	John Montgomery	Barcelona
1793	Dominick Castillini	Cartagena
1794	Thomas Vague	Valencia
1795	Roberto Ryan	Benicarló
1795/1800	Lewis M. O'Brien	Santander
1806	John J. De Slanas	Valencia
1807	George Clark	Torrevieja
1807	Bartolome McDonnel	Benicarló
1809	William Goodwin	Tarragona
1814	Francis de Llamo	Valencia
1814	Nicolas Biale	Cartagena
Before 1814	Josef Innocencio de Llamo	Valencia
Before 1814	Bartolome Miquelote	Cartagena
?	Anto H. Sanchez	Torrevieja

[1] Sources: Montgomery and Castillini, Oct. 10, 1793, in Alicante
    Despatches; Thomas Vague Files, Consules Estranjeros, Inglaterra
    Valencia 1792 and Estados Unidos Valencia 1794; Roberto Ryan File,
    Consules Estranjeros, Estados Unidos (PARES); Lewis M. O'Brien File; De
    Slanas, July 31, 1806, in Alicante Despatches; Bartolome McDonnel File,
    Consules Estranjeros, Estados Unidos; William Goodwin, May 26, 1809,
    in Alicante Despatches; Francis and Josef de Llamo, Viale, and Miquelote,
    Dec. 16, 1804, in Alicante Despatches; Sanchez, June 19, 1823, in Alicante
    Despatches; G. Clark, B. McDonnel Files, Expedientes de la Junta de
    Dependencia de Extranjeros, Archivo Nacionales, Madrid.

from Henry Tawson of Cartagena, which he denied due to questions
about his character and conduct. In at least some cases, he asked appoint-
ees to pay a bond to insure good behavior, which he transmitted to the
State Department.[16] Montgomery, like other Spanish consuls, wrote up
appointment patents for his vice-consuls, which he transmitted to the
American minister or chargé d'affaires in Madrid who, in turn, transmit-
ted them to Spanish authorities. The one surviving patent issued by
Montgomery during this period, for vice-consul Roberto Ryan of
Benicarló, was extremely broad, calling on Ryan to take care of all
Americans in Benicarló, and to issue patents or passports. By contrast

---

[16] Montgomery to Sec. State, Oct. 10, 1793; Jan. 8, 1794, both in Alicante Despatches.

the British consul in Galicia only granted his vice-consul jurisdiction over disputes between merchants and captains and between captains and mariners, promising him unspecified emoluments.[17]

The Spanish authorities, however, had a very clear procedure for vice-consular appointments and scrutinized applications carefully to make sure they conformed. Montgomery's vague appointments did not please them. His appointment of Ryan "only during my pleasure" (durante tan sólo mi voluntad) struck the Spanish authorities as undercutting the king's right to terminate such appointments. More importantly, the Spanish authorities also expressed dissatisfaction with Montgomery's own appointment as United States consul to the port of Alicante and to all ports closer to Alicante than to the residences of any other American consuls. In practice, Montgomery interpreted this broad mandate as consul to the realms (*reinos*) of Murcia and Valencia, the principality of Catalonia, the Isles of Baleares, and the port of Santander and its dependencies. Montgomery's attempt to appoint Lewis Meagher O'Brien as vice-consul to Santander – more than 500 miles from Alicante as the crow flies and much further by the usual shipping routes – proved to be too much for the authorities, who launched a detailed examination of Montgomery's patent which concluded that the lack of clarity, and especially the failure to specify the particular places under Montgomery's authority, needed to be remedied. After this incident, Montgomery mostly confined his appointments to the portions of Valencia and Murcia abutting Alicante, and he appears to have circumvented the entire process at times by appointing informal consular agents rather than vice-consuls.[18] Rather than some sort of megalomania on Montgomery's part, these conflicts more likely reflected how inexperienced and understaffed the State Department was at this time.

Like the larger consular network, Montgomery's sub-consular organization created an infrastructure for the developing trading nation, providing resources for American ships throughout the busy eastern portions of Spain. But, even more so than the larger Mediterranean consular network, these vice-consuls had little connection to the United States. They were appointed by and reported to Montgomery rather than to

[17] Roberto Ryan File, Consules Estranjeros, Estados Unidos (PARES) 16; Lewis M. O'Brien File, 2.

[18] Ryan File 1, 2, 7, 16; Robert Montgomery File, Consules Estranjeros, Estados Unidos, 4–5, 27–52; Lewis M. O'Brien File, 2, 8–15; Montgomery to Sec. State, July 3, 1806; Dec. 16, 1814, both in Alicante Despatches.

State Department officials. Furthermore, only two of Montgomery's appointments, his brother John and George Clark, appear ever to have set foot in the United States. Nearly all of them, including John, were Anglo-Irish merchants residing in Spain. At least two of these appointees – Thomas Vague of Valencia, and Lewis Meagher O'Brien of Santander, were also serving as British consuls in their respective ports. O'Brien, a merchant residing in Santander did have ties to American merchants and consuls, although it is unclear whether these ties predated his appointment to the vice-consulship and subsequent consulship in Santander or whether they developed as a result of his appointment. Vague was likely of British or possibly French descent and was well integrated into the Mediterranean world with no apparent American connections.[19] A third appointee, Roberto Ryan of Benicarló was an unmarried Irish merchant, described as a lapsed Catholic by Spanish authorities. He worked with the firm of Bartolome and Reynaldo McDonnel (or Magdonel), who were likely part of the large, important Irish family of Enrique Reynaldo MacDonnel, an admiral in the Spanish Navy and later a major figure at the Battle of Trafalgar. Ryan was also associated with Jorge Moore, an important Irish merchant in Alicante with whom Montgomery was well acquainted.[20] All in all, Montgomery and these vice-consuls made up a tight little trading network connected to many of the major Anglo-Irish players in the eastern parts of Spain and with very few American contacts.

***

At the same time as Montgomery was building connections to the Anglo-Irish mercantile network and becoming integrated into Alicante society, he was also strengthening his ties and those of others to the American trading nation. As with Simpson, the Barbary crises accelerated this

[19] Lewis M. O'Brien File and Thomas Vague File both in Consules Estranjeros, Estados Unidos; Margaret L. O'Brien to Mr. Bowdoin, May 2, 1806; Strange and Co. and others, petition, Nov. 5, 1806; John White and Sons to Samuel Welles, May 21, 1806, all in Lewis O'Brien File, Letters of Application and Recommendations during the Administration of Thomas Jefferson, NARA; Joseph Townsend, *A Journey Through Spain in the Years 1786 and 1787* (London: C, Diely, 1792) 285, 292; Thomas Vague to the Royal Economic Society of Friends of the Country of Valencia, May 23, 1786, www.riconet.upv.es.

[20] Roberto Ryan File; Bartolome McDonnel File, Consules Estranjeros, Estados Unidos; Moore, who was a character in Thomas Flanagan, *The Year of the French*, was an important wine merchant who represented one of Montgomery's creditors in a lawsuit against the consul, as discussed in Chapter 6 below. Luisa Montgomery married Ricardo Ryan, most likely Roberto's younger brother. See Chapter 5 below.

process. Because of Alicante's location along an important shipping route to Algiers, the captivity crisis of 1785–96 with Algiers, particularly, and tensions with North Africa, generally, shaped Montgomery's earliest years as a consul. Montgomery's concern with North African events was in accordance with all facets of his identity – as an American, a merchant in the Anglo-Irish network, and a *vecino* of Alicante. As a merchant, any disruption to trade would be troubling to him, and in particular, considering his position as one of the only American merchants in the region, disruption of American ships would affect his interests. As a resident of Alicante, he was very much aware of and concerned by Algerian corsairs. In the very Huerta where he was buying agricultural land, he could view numerous small stone towers that had allowed residents to scout out the approach of invading Algerians for centuries and stood as daily reminders of the dangers emanating from across the Mediterranean. (See Figure 3.2.) More recently, in 1776, 1783, and 1784, the Spanish military launched missions against Algiers from nearby Cartagena with varying degrees of success. Even closer to home, in 1783 Algerian corsairs threatened the beach of Altea, located only 36 miles up the coast from Alicante.[21]

Montgomery hoped to use his location in Alicante and the connections he had developed over the years around the Mediterranean to assist the United States in its conflicts with North Africa. He once told Secretary of State John Randolph that "a consul should be as much a man of intrigue as any foreign minister," and he tried to follow this advice in his early career. Shortly after Algerians captured eleven American ships in 1793, Montgomery had written the secretary of state, "The success of my private negotiations with some of the first men in Morocco during the reign of Muley Ishmael and my proximity to the city of Algiers with some weighty correspondents in that place induced me officiously to use their influence ... to endeavor to conciliate the mind of the Dey towards the United States." Oblivious to Philadelphia's dissatisfaction with his earlier intrigues in Morocco, he praised himself profusely on that count. He derided previous American agents as "little respecting the artful intrigues of courts and

[21] Óscar Recio Morales, *Ireland and the Spanish Empire 1600–1825* (Dublin: Four Courts Press, 2010) 269–74; Emiliano Fernández de Pinedo, Alberto Gil Novales, and Albert Dérozier, *Historia de España* (Barcelona: Editorial Labor, 1987) VII: 245–44; Roberto Montgomery Fiansa por Dn. Alejandro Gozpoll y otros, May 6, 1783, Francisco Aracil, PN.

FIGURE 3.2 The Torre de Santiago outside Alicante, constructed in the sixteenth century, served as a watchtower for Algerian cruisers (author's photo)

statesmen" and of foolishly relying upon interpreters and others, "whose very business it was to counteract them in every part of their commission."[22]

Despite Montgomery's self-serving puffery, or perhaps because of it, the State Department soon asked him to take on an important role in the negotiations for the American captives in Algiers. His break came when David Humphreys, the American minister to Spain, arrived in Alicante, a traditional hopping-off point to Algiers, on his way to negotiate with the Dey in late October or early November 1793.[23] While stopping in Alicante, Humphreys heard the first rumors of the capture of the eleven additional American ships. When a large Algerian ship arrived in Alicante,

[22] Memorial of Robert Montgomery [1793], Montgomery to Sec. State, Oct. 9, 1795, Alicante Despatches.
[23] Humphreys's last letter from Gibraltar is dated Oct. 13, 1793, and O'Brien received a letter from him sent from Alicante on Nov. 5, 1793. See David Humphreys to Sec. State, Oct. 13, 1793; Lewis O'Brien to Humphreys, Nov. 12, 1793, both in Despatches from US Ministers to Portugal.

Humphreys prodded Montgomery to take a boat out to it and get information. The Algerian captain responded he had personally captured seven
American vessels, and his information provided some of the first definitive
news of the captive crew members.[24]

In the meantime, much to Humphreys's surprise, the Dey refused to
treat with him, leaving him stuck in Alicante with Montgomery. His plight
was similar to that of Thomas Barclay some years earlier when (as discussed in Chapter 2) he was stuck in Gibraltar for months with James
Simpson in a stalled effort to negotiate with the Moroccan emperor. And
much as Barclay and Simpson built a relationship then, Humphreys and
Montgomery got to know each other well in the roughly two months that
Humphreys spent in Alicante.[25] During this period, Alicante became the
default location of the Spanish ministry as Humphreys carried out his
business there, most likely in Montgomery's house. In another parallel to
Simpson's experience, Humphreys had a number of goods delivered from
Gibraltar to Alicante to be used as gifts during the expected negotiations
with the Dey, some of which, if not all, were the exact items Barclay had
intended to use in Morocco.[26]

More importantly, as Humphreys realized he would not be able to
continue to Algiers, he arranged for Montgomery to handle the captivity
situation for the time being from Alicante. Because the State Department
did not expect Humphreys to be unable to reach Algiers, they had not
given him authority to delegate his negotiating power. As a result,
Humphreys had to turn down an offer from Sweden's Algerian consul
Pierre Skjoldebrand to take his place. Instead, he gave Montgomery
permission to try to open a direct line of correspondence to the Dey. He
also left Barclay's old materials and $40,000 in cash with Montgomery in
anticipation of future negotiations and to assist the captives. The
Washington administration was concerned that if they appeared to pay
too much attention to the captives, it would only drive up the price the
Algerians demanded for their redemption as the Algerians would see that
the Americans placed a high value on them. Montgomery had already
been quietly sending small amounts of money to the crews of two ships
that had been captured in 1785 and still not redeemed. Humphreys asked
him to continue his efforts by sending a modest stipend of $8 a month to

---

[24] Humphreys to Sec. State, Nov. 19, 1793, Despatches from US Ministers to Portugal.
[25] Humphreys was back in Madrid by Jan. 1, 1794.
[26] Montgomery to Sec. State, Dec. 17, 1793; Receipt dated Dec. 9, 1793; Invoice dated
Dec. 17, 1793, all in Alicante Despatches.

the captains, $6 to the mates, and 12 cents per day to the common sailors. He also directed him to send each of the sailors a new suit of clothing. By March 1795, roughly three months after Humphreys left Alicante, Montgomery had already reported spending $6,000 on the captives. His actions were met with appreciation from Humphreys's assistant, Nathaniel Cutting, who referred to Montgomery as a "steady, active and zealous friend."[27]

American affairs in Algiers continued to occupy Montgomery well after Humphreys's departure. In addition to sending the monthly allowances, Montgomery also directed Skjoldebrand to move the captains and mates into the countryside when he learned that the plague was ravaging Algiers, and he sent Skjoldebrand money to pay for their transport and lodging. In the meantime, Skjoldebrand began working on the Dey to accept an American negotiator. He sent George Smith, a recently redeemed American captive, to Alicante to deliver this news to Montgomery. Unfortunately, the Swedish consul to Alicante ordered Smith's ship burnt when it was stranded on a beach to the east of Alicante, forcing Montgomery to find lodgings for the crew and to search out a new ship for them to continue their journey. He soon sent Smith on to Cádiz and provided payment for his passage to Philadelphia. Even after the captives were freed in 1796, Richard O'Brien, now consul to Algiers, drew on Montgomery to provide cloth as part of the annual payment in goods the Americans had agreed to send the Dey under the Algerian–American peace treaty. As late as 1807 Montgomery was still providing cash to the Algerian consul for the annuity the United States paid the Dey each year.[28]

In addition to being a man of intrigue, Montgomery believed a consul should have "a facility of being on friendly footing with the most leading

---

[27] James Carmichael to Lewis O'Brien, Sept. 13, 1793, Cathcart Family Papers, New York Public Library; Lewis O'Brien to Montgomery, Nov. 16, 1793; Montgomery to Sec. State, Dec. 17, 1793; Receipt dated Dec. 9, 1793; Montgomery to Sec. State, Feb. 20, 1794; Mar. 29, 1794, all in Alicante Despatches; Humphreys to Pierre Skjoldebrand, Mar. 29, 1793; Humphreys to captive American captains, Nov. 29, 1793; Instructions to Robert Montgomery, n.d. [1793], all in Despatches from US Ministers to Portugal; Nathaniel Cutting to Sec. State, Feb. 10, 1794, Algiers Despatches. On the Washington administration's policy, see Lawrence Peskin, *Captives and Countrymen: Barbary Slavery and the American Public, 1785–1816* (Baltimore: Johns Hopkins University Press, 2009) 50–67.

[28] Humphreys to Montgomery, Jan. 12, 1794; Montgomery to Humphreys, Apr. 29, 1794; Pierre Skjoldebrand to Humphreys, Oct. 10, 1794; Montgomery to Humphreys, Oct. 18, 1794, all in Despatches from US Ministers to Portugal; Montgomery to Sec. State, Dec. 15, 1807; Montgomery to Humphreys, Jan. 29, 1795; Richard O'Brien to Montgomery, June 18, 1801; Montgomery to O'Brien, July 22, 1801, all in Alicante Despatches.

people as well in the capital as in the town where they reside."[29] As with Simpson, his broad network of correspondents was the basis for his applications to represent the United Sates in Alicante and Algiers, and through his work for the United States, particularly in connection to events in North Africa, he came to know most of the important Americans in the region. While no letterbooks like those of Simpson have survived for Montgomery, his despatches from Alicante alone reveal the breadth of his network. (See Table 3.5.)

Nearly all of these correspondents were American.[30] Montgomery wrote to many of them quite frequently, developing long relationships that could also veer into personal friendships and business partnerships. Because of Alicante's location he met a number of them in person as they traveled to and from Algiers. In addition to Humphreys, examples include Joseph Donaldson, George Smith, Hans Heysell, and naval officers such as William Bainbridge and Stephen Decatur. Montgomery met others on his travels to Madrid, most notably George Erving. He wrote to others throughout multiple stages of their lives. For example, he began writing to James L. Cathcart when he was a captive in Algiers, continued the correspondence when Cathcart was consul to Tripoli, and likely remained in touch during Cathcart's time in Livorno and Madeira, though no correspondence from that period survives. In addition, most of these individuals also had large correspondent networks of their own to which Montgomery would obtain access, creating further connections between him and others in the American orbit.[31]

***

While he never took part in high-level diplomacy comparable to Simpson's treaty maintenance in Tangier, Montgomery, the "man of intrigue," nonetheless played an outsized diplomatic role in the Barbary conflicts and in the Napoleonic Wars. He represented the United States to the aggressive powers and represented Americans who were caught up in

[29] Montgomery to Sec. State, Oct. 9, 1795, Alicante Despatches.

[30] Since the source of these correspondents is Montgomery's consular despatches, Americans may well be overrepresented. His business correspondence, if it survived, would no doubt be filled with non-Americans. However, the larger point is that he was in touch with a very large number of Americans as he pursued his duties.

[31] Montgomery to Sec. State, Aug. 20, 1795; to Humphreys, Jan. 27, 1795; to Sec. State, Mar. 14, 1795; Feb. 19, 1800; Sept. 17, 1805; July 3, 1806; Mar. 30, 1801, all in Alicante Despatches; Robert Montgomery to James L. Cathcart, Apr. 16, 1795, Cathcart Family Papers, New York Public Library.

TABLE 3.5 *Montgomery's correspondents (from Alicante Despatches 1790–1807)*[1]

Name	Location	Position	First Mention
William Bainbridge	US Navy	Captain	Feb. 19, 1800
Hugh Campbell	US Navy	Commodore	Jan. 2, 1807
James Carmichael	Madrid	Chargé d'affaires	
James Cathcart	Algiers/ Tripoli	Captive/consul	Mar. 8, 1801
George Davis	Tunis	Consul	Dec. 24, 1807
Stephen Decatur	US Navy	Captain	Sept. 17, 1805
Joseph Donaldson	Algiers	US envoy	Aug. 20, 1795
J. B. Ducoster	Naples	US vice-consul	Nov. 9, 1807
George Erving	Madrid	US chargé d'affaires/ minister	June 17, 1806
John Gavino	Gibraltar	US consul	July 22, 1801
John Graham	Madrid	US secretary	Feb. 2, 1803
Hans Heysell	Algiers	US consul	Mar. 14, 1795
David Humphreys	Madrid	US minister	
William Jarvis	Lisbon	US consul	Jan. 9, 1804
Tobias Lear	Algiers	US consul	Jan. 7, 1804
T. J. Mountford	Algiers	US acting consul	Aug. 5, 1805
Richard O'Brien	Algiers	US Captive/consul	
Plenipotentiaries	Aranjuez	US plenipotentiaries	July 23, 1793
William Short	Madrid	US plenipotentiary	July 23, 1793
Skjoldebrand	Algiers	Swedish consul	
George Smith	Algiers	US captive	
Young, Mr.	Madrid	?	July 3, 1806

[1] First mention is for Alicante Despatches only. In some cases, earlier letters between Montgomery and these individuals survive in other record groups.

the conflicts. He kept Americans at home informed on events in the Mediterranean, and he hatched schemes to improve the United States' commercial position in the region. Above all else, he tried to keep American ships and commerce moving, unimpeded by outside forces. His consular work brought him to the attention of Americans and brought Americans to his attention. Like Simpson and others, it helped to forge stronger connections between Americans in the region at the same time that it connected him more tightly to those same Americans.

Montgomery insisted that, a consul should "at least have the first information of any new laws that are about to be promulgated as well as of matters relative to peace or war." His connections with the American network combined with Alicante's proximity to Algiers and its eventually heavy American ship traffic made Montgomery an ideal conduit of such information to the United States. He frequently reported on political developments in Algiers and on ship movements in the region. He quickly relayed news of the capture of the *Philadelphia* in Tripoli during the first Barbary War. He also occasionally sent news of other ship captures around the Mediterranean; for example, he forwarded information he received from the American consul in Marseille that the French had condemned several American ships as prizes there. He used his Madrid contacts to inform American authorities very early on that Spain intended to make New Orleans a free port.[32]

Montgomery frequently sent news about American officials' efforts to redeem the captives and broker peace with the Algerians in the 1790s, much of it very critical. He wrote the secretary of state that James Simpson's friend, Joseph Donaldson, the American envoy who finally negotiated peace with Algiers in 1795, would likely not succeed on his mission because he spoke only English, and he warned that Hans Heysell, the Danish captain briefly appointed to be American consul to Barbary, lied about his powers and was "in many other matters wanting in veracity." Montgomery's advice on Heysell at least proved discerning when the Algerian Dey refused to accept his appointment and apparently denounced him as an imposter.[33] Montgomery's superiors did not entirely trust these missives, suspecting that he might be criticizing others in order to advance his own career. Shortly before the Donaldson mission, Montgomery's brother and sometimes business partner expressed interest in being a consul to one of the salaried posts in North Africa but was turned down despite a recommendation from Joel Barlow, the Algerian consul. Donaldson then informed David Humphreys that Montgomery "was excessively mortified upon his (Donaldson's) arrival in Alicante, to find that he (Montgomery) was not employed in the Barbary negotiations." Montgomery badmouthed Donaldson to O'Brien and considered

[32] Montgomery to Sec. State, Oct. 9, 1795; Apr. 6, 1794; Jan. 7, 1795; Apr. 26, 1798; Apr. 28, 1803; Jan. 7, 1804, all in Alicante Despatches; David Humphreys to Joel Barlow, Apr. 22, 1797, Box 2, Folder 41; Robert Montgomery to Timothy Pickering, Feb. 13, 1798, Box 1, Folder 9, both in David Humphreys Papers, Humphreys-Marvin-Olmsted.

[33] Montgomery to Sec. State, Mar. 14, 1795; May 2, 1795; Aug. 20, 1795, all in Alicante Despatches.

travelling to Philadelphia and meeting with State Department officials personally "in order to lay facts with clearness before them" if Donaldson failed. O'Brien and Humphreys wondered if Montgomery might have some "ulterior object in view," particularly since he had recently sent a nephew to Algiers, supposedly as a wheat merchant. Perhaps remembering Montgomery's earlier proposal to disguise himself as a wheat merchant in Algiers as cover for diplomatic activity, Humphreys speculated that Montgomery might be contemplating "the establishment of a branch of his house in some of the Barbary states, in a consular character."[34]

Like nearly all Mediterranean consuls, Montgomery urged the United States to develop its navy in order to protect regional commerce. In 1795, he recommended commissioning at least ten forty-gun frigates and as many smaller vessels to show the Algerians the United States could enforce the peace if necessary. He also hoped the new navy might use his home port as a provisioning station, an arrangement that could prove profitable to him, particularly if, as was customary, he was also appointed naval agent. He maintained that the port of Alicante was "the cheapest in the Mediterranean for every kind of provisions for the navy" and pledged that should the Navy make use of its facilities, he would be "happy to supply them as well with money as with anything else they may want." Finally, in addition to promoting commerce to Alicante, he also urged the State Department to consider a commercial treaty with Naples. He provided the State Department with a long list of items that could be traded between Naples and the United States and volunteered to work his own connections in order to negotiate a treaty. In addition to its commercial benefits, he argued that such a treaty would provide the United States with the use of a convenient, friendly port "in case we should ever be compelled to act offensively against the Algerians."[35]

Like Simpson and other Mediterranean consuls, Montgomery also had to deal with issues relating to epidemics. In his case the primary issue was yellow fever. Alicante suffered from a massive outbreak in 1804–5 that killed one-fifth of the city's inhabitants. It also completely disrupted what was by then the town's considerable US commerce. Montgomery wrote

---

[34] Pickering to David Humphreys, Dec. 7, 1796, Box 1, Folder 4; Humphreys to Pickering, Apr. 20, 1797, Box 1, Folder 20, both in David Humphreys Papers, Humphreys-Marvin-Olmsted.

[35] Montgomery to Sec. State, Jan. 16, 1795; Aug. 13, 1806; Nov. 30, 1794, all in Alicante Despatches.

that not a single American ship arrived in port during the second half of 1804. While devastating to the town's fortunes, this figure also points to the effectiveness of Montgomery and the broader Mediterranean network in warning ships to stay out of dangerous ports. By the spring of 1805 Montgomery wrote that commerce was "beginning to revive" but he warned the State Department (and probably other correspondents) that "no foreign grain would be wanted for some time after the harvest" which looked to be particularly good.[36]

The larger problem for Alicante's commerce was the United States' reputation as a hot spot for yellow fever, which was warranted considering the massive Philadelphia outbreak in 1793 and less massive outbreaks in subsequent years, including 1806. Consequently, amidst fears of a new Spanish outbreak in 1806, Alicante officials were very vigilant about quarantining American vessels. The American minister to Spain, George Erving, wrote to Montgomery and other consuls to gather more information. Montgomery complained to him that merchants in Alicante's fish trade were suffering from what he viewed as unnecessary detention of American ships. Fish, he argued, is "an article of commerce incapable of receiving or conveying any infectious disorder," a quality enhanced by the fact that ships in the cod trade spent many months in disease-free fishing areas off the Canadian shore before arriving in Spain. Furthermore, Montgomery argued that American yellow fever outbreaks were occurring from Philadelphia southward, while the cod ships mostly came from Massachusetts where yellow fever was not known. He suggested that the United States adopt measures to avoid quarantine and keep the trade flowing. US consuls should be ordered to meet all incoming American ships and certify that they were disease free in order to shorten their Spanish quarantine time. Unfortunately, the next spring a Massachusetts cod ship arrived in Alicante with two sick sailors, triggering further quarantine measures.[37]

Montgomery, like other consuls, also faced the problem of ships falsely claiming to be American in order to gain neutral shipping rights as well as hostility from his own countrymen. Both groups posed threats to the long-term viability of American shipping. In 1795 Montgomery wrote, "The peace which has now happily taken place with Algiers, opens an immense field and prospect of advantage to the commerce of the United States, and

---

[36] Montgomery to Sec. State, Sept. 18, 1804; Apr. 10, 1805, both in Alicante Despatches.
[37] Montgomery to George B. Erving, June 17, 1806; to Sec. State, Mar. 25, 1807, both in Alicante Despatches.

[in] the present state of affairs in Europe, the American flag will have a decided preference in the Mediterranean." Nevertheless, he continued, "it will be the business of consuls to [be] extremely vigilant in detecting forgeries and counterfeits of the papers and documents belonging to our vessels." While a portion of Montgomery's concern may have been that he did not want ships unentitled to the benefits of the neutral trade to compete with his personal business, the larger issue was the need to protect American shipping rights. Captains from other countries who sailed under phony American papers put the entire trading nation at risk, threatening neutral shipping rights at large and also making seizures of American ships on suspicion of smuggling a more likely prospect. These concerns also prompted Montgomery to be particularly careful to keep the State Department abreast of local shipping regulations. Verifying American identity, in this sense, became crucial to protecting American commerce.[38]

But the need to weed out fake papers called for powerful consuls. In actuality, American consuls had very little leverage to force any captain to do anything beyond holding on to their papers – assuming they could get them in the first place. Montgomery reported that even in apparently innocuous situations – when an American ship was stranded and sold but the captain refused to give up the papers, or even when Montgomery requested information on cargoes as he was required to do by the State Department – captains could be recalcitrant and even hostile. He complained that "the independent principal natural to people under our government leads masters and supercargoes of vessels to believe that any submission to consuls would be deletory [*sic*] to the right of an American citizen." On the other hand, even if consuls were given unlimited power, antagonizing these Americans would not be to the merchant-consuls' advantage since "becoming generally disliked forfeits the very business in commerce that his employment eventually entitles him to."[39]

These issues all coalesced in the spring of 1803 when the brig *ABC*, commanded by Captain de la Mare, sailed into Alicante from Guernsey, a British Crown Dependency. Montgomery was immediately suspicious because the captain was not an American but a native of Guernsey. His papers seemed counterfeit to Montgomery, particularly the Mediterranean pass, but "so well executed as to baffle the nicest judge." The consul decided

---

[38] Montgomery to Sec. State, Oct. 9, 1795; Spanish Regulations, Oct. 20, 1798, both in Alicante Despatches.
[39] Montgomery to Sec. State, Feb. 19, 1802; May 20, 1807, both in Alicante Despatches.

to hold on to the papers and consult with Charles Pinckney, who had replaced Humphreys as minister to Spain. Pinckney advised him to use his judgment but remember he should use his right to detain the ship "discreetly and attentively ... to avoid personal [liability] or preclude complaint." Montgomery personally believed that de la Mare's cargo should be seized for the benefit of the United States. But, he feared that due to the valuable cargo on board the ship, the captain would only drag him through an expensive Spanish court case in which "the owners of the cargo could afford to pay high, and with the great likeness of the papers there is no doubt a sentence would go in their favor and the charges go very heavy on myself." Without strong support from Pinckney, he felt obliged to return the papers and allow the *ABC* to continue its journey protected by the American flag.[40]

Montgomery also had to deal occasionally with French and English captures of American ships, though such episodes were initially rare, as Alicante was on the periphery of the war in the 1790s and early 1800s. In 1797 French privateers captured eight American vessels in the Mediterranean near Alicante, four of them actually in the Bay of Alicante. One of them, the *Pomona*, commanded by Captain Crafts and owned by the prominent Boston merchant house of Amory and Head, had originally intended to ship to Málaga but had found better prices for its cargo of fish, butter, and peppers in Alicante, where Montgomery certified their shipping papers after a crew member was discharged. About two hours after leaving Alicante, on May 15, a French privateer detained and boarded the *Pomona* but found its papers in good order. Crafts then returned to Alicante and tried to sail out again on May 18 with an American convoy but was again stopped, this time within the Bay of Alicante and probably within sight of Montgomery's merchant house, at a distance of less than 3 miles from land (3/4 of a league) by the corsair *Revenge*. Now the French judged his papers insufficient, condemned the boat, and sailed it into Cartagena as a prize. News of these captures reverberated throughout Massachusetts.[41]

Montgomery spent a good deal of time and money attempting to convince Spanish authorities to release the *Pomona* and the other captured ships with no success. Ultimately their cases were heard at the

[40] Charles Pinckney to Montgomery, Aug. 16, 1803; Montgomery to Pinckney, Aug. 20, 1801; Montgomery to Sec. State, Aug. 22, 1803, all in Alicante Despatches.
[41] Protest Against the Capture of the Barque Pomona, Oct. 10, 1797, Box 1, Folder 9, David Humphreys Papers, Humphreys-Marvin-Olmsted; Thornton, *Nathaniel Bowditch*, 50.

French Tribunal of Aix, where Stephen Cathalan, the American consul to Marseille, defended Crafts. Once again, the Americans had no success and Montgomery bitterly concluded that the outcome was "the ultimate proof that the French directory are determined to protect and support the robberies made upon us by their privateers."[42] In 1803, Montgomery claimed to have spent over $2,000.00 defending captured American ships in Spanish and French tribunals. When the State Department appeared reluctant to reimburse him, he stressed that he took these actions entirely in his official capacity as American consul without any personal interest in the ships or their cargo. He always expected to lose the cases, but, as he explained, his hope was "I should succeed [in] preventing the [prize] amount coming into the hands of the captors for one, two, or more years and thereby throw a damp on their passion for cruising against us."[43]

British and particularly French captures started to become a bigger problem in 1807 as the Napoleonic Wars moved ever closer to the Spanish Mediterranean. Meanwhile, rumors of new Algerian captures spread through the American consulates around the Mediterranean, though Montgomery believed that the hostilities were not generally directed against the United States but instead limited to a specific ship suspected of carrying French cargo, a conclusion he presumably reached on the assumption that the Algerians were supporting their frequent allies, the British, in opposition to France. Montgomery also reported that British captures of American ships suspected of trading at French ports had cut into the American trade at Alicante during 1807.[44]

But the most trouble came from the French privateer *Le Serpent*, which Montgomery claimed was commanded by Louis D'adero, "a noted smuggler from Genoa." On December 26, 1807, D'adero encountered two Boston ships carrying cargoes of fish near the Alicante coast and detained them; according to Montgomery, "under pretext that the cargoes on board these vessels were English fish." Montgomery attempted to free them through official and unofficial challenges, but having no success, he sent the matter to George Erving, the American minister in Madrid and requested a naval force from Commodore Hugh Campbell in Gibraltar.

---

[42] Montgomery to Pickering, Feb. 13, 1798, Box 1, Folder 9, David Humphreys Papers, Humphreys-Marvin-Olmsted.
[43] Montgomery to Sec. State, Aug. 22, 1803, Alicante Despatches.
[44] Montgomery to Sec. State, July 21, 1807; to George Erving, June 17, 1806; Dec. 19, 1806; Charles D. Cox to John Leonard, Nov. 5, 1807; Montgomery to Sec. State, Dec. 8, 1807, all in Alicante Despatches.

Erving had been worried about French captures since a French imperial decree in November 1806 had raised questions about neutral rights. French authorities assured him that American ships and citizens resident in Spain should remain safe and that they had ruled in favor of a captured American ship in a previous case. After notification from Erving, they urged the French Council of prizes and the consul at Alicante to expedite a decision on the matter. Within the month Montgomery was able to report that one ship was freed and the other would likely join it soon. He expressed confidence that the councils' decisions would help him free any future American prizes. Little did he realize that within months the Peninsular War would dramatically escalate the pace of captures and would ultimately lead to his ruin and the demise of American trade in the Alicante region.[45]

---

[45] Montgomery to Sec. State, Jan. 2, 1807; Mar. 25, 1807, both in Alicante Despatches; "Decision of the Consul of Prizes . . .," Dec. 24, 1806; "Extract of the Decision Made by the Council of Prizes . . .," Mar. 25, 1807; "Marine Prizes," Mar. 20, 1807, all in George W. Erving Papers in Humphreys-Marvin-Olmsted.

4

Thomas Appleton

Community and Conflict in Livorno's American Community

Livorno Italy, known as Leghorn to the English, was much farther removed from America than Alicante and Tangier, located roughly 1,000 and 1,400 miles to the west respectively. Yet, in many ways it seemed more tightly connected to the United States when Thomas Appleton arrived there in the late 1790s. Unlike Alicante and Tangier, Livorno contained a good-sized American community which was augmented by frequent comings and goings of American ships. During one crisis in 1807, thirty-one American citizens in Livorno (not including Appleton) signed a petition. Many of these, undoubtedly, were just passing through, but when combined with the wives, children, clerks, servants, and other dependents of American Livornese such as Appleton and other major merchants, a conservative estimate would have fifty or so Americans in the city at that time.[1] This population was due to Livorno's position as one of the most important Mediterranean ports (see Figure 4.1), and, in turn, heavy traffic in American ships made Appleton's job quite different from consuls in quieter locations with few Americans. Unlike Simpson and Montgomery, much, if not most, of Appleton's time was devoted to dealing with other Americans. In this respect the Livorno consulate conformed more closely to the norm Congress

---

[1] The petitioners may be found in petition to Gen. Miollis, Oct. 1, 1807, GL. Appleton, Robert and William Purviance, William de Butts, and Charles Degan were some of the American merchants known to have resided in Livorno. De Butts had died by 1807, but if the others each had five people in their households that would be twenty individuals, bringing the total up above fifty. If one-third of the other thirty lived permanently in Livorno, with households of five people each, that would bring the total closer to 100. Other non-citizens like Philip Felicchi and his household, were also part of the American community.

Veduta del Lazzeretto di S. Rocco

FIGURE 4.1 Livorno harbor with the *lazaretto* in the foreground (Painting by P. Lapi. Source: Wellcome Collection. Attribution 4.0 International (CC BY 4.0).)

had envisioned for consular posts as centers of American trade. Yet, Livorno ultimately was connected to the same Mediterranean network as the other consulates and faced the same trade interruptions from Barbary cruisers, French ships, and British vessels, all of which meant that Appleton also dealt with many of the same issues as his colleagues to the south and west.

For Appleton, the relatively heavy and persistent volume of American trade served as Livorno's chief attraction (although he continued to angle for the Paris job for decades). Between 1768 and 1772, Livornese–US trade was extremely minimal, but it began to gain steam during the latter parts of the Revolution and into the confederation period, with fifty North American vessels arriving between 1770 and 1774. In the Revolutionary years the typical US Mediterranean traffic in cod and flour predominated, with a good number of Italians and Americans seeking to formalize trade relations with treaties and to expand US–Tuscan trade generally.[2] By the

---

[2] Maria Argiero and Algerina Neri, *Bostoniani a Livorno: il Console Thomas Appleton e I suoi conterranei* (University of Pisa, 2012) 11–17; Luca Codignola, "Relations between North America and the Italian Peninsula, 1763–1799: Tuscany, Genoa and Naples," in S. Marzagalli, J. R. Sofka, and J. J. McCusker, eds., *Rough Waters: American Involvement with the Mediterranean in the Eighteenth and Nineteenth Centuries* (Newfoundland: International Maritime Economic History Association, 2010) 25–30. Argiero and Neri

time Appleton arrived, in 1798, US–Livorno trade was again relatively stagnant, with the arrival of only four US ships recorded that year. Much of the decline was due to the French occupation of Livorno, which had begun in 1796 and which seriously impacted commerce.

However, using ship arrivals or merchandise delivered in US ships as a marker of trade seriously underestimates the importance of US merchants in the region, because much American commerce appears to have been carried on by non-American, neutral ships. At the time of the French occupation in 1796, British merchants claimed to hold a great deal of American produce, very little of which was carried by American ships. The house of John Webb reportedly held perhaps £7,000-worth of merchandise owned by merchants in the United States, which arrived by Danish and American ships, while Earle, Hodgson, and Drake reportedly held another £8,000-worth of goods belonging to Americans carried by Swedish, Danish, and Ragussian vessels. Appleton's predecessor, Philip Felicchi, reported that Earle provided him with a list of American goods held and credits owed him amounting to perhaps £25,000 in all. These claims may well have been exaggerated as they were made to protect the allegedly American property from seizure by the French under the 1778 Franco-American commercial treaty. Nevertheless, the magnitude of the sums suggests the Livorno trade was far more significant for American merchants than an exclusive focus on US ship arrivals would indicate. The claims also suggest a transition in the American–Livorno trade from the earlier focus on fish and flour toward a new emphasis on tropical reexports from Latin America and the Caribbean. While the list included some flour and bacon, these items were overshadowed by cocoa, sugar, rum, coffee, and pimentos.[3]

---

have the annual average of Livornese exports to the United States rising steadily from 1768 to 1792 with the 1768–72 average at 742 lire tornesi and the 1788–92 average at 409,165. John J. McCusker, *Money and Exchange in Europe and America 1600–1795* (Chapel Hill: University of North Carolina Press, 1978) 97, suggests that one "Livre Tournois" would be equivalent to ten pennies sterling, creating an exchange rate of 24 livre to the pound, and indicating fairly small total numbers in the Livorno–US trade (if accurate, this would translate to roughly £17,000-worth of Livornese exports to the United States annually as late as the 1788–92 period). It should be noted that, while Codignola finds fifty North American ships bearing cod to Livorno in the 1770–74 period, most of them were from Canadian ports.

[3] Testimony of John Webb and others, July 26, 1796; Philip Felicchi to John Randolph, Sept. 14, 1796, both in Leghorn Despatches. I have converted Livornese pezza (pieces of 8) to pounds at the rate of 1:4, which was the ratio used in the earlier part of the eighteenth century according to Francesca Trivellato, *The Familiarity of Strangers: The Sephardic Diaspora, Livorno, and Cross-Cultural Trade in the Early Modern Period* (New Haven:

On his arrival, Appleton was particularly concerned about the relatively small number of American ships arriving in the region, and he attempted to drum up business for the port. Researching local records he found that only twenty-three had arrived from the end of the Revolution to 1798. Although he may not have known it, this was a steep drop from the 1770s. It was not really due to lack of interest, as Italians such as Philip Mazzei and the Felicchi family were actively promoting the Italian–American trade during the late 1780s. Rather, the problem was more likely due to the Algerian cruisers which had captured US ships in 1785 and 1794 and created numerous scares that hobbled American shipping in the region.[4] Appleton wrote lengthy descriptions of the Livorno trade and its prospects to the secretary of state. He stressed that low tariffs made the port desirable, even after 1802 when an Anglo-French peace had lessened the benefits of neutral trade in much of the Mediterranean. He mentioned that the Livorno trade in reexported West Indian products was among the "most lucrative" in the Mediterranean, with profits regularly ranging from 50 to 100 percent for cargoes of West and East Indian reexports, chiefly sugar, coffee, and cochineal. He also reported that return shipments of items such as oils, soap, silks, drugs, marble, anchovies, and capers proved profitable, particularly when carried back to the West Indies. He estimated that from 1798 to 1802, 154 such cargoes had arrived in Livorno, selling at an average of $110,000 for a total of roughly $17 million. Thus, the Livorno trade appeared to offer enormous profits to American shipping, although it almost entirely bypassed American producers and consumers, since most of it involved West Indian products.[5]

Appleton attributed the relative lull in US–Livorno trade before his arrival to lack of information, or the "plain reason that it was but little known." While this explanation ignored the general disruptions in the region, it underscored his assumption, indeed the assumption of most merchants, that accurate information was vital to the smooth functioning

---

Yale University Press, 2012), xi. Charles A. Keene, "American Shipping and Trade, 1798–1820: The Evidence from Leghorn," *Journal of Economic History* 38 (Sept. 1978) 681–700 also finds a shift to the reexport trade by the 1790s, estimating that 70% of American ships arriving between 1798 and 1808 carried tropical reexports, but his figures account only for goods on US ships, not those carried by other nations. *Ibid.*, 695.

[4] Appleton to Sec. State, June 15, 1802, Leghorn Dispatches; Codignola, "Relations between North America and the Italian Peninsula," 28–32.

[5] Thomas Appleton to Sec. State, Dec. 12, 1801; Jan. 15, 1802; June 1, 1802, all in Leghorn Despatches.

of international trade. This assumption also explains why, in addition to his missives to the secretary of state, Appleton reported sending "a great variety of letters to America [that] pointed out advantages which would result from sending their ships to this place." They were similar to the many other letters sent by merchants and consuls at this time, usually enclosing lists of prices (known as price currents) to inform their counterparts of what to ship (and not to ship) in order to take advantage of needs in other ports.[6]

Whether or not Appleton's efforts were responsible, US–Livorno trade did increase dramatically during the early years of his consulship, reaching a peak in 1806 and 1807, the two years following the end of the First Barbary War. We know this, in part, due to Appleton's unusually meticulous record-keeping, another indicator of his efforts to spread commercial information to American traders.[7] In 1805, Appleton estimated American ships sold cargo worth nearly $3.4 million to Livorno, and in the second half of 1806 they brought in nearly $1.5 million. The majority of these ships came from New England, with significant numbers originating in mid-Atlantic and Chesapeake ports. Most carried reexported tropical items (81% in July–Dec. 1805 and 60% in Jan.–June 1806), most commonly sugar, which was found in a majority of cargoes, but frequently also coffee and cacao. By early 1806 fish was making a comeback, appearing in more than a third of cargoes as opposed to virtually none in late 1805. These ships carried cargoes out of Livorno that tended to be about half as valuable as those they carried in. Appleton reported elsewhere that about half of sales in Livorno were paid in bills of exchange on London, which would explain the gap. Only about half of these ships returned directly to the United States (58% in late 1805 and 45% in early 1806). The rest sailed on, mostly to points in Europe and Asia, including Asia Minor.[8]

***

---

[6] Quotes from Appleton to Sec. State, Dec. 12, 1801; Jan. 15, 1802; June 1, 1802; May 26, 1804, all in Leghorn Despatches. These letters were quite self-serving and a common practice for consuls. The issue of conflicts of interest is discussed in detail in Chapter 6 below.

[7] For a full examination of these records see Keene, "American Shipping and Trade."

[8] Statistics found in "List of American Vessels Sailed from the Port of Leghorn from the 1st of July to the last of December 1805" and "List of American Vessels ... from the 1st of January to the last of June 1806," both in Leghorn Despatches, and in Keene, "American Shipping and Trade," Table 1, 687. On bills of exchange, see Appleton to Sec. State, June 1, 1802, Leghorn Despatches.

As a result of this activity, Appleton interacted with multitudes of Americans ranging from common seamen to some of the most famous names in the early republic. Seamen were the lowest ranking and most numerous members of the American community. A total of 755 arrived on US ships in the first half of 1806 alone, and many others found their way to Livorno on other ships or by land. While some other American consuls, particularly in England and Ireland, exerted a good deal of energy attempting to identify whether sailors were actually American and to certify their nationality in order to prevent impressment, Appleton did not ever record questioning sailors' purported nationality or providing certification.[9] French control of Livorno during this period might have made a difference if their presence could deter British ships from coming close.

For Appleton the issue with sailors was charity rather than identity. Consuls were responsible for providing support to destitute American sailors arriving in their ports. Generally, these men had been too sick to continue their journeys or had been discharged by their captains. Appleton advanced a great deal of his own money toward this end – close to $500 in 1801 and nearly $900 in 1802. He drew these funds from his brother-in-law in Philadelphia and others who, in turn, charged it to the State Department. Appleton attributed the high expenses partly to the fact that, in addition to sailors stranded in Livorno, he had to assist distressed seamen who traveled on their own power from as far away as Naples and Trieste, often arriving very hungry and "bordering on the most extreme wretchedness."[10] Appleton also distributed his own money to destitute English sailors during a period when the British consul had been expelled from French controlled Livorno. Assisting people from countries without consuls was a tradition from which Americans had benefitted in Algiers, Morocco, and other places when US consuls were absent or nonexistent.[11]

Congress took action to lessen the expenses of caring for destitute sailors in February 1803. Rumors of this measure reached Appleton by

---

[9] Nathan Perl-Rosenthal, *Citizen Sailors: Becoming American in the Age of Revolution* (Cambridge: Harvard University Press, 2015); Matthew Taylor Raffety, *The Republic Afloat: Law, Honor and Citizenship in Maritime America* (University of Chicago Press, 2013); Bernadette Whelan, *American Government in Ireland, 1790–1913: A History of the US Consular Service* (Manchester University Press, 2010) 54–71.

[10] Appleton to Sec. State, Mar. 5, 1801; Dec. 12, 1801; Jan. 15, 1802, all in Leghorn Despatches.

[11] Entry for Mar. 10, 1801, Register of Events.

July but, as he had not received any communications from the State
Department for three years, he did not yet have official word. He apparently finally received notification by January 1804. The act was designed
to protect American seamen from abusive captains as well as from bad
fortune. It stipulated that captains must maintain a list of all crew members, their birth places, and physical descriptions. An important motivation for this stipulation was the need to identify the nationality of seamen
who could be liable to impressment, particularly by British officers who
would question their American identity. But a second concern appears to
have been some captains' tendency to discharge recalcitrant, superfluous,
or sick seamen at will in overseas ports. As Appleton's correspondence
made clear, this treatment could be very harmful to the discharged seamen
and very costly to consuls and the federal government, which had to pay
for seamen's support and often for their return voyages home. The new
legislation sought to prevent such casual discharges. It stipulated that the
returning crew had to be checked against the original list, and captains
would become liable to forfeit a $400 bond if any of the original crew was
missing and unaccounted for either by a discharge certificate assented to
by a consular official or by proof of death, impressment, or desertion.
Additionally, the new law stipulated that any captain discharging a crew
member must provide the local consular official with three months' pay
for the discharged man. Consuls were expected to find passage for these
men and pay them two-thirds of the wages while depositing the remaining
third into a fund to assist destitute seamen. This measure would serve the
dual purpose of reducing distress for seaman and reducing government
expenditures.[12]

Appleton very much appreciated the new measure. In its first year in
force, he reported that his six-month expenses for relief of seamen had
dropped by at least 50 percent to $222.88, and would presumably drop
further once the seamen's fund became established. The improvement, he
wrote, "is at once a proof of the salutary effect of the late law of Congress
[against] the discharging of sailors by the masters of merchantmen . . . ."
Appleton also believed the act was forcing captains to be less dictatorial
toward their crews and, therefore, minimizing desertions. He wrote the
secretary of state that since the law had become known, "not a citizen has

---

[12] "An Act Supplementary to the 'Act Concerning Consuls and Vice-Consuls,' and for the
further protection of American Seamen," Feb. 28, 1803, 7th Congress Sess. II, Chap. IX.
On this act see also Perl-Rosenthal, *Citizen Sailors*, 219–20 and Raffety, *A Republic
Afloat*, 54–55.

evaded from this port or entered into foreign service, the captains are less unjust in their treatment of their sailors, and ... we can compel [them] to their duty."[13] He probably also did not mind the new 50-cent fee paid to consuls for receiving each certificate of discharge or the $2.50 commission for paying and discharging each seaman.

Nevertheless, Appleton continued to face the problem of unruly American sailors. Two who had been imprisoned for shipboard crimes in Naples demanded the usual allowance from Appleton "with much insolence" despite already being "well provided" by the captain of the ship Appleton found to carry them home. Numerous American deserters became so troublesome that in 1804 Appleton resolved "that every sailor after having been warned to return to his duty and should still be refractory shall be confined in the prison of the city until the departure of the vessel they belong to." Later that year, in response to a riot on board the schooner *Dolphin* in which a seaman struck the captain, Appleton saw to it that several crew members were imprisoned in the *lazaretto*. These, and other frequently drunken incidents led Appleton, like social welfare agents in the United States, to distinguish between deserving and undeserving recipients of his charity. He assured the secretary of state that "Every possible care has been taken to discriminate between the unfeigned distressed seaman, entitled to charity, and the vagabond profligate who was undeserving the [aid] of government."[14]

If common seamen served as a troublesome working class within the trading nation, captains and their mates served as a more respectable middle class, perhaps analogous to the prosperous tradesman in port cities who, like captains, were referred to as masters. Captains acted as postmen, delivering mail to and from the consulate, and they provided Appleton and others with a good deal of vital information about trade and ship movements. Appleton's detailed semi-annual reports on American arrivals depended on information provided by captains who reported on the size of their crews, nature of their cargoes, point of origin, and future destination. While other consuls, including Montgomery, occasionally complained about their inability to get captains to comply with these procedures, Appleton does not seem to have had much trouble. The 1803 legislation certainly should have helped with compliance since captains could forfeit their bonds if they did not at least provide

---

[13] Appleton to Sec. State, Jan. 20, 1804; Jan. 20, 1805, both in Leghorn Despatches.
[14] Entries for July 20, 1801; May 17, 1804; June 14, 1804, Sept. [?], 1804; May 22, 1805, all in Register of Events; Appleton to Sec. State, July 8, 1803, Leghorn Despatches.

information on their crews. Even so, captains could provide a fair deal of trouble for Appleton, either through shipboard issues or through their interaction with local authorities.

As the leading American authority in the port of Livorno, Appleton was called on to settle a multitude of shipboard problems that captains were unable to fix. A mate complained that his captain refused to pay his wages. A passenger aboard a ship accused the captain of disguising an English vessel as American. A captain sold a ship and needed Appleton's assistance with the ship's paperwork. A captain, unable to put down a shipboard riot, needed his assistance. A woman from Bristol who arrived in Livorno sought out Appleton to make a complaint against an American captain who she claimed had raped her repeatedly and fathered her child. After a Baltimore ship was destroyed by fire in the port, the captain left the surviving sails with Appleton for safe-keeping.[15]

Like Montgomery, Appleton also took proactive measures to solve a vexing issue for captains: the complicated quarantine regulations. Public health officers relied on periods of quarantine to ensure that ships were not carrying disease into their port. Alarmed by the well-known Philadelphia yellow fever outbreak of 1793 and an outbreak in Spain in 1801 tied to American shipping, by 1803 Livorno authorities were very strict in demanding quarantines for American ships, often above and beyond the standard fourteen-day "quarantine of observation." American ships potentially faced quarantine of up to forty days, during which some goods had to be stored in the *lazaretto* where they could be taxed at up to 2 percent of their value, thereby making trade much slower and less profitable than anticipated. Appleton claimed that the extra expense could rise up to $1,000 for a single cargo. Appleton, who had frequent interaction and apparently good relations with local authorities, discussed the matter with the secretary of the Board of Health. Appleton was particularly concerned that even though ports such as Baltimore and New York had received clean bills of health during the most recent yellow fever outbreak in Philadelphia, all American ships had been subject to the same twenty-day quarantine. Eventually he was able to convince Livorno's authorities to reduce the quarantine back to the usual fourteen days on any American ship bearing a certificate signed by authorities in its home port that it was free of fever and to allow all merchandise aboard

---

[15] Entries for Mar. [?], 1801; Mar. 1, 1801; Sept. [?], 1804; Sept. 1, 1804; Nov. 24, 1805, all in Register of Events.

these ships to remain on board, thereby avoiding the storage fees for the *lazarettos*.[16]

As consul, Appleton also met merchants and other elite Americans travelling through Livorno. He occasionally met their corpses, too, since consuls had the responsibility of burying Americans who died in their jurisdiction and disposing of their estates (for a fee). In December 1803, he received word of the death of Philip Felicchi's trading partner and prominent New York merchant, William Seton. Seton, whose widow would become the first Catholic saint born in the United States, had just arrived in Livorno days before and suffered a difficult stay in quarantine. Appleton no doubt would have had much contact with him at that time, and probably on earlier visits as well. That same year, Appleton also had to raise funds for the burial of Thomas Pollock of New York, who died in Lucca in September. Pollock was the son of a prominent North Carolina family involved in planting and commerce. Family legend has it that he was refused burial in the Catholic cemetery in Lucca and then had to be buried in Livorno's Protestant cemetery.[17]

Appleton also occasionally had to certify that live merchants were American. In 1800, he provided a certificate for Julius Ceasar Alberganty (or Alberganti) a representative of the Livorno firm Jaume and Swartz who had spent some time in Philadelphia and claimed to be a naturalized citizen. This claim was also supported by John Baptiste Sartori, the Italian-born American consul in Rome who had known Alberganty in Philadelphia. However, William Eaton, the American consul in Tunis disputed the claim and refused to recognize Alberganty as a citizen. When Alberganty showed Eaton Appleton's certificate, Eaton claimed that it was "insufficient." Eaton's concern was that Alberganty, whom he felt had insulted him, was falsely claiming to be a citizen and that his firm's impending bankruptcy would leave American agents in the Mediterranean liable for his debts.[18]

---

[16] Appleton to Sec. State, May 23, 1803; May 29, 1803, both in Leghorn Despatches; Entry for May 27, 1803, Register of Events.

[17] Entries for Sept. 14, 1803; Dec. 27, 1803, both in Register of Events. George Frederick Tuttle, *The Descendants of William and Elizabeth Tuttle* (Rutland VT: Tuttle and Co. 1883) 425; *Dictionary of North Carolina Biography* (Chapel Hill, University of North Carolina Press, 2000) V: 117.

[18] Letterbook 1799–1801, 23, 26, 127, Eaton Papers; Lawrence A. Peskin, "American Exception?: William Eaton and Early National Antisemitism," *American Jewish History* 100 (July 2016) 299–317, 306; Robert Alison, *The Crescent Obscured: The United States and the Muslim World 1776–1815* (University of Chicago, 2000) 173–74; *American State Papers: Documents Legislative and Executive of the Congress of the US* (Washington DC: Giles and Seaton, 1834) IX: 305. For the alternate spelling, see *ibid*. II: 445.

The American merchants with whom Appleton had the most contact were Samuel and William Young Purviance, who were Livorno's most prominent resident Americans. They initially worked in partnership under W. H. de Butts, an American citizen, and after de Butts died in 1801, with Charles F. Degan.[19] The Purviances belonged to an important and well-connected Baltimore family. Their kinsman, Robert Purviance, was collector of Baltimore's port and politically connected to Samuel Smith, Maryland's powerful merchant congressman.[20] Appleton clearly resented the Purviances, viewing them as rivals. The Purviances's habit of frequently meeting incoming American ships and entertaining their captains and other officials, a role often associated with consuls, may well have irritated Appleton, who appears to have occasionally been ignored altogether by these visitors. Despite claiming not to pursue mercantile affairs, Appleton did so to some extent, and the Purviances's presence and evident success could have been a source of bitterness as well. The Purviances certainly moved in more elevated social circles than Appleton. In 1805, Samuel paid an outrageous sum for tickets to attend Napoleon's coronation as king of Italy in Milan along with Nathaniel Amory, a member of one of Boston's most prominent mercantile families. Another Amory, Rufus, had signed one of the petitions supporting Appleton's appointment in 1797, indicating that they saw Appleton as a suitable person to receive their patronage, but not necessarily as an equal.[21]

But for Appleton the larger issue was the appointment of the House of Purviance as naval agents in Livorno. Their firm certainly profited from the appointment, providing goods and financial services to the recently established Mediterranean squadron. All activities provided commissions, and as merchants they would have found multiple ways to benefit from the contacts and reputation that came with the job. But Appleton stressed that "the pecuniary emoluments which might arise [had] the smallest share" in his desire to replace the Purviances as Livorno's naval agent. Instead, he saw it as a matter of dignity and reputation. He felt he had provided exemplary service to the United States as consul, and, he wrote Thomas

[19] Degan was also frequently spelled "Degen." The two spellings were so frequently interchanged (and handwriting of the day sometimes blurred "e" and "a") that it is difficult to know which was preferred. I have standardized it to Degan here for the sake of consistency.

[20] See R. Purviance application, May 19, 1789, Washington Papers.

[21] Entries for Aug. 4, 1801; Feb. 6, 1802 (in French); June 15, 1804; July 27, 1804; Oct. 10, 1805, all in Register of Events; Appleton to Sec. State, July 5, 1805, Leghorn Despatches; Petition supporting Thomas Appleton, Apr. 4, 1797, Adams Recs.

Jefferson, all other American consuls in the Mediterranean and all the foreign consuls in Livorno also served as naval agents for their respective government. Indeed, he wrote, "It is a *rule here* and hitherto without exception, that the consuls are the agents of the navy of their respective nations." In short, Appleton wrote elsewhere, the "disgrace" of being the only consul in his position "may tend to weaken a respectability which was my first object to establish, and shall be my last to maintain."[22]

Washington's seeming disregard for Appleton particularly troubled him at the time of the death of the Purviances's senior partner, W. H. de Butts. De Butts was an American citizen, and subsequent events suggest what may have already been evident to Appleton – the Purviances, though well connected, were not always temperamentally suited for diplomatic work – or at least William was not. The fact that, even after de Butt's death, the house of Purviance retained the naval agent position, therefore, must have been a blow. Perhaps Appleton was correct that Purviance's continued appointment reflected badly on his own reputation. William Eaton, consul to Tunis, viewed Appleton as "harmless" but lacking character. By contrast, he lauded the naval agents at Livorno and other ports as "judiciously selected" and worthy of serving as consuls. But Eaton was a volatile character who was hostile to most other consuls. Tobias Lear, consul to Algiers and far more even tempered than Eaton, did in fact support Appleton's request, so it may well have been that the Purviances's superior connections and no fault of Appleton's led to their continued appointment.[23]

William Purviance's difficult temperament became apparent in 1805 when, in short order, he got into angry confrontations with, first, Livorno's governor and then its health officer. In May, William barged into the home of a government official named Armano and "spoke to him in an unbecoming manner." The governor told Appleton he did him a favor by not arresting William, but that this was his second offence and "he must be taught to curb his temper." When William learned of the governor's remarks from Appleton, he vowed that should Armano offer him the least provocation "he would take a pistol in one hand and a horsewhip in the other and chastise him." When Appleton tried to calm him, pointing out that Americans were only permitted to reside in

---

[22] Appleton to Sec. State, Sept. 28, 1801; Jan. 15, 1802; June 1, 1802, all in Leghorn Despatches. Original emphasis.
[23] Entry for [Dec. 1801], Register of Events; Letterbook, Jan. 2, 1804–June 17, 1805, 11, Eaton Papers. On Lear, see entry for Oct. 1805, Register of Events.

Livorno at the courtesy of the government, William reportedly replied, "By G[od] if the governor arrests me the first time I meet him in the street, I will shoot him."[24]

In August the governor ordered Livorno's health secretary to complain to Appleton of William Purviance's "unwarrantable behavior" in frequently "outrageously" insulting the health commissioner while doing his duty, which included quarantining ships at some cost and disruption to merchants. The health officer informed Appleton that on his next offence William "shall be immediately punished in the most severe manner." This time Appleton decided to bypass William and instead spoke to his partner, Charles Degan, who was married to William's sister, Jemima Purviance Degan. Degan told Appleton he regretted Purviance's "unhappy and ungovernable temper." According to Appleton, Degan added that "no consideration should induce him to have any further contact with Mr. P. from the continual uneasiness he excited but from the consideration of his having married his sister."[25] Clearly all was not well with Livorno's American colony.

Rather than calming the Americans, the arrival of naval officers only exacerbated the conflicts. Because Degan and Purviance were among only a handful of naval agents scattered throughout the Mediterranean charged with funding and provisioning the fleet, American warships were frequent visitors to Livorno during the Barbary Wars. Perhaps because of tight, sometimes violent shipboard discipline, sailors and officers could become particularly difficult on land. The officers were sensitive to perceived insults from the Livornese and their own countrymen, thereby creating a number of volatile situations that Appleton attempted to defuse. Captain Samuel Evans of the USS *Nautilus* violated quarantine and illegally entered into Livorno, according to Appleton due to bad advice from Degan and Purviance. He took offense at the hand gestures used by an Italian guard attempting to forbid him from coming ashore, and rushed him several times with his sword. Seeing that Evans was drunk and had probably misunderstood the guard's intent, Appleton used his influence to get the courts to

[24] Entry for May 25, 1805 [2], Register of Events.
[25] Entry for Aug. 4 [1805], Register of Events. On Jemima Purviance see William Edwin Rudge, *Gilbert Stuart: An Illustrated Descriptive List of His Works* (New York: William Edwin Rudge, 1926) 683, www.Archives.org. This source correctly notes the Purviances's marriage but omits their residence in Livorno. Appleton's complaints against Purviance may have been exaggerated for effect or for future utility but the Register in which they are recorded does not appear to have been shared with American officials and he does not appear to have used these incidents to support his requests to be appointed naval agent or to impugn the Purviances to the State Department.

overlook the offense. Appleton also had to work to resolve two incidents involving the USS *Enterprise*, one in which an officer struck an Italian guard and one in which Captain David Porter's clerk was involved in a street fight with the captain of an American merchant vessel.[26]

The most potentially explosive incident occurred when Commodore John Rodgers believed Italian guards insulted him twice. Rodgers had landed in 1805 with Algerian consul Tobias Lear as a passenger in order to procure funds from Purviance and Degan. On September 29, he complained that a guard had erroneously detained him, and the governor of Livorno jailed the man for his mistake. Three nights later Rodgers and Samuel Purviance were together refused permission to enter into Livorno's mole by a different guard. Rodgers threw rocks at him, he said, to get the guard's attention. Rodgers claimed the guard then leveled a gun at him, though Purviance stated he only verbally threatened to shoot Rodgers. An English witness claimed that Rodgers actually attempted to climb a wall and enter the guardhouse window and that he threatened to "send on board for a twelve pounder and force a passage into town." The commodore made similar threats to Appleton when he met with him. Appleton reported Rodgers told him that he would "come with a 12 pounder ... to obtain by force his satisfaction" and that "if the governor was not so old (he is past 80) he would demand personal satisfaction." He added that "the first Tuscan officer who should even touch his coat in the street he would take his nose from his face – with many other threats, all which prudence prevented me from imparting to the Governor." Rodgers apparently was able to calm down enough to stay on board his ship because, as he told Appleton, he feared he might kill someone if he came on shore. Luckily for everyone, he sailed for Algiers about a week later without pursuing the matter further.[27]

Livorno's status as a naval station during the Barbary War eventually brought Appleton into personal contact with all of the important US naval figures of the time. He became especially well acquainted with Commodore

[26] James A. Field, *America and the Mediterranean World, 1776–1882* (Princeton, NJ: University Press, 1969) 55–56; Entries for Mar. 3, 1806; Dec. 24, 1806; Dec. 29, 1806, all in Register of Events. On shipboard discipline and violence, see James E. Valle, *Rocks and Shoals: Naval Discipline in the Age of Fighting Sail* (Annapolis: Naval Institute Press, 1980). He reports a duel between sailors in Sicily in 1804 and suggests there could have been others (*ibid.* 137).

[27] Charles Oscar Paullin, *Commodore John Rodgers: Captain, Commodore and Senior Officer of the American Navy 1793–1838* (Cleveland: Arthur B. Clark, 1910) 160–61; Entry for Oct. 12, 1805, Register of Events.

John Rodgers, for better or worse, as well as Commodores Samuel Barron, Richard Morris, and Edward Preble, all of whom frequently sailed in and out of Livorno for supplies. At one time in 1803, Preble's entire squadron docked in Livorno, including ships captained by such well-known naval officers as William Bainbridge, Stephen Decatur, and Richard Somers. As usual, Appleton felt that some of the naval officers slighted him by refusing to call on him. In the case of Stephen Decatur, Appleton believed the slight "arose from undue prejudices he had received" from Degan and Purviance.[28]

Naval ships also transported a number of Appleton's fellow consuls into and out of Livorno. Most notable was the arrival of James Cathcart, American consul to Tripoli, on June 1 or 2, 1801. Cathcart had been ejected from Tripoli due to the onset of the war. He would remain in Livorno on and off until approximately December 1803. Appleton already knew of Cathcart from his many circular letters. While Cathcart was in town, Livorno essentially became the American Tripolitan consulate in exile as Cathcart continued to receive information and issue circular letters. As he had in Africa, he also created personal conflict, alienating Degan, who told him, "Your self-importance puts me in mind of children when they are armed with a wooden sword and imagine themselves kings." Cathcart was also interested in doing business in Livorno for himself and his sometimes partner, William Eaton, the consul to Tunis. Appleton must have met Eaton when he arrived in Livorno in early 1802 aboard the USS *George Washington* in part to discuss business with Cathcart and to work on the plan that would lead to Eaton and Hamed Karamanli's famous march across the desert to capture Derna. Appleton also later met Colonel Tobias Lear, US consul to Algiers, who had come up to Livorno overland from Naples, and the American consul to Sicily, Joseph Barnes, who met with Lear while he was in Livorno tying up his business concerns before heading to Sicily to begin his appointment.[29]

These contacts between consuls and naval officers helped American officials to work together more closely in their public capacities. But they

---

[28] Entries for Nov. 26, 1801; Mar. 26, 1802; Nov. 3, 1802; Nov. 23, 1802; Aug. 12, 1803; Aug. 20, 1803; Nov. 12, 1803; Nov. [?], 1803; Nov. 27, 1803; May 30, 1805, all in Register of Events. Appleton to Sec. State, Dec. 7, 1802, Leghorn Despatches.

[29] Louis B. Wright and Julia H. Macleod, *The First Americans in North Africa* (New York: Greenwood Press, 1969) 101–3; Brett Goodin, "Opportunities of Empire: Three Barbary Captives and American Nation Building, 1770–1840," Phd dissertation (Australian National University, 2015) 134–35; Paullin, *Commodore John Rodgers*, 160; Entries for June 2, 1801; Aug. 4, 1801; June 3, 1802; Aug. 20, 1803; Nov. 12, 1803; June 4, 1804; Oct. 25, 1804; Nov. 14, 1804, all in Register of Events; Appleton to Sec. State, June 3, 1801; July 9, 1801; June 7, 1802, all in Leghorn Despatches; Joseph Barnes to Thomas Jefferson, June 7, 1803, Jefferson Papers.

also served to bring together a number of merchant consuls or would-be-merchant consuls who, as in the case of Cathcart and Eaton, would come to rely on each other for their private business concerns. In this way the public and private business world came to be intertwined in the Mediterranean, and, as described below, all this would further strengthen the networks connecting the participants in the trading nation.

***

In addition to overseeing Livorno's American community, Appleton, like Simpson and Montgomery, had to engage in the delicate diplomacy of preventing or mitigating ship captures and other disruptions to American commerce. In doing so, he had to convince foreign officials of the rights and identity of American ships, sailors, and goods. Unlike in Morocco and Alicante, the effect of the Barbary Wars was not the primary issue in Livorno, although, like all Mediterranean consuls, Appleton was kept busy monitoring events in North Africa and warning American ships of any danger. Additionally, as hosts to the Degan and Purviance naval agency, Livornese frequently saw warships from the Mediterranean fleet at their port, potentially providing more protection than was afforded Americans in other ports. For Appleton, however, the larger concern was the serious and immediate threats from British and French vessels due to Livorno's strategic importance during the Napoleonic Wars.

Livorno had served as a free port since 1692, meaning trade was theoretically free of duties and open to all. This status began to change due to a series of invasions and blockades during the Napoleonic Wars, and it was during these turbulent times when American commerce was most disrupted and the American consul kept busiest trying to lessen the impact on American shipping. The first such period was Napoleon's initial invasion and occupation in 1796–97. A second turbulent period occurred in 1800–1801, when Napoleon once again occupied Livorno. Because these disruptions occurred simultaneously with the outbreak of the First Barbary War, this was a particularly hectic and difficult period for Appleton. During the subsequent two-year Treaty of Amiens, neither the British nor French troubled American shipping, but with the reoccurrence of war in 1803, Appleton once again was forced to deal with British and French disruptions to American shipping, while also dealing with the disruptions associated with the ongoing Barbary War.[30]

---

[30] Katerina Galani, "The Napoleonic Wars and the Disruption of Shipping and Trade: British, Greek, and American Merchants in Livorno," *Historical Review* VII (2010) 179–98 provides a brief overview.

The 1796–97 occupation took place on Philip Felicchi's watch. He reported that about 6,000 French troops occupied Livorno on June 27, 1796 though the number that stayed was only about 2,000. Having been warned just before the invasion, the large cohort of British merchants was able to flee the French, who confiscated their property under the notion that British merchant houses should be considered the same as ships taken as prizes on the high seas. British merchants were holding a good deal of American property, which the French confiscated as though it were British. Felicchi himself suffered. He demanded his goods "be considered as vessels under American color" (i.e., as neutral ships that could not be seized). The French ignored this demand, sealing off his stores, rummaging through the goods, and even sealing off his country house. Felicchi claimed he "suffered a great deal of vexation" due to these actions. At the same time, the British blockaded Livorno, and the Tunisians reportedly captured an American vessel. "These events have thrown so great a confusion in the affairs of all the mercantile houses," Felicchi wrote, "that a general bankruptcy must be the inevitable consequence of it if not soon remedied."[31]

At the same time Felicchi reported working diligently to negotiate with the French authorities in order to protect confiscated American property. He spent the rest of June and most of July chasing down French officials and trying to get assurances that American property would be treated as neutral goods and that France would obey the twenty-third article of the Treaty of Amity and Commerce, which forbade either power from capturing the other's ships. Felicchi hinted that the local authorities were corrupt and accused the French consul of "ground[ing] his pretensions merely on his force . . . ." He tried, without success, to go over their heads by appealing to the Grand Duke of Tuscany. In the end he had to report to the State Department that "the American property that unfortunately was consigned to the English merchants resident here has been violated and taken possession of notwithstanding the remonstrances on my part . . . ."[32] Clearly the French were unable or unwilling to distinguish between American and British goods, nor were they convinced by a man they likely viewed as a self-interested Italian merchant.

---

[31] Felicchi to Sec. State, July 7, 1796 (with numerous attachments); Sept. 14, 1796, both in Leghorn Despatches.
[32] "Treaty of Amity and Commerce between the United States and France, Feb. 6, 1778," https://Avalon.law.Yale.edu; Felicchi to Sec. State, Sept. 14, 1796, Leghorn Despatches.

While similar to the 1796–97 occupation, that of 1800–1801 forced Appleton to prove the identity of American ships rather than of American goods. As conflict in the region heated up in late summer and early fall of 1800, the immediate threat was from the British, who stopped at least four American ships sailing from Livorno, apparently on suspicions that they carried French cargo. The day before the French invasion, Appleton was busy at court trying to use his influence to get this cargo cleared.[33] From the time of the French invasion on October 16, the authorities changed but Appleton's task remained more or less the same. The French immediately laid an embargo on the port and demanded that consuls for countries allied with France, including the United States, prove that their ships did not carry the property of other nations. Appleton, realizing that this decree could entirely shut down the port and paralyze American shipping, immediately tried to ascertain how Americans might be able to comply with it. On the day the French arrived he waited on their general in an effort to get clarity, but he was replaced by a second general three days later, and, due to conflict and confusion between civil and military authorities, Appleton passed a number of days "continually calling on one authority and another without anything effectual … ." This situation continued into November, and Appleton continued to make the rounds in search of authorization for American ships. During the first week of November, he called on military officials several times a day, sometimes even having to track them down when they changed their lodgings. He reported "many promises" but no successes. Finally, on November 6, as another American brig arrived in port, Appleton received word that the authorities had drawn up a declaration form for American ships.[34]

All this time, at least five American ships (*Mechanick*, *Lucy*, *Tamerlane*, *Greyhound*, and *Boston*) had been grounded at Livorno and another (*Louisa*) at nearby Portoferraio on the island of Elba. The unfortunate brig *Lucy*, Captain Tappan of Newburyport, Mass. had first been captured by British privateers just before the French occupation. When the French arrived, they claimed it was an English prize, not an American ship, and therefore subject to seizure. Appleton spent a good deal of effort shuttling the ship's paperwork between officials. All this time the stranded sailors were becoming restless, and Appleton had to get permission from the authorities to arrest six sailors from the Purviances's ship, *Mechanick*,

---

[33] Entries for Aug. 2, 1800, Sept. 12, 1800; Oct. 15, 1800, all in Register of Events.
[34] Entries for Oct. 16, 1800; Nov. 2–7, 1800, all in Register of Events; Appleton to Sec. State, July 9, 1801, Leghorn Despatches.

who were suspected of stealing and subsequently deserted. By November 7, French authorities had decided that, in addition to the forms, American ships would need to pay a duty of up to 2 percent of their cargo before being allowed to embark. Finally, on November 12, almost a month after the French arrival, Appleton was able to secure permission for the American ships to continue on their journeys. Despite the short-term damage to American shipping, the situation also offered advantages. As Appleton noted, the American ships were the first of any nation to be granted permission to sail, and their relatively good treatment would have given them a trading advantage over their slower rivals.[35]

Appleton encountered a few more problems in the second and last year of the French occupation when authorities detained at least two American ships on suspicion that they were actually British. Just as British officials sometimes impressed American sailors believing that due to their linguistic and cultural similarities they were actually British citizens, so French officials must have had difficulty discerning between American and British crews. As with impressment of sailors, it fell on consuls to verify that such ships were in fact American. The two ships in question were the *Raven*, a 58-foot-long two-masted schooner owned by Nathan Brown of Marblehead, Massachusetts, and the *Columbia*, apparently owned by an American in Livorno named Abernathy. Upon learning of the detentions, Appleton immediately vouched for their identity to local authorities. He insisted that under the Treaty of Amity and Commerce the ships' possession of sea letters was sufficient to identify them as American, but the authorities continued to detain the *Columbia* until Appleton took the case to General Joachim Murat, who ordered the ships released.[36]

With the advent of the Treaty of Amiens between France and Britain in 1802, shipping returned more or less to normal, only to be interrupted again when war resumed in the spring of 1803. Official news of the resumption of war reached Livorno on May 28. The next day authorities declared the city under siege and laid an embargo on vessels in the port. According to Appleton, "A few fortunate adventurers from the United States" soon arrived at the port hoping to "profit of the enthusiasm which generally ensues hostilities [and] sell their cargoes at least for 100 percent

---

[35] Entries for Nov. 7, 1800; Nov. 9, 1800, both in Register of Events; Appleton to Sec. State, July 9, 1801, Leghorn Despatches.

[36] Entries for Apr. [?], 1801; Apr. 2, 1801; May 8, 1801, all in Register of Events; Appleton to Sec. State, July 9, 1801, Leghorn Despatches. In the May 8, 1801 entry, Appleton mistakenly cited Article 4 of the treaty as requiring sea letters, rather than Article 27.

[above] the original cost." Unfortunately for those adventurers, the French seized two American ships entering Livorno on June 15 (*Syren* and *Adelaid*) and another (*Boston*) on July 7, the first two on the pretext that their cargo was consigned to a British merchant house and the third because it had unloaded its cargo in Mahon, which was under British control, after being loaded in the French ports of Guadelupe and Marseille. French authorities also seized a non-American ship with an American supercargo and a cargo claimed by Degan and Purviance. As he had before, Appleton tried to get the local officials to abide by the Franco-American Treaty of Amity and Commerce which forbade the detention of ships carrying prohibited goods as a part of their cargo.[37]

Unfortunately, Appleton's efforts were ineffectual this time and he was compelled to try additional measures. First, he wrote to Robert Livingston, the American minister to France to persuade the government in Paris to "obtain a security to our vessels and the respect which is due to our flag." Then, in August, Commodore Richard Morris fortuitously arrived in Livorno with a Tripolitine prize captured in the Barbary Wars. It is unclear who initiated it, but about the time of Morris's arrival he and Appleton must have determined that, as leaders of the American trading nation they should take the American captains' case to the Tuscan queen. But first Appleton wrote a circular letter to Livorno merchants (presumably both American and non-American) prompting them to draw up a petition to the queen decrying the local officials' detention of the ships, "stating how destructive it would be to the commerce of this place," and urging the Queen's interference. Appleton and Morris then took the petition with them to Tuscan officials on August 20. The officials were sympathetic and promised to write General Murat and Napoleon to confirm that "American vessels loaded in [part] or wholly with the manufactures of Great Britain or her colonies, should not be subject to any undue detention [or] vexatious suits." Unfortunately, local officials still controlled the situation, and at least one of the American ships, the *Boston*, was still struggling to get permission to sail in late October, more than three months after it was detained.[38]

---

[37] Entries for May 27, 1803; June 15, 1803; June 19, 1803; July 7, 1803; July 27, 1803, all in Register of Events. Appleton to Sec. State, June 4, 1803; July 8, 1803, both in Leghorn Despatches.

[38] Appleton to Livingston [July 8, 1803]; to Sec. State, July 8, 1803; Aug. 29, 1803, all in Leghorn Despatches. Entries for Aug. 12, 1803; Aug 28, 1803; Oct. 20, 1803, all in Register of Events.

Livorno was not immediately affected by the Barbary Wars in the same way that it was by the Napoleonic Wars, but events in North Africa did occupy a good deal of Appleton's time and efforts. Because Livorno was one of the busiest and most important Mediterranean ports for the American trading nation, it occupied a crucial node in the American communications network. Tangier and other North African ports such as Tunis and Algiers received more Barbary news earlier than did Livorno, but officials in those locations could not easily get it to the United States because they were cut off by geography and by military actions such as Barbary cruisers, European privateers, and shipping embargoes in Europe and North Africa. Simpson's frequent inability to get important information across the fewer than 40 miles of Mediterranean separating him from Gibraltar is a prime example. Because of Appleton's wide range of Mediterranean contacts and frequent ship arrivals and departures to and from Livorno, he was able to gather a good deal of information from Americans and others in their network about North African events and to convey it to the State Department and others in the United States. Additionally, Livorno's location and the presence of US naval agents, made it an important stopping point for key American officials, furthering Appleton's importance and cementing his connections.

As in Morocco, the major concern for the Americans was to keep commerce open in the Mediterranean, which entailed avoiding threats from North African cruisers that could shut down trade by declaring war on the United States and capturing American ships, crews, and cargoes. Even before Appleton, Philip Felicchi had been aware of these concerns, as he received and disseminated information about the Algerian cruisers and the American captives in Algiers. After learning of the treaty ending hostilities in Algiers, he wrote the secretary of state that "the navigation of American vessels in the Mediterranean can not be secure without a like treaty with Tripoly and Tunis."[39]

During the five years of the First Barbary War, Appleton received at least twenty letters from correspondents with information about Barbary affairs. These were probably only the tip of the iceberg, as none of his consular letterbooks have been preserved and the figure, therefore, only reflects those items mentioned in official State Department documents. Simpson's one extant letterbook contained dozens of letters that did not find their way into consular despatches, and the case with Appleton is likely similar. Of Appleton's twenty documented letters, the majority

---

[39] Felicchi to Sec. State, Oct. 23, 1795, Leghorn Despatches.

came from US officials, with five from consuls in North Africa and Spain and four from naval officers. The remainder came from consuls representing neutral countries, unspecified sources, and a personal friend. The large majority (fourteen) came in the first two years of the First Barbary War, when Americans needed to know about the declaration of war, rumors about Tripolitan (and other) cruisers, and details of the blockade.[40]

Appleton often passed information from these letters on as circulars to warn Americans and others. "The frequency of intercourse between Barbary and this place gave me an opportunity of affording the most timely information to our consuls in Europe of the gradual steps of the Bashaw of Tripoli," he wrote the secretary of state. "I may with much truth say, that there is scarcely a seaport in Europe (and even some in Asia Minor) to which I have not sent circulars apprizing them of the danger which threatened the commerce of the United States in the Mediterranean," he later added.[41] Among the places to which he sent circulars were Genoa, Barcelona, Alicante, Málaga, Paris, Amsterdam, Hamburg, London, Trieste, Smyrna, Ragusa, and Naples, and even as far afield as Sweden, Denmark, and Russia. Eventually he just reported sending circulars to "all our consuls on the European side of the Mediterranean." He also frequently sent circulars to Americans in the port of Livorno as well as notifications to the *Florence Gazette*, and, on the occasion of the peace with Tripoli, to "fourteen consuls of different nations in Leghorn."[42]

Appleton also took further actions to try to prevent captures, actions that were typical of consuls in his situation. In response to the circular letter from James Cathcart advising of Tripoli's declaration of war against the United States, Appleton placed the American ships in Livorno under embargo (meaning they could not leave port) and apparently encouraged other consuls to do the same in their respective ports. He justified the action on the grounds that if any ships were to be captured "the government of the United States of America would be obliged to redeem the

---

[40] James Cathcart to Appleton, Jan. 3, 1801; Appleton to Sec. State, Mar. 5, 1801; Aug. 10, 1801; Dec. 4, 1801; July 10, 1802; Circular Nov. 25, 1803; Appleton to Sec State, Dec. 7, 1802; to R. Livingston, Oct. 7, 1803; to Sec. State, Oct. 7, 1803; Jan. 20, 1804; Apr. 13, 1804; Mar. 20, 1805, all in Leghorn Despatches. Entries for Feb. 2, 1801; Apr. 14, 1801; May 11, 1801; Aug. 14, 1801, [Dec. 1801], June, 3, 1802; June 26, 1802; June 16, 1802; July 6, 1802; July 9, 1802; Sept. 20, 1802; Nov. 9, 1802, all in Register of Events.

[41] Appleton to Sec. State, Aug. 10, 1801; Sept. 28, 1801, both in Leghorn Despatches.

[42] Entries for Feb. 2, 1801; Aug. 4, 1801; July 6, 1801; July 9, 1801; Sept. 20, 1802; Nov. 25, 1802; July 1, 1805; July 18, 1805, all in Register of Events. Appleton to Sec. State, Mar. 5, 1801; Aug. 10, 1801; Dec. 4, 1801, all in Leghorn Despatches.

captives, and that [Tripoli's] demands will increase in proportion to the number of slaves." Appleton admitted that taking this step without consulting the State Department might be seen as exceeding his consular duties, but he argued that the sketchiness of the consuls' instructions and the long delays in communicating with the US necessitated that in all events for which there were not clear instructions the consuls' "judgement must be the only guide that we should follow." At the same time, Appleton also worked on arranging convoys for American ships to allow them to sail out of port with protection. For example, in September 1804, he arranged for them to join a convoy led by a Swedish frigate that would afford them protection while they continued their journeys through the Mediterranean.[43]

Finally, Appleton unsuccessfully floated two less conventional projects to reduce the risk of captures. Immediately after receiving Cathcart's circular warning of the war with Tripoli, he asked Godefroy Redon de Belleville, the former French consul to Livorno who was recently appointed Italian commissioner general for commercial affairs, to ask French officials in Tripoli to convince the ruling Bashaw to suspend his declaration of war. Appleton reasoned that since Belleville had influence with Napoleon and the French had earlier offered to assist the United States in negotiations with Algiers and had recently completed a treaty with Tripoli, Belleville's intercession might succeed. Belleville apparently received permission from Charles Talleyrand, then Napoleon's foreign minister, and Cathcart was supposed to carry a letter to North Africa, but Cathcart's sudden departure from Livorno scuttled the plan. Having failed to stop the war, Appleton drew up a scheme to establish a naval registry in Gibraltar where US captains would be required to dock on entering the Mediterranean in order to be informed of the most recent dangers to shipping in the region. This scheme would alleviate "the continual hazard our ships encounter, in these seas arising from the captains being totally uninformed, whether the Barbary powers are friendly or inimically disposed toward the United States."[44] He does not seem to have received a response to this suggestion, and the idea died almost before it was born.

---

[43] Entry for Apr. 16, 1801; Sept. 23, 1801, both in Register of Events; Appleton to Sec. State, July 9, 1801, Leghorn Despatches. For other examples of convoys, see Lewis O'Brien to Appleton, Dec. 5, 1801, Leghorn Despatches; Entries for Mar. 26, 1802; Nov. 12, 1803, both in Register of Events.

[44] Entry for Feb. 2, 1801, Register of Events; Appleton to Sec. State, Mar. 5, 1801; July 10, 1802; Feb. 4, 1804, all in Leghorn Despatches.

It is hard to overestimate the importance of disseminating this information throughout the trading nation. Awareness of the threat of captures was the best preventative. As Appleton wrote, "I am satisfied that in no port of Europe can ignorance of our situation with Tripoli be pled, as an apology for hazarding themselves in the Mediterranean."[45] Additionally, these frequent correspondences had the unintended consequence of binding American consuls, captains, and merchants more tightly together both for business and for pleasure, as detailed in Part II.

[45] Appleton to Sec. State, July 9, 1801, Leghorn Despatches.

PART II

COMMUNITY STRUCTURES

5

The American Social Network and National Identity

At the time of their arrival at their posts, the three consuls who are the subjects of this book, were more-or-less alone. They were young men without much family nearby and with few acquaintances or friends. Over time they all built dense social networks of family, friends, acquaintances, and business associates that became the core of the broader American community in the Mediterranean. They did so in a number of ways. All married (though quite late) and had children and grandchildren who remained nearby for a time at least. Further family marriages brought more in-laws and others into the family circle. All also had siblings or other relatives nearby for a time. As merchants they brought in clerks to their business. These young clerks were often Americans and frequently relatives. They, in turn, married and brought more children, spouses, and in-laws into the network. When they set up their own mercantile businesses, they brought in their own clerks. As already discussed, consuls also brought vice-consuls and other business associates into the network. As the US State Department expanded, they also got to know other US officials stationed within the Mediterranean, most frequently other consuls and those associated with the US Navy.

Yet, even as the American community grew, the consuls inhabited a liminal social world teetering between American and foreign identities and on the boundary of nationalism and cosmopolitanism. On the one hand, they represented a particular nation-state. But on the other, they spent most of their time in transnational networks composed of European consuls and merchants. Whom they associated with was limited both by availability and choice. With few countrymen in the region, particularly early on, even if they wanted to socialize primarily with Americans it was impractical to do so, at least face-to-face. Thus, in Catholic Europe, Mediterranean consuls would most frequently associate with Europeans, either Catholic natives of the areas where they were posted or Protestant representatives of other countries posted in the same port. In Islamic North Africa, where there were virtually no Americans and social interaction with Muslim residents was even more constrained, consuls' face-to-face interaction would be limited almost entirely to non-American European officials and their families. Over time, as the number of Americans living in the Mediterranean engaged in regional trade grew, their personal networks became more Americanized, although the extent to which this was true varied from consul to consul and, for all, the tension between nationalism and cosmopolitanism remained even when the American community was at its largest and most powerful.

As a result, Simpson, Montgomery, and Appleton all faced accusations of excessive cosmopolitanism and insufficient Americanism at one time or another. At the time of his appointment, Appleton's recommendation letters acknowledged possible concerns, with one recommender concluding, "In short, he is an American and not a Frenchman [because] he had, in the morning of life, those seeds planted in the mind, which are now producing that fruit without which the most perfect confidence cannot be placed in any man." Similarly, his father, Nathaniel Appleton stressed his attachment "to the interest and reputation of his native country in opposition to many Americans who have sacrificed both, to their private interest or French enthusiasm."[1] There are many hints that Montgomery, too, was looked on with suspicion by some Americans, but the most obvious instance occurred in 1815 when Colonel John R. Fenwick was appointed to replace him as consul to Alicante. Montgomery deduced that Fenwick's supporters had claimed he was not a citizen due to his faulty original appointment which stated he was "of Alicante" despite his receiving the oath of allegiance from Franklin and the other American commissioners. No doubt he was correct, as by this time it was relatively common for ambitious or dissatisfied Americans to attempt to replace noncitizen consuls.[2]

[1] Benjamin Lincoln recommendation for Appleton, Oct. 12, 1797; N. Appleton to the President, Oct. 16, 1797; Arthur Fenner to the President, Oct. 19, 1797, all in Adams Recs.
[2] Robert Montgomery to Sec. State, June 25, 1815; June 29, 1815; Memorial of Robert Montgomery, Mar. 17, 1816, all in Alicante Despatches.

Two contemporary commentaries from the 1810s offer seemingly contradictory views on James Simpson's Americanism. James Riley, a captive whom Simpson redeemed and who later represented Simpson in Washington, claimed that the consul "is a native of Scotland, but a firm American in principle, and an enthusiastic admirer of our excellent institutions." On the other hand, Mordecai M. Noah, American consul to Tunis and a critic of foreign-born consuls, complained that, "Although enjoying the patronage of the people for a number of years, [Simpson] never fails to let it be distinctly understood, that he has the honor to be born in Scotland, and has lost none of his veneration for 'Kings, Lords and Commons.'"[3] It is not surprising that Noah viewed Simpson's attachment to the United States with suspicion. In addition to a general lack of social and familial connection with Americans, neither Simpson nor any of his children ever appear to have set foot in the United States, and his inability to conduct much mercantile business in Morocco also forestalled further connections with people engaged in American trade. However, Simpson's relative lack of American friends and relations does not necessarily contradict Riley's point about the Moroccan consul's admiration of American institutions. The most interesting piece of evidence here is Simpson's decision to dub the family seat Mount Washington when he purchased it in 1797, shortly before Washington retired from public life. This was the period when Washington was coming to be seen as the father of his country, the personal embodiment of the nation. For Simpson, a young father himself, naming his own family's home after George Washington sent a powerful message of fealty and admiration.[4] Simpson did not and could not claim to be an American based on birth or any territorial notions of citizenship. Instead. he drew on an enlightened, cosmopolitan sense of the unity of free people who support liberal institutions. In this sense, Simpson went a long way toward reconciling cosmopolitan and national identities.

The accusations of insufficient Americanism aimed at the three consuls reflected the distance between two diverging perspectives. From the point of view of Americans within the United States, even Montgomery and Appleton, who were both American citizens, seemed somehow

[3] James Riley, *An Authentic Narrative of the Loss of the American Brig Commerce* (Hartford: James Riley, 1817) 519–20; Mordecai Manuel Noah, *Travels in England, France, Spain, and the Barbary States* in the Years 1813–1814 and 15 (New York: Kirk and Mercein, 1819) 98–99, 217–18.

[4] James Simpson to David Humphreys, June 8, 1796 [misdated, should be 1798], Simpson NARA.

insufficiently American due to what appeared to be excessive ties to
Spain and France, respectively. Yet viewed from within the American
circle in the Mediterranean, they and even non-American citizens like
Simpson were leading personages within the American community due
to their strong personal, financial, and professional ties to the broad
American network. For Americans outside of the United States at this
time, identity was less a matter of citizenship, or even birth than of
whether they associated with Americans, and shared American interests
and ideals.

***

Unlike Jewish merchants or British officials, American consuls and their
associates did not seem to have a particularly strong group identity, at
least not initially. As in the United States, ethnic identities coexisted with
national affiliation. Montgomery's and Simpson's circles continued to be
dominated by Irish and Scottish people with few ties to America. Even
decades later many in this network still had fairly loose connections to the
United States compared to their ethnic identities. Nevertheless, the
increasing time spent associating with others in the American community
reinforced identification with the United States and helped make the
community more distinctive. Over time, a stronger US identity certainly
emerged, and it evolved into a more modern nationalism based on citizenship, as opposed to the traditional ethnic affiliations of many overseas
merchants.

Perhaps the most obvious route for expanding the American community was for consuls to follow the biblical injunction to be fruitful and
multiply. However, family formation was a difficult task reflecting directly back on the consuls' positions within a region with few other
Americans. Montgomery and Appleton were both Protestants surrounded by Catholics while the Simpson family, once they moved to
Tangier, was surrounded primarily by Muslims. These Protestants
clearly were reluctant to marry Catholics, let alone Muslims, and, despite the heterogeneity of Mediterranean society, Catholics and Muslims
were in no hurry to marry Protestants. Distance from home coupled with
their already weak ties to the mother country, also made it difficult for
them to import brides.

Despite achieving great prosperity in his twenties, Robert Montgomery
delayed marriage until 1786 or 1787 when he was in his early thirties. His
bride, Elizabeth McNeill, was a native of Larne, an important northern

Irish seaport located roughly 60 miles from the Montgomery family seat of Antrim.[5] The Spanish government described her as "English" in 1794, suggesting that they viewed her as a foreigner and a Protestant. Beyond that, Mrs. Montgomery's origins remain obscure. She might possibly have been part of another Irish family residing in Spain, though there is no evidence of any McNeills in that position and Protestants were relatively rare within Irish-Spanish circles. More probably, Robert met her while visiting Ireland or England. There are long periods in 1786 and 1787 when there is no evidence of his presence in Alicante, suggesting a possible voyage during that time.[6] Robert's choice of spouse not only illustrates his social distance from Spanish families but also his continuing ties to Ireland, bonds that may well have been stronger than those connecting him to the United States.

His brother, John Montgomery, spent a good deal more time in the United States as a merchant in Boston and appears to have met his wife, Louisa Lang, during that period. Even less can be gleaned about Ms. Lang than about her sister-in-law, Elizabeth. The Spanish government describes her only as a "foreigner" in a brief report on John's 1795 appointment as US consul to Barcelona. Her daughter, Ana was married in 1809, suggesting

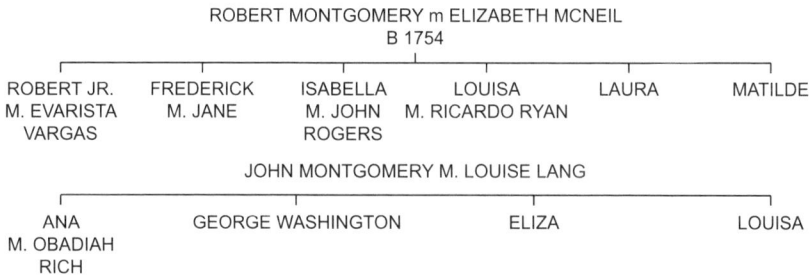

```
            ROBERT MONTGOMERY m ELIZABETH MCNEIL
                          B 1754
   ┌──────────┬──────────┬──────────┬──────────┬──────────┐
ROBERT JR.  FREDERICK  ISABELLA    LOUISA      LAURA     MATILDE
M. EVARISTA M. JANE    M. JOHN   M. RICARDO RYAN
VARGAS                 ROGERS

             JOHN MONTGOMERY M. LOUISE LANG
   ┌──────────────────┬──────────────┬─────────────┐
  ANA          GEORGE WASHINGTON       ELIZA        LOUISA
M. OBADIAH
RICH
```

FIGURE 5.1 Montgomery family tree

[5] Thomas Harrison Montgomery, *A Genealogical History of the Family of Montgomery* (Philadelphia: Printed for Private Circulation, 1863) 149.

[6] Exp. 34, Feb. 6, 1794, "Nombramiento de Roberto Montgomery como consul de Alicante y su Distrito," Estado 632–2, Archivo Histórico Nacional, Madrid. I am speculating on Montgomery's possible absence from Alicante based on the lack of documents notarized for him in late 1796 and early 1797, but gaps could also be due to missing documents or Montgomery simply not needing the use of a notary at those times.

```
              JAMES SIMPSON          M. HARRIET MAWBY
               b. Circa 1747          b. Circa 1769
        ┌──────────────────────┬──────────────────────┐
 JOHN JAMES b.1792          HELEN b.1794        THOMAS SEBRIGHT
   M. HELEN ANN           M. PETER WILSON            b.1803
                                              M. JANE REYNOLDS
```

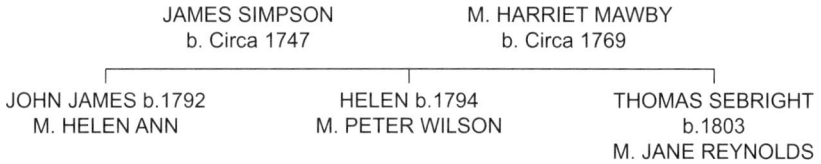

FIGURE 5.2 Simpson family tree

she was likely born around 1789 give or take a few years.[7] We know that John lived in the United States from at least 1789 to 1793 and possibly from as early as 1786. Therefore, it seems likely that his daughter was born in the United States and that he met and married his "foreign" wife there rather than in Spain.[8] If so, then Mrs. Montgomery may well have been an American or Irish-American. (See Figure 5.1.)

Like Montgomery, James Simpson married late due to the small pool of eligible spouses on the tiny rock of Gibraltar. He wed Harriet Mawby in December 1789 when he was in his early forties and she was 20. Simpson likely met her due to his friendship with the soldiers at the garrison, one of whom, Major Sebright Mawby of the 18th (Royal Irish) Regiment of Foot, was Harriet's brother. The Mawby family was an important English military family, apparently from Leicestershire. Harriet's father, John Mawby rose to be a major in the 18th Regiment of Foot and fought against the patriots during the American Revolution. It is likely that Harriet was born in the United States during the war, though there is no evidence that she or any of the other Mawby family members had any attachment to the rebellious former colonies. Major Mawby died back in Leicestershire shortly before Simpson would have met Sebright and Harriet.[9] (See Figure 5.2.) Thomas Appleton also married late and under circumstances so unusual that they will be discussed more fully at the end of this chapter.

Being a consular wife could not have been easy. While consuls maintained face-to-face social connections with a fairly constant stream of fellow

---

[7] Dna. Ana Montgomery y Dn. Obadiah Rich, recepción de dote, July 1809, Protocolo Notarial de Francisco Aracil, PN (Note: "Protocolo de Notariales" (notarial notebooks) are identified by name of the notary and date in the archives throughout this chapter).

[8] Exp 18 "Nombramiento de vice consul a d. Juan Montgomery en el Puerto de Barcelona," Aug. 22, 1795, Estado 628, Archivo Histórico Nacional, Madrid; Dna. Ana Montgomery recepción de dote a Dn. Obadiah Rich, July 4, 1809, Francisco Aracil.

[9] *Scots Magazine* 52 (Jan. 1790) 49; Steven M. Baule, *Protecting the Empire's Frontier* (Athens: Ohio University Press, 2014) 188–91, 210–14; John Throsby, *The Supplemental Volume to the Leicestershire Views* (London: J, Nichols, 1790) IV: 210; *Gentleman's Magazine*, Feb. 1851, 202–3; Gibraltar Inhabitants 1704–1914.

American and foreign officials, merchants, and American seamen, their wives' social lives would have been less rich. The consular world was a male-dominated one with women largely absent other than the occasional wife or daughter or still more occasional female traveler. Nevertheless, the women of the consular families seem to have adapted well to this environment and even thrived. No doubt, as members of a very small subgroup, they found that they had important roles to play within the American community. Unfortunately, the documentary record is far less useful in unearthing their lives and concerns than it is for their husbands.

The available evidence suggests that Elizabeth Montgomery was a strong woman who took an active part in the family business. Coming to a strange land to marry Robert Montgomery, whom she could not have known well, and living in a place with very few English speakers, let alone familiar faces, would have been a difficult trial for anyone. The best picture we have of her comes from 1798, roughly eleven years after she married Robert. At that time Henry Prince, the supercargo of an American ship docking in Alicante, described how Montgomery aggressively solicited potential consignees to dine at his house. Once there, Prince met Mrs. Montgomery, whom he described as "forcing you to eat in such an overbearing manner and insist[ing] on you not refusing and in such a manor [*sic*] that one must a[f]front her or kill him self with eating." He concluded that, rather than politeness, this behavior came from the Montgomerys' self-interested pursuit of business. Prince's description of Elizabeth as "over bearing" and impolite hints at a perception that she overstepped the accepted role of a wife as a helpmeet concerned only with affairs of the household with her active efforts on behalf of her family's business.[10] The suggestion of strength and business sense is furthered by the only document Elizabeth is known to have written, or had written, a petition to President Monroe in 1823 just after Robert's death. In her petition, Elizabeth requested that the president appoint her son, Robert Jr., consul to Alicante in recompense for his father's "long and faithful service" in that position and that, if such an appointment was not possible, he allow her a pension "sufficient for her subsistence." This request, according to one knowledgeable contemporary, was the primary reason why the younger Montgomery succeeded in gaining the appointment.[11]

[10] [Henry Prince] Log, Astrea, 1798–99, Nov. 24, 1798, Philips Library, Peabody Essex Museum, Salem, MA.
[11] Thomas Adams to Henry Clay, Sept. 4, 1827, in *The Papers of Henry Clay*, VI: *Secretary of State, 1827* (Lexington: University Press of Kentucky, 1981) 995–96; "The Petition of Elizabeth Montgomery . . .," Sept. 6, 1823, Alicante Despatches.

Harriet Simpson lived a similar life and demonstrated similar qualities. While in Gibraltar her social life would have been more stable and more active than Elizabeth Montgomery's. She lived in close proximity to her brother Sebright (when his regiment was not away) and to her unmarried sister Charlotte, as well as to friends and possible in-laws and relations, such as the Simpsons and a Sebright family which may have had some connection to the Mawbys.[12] As James devoted more and more of his time to his consular duties, she would likely have found his official routine and concerns familiar, considering that she had spent her life among men and women who lived within the vast imperial bureaucracy. Like Mrs. Montgomery in Alicante, she helped her husband to establish sociability with the Americans and others who came into port. Mr. Simpson often conveyed her regards, and occasionally her sister's to officials whom they had met in person, such as Thomas Barclay, the Danish consul to Gibraltar Michael Classen, and American Commodore Richard Morris and his wife Ann Walton. She seems to have developed a particularly close relationship with David Humphreys and his wife Anne Bulkeley. Mrs. Humphreys was the daughter of a British national serving as a US consul and the wife of a US diplomat. As such she was in a similar position to Mrs. Simpson, daughter of a British official and wife of a Scotsman serving as American consul. Harriet Simpson also somehow became acquainted with Robert Montgomery's wife, Elizabeth, most likely when the Montgomerys passed through Gibraltar on their travels to Britain. Both women were British Protestants of roughly the same age married to American consuls for roughly the same amount of time. They apparently remained friends for some time, as there is evidence they continued to correspond.[13]

At one point, between late June and September 1795, Harriet Simpson even served as de facto US consul to Gibraltar while her husband traveled to Morocco to negotiate with the emperor. Before embarking on this mission, James Simpson wrote William Short, "Your letters for me during

[12] James Simpson to Thomas Barclay, Dec. 13, 1792, Gibraltar Despatches; Sebright Mawby Will Probate 11/2126/1, National Archives, Kew; Gibraltar Inhabitants 1704–1914. I am guessing that there was a Sebright Mawby connection based on the Mawbys'/Simpsons' frequent use of Sebright as a first or middle name and the general rarity of the name "Sebright."

[13] Simpson to Barclay, Dec. 13, 1792; Michael Classen to Simpson, Jan. 21, 1795; Simpson to David Humphreys, Feb. 5, 1795, all in Gibraltar Despatches; James Simpson to David Humphreys, July 7, 1794, Simpson Letterbook; Simpson to Humphreys June 8, [1798] 1796; June 22, 1799, both in Simpson NARA; James Simpson to Richard Morris, June 20, 1803, Tangier Despatches.

my absence from Gibraltar will be opened by Mrs. Simpson, and if any information inclosures for America or other, they will be carefully forwarded and if any thing interesting occurs here you will be advised of." Following Simpson's departure, his letterbook contains a number of letters which are little different from his usual work other than being composed in a neater hand, presumably that of Mrs. Simpson. She was often careful to indicate in official correspondence that the information she imparted came from the absent Mr. Simpson who kept in close touch with her from Morocco. These letters reflect not only Mrs. Simpson's willingness to assist her husband in his official duties and her understanding of official business, but also a high degree of literacy befitting the daughter of a high-ranking British officer.[14]

For Mrs. Simpson and her family, the major and, likely, traumatic change occurred when they moved across the Strait of Gibraltar to Tangier in early 1798. Though not far when measured by miles, this move took the Simpsons into a different world. Literally, they were on a different continent, and one on which they had limited mobility due to restrictions placed on Europeans by Morocco's Islamic leaders. But most importantly, Mrs. Simpson and her two children – 5-year-old John and 3-year-old Helen – were ripped from the comfortable social fabric of Gibraltar. They left behind friends and relations as well as frequent contact with the many travelers who had to pass through the most important crossroads between the Atlantic and Mediterranean. By contrast, in Tangier she had only a very small circle of European women with whom to socialize, namely those associated with the other consulates, primarily England, Sweden, Denmark, France, and Spain.

***

The next generation, the first born in the Mediterranean, also suffered from social isolation. As residents in places where they could have had few childhood companions other than family members, their situation was perhaps even worse than that of their parents, who retained stronger connections to the homeland forged before moving to the Mediterranean. As children, they knew few to no Americans, and encountered few English speakers. Most, if not all, spoke the local language. As young adults, they faced even more difficulty finding suitable spouses than had their parents. As a result, this creole Mediterranean generation would

---

[14] Simpson to William Short, June 11, 1795; Entries for June 23, 1795; Aug. 6, 1795; Sept. 3, 1795; [Mrs. Simpson] to Michael Morphy, Sept. 3, 1795, all in Simpson Letterbook.

become particularly closely tied to family members in the Mediterranean and to any other American and European consular and merchant families in the area.

Both Robert and John Montgomery had large families and continued producing children relatively late in life. Robert and Eliza had six – two boys and four girls. Isabella was likely the eldest daughter as her 1808 marriage date suggests she was born shortly after the Montgomerys married in 1787. The elder son, Robert Jr., was born in 1791, and his brother Frederick shortly thereafter, when Robert was nearing 40.[15] John and his wife had four children – three daughters and a son born over a roughly twenty-year span, with the youngest likely born when his father was in his early forties. Based on marriage dates, one daughter, at least, was born in America before John came to Alicante in 1793. The only son, George Washington, was born in Alicante in 1804.[16] By the time of George's birth the two branches of the Spanish Montgomery family numbered fourteen people.

The children were mostly named for family members, sometimes those back home whom they wanted to remember. John's daughter Eliza would have been named for her grandmother, Eliza Hamilton Montgomery, and his daughter Louisa possibly for her mother. However, the presence of two Louisas also suggests a common ancestor with the same name. Robert Jr., of course, was named for his father. The name of Robert's daughter, Isabella, may perhaps reflect something of a Mediterranean influence as it appears to be neither a family name nor very Irish.[17] Finally, John and his wife's decision to name their only son George Washington Montgomery seems pregnant with meaning. Foregoing the opportunity to have a "John Jr." in the family, particularly when Robert named his eldest son Robert Jr., seems a significant decision. Naming him instead after the relatively recently deceased hero certainly demonstrated John's political sympathies. It is also the clearest signal of the Montgomerys' identification with the United States, and it is perhaps not surprising that it came from the brother who had spent more time there.

---

[15] Montgomery, *Genealogical History*, 149; Josiah Rogers to John Rogers, Jr., n.d. [1808], Rogers-Bridges Family Collection.

[16] Montgomery, *Genealogical History*, 149; Salvador García Castañada, "Acerca de George Washington Montgomery, Washington Irving y Otres Hispanistas Norteamericanos de la Época Fernandinas," in *Ideas en sus parsajes Homenaje al Profesor Russell P. Sebold* (Universidad de Alicante, 1999) 195–201; J. G. Marvin, *Bernado del Carpio Translated from the Spanish of Don Jorge Montgomery* (Boston: Brain and Co., 1843) 4.

[17] Montgomery, *Genealogical History*, 149–50.

Two of the Simpsons' three children were born in Gibraltar, while the youngest was born in Tangier. The eldest, John S., was called James by the family, suggesting he was named for his father. It is unclear who the daughter, Helen, was named for. The youngest, Thomas Sebright, was born in Tangier, an event that must have been particularly difficult for Mrs. Simpson considering the distance from family and from western medicine. A miscarriage two years later must also have been terrifying. Thomas's middle name honored Harriet's brother through whom she and James probably met. The elder Sebright, who would rise to the rank of general, remained an important part of the Simpson family circle for many years and was clearly an important family patron. No doubt his name and influence around the Mediterranean was of great utility to the Simpsons. Many years later, at his death, in 1851, General Sebright Mawby made his nephew Thomas Sebright Simpson his executor and left a substantial sum to the Simpsons' daughter, Helen.[18]

***

Marriage prospects were no better for the creole Mediterranean generation than for their parents and perhaps worse, since they were even more cut off from the homeland than their parents had been. The lack of suitable partners was in particular a function of religion since all were Protestant Anglo-Americans living in a world of Catholics and Muslims where intermarriage was strongly discouraged. It is likely that the Protestant Montgomerys also had little interest in mixed marriages, leaving them in the same difficult position as other merchants, such as Sephardic Jews and Armenians, who found themselves part of a tiny

---

[18] Simpson to Humphreys, Jan. 16, 1794; July 17, 1794, both in Simpson Letterbook. Simpson to Hugh Cahill, Sept. 5, 1800, Simpson NARA; Sebright Mawby Will Probate. Helen calls John "James" in her letters, but he signs his name John S. in his Tangier Despatches during his time as consul. It is possible that he too was named for Sebright, given the middle initial, though there is a John M. Simpson his age listed as living in Gibraltar in 1834, suggesting he might possibly have switched his middle initial (perhaps for Mawby). John was born in 1792 according to the Konsulatarkiv, making it very likely that he was the John M. listed in Gibraltar as they would be the exact same age. The Simpsons were quite concerned about Sebright's safety during the active phase of the Napoleonic Wars and grateful to David Humphreys for providing them with information on events in Toulon that would give them some idea of what Sebright's regiment was up to. They were even more relieved when Sebright and his sons returned to Gibraltar briefly in January 1794. On the miscarriage, see entry for Apr. 22, 1805, Konsulatarkiv. The author is grateful to Emil Kaukonen for identifying and translating portions of this document.

foreign minority. As a result, two of Robert's four daughters and two of John's appear never to have married.[19]

Robert's other daughters, so far as is known, both married men in Irish-American circles. Louisa wed Richard (Ricardo) Ryan. He was a merchant, most likely a relation to Roberto Ryan whom Montgomery had appointed vice-consul to Benicarló in 1795. Roberto was Irish born and worked as a clerk for the Irish merchant firm of Reynaldo Magdonnel (probably Reynolds McDonnel). He had connections to Jorge (or George) Moore, one of the most prominent Irish merchants in Alicante and a probable link between him, Ricardo Ryan, and Robert Montgomery. The Ryans were lapsed Catholics, which likely would have made Ricardo less desirable than a Protestant, but explains why he was able to marry Louisa. Still, his general prosperity, the two families' friendly connections, and the paucity of marital prospects for Protestant Irish-Americans in the region no doubt made him acceptable to Robert and Elizabeth.[20]

Louisa's sister, Isabella, was the only one of Robert and Elizabeth's children known to have married an American. She wed John H. Rogers, a Protestant merchant from Newton, Massachusetts, in 1808. Rogers moved to Alicante in 1802 where he set up as a rival to the Montgomery family during a period of lucrative trade in the region. For most of the decade he was one of only two or three American men in Alicante not related to Isabella, so the marriage was certainly a convenient one. Rogers was sociable, successful, and apparently friendly with his new father-in-law. His younger brother, who had come out to Spain, wrote that Rogers was "completely happy in his new situation" shortly after the wedding.[21] Rogers' roots were, as far as can be determined, completely in the United States. The Montgomerys' connection with him and his family may well have further Americanized them. However, it is also possible that the Montgomerys "Irish-ized" Rogers. While there is no evidence that the Rogers ever visited the United States, they did take a long trip to Belfast,

[19] Robert's unmarried daughters were Laura and Matillde, while John's were Eliza and Louisa. See Montgomery, *Genealogical History*, 149–50 and author's private correspondence with Luis Dunoyer.

[20] Montgomery, *Genealogical History*, 149; File of Roberto Ryan, May 14, 1796, Estado 628, Exp. 41, PARES; Ricardo Ryan appears as a merchant in *Diario De Alicante*, Dec. 17, 1816. As will be seen in Chapter 6, below, Montgomery also sold a large portion of land adjacent to his own home to Ricardo.

[21] Montgomery, *Genealogical History*, 149; Josiah Rogers to John Rogers, n.d. [1808], Rogers-Bridges Family Collection. The best evidence of Rogers and Montgomery's friendship is Montgomery's willingness to notarize a false bill of lading for Rogers. See certificate dated May 4, 1809, Rogers-Bridges Family Collection.

where Isabella spent a good deal of time with her Irish relations. Unfortunately, on this trip they also lost their infant son, who died in London.[22]

John Rogers' relatively well-documented early adulthood in Alicante provides a good sense of the difficulties a young American faced in finding a spouse. He arrived in Alicante in 1802 from Massachusetts as a 29-year-old bachelor. He clearly had marriage on his mind. Less than a year after his arrival he informed his father, "I am not married yet," as though perhaps the family might have expected him to find a bride immediately on arriving in Spain. He added, "I cannot tell when I shall have time to be [married]" and lamented, "[O]ne thing I know [is] that I am growing old very fast and by and by shall find no young lady that will marry me." He joked (apparently), "[I]f you can engage any one to come out on trial, if she and I can agree, we will tie the knot; if not I will pay her passage back again." A month later he asked his father to "Say to Sally Wessan I wish her all desired happiness," most likely because she was getting married. Perhaps she was an old girlfriend. His admonition to his father two sentences later to, "Tell the young ladies of my acquaintance I am still a bachelor" and to "say to every one who may enquire after me that I send them my compliments" may well be an indication that news of Sally Wesson brought his mind back to his own unmarried state.[23]

Rogers made some impressive efforts to find a wife or at least to create a social circle in Alicante. Not long after his arrival he began holding an annual party to celebrate the St. John's Day midsummer feast. He explained to his father, "On the 24th of [June] I have a great party at my house [and] shall dine 24 [or] 26 persons, and in the evening shall give a dance to the young ladies." The party served as a "species of Thanksgiving" since it occurred at the time of year when he closed his books. But it also clearly was an effort to meet girls, a notion reinforced by the fact that he began discussing it in the sentence immediately after inquiring about his recently married sisters and hoping that "fortune smiles on their husbands."[24] To invite twenty-four to twenty-six people, Rogers would have had to invite the entire American community in Alicante and a good number of the British, assuming he did not invite many locals – which seems unlikely, particularly if matrimony were on his

---

[22] John H. Rogers to John Rogers, Aug. 26, 1811; Mar. 2, 1814; Oct. 20, 1816, all in Rogers-Bridges Family Collection.

[23] John H. Rogers to John Rogers, Jr., Oct. 28, 1803, Rogers-Bridges Family Collection.

[24] John H. Rogers to John Rogers, Jr., June 20, 1806, Rogers-Bridges Family Collection.

mind. No doubt the Montgomery girls, daughters of the leading American in the region, would have been at the top of his invitation list.

Ana, the only one of John Montgomery's daughters to be married, wed an American, Obadiah Rich, in Alicante in July 1808. Rich was a Protestant New Englander, the son of a Cape Cod ship captain. He was actively shipping books from France back to New England by 1807 and shortly after his marriage boasted of carrying on a "considerable business" in Valencia, where he most likely was involved in the *bacalao* (salted cod) trade. The sizable dowry granted to the Riches and the fact that Montgomery specified that he granted it "according to the circumstances of Dona Ana Montgomery and the affection he has for Don Obadiah Rich" suggests that the family was very pleased with Ana's choice.[25] Ana's marriage to Rich would have tied John Montgomery's family even closer to the United States. The groom's business ties were much more American-oriented than his in-laws'. He provided European books to many American bibliophiles including the nucleus of the collection of the Boston Athenaeum, for which he had become a charter member just prior to his marriage. The couple moved back to the United States for a period, living in Boston and Georgetown, Maryland (now DC) from roughly 1812 to 1815 where she gave birth to at least one of their five children. The young family returned to Spain in 1816, where Rich served as US consul to Valencia, located about 100 miles from Alicante.[26]

None of the three Montgomery boys in the second generation was able to find a spouse in Spain. The gender ratio would have been in the girls' favor since a good number of single men made their way to Spain to seek a fortune, but to my knowledge the only young American ladies there would have been born to the few settled American families. Of course, the boys could also seek out English or Protestant-Irish spouses, but again the pickings would have been relatively slim. John's son George Washington attained a good deal of prominence, but none of the material written about him nor any documents thus far uncovered refer to a spouse or children until he left Europe. Likewise, neither of

---

[25] Dna. Ana Montgomery y Dn. Obadiah Rich, recepción de dote, July 14, 1809; Norman Paul Tucker, "Obadiah Rich, 1783–1850: Early American Hispanist," PhD dissertation (Harvard University, 1973) 1–2, 7–9, 24.

[26] Tucker, "Obadiah Rich," 7, 16, 31–32; Obadiah Rich to William Maclure, Feb. 8, 1824, New Harmony Manuscripts; Obadiah Rich to Thomas Jefferson, July 15, 1815, Jefferson Papers.

Robert's sons – Frederick and Robert Jr. – married until immigrating to Latin America. Both would have been at least well into their thirties.[27]

As with the second generation of Montgomerys, the Simpson children married late. Unsurprisingly, none could find spouses in Morocco. The eldest son, John, appears to have been recently married by 1817, when he would have been about 25, and living in Italy. Thomas Sebright only married after moving to England where he met Jane Reynolds. They married in 1833 when the groom was about 30 years old. Daughter Helen remained single, living with her parents in Tangier throughout their years there. She did not marry until 1840 when she was about 45 years old and had returned to Gibraltar. Her husband, Peter Wilson, was an English doctor. Like her father and grandfather, and so many others in that citadel, he was a government official – the director of the British hospital.[28]

***

Finding schools for children in such an isolated situation was also a difficult proposition for American mothers and fathers. Eighteenth-century Spain, with its largely Catholic educational system did not provide much for the Montgomery boys, and the parents seem to have had little interest in their daughters' educations. This issue would persist for generations. John Montgomery's son-in-law, Obadiah Rich, complained that the prospect of his own children's education gave him "considerable uneasiness" because he could not afford to send them abroad and "the present Spanish schools and Spanish instructors are worse than none."[29]

---

[27] Montgomery, *Genealogical History*, 149. Robert Jr. was in Colombia by 1827, when he would have been 36. See Adams to Clay, Sept. 4, 1827, *Papers of Henry Clay*, VI. Frederick did not leave Alicante until after 1823. He was born sometime after 1791. He was working in the family business in Marseille by 1814, suggesting he was likely born well before 1800.

[28] James Riley, *Sequel to Riley's Narrative* (Columbus: George Brewster, 1851) 330; Helen Ann Wilson to Donald McLean, May 1, 1854; May 19, 1854, both in McLean Letters; "Wilson, Helen Ann Simpson," in *Te Ara: The Encyclopedia of New Zealand*, https://teara.govt.nz/en/biographies/1w29/wilson-helen-ann. Information on Thomas's marriage is from a family discussion on RootsChat.com, www.rootschat.com/forum/index.php?topic=703783.0.

[29] G. W. Montgomery, *Bernardo del Carpio* (Boston: Brainard and Co., 1843), 4; Castañada, "Acera de George Washington Montgomery," 1; Montgomery to Sec. State, Feb. 19, 1802; Jan. 20, 1821, both in Alicante Despatches; Rich to Maclure, Feb. 8, 1824, New Harmony Manuscripts.

Burdened with these same concerns, Robert and John had earlier rejected local Spanish options, instead sending their sons away at young ages. They also rejected schools in Ireland and America in favor of elite English academies. John sent George Washington to Exeter (not to be confused with Philips Exeter in the United States), and Robert's two sons also attended schools in England from roughly age 10 onward. Though it is unclear which school they attended, their father's boast that they received "a classical education with the most liberal sentiments" suggests it was also a high-class public boarding school. Certainly, the choice of English public schools for their sons reflected the Montgomerys' Protestant affiliation and their sense of themselves as part of a rising anglophone elite as well as the problematic nature of Spanish schools. This education was calculated to allow the Montgomery boys to continue the family's avocation representing anglophone interests in the Spanish-speaking world.

The Simpsons took a similar approach to educating their children. There were no appropriate schools in Tangier. Simpson rarely mentions the boys in his correspondence, and in 1799, when the family was evacuated during the plague, 7-year-old John did not accompany them, suggesting that both boys spent considerable time away from Tangier at school. Both spent at least part of 1808 in Britain, most likely for educational purposes. John went to Gibraltar in 1810 at the age of 17 to serve as a clerk for the British commissary general, a job no doubt landed through the Simpson and Mawby families' connections and typically used as a sort of mercantile training. Again, in 1818, when they were evacuated, 15-year-old Sebright was not included, suggesting he was away at school or a clerkship. After Simpson died, John's education allowed him to take over his position as consul without difficulty. His letters demonstrate a firm command of English, no doubt a product of his education as well as living in an anglophone family.[30]

With the Simpson boys frequently away, young Helen Simpson would have been brought up among the other consular families and their daughters – assuming that most others also sent their sons to be educated abroad. She was able to visit with one of her young cousins who came over the Strait from Gibraltar in 1805 and she also visited Europe occasionally. In adulthood Helen was a clear and well-informed letter writer as is demonstrated by her extensive surviving correspondence. In addition to

---

[30] Simpson to David Humphreys, Aug. 20, 1818, Tangier Despatches; Entry for June 15, 1810, Konsulatarkiv.

her good command of English, she also spoke Spanish late into life. Since there is no evidence that Helen received any formal education, she most likely learned to read and write from her very literate mother.[31]

***

Consuls also maintained ties with more distant relatives. The clerks whom they recruited to come to their merchant houses were often, though not exclusively, family members. Bringing these clerks from the United States or elsewhere was also one of the ways in which the American community grew. By 1798, Henry Prince of the *Astrea* implied that Montgomery had multiple clerks, some of whom may have been Spaniards. He probably also employed his sons to teach them the trade but, considering that much of his work was done in English and family members were traditionally used as clerks, it is not surprising that he would have brought in young men from the United States or Great Britain. George Clark, whom Montgomery sent to Algiers to assist the American captives, appears to have been one. Montgomery described him as his nephew, although the exact relationship is unclear. Whichever side of the family Clark was from, it is likely that Montgomery was happy to have another family member to converse with and that Clark hoped the arrangement would set him on his way to fortune. A second Montgomery clerk, whose residence overlapped with Clark's, was Asa Fitch, who does not appear to have been related to Montgomery. A pale, sickly Connecticut Yankee, the 18-year-old Fitch, like Robert Montgomery, came to Alicante in the hope that the Mediterranean climate would benefit his health. Perhaps he reminded Montgomery of his younger self. At any rate, he would prove an excellent clerk, and Montgomery would later trust him to open up a branch of the firm in Marseille along with his two sons.[32]

Almost from the time he left Massachusetts, Montgomery's future son-in-law, John Rogers, began to think of having his younger brother, Josiah, join him as a clerk. In the spring of 1803 he wrote his father, "I shall want my brother out next fall; although in the beginning he will be of little service to me, yet he will be preparing himself for a career thro life." The elder Rogers maintained that it was too soon and kept Josiah in

---

[31] Simpson to Sec. State, June 24, 1799, Tangier Despatches; Simpson to Humphreys, June 22, 1799, Simpson NARA; Wilson to McLean, May 9, 1857, McLean Letters; Entry for Sept. 16, 1805, Konsulatarkiv.

[32] Montgomery to Sec. State, May 17, 1818; July 26, 1818 [misdated as July 26, 1817], Alicante Despatches; "Lista de los Individuos Americanos residentes en esta plaza," [1807], Matricula de Extranjeros, Legajo 96, Numero 94, Municipal Archive, Alicante; D. Hamilton Hurd, ed., *History of New London County, CT* (Philadelphia: J. W. Lewis, 1882) 379.

school for another year. Yet John continued to plan, writing that after the 1804 school year Josiah should come to France at John's expense to learn the language before making his way to Alicante. There, John wrote, "I shall exert myself to make a man of him." The youth finally arrived at Nantes in early 1806, nearly three years after John first asked for him. There he enrolled in a French school, as per his brother's instructions. Josiah remained in Nantes that spring, studying French and sending out occasional letters to his brother. John wrote from Alicante that he "wish[ed] very much" to see Josiah as "I think he will make a bright youth." Finally, in 1807 or 1808 the brothers were reunited at Alicante at about the same time John married Isabella Montgomery.[33]

When consuls visited with, wrote to, or brought over family members from the United States it certainly strengthened connections to the new republic. But, in many cases these cosmopolitan Mediterranean consuls had stronger connections to family members in other locations. Such ties, no doubt, stoked concerns about whether the consuls were sufficiently American. When the Montgomerys thought of home it seems just as likely that they looked to Ireland as to the United States. Many relations still resided in northern Ireland, while their remaining relations in the United States were few and distant. As discussed in Chapter 6, they maintained business contacts in Ireland. But they also continued to buttress familial connections there, and family and business were almost always inter-twined. In 1789, when John and Robert's sister Elizabeth Cron (possibly Carr) and her husband William died in Newry, Robert appointed a guardian for their young daughter, Anna. The man he appointed, Acheson Thompson, was a prominent Newry linen merchant who had lived in New York during the 1760s, when he may well have been in contact with Robert in Philadelphia or John in Boston. John appears to have bought a substantial plot of land in Northern Ireland sometime before 1809 along with a Malcolm McNeill of Lairne. The latter likely was a relation of Robert's wife, Elizabeth McNeill, also of Lairne.[34] Clearly John and Robert both continued to be connected to extended

[33] John H. Rogers to John Rogers, Jr., Mar. 30, 1803; Jan. 24, 1804; Mar. 12, 1804; May 1, 1805; Josiah Rogers to John Rogers, Jr., Jan. 30, 1806; John H. Rogers to John Rogers, Jr., June 20, 1806; May 15, 1808, all in Rogers-Bridges Family Collection.

[34] Dn. Roberto Montgomery poder (power of attorney) a Dn. Achison Thompson, June 19, 1789, Vicente Izquierdo y Suredo, PN; Mortgage reconveyance dated 1809, D509/1703, Public Records of N. Ireland, Belfast cited in "The Family History of the Patons," http://chrispatonscotland.tripod.com/id19.html; Thomas M. Truxes, *Irish American Trade 1660–1783* (Cambridge University Press, 2004) 115–16.

family in Northern Ireland long after settling in Spain and perhaps they also had hopes of returning there during their retirement.

The Simpsons' extended family lived almost exclusively in Britain and Gibraltar. As mentioned earlier, in addition to Harriet's immediate family, there were numerous Simpsons in Gibraltar, and, after the Simpsons left for Tangier, Simpson's nephew, John Duguid settled in Gibraltar with a large family.[35] The Simpsons were able to maintain close contacts with Scottish relatives in the Mediterranean, even staying in Gibraltar for long periods when they were ejected from Tangier due to plague or threatened hostilities against the United States and receiving at least one visit from the Duguids in Tangier. As noted above, they also remained in contact with Harriet's brother in England. By contrast, Simpson had no family and only a few acquaintances in the United States. One was the ship captain Ozias Goodin of Boston, whom Simpson likely met in Gibraltar. More tantalizing was Simpson's mention of his "friend" Alan Simpson who was in Philadelphia in 1792. It is unclear if this Simpson was a relation or if he lived in Philadelphia permanently, but if so, it could point to a branch of Simpson's family that, like so many other Scots families, had found its way to Pennsylvania. A family connection might explain Simpson's interest in backcountry Pennsylvania and the Whiskey Rebellion.[36]

Others attempted to maintain closer ties to the United States. The Montgomery son-in-law, John Rogers, badly missed his home and family in Newton, Massachusetts. After less than a year in Alicante, he was already thinking of taking a trip back home. He wrote frequently to his father and his numerous brothers and sisters (though the latter letters were not preserved) always expressing concern about family members and happy to exchange news and gossip about them and townspeople. He was particularly concerned about his aging grandfather who, despite expectations to the contrary, survived for many years after John left home. It was a notable event for him when two Newtonians briefly visited Alicante. After a particularly long period without a letter from home he wrote his father, "[I] intend to keep you six months without a letter from me, that you may figure to yourself little more or less how I feel not having

[35] List of Inhabitants 1814, 1834, Gibraltar Inhabitants 1704–1914; Wilson to McLean, n.d. [probably early 1860s], McLean Letters.

[36] Simpson to Humphreys, Feb. 23, 1795, Gibraltar Despatches; Simpson to Short, Dec. 18, 1794; to Lt. Col. Drinkwater, Aug. 17, 1796, all in Simpson Letterbook; Simpson expressed interest in a book recently published on Pennsylvania's Back Country, probably [Thomas Anburey], *Travels through the Interior Parts of America* (London: Wm. Lane, 1789), Simpson to Humphreys, Feb. 23, 1795, Gibraltar Despatches.

received one from you during that time." After his marriage, Rogers less frequently mentioned or alluded to missing the folks back home. But when communications to Alicante were cut for several years during the War of 1812, he once again became quite worried. That long gap, his own aging, and continual inability to find time to visit the United States clearly concerned him. As a substitute, he had his and Isabella's portraits done and shipped back to Newton. "As you can not yet see the originals," he wrote, "you must be content with the pictures," though he complained that his was "flattened" and "made me too fat."[37]

Appleton, too, maintained close connections with American relatives. He wrote regularly to his mother, Mary Henderson Appleton, in Massachusetts. He was also very close to two of his sisters – Mary, three years his senior and the eldest of the three Appleton girls, and Charlotte, three years his junior. As with his mother, no actual letters to them have been preserved in his letterbook as Appleton seems not to have wanted such private letters to be exposed to the eyes of clerks and others. However, there are several instances of Appleton sending greetings to Mary with passengers on ships heading toward her hometown of Philadelphia and also of sending her gifts, such as a set of amber beads earmarked for "my dear sister Mary."[38] Charlotte, the younger of the two, took sick and died in Boston while Appleton was in the midst of preparing to move to Livorno in late 1798. Her death was traumatic enough that it prompted unusually emotional outbursts from her grieving brother. Shortly after she died, he wrote her brother-in-law George Perkins in Smyrna that the death of his "beloved sister" was "a circumstance of that deep rooted anguish which I feel hourly can never diminish." He continued, "She has left a most inconsolable family and three charming children" but added that "it is so painful to dwell on this subject" that he would leave it to the man delivering the letter to elaborate further. In a rare letter to a female correspondent two years later offering sympathy to the marquise de Chastellux (Charlotte Brigitte Plunkitt) who had recently lost her brother, he commiserated, "I have lost a sister. She possessed all the charms of nature, joined to an understanding ornamented by the most cultivated society."[39]

---

[37] John H. Rogers to John Rogers, Jr., Mar. 30, 1803; Aug. 3, 1803; Mar. 12, 1804; Feb. 26, 1806; Mar. 2, 1814; Sept. 2, 1814, all in Rogers-Bridges Family Collection.

[38] W. S. Appleton, *A Rough Sketch of the Appleton Genealogy* (Boston: T. R. Marvin and Co., 1873) 14; Thomas Appleton to Robert H. Rose, May 17, 1801; to Samuel Emery, Aug. 11, 1801, both in GL.

[39] Appleton to George and Samuel Perkins, Jan. 27, 1799; to Marquise de Chastellux, Sept. 2, 1801, both in GL.

Appleton was also close to his brothers-in-law, both of whom, Thomas Perkins of Boston and Samuel Emery of Philadelphia, were wealthy, well-connected merchants and, therefore, very valuable contacts for Appleton. Perkins was one of twenty-eight prominent Boston merchants who signed one of the petitions that helped Appleton get appointed to his Livorno position. Once Appleton arrived in Livorno he drew on the Perkins connection when he reached out to Thomas's brothers George and Samuel Perkins, who were American merchants in Smyrna. Appleton established commercial ties to the Smyrna Perkinses, and eventually they would become one of his most important business contacts as discussed in Chapter 6. He would also pursue various business schemes with Thomas Perkins and would depend on him to handle his US business, granting him power of attorney to handle his portion of his father's estate and regularly having him advance money due to him from the State Department and to serve as a bondsman when needed.[40] He maintained a similar relationship with his sister Mary's husband, Samuel Emery. A Harvard graduate who likely met Mary while living in Massachusetts, Emery had moved to Philadelphia by the time Appleton left for Livorno. A merchant and ship broker, Emery was somewhat less prosperous and less well connected than Perkins, and his financial situation had been precarious in the 1780s. Nevertheless, he was a valuable connection for Appleton, particularly due to his location in Philadelphia, near the State Department and the rest of the federal government. Appleton frequently drew his State Department reimbursements from Emery, particularly in the years when Philadelphia was the national capital. He also used Emery's services to deliver goods directly to President Jefferson occasionally. Additionally, he frequently suggested business proposals to both Emery and Perkins together.[41]

---

[40] Petition dated Boston, Apr. 4, 1797, Appleton File, Adams Recs; Appleton to George Perkins, May 15, 1800; to George and Samuel Perkins, Jan. 27, 1799; Circular to Thomas. Perkins and others, n.d. [June 1799]; Appleton to George and Samuel Perkins, Sept. 13, 1799; Circular to Thomas Perkins, Mar. 1, 1800; Power of attorney, Nov. 4, 1801; Entries for Dec. 16, 1801; Jan. 28, 1802; Nov. 12, 1802; Aug. 17, 1803; May 20, 1804; June 28, 1804, all in GL; Thomas Appleton to Sec. State, Dec. 8, 1808; Sept. 3, 1801, both in Leghorn Despatches.

[41] James P. McClure, ed., *The Papers of Thomas Jefferson* (Princeton University Press, 2017) XLIII: 180. J. Russell Smith, *Ocean Carrier* (New York: G. P. Putnam's Sons, 1908) 97–98; Bruce H. Mann, *Republic of Debtors: Bankruptcy in the Age of American Independence* (Cambridge: Harvard University Press, 2009) 318; *Harvard Gazette*, Oct. 2, 2003, "This Month in Harvard History"; Circular, Nov. 30, 1799; DuPouy Bros. to David and John Stewart, Aug. 11, 1801; Appleton to Samuel Emery, Aug. 11, 1801; Entries for Dec. 16, 1801; Jan. 28, 1802; Oct. 7, 1803; Jan. 20, 1804; May 20, 1804,

Appleton also maintained close relations with family members in France. Elder brother John arrived in Europe in 1780 when he was in his early twenties and Thomas was only 12. John likely influenced young Thomas to join him in Paris when the future consul set off for Europe in his late teens. The two doubtless spent a good deal of time together during the following decade, when both lived in France. The brothers appear to have had mutual Paris friends, including the poet and diplomat Joel Barlow.[42] It is evident that Thomas remained in close contact with John while living in Livorno. As with other close family members, he did not copy out any of his letters to John into his letterbook, but his concern when an unusually long period passed without news from John suggests regular correspondence.[43] Like Thomas, John followed a diplomatic path. He set up a merchant house in Calais, France, and was appointed US agent there. He had married and begun a young family there consisting of two sons. The eldest, John James Appleton would soon leave Calais to be educated in the United States. In 1801 John carried the convention ending the Quasi-War between France and the United States back to Philadelphia. A proud Thomas Appleton frequently mentioned to correspondents that John had been given this honor.[44]

Like other Mediterranean merchants, Thomas brought his younger brother to the region. George Appleton arrived in Livorno in 1803 to look for mercantile work with his big brother's assistance. Although not yet 29 years of age, George already had a good deal of experience. He worked as a clerk in the merchant house of Boston's prominent Russell family for nine years after graduating from Harvard, a position that the Appletons' Perkins connection may well have facilitated. After that, he captained an American ship around the world, from Boston to the Northwest American coast and then on to China and Europe. Unfortunately, the brothers' plans for Livorno were spoiled when the port came under siege and the French declared it part of the French Republic, thereby killing the American trade which flourished only so

all in GL. Appleton to Sec. State, Mar. 5, 1801; June 4, 1803; July 8, 1803; Jan. 20, 1804; Jan. 20 1805; July 5, 1805, all in Leghorn Despatches.

[42] Appleton, *Rough Sketch*, 14; Nathaniel Appleton to Timothy Pickering, Oct. 16, 1797, Adams Recs; John Appleton to Thomas Jefferson, Oct. 1, 1802 annot., Jefferson Papers; Appleton to Joel Barlow, Apr. 22, 1801; to __ Mountflorence, Apr. 18, [1801], both in GL.

[43] Appleton to Mountflorence, Apr. 18, [1801], GL.

[44] John Appleton to James Madison, Apr. 18, 1802, Leghorn Despatches; Thomas Appleton to Joseph Barnes, Aug. 31, 1801; to __Woolaston, Sept. 2, 1801; to William Eaton, Sept. 24, 1801, all in GL; "John James Appleton" in *Appleton's Cyclopaedia of American Biography* (1888) I: 85; Appleton, *Rough Sketch*, 22.

long as Livorno remained a free port. Appleton attempted to work his connections in Paris to find George a position there, writing to Massachusetts expatriate merchant Daniel Parker and to Joel Barlow. He assured the latter that he could not "place [his] favors in any one, who possesses a more grateful heart" than young George. By early 1804 Appleton learned that George had "entered into certain engagements in Paris," presumably within a merchant house. As long as George remained in Paris and John's sons had not yet left Calais for school, six members of the Appleton family were now settled in France and Italy.[45]

***

Beyond family, consuls also maintained a broad circle of friends. Friendship had at least two definitions. Sometimes it took on the more modern tone of personal affinity, but often it connoted a more diplomatic sort of alliance referring to what Webster's original 1828 dictionary termed "one not hostile; opposed to an enemy in war."[46] Most frequently consuls maintained friendships with non-Protestant Europeans, with other consuls whether American or not, or with mercantile contacts. Often these groups overlapped, and over time, as more and more Americans came to be involved in Mediterranean trade and diplomacy, their circles took on an increasingly American tone.

Friendships of affinity with local Catholics and Muslims appear to have been relatively rare, but consuls did see locals as friends in the more diplomatic sense of allies. When volunteering to negotiate for the United States in Algiers, Montgomery wrote that he had "friends there of importance and of good influence." He claimed the new Dey of Algiers as an "old friend" who could be helpful to the United States. Similarly, Simpson hoped that he could seize the earliest opportunity to secure "the friendships of whoever may be appointed minister [in Morocco]." Consuls also often referred to European informants in a similar manner. Montgomery, for example, credited "friends in Valencia" for providing diplomatic information and wrote of his request to a "friend in London" to prosecute a libel suit in England. Sometimes consuls referred to a "particular" friendship with individuals that seemed to indicate a more personal bond. Both Simpson and Montgomery had such personal friendships with David Humphreys, the American minister in Madrid. And, as

[45] Appleton to Daniel Parker, Sept. 14, 1803; Entry for Oct. 16, 1803; Appleton to Barlow, Dec. 14, 1803; to Philip Jaume, Jan. 10, 1804, all in GL.

[46] http://webstersdictionary1828.com/Dictionary/friend.

discussed earlier, Simpson developed a particularly close personal friendship to the American consul and agent Thomas Barclay while in Gibraltar.

Because of his isolated situation in Tangier, Simpson formed particularly close friendships with a number of European consuls who made up his and his family's primary social community. Consuls in Tangier represented England, Spain, France, Holland, Denmark, Sweden, Portugal, Genoa, Ragusa, and Venice, with the Genoese consul representing the latter two city-states as well as his own. These consuls, Simpson noted at the time of his appointment, were all his "old acquaintances."[47] As a contemporary observer noted of European consuls there, "They can form no society but among themselves."[48] Rather than nationalistic rivals they acted more as a guild of professional representatives, a situation made still more natural for Simpson and others who represented countries other than their own. They looked after each other personally and professionally, and in situations where one was threatened, all realized that they, too, were in danger. They occasionally met as a group to discuss issues concerning all of them, such as when Arab raiders became more aggressive in capturing European ships in 1806. The emperor also occasionally treated the Christian consuls as a unit – for example, when he announced his upcoming visit to Tangier to them *en masse* or when he would address all of them on matters of shipping and trade.[49]

In addition to acting as professional colleagues, the Christian consuls also served as the Simpsons' social circle. In Tangier the Simpson family lived in the small American house attached to Simpson's good friend, Swedish Consul Peter Wyk's verdant garden near what is today Tangier's Petite Sacco. Though Simpson constantly complained that the house was not suitable to represent the United States and unsuccessfully pushed for a better one for decades, he nonetheless frequently hosted

---

[47] Simpson to Sec. State, Dec. 16, 1797, Tangier Despatches.

[48] William Lemprière, *A Tour from Gibraltar to Tangier* ... (London: J. Walter, 1793) 9.

[49] Simpson to Sec. State, Sept. 3, 1802; Sept. 26, 1803; June 22, 1805; May 26, 1806; Oct. 2, 1806; Sept. 5, 1807; Jan. 4, 1809, all in Tangier Despatches. Simpson benefitted from this consular unity when Moroccan officials detained and insulted him during the crisis over the US capture of the ship *Meshouda* (see Chapter 2). Simpson remained a captive for some time, until, he wrote, "my brother consuls came in a body to demand my [enlargement] on the principle of the person of a consul in this country as representative of his nation being exempt from all arrest." The consuls' intervention, and their willingness to provide security for their "brother" effectuated Simpson's release and further legitimated the notion of consular immunity for the entire group. See Simpson to Sec. State, Sept. 5, 1803; Sept. 26, 1803, both in Tangier Despatches.

dinner parties of up to twelve people.[50] Guests usually included other consuls, their families and staffs, and the occasional American visitor, most notably Captain Stephen Decatur and Commodore Samuel Barron. The Simpsons also frequently attended dinners at their fellow consuls' homes in town, often at Wyk's adjacent house. In November 1803, to choose a fairly random month, the Simpsons dined at Wyk's house along with British consul James Matra and his wife as well as some Spanish travelers and others on the first Monday of the month. The following Tuesday Simpson hosted a dinner for eleven, including the Matras, Wyk, and others. On the final Monday of the month, the Matras hosted a dinner for eleven in the Simpsons' honor. Despite their frequency, there are indications that these dinners could be rather stilted due to the need to maintain propriety among potential rivals. Simpson's successor once explained that "all the intercourse between the Consuls and their families was carried on with more regard to ceremony and etiquette than to pleasure, and the enjoyment of each other's society."[51]

Typically, the Simpsons would leave Tangier's crowded, hot old city in May and travel a half hour by horse or an hour on foot to spend the summer months at their verdant country estate, where they could enjoy cool breezes off the Strait. Immediately on arriving in Morocco, Simpson had purchased this house for $2,000 from the Danish consul and renamed it Mount Washington. It had a fine garden and views in one direction over the Bay of Gibraltar. In the other direction, according to a later visitor, "the eye might wander at pleasure over the wooded hills, the town of Tangier with its old castle and ruined walls, the low sea-beach and culti-vated plains, with here and there the white tomb of some Mahometan saint peeping out from amidst a group of dark evergreens; the high ridge of mountains that stretch to the eastward; and far beyond, the dim outline of the lofty Atlas rearing their snowy tops till they mingle with the clouds!" Today the location is part of the popular Cap Spartel Park located above what is still the city's most exclusive residential section.[52]

---

[50] On Simpson's housing problems, see Simpson to Sec. State, Dec. 16, 1797; July 17, 1798; Feb. 27, 1799; Mar. 11, 1799; Apr. 30, 1799; Nov. 15, 1800; Feb. 20, 1802; Mar. 19, 1802; May 13, 1802; June 26, 1802; Dec. 24, 1802, all in Tangier Despatches; Lemprière, *A Tour from Gibraltar to Tangier . . .*, 10; John Buffa MD, *Travels Through the Empire of Morocco* (London: J. J. Stockdale, 1810) 25; Riley, *An Authentic Narrative*, 517; Riley, *Sequel*, 330; John Mullowney to Sec. State, Sept. 7, 1825, Tangier Despatches.

[51] Entries for Nov. 1803, Konsulatarkiv; G. Fort, *Coos-Coo-Soo: Letters from Tangier, in Africa* (Philadelphia: J. S. M'Calla, 1859) 98.

[52] [NA], *Spain and Barbary: Letters to a Younger Sister, during a visit to Gibraltar, Seville, Cadiz, Tangier etc. etc.* (London: John Hatchard and Son, 1837) 181–82; Simpson to

At Mount Washington the Simpsons were close to other consuls, including Wyk, Matra, and the Danish consul, who also had country homes located nearby. According to Lemprière these consuls "occasionally retire and enjoy those amusements which the country affords … chiefly gardening, fishing, and hunting." The round of consular entertainments continued in this location throughout the summer. The Swedish consul and his assistant were frequent guests at Mount Washington, and the house was a popular walking destination in nice weather. When the Simpsons were away, yet another European friend and neighbor, the Spanish consul to Tangier, looked after the property.[53]

As an unmarried man, Thomas Appleton's social situation was very different from those of Robert Montgomery and James Simpson. Friendship, in particular, was crucially important to Appleton, who comes across in his letters as a gregarious and thoughtful individual, prone to sentimentalizing friendship. Before his appointment as a consul, he had a wide circle of friends in France, with whom he continued to correspond regularly after moving to Livorno. A large number were merchants from the Northeast United States, especially Massachusetts. This group, which included Daniel Parker, Joel Barlow, James Swan, Jonathan Amory, Allan Melville, and Appleton's brother John, were mostly aggressive traders who sometimes stepped over the law in their business practices. Most could be viewed either as patriotic conduits between the emerging American republic and its French supporters or as war profiteers depending on how one looked at it and what day it was.[54] After arriving in Italy, Appleton added many new friends to his group, the majority of whom were either American or connected to American circles.

Humphreys, Dec. 18, 1797, Simpson NARA; to Sec. State, Dec. 16, 1797; Mar. 11, 1799; July 6, 1812, all in Tangier Despatches; Simpson to Sec. State, Nov. 14, 1800, Simpson NARA.

[53] Lemprière, *A Tour from Gibraltar to Tangier …*, 10; Entries for Aug. 28, 1801; Feb. 29, 1804; July 18, 1804; Feb. 26, 1805; Mar. 7, 1805; Aug. 7, 1807; Aug. 18, 1808; Oct. 31, 1808; Feb. 24, 1809; June 24, 1811; Aug. 13–15, 1811, all in Konsulatarkiv; Simpson to Sec. State, June 26, 1802, Tangier Despatches.

[54] On Parker, see Tom Cutterham, "'A Very Promising Appearance': Credit, Honor, and Deception in the Emerging Market for American Debt, 1784–92," *WMQ* 75 (Oct. 2018) 623–50. On Swan, see www.newenglandhistoricalsociety.com/james-swan-the-man-who-financed-two-revolutions/; on Barlow, see Richard Buel, Jr., *Joel Barlow: American Citizen in a Revolutionary* World (Baltimore: Johns Hopkins University Press, 2011). On Amory, see J. and J. Amory records, https://hollisarchives.lib.harvard.edu/repositories/11/resources/7593.

Appleton was also a shrewd operator, both as a consul and a businessman, and friendships usually had a utilitarian dimension for him. His declarations of personal friendship were typically tinged with pecuniary and consular concerns as personal and professional relationships merged together. He asked Boston merchant Allan Melville (future father of Herman) for help locating an important box and getting it sealed by an American official and suggested they attempt a small speculation in sugar together. He floated the idea of a speculative venture in snuff with James Swan, another Boston merchant who played an important and very profitable role in supplying the French Revolution. He asked yet another Boston merchant, Daniel Parker, to help his younger brother George find a job in Paris. Finally, he enrolled the writer and diplomat Joel Barlow to be his advocate in his efforts to gain the Paris consulship.[55]

Yet Appleton's friendship with these men could also be affective or "disinterested," to use a contemporary term. He genuinely looked forward to the possibility that James Swan might visit Livorno. He wrote that he hoped Swan "may put into effect what you give me some reason to expect and that you will take very speedily a journey to Italy," pledging "all my best endeavours to make it agreeable either by accompanying you in different parts . . . or by pointing out those objects most worthy of your attentions." He struck a nostalgic note with Barlow, begging him to send "affectionate regards" to their old friends Mr. and Mrs. Lavenworth and to write a letter of at least four pages detailing "what has become of those we formerly knew, from the Marquis de La Fayette down to poor Hickson, the man of tenses."[56]

Appleton's friendships also had a political dimension. While in Paris, he associated with a number of liberal aristocrats, as the mention of LaFayette suggests. His entrée into this circle seems to have been the duchess of Brancas, who took over the house that Gouverneur Morris, the former American minister to France once occupied. After his arrival in Livorno Appleton maintained a vigorous correspondence with her, sending frequent, long letters, which he did not transcribe into his letter book, an indication that they were personal and not related to business.[57]

---

[55] Appleton to Alan Melville, Oct. 28, 1801; Nov. 17, 1801; to James Swan, June 1803 (not copied); to Swan, Sept. 14, 1803; to Parker, Sept. 14, 1803; to Barlow, Dec. 14, 1803; Mar. 25, 1804, all in GL.
[56] Appleton to Swan, Sept 14, 1803; to Barlow, Apr. 22, 1803, both in GL.
[57] Appleton to Parker, Oct. 18, 1804; Notations for Oct. 13, 1803; Mar. 27, 1804; May 24, 1804; Nov. 9, 1804; May 10, 1805; Aug. 15, 1805; July 4, 1806; Aug. 5, 1806; Oct. 16, 1807, all in GL.

He also became friends with Mdm. de Branca's sister, Mdm. de Champcenetz (Albertine Elisabeth de Nyvenheim), who was living at Fontainbleu while her husband, an early supporter of the American Revolution and former governor of the Tuileries, was in exile in England.[58] At one point Appleton even asked his friend Daniel Parker to advise her on how to recover her considerable fortune in Surinam from the British government. Appleton also wrote her frequently, sending gifts such as wine and oranges.[59]

Through Mdm. de Brancas and possibly others, Appleton became acquainted with the widowed marquise de Chastellux (Brigitte Plunkett), whose husband wrote an influential book on the United States, served as a general in Rochambeau's army, and befriended Thomas Jefferson. Appleton had somehow acquired a portrait of her dead brother, which prompted an unusually intimate correspondence. Chastellux was lady-in-waiting to Louise-Marie-Adelaide, duchesse d'Orléans, whose daughter, at Madame Chastellux's direction, spent a good deal of time with Appleton during a six week stay in Livorno. Appleton was impressed by the wealthy Bourbon heiress, whose mother had been an early supporter of the French Revolution. On her departure Appleton profusely thanked Madame Chastellux for introducing them and wrote of the "pain in bidding adieu to as much worth and such a degree of amiableness ... For I hold it as a maxim forever true with ingenuous minds that depravation more than countervails happiness of any kind." To the duchess he lamented, "I should ever have thought it too speedy your departure, even had it been delayed to the last hour of my life."[60] Likely these flirtations with French women of a much higher social station and either a decade older or a decade younger than Appleton were not serious, yet clearly they played an important role in his social life – and reflected his continuing fascination with all things French and republican.

In Livorno Appleton counted many American merchants as his friends both in the sense of trusted allies and in the more romantic or affinitive sense.[61] He frequently sought business connections as well as small favors

---

[58] www.nationaltrust.org.uk/features/a-noble-return-gainsboroughs-portrait-of-a-french-marquis; https://reader.exacteditions.com/issues/52160/page/56.

[59] Appleton to Parker, Oct. 18, 1804; Notation for Mar. 27, 1804; June 27, 1804; Appleton to Mdm. Champcenetz, Oct. 18, 1804, all in GL.

[60] Appleton to Marquise de Chastellux, Sept. 2, 1801; to Joseph Pitcairn, Mar. 19, 1802; to Marquise de Chastellux, Mar. 17, 1802; to the Duchesse d'Orléans, Mar. 17, 1802, all in GL.

[61] On the two senses of merchant friendship, see Toby Ditz, "Shipwrecked: or, Masculinity Imperiled: Mercantile Representations of Failure and the Gendered Self in Eighteenth-Century Philadelphia," *Journal of American History* 81 (June 1994) 51–80.

from merchant friends in America and Europe. Most frequently he would request that they forward letters, pass on greetings to other friends and relations, pass on packages and gifts to others, or inform him of local prices and business conditions. Yet Appleton also had deeper relations with those he sometimes termed "particular friends." One was Nathan Amory, part of a prominent Massachusetts merchant family that Appleton knew well, including his friend Jonathan Amory from his Paris days. Another was Nathan Robinson of Salem, whom Appleton met while he was on business in Livorno. Shortly after the visit, Appleton wrote him, "I believe you will agree with me that a few months are sufficient to have formed a [compleat] idea of each other, and what I am equally sure of is, that no event in life will alter the indelible esteem and friendship which our intimacy has cemented."[62]

Appleton became particularly friendly with his fellow American consuls who were almost uniformly also merchants. For William Willis, American consul to Barcelona, he distributed circulars advertising his business and, according to Appleton, "never deviated from that strict path of friendship which our friendly intercourse for a long time has inspired me with." He maintained a long-standing friendship with Stephen Cathalan, American consul to Marseille, including a personal visit in 1803. He met the new American consul to Trieste, John Lawson when he stopped in Livorno on his journey from Massachusetts and immediately began providing him with friendly advice. He suggested Lawson set up shop in Trieste with some merchant friends for whom Appleton had "the most friendly regards" as they had "shown me many disinterested marks of their esteem and friendship."[63]

The best example of the intersecting strands of interest and affection in these friendships might be Appleton's relationship with Joseph Barnes, US consul to Sicily. The two were friendly even before Barnes's 1802 appointment and they plotted together to turn out Barnes predecessor, who was not a US citizen. Appleton also wanted Barnes to split commissions with him for ships he directed to his merchant house in Naples, a common arrangement between Appleton and his merchant friends.[64] Beyond these shared interests, Appleton also viewed Barnes as a friend due to their shared political

---

[62] Appleton to Mr. Robinson, Sept. 2, 1800; to Mr. Wagner, Nov. 6, 1801, both in GL.
[63] Appleton to Mr. Willis, Aug. 31, 1801; to Mr. Lawson, Jan. 3, 1802, both in GL.
[64] Appleton to Robert Rose, May 17, 1801; to Barnes, Oct. 19, 1801, both in GL; Joseph Barnes to Thomas Jefferson, Sept. 27, 1800; Robert H. Rose and others, petition, Mar. 11, 1801, both in Joseph Barnes File, Jefferson Recs.

sentiments. He wrote that he was prepared to greet Barnes on his arrival to Livorno "because I feel the firmest reliance on your political principles and ... because I am persuaded of your most friendly disposition towards me." Sometime later, he assured Barnes he was one of the "very few men in life whom I have thought proper to view in the relation of friend." The designation, he explained was due to "the similarity of our ideas on most subjects [being] embarked in the same public occupations and ... the thousand little acts of regard which have cemented our esteem."[65]

Yet, in the end, friendship only went so far and was subject to betrayal. Appleton had long hoped to return to Paris as US consul and had enlisted many friends to assist him, including Barnes. What he did not know was that Barnes and another purported friend, Philip Mazzei, were smearing Appleton in their efforts to have him replaced with Barnes. Mazzei wrote Jefferson complaining that the administration's snub of Appleton in favor of awarding the lucrative naval agent position to the Purviances "deprived [Appleton] of the income which may provide him with the means to hold his post with decorum" and undermined his ability to do his job because it showed "the government has no confidence in him." Mazzei therefore determined that Appleton "should pack up and leave, since he can no longer be loved nor held in esteem, not even if his manners were not so displeasing to both his compatriots and the locals." Since Appleton had not really done anything wrong, "it would seem right that he be compensated with some other position." A few months later, Barnes also wrote the president noting that Mazzei had explained to Jefferson "the political necessity, for the reasons he had given, of removing Mr. Appleton to some other place which the *good* of his country and even *his own Interest* demands, and warmly solicited me to consent to accept" the Livorno consulship. Barnes concurred with Mazzei, arguing that while Appleton had done nothing wrong, he had "unfortunately rendered himself so generally disrespected not only by the people of the place, but by his countrymen, that 'tis impossible he can ever be esteemed here." However, Barnes concluded, it was possible he might command more respect elsewhere, "particularly in France, for which he is best qualified."[66]

***

[65] Appleton to Barnes, Oct. 19, 1801; Oct. 25, 1803, both in GL.
[66] Philip Mazzei to Jefferson, Dec. 28, 1803; Barnes to Jefferson, Feb. 4, 1804; Mar. 25, 1804, both in Jefferson Papers. One might read this as a sneaky plot to send Appleton to Paris, where he wanted to be, but it seems unlikely that the criticism of Appleton's behavior would have commended him for the Paris position.

But, in fact, all was not quite as it seemed with Appleton. He was not actually an unmarried man – at least not after 1812 or so. For some years he had been living with Vincenza Trentanove, sister to the sculptor, Raimondo Trentanove. In 1813 the couple had a daughter, Minerva Eufrosina Appleton. They had certainly married by the time of her birth as she was considered his legitimate daughter when he died. While the existence of this family was probably an open secret to many of his acquaintances, Appleton never once confirmed it in any of his multitudinous letters. In fact, I have been able to find only three rather circuitous allusions. The first is in an 1812 letter to Giuseppe Luciani, his partner in a marble venture in Carrara, when he noted that "Vincenza is in perfect health." Ten years later, in a long letter to his good friend William Shaler, the Algerian consul, he wrote, "My own health is as usual, and my family, as you term them, are the same."[67]

While at least some of Appleton's friends in the region seem to have known about his wife and daughter, he refused to acknowledge them to his American family. When Appleton's nephew Charles Appleton visited in 1823, Appleton declined to invite him to sleep at his house on the excuse that there was no room. Instead, he paid for him to stay in a hotel room and dined with him daily, possibly at his house. While it is possible that Appleton genuinely did not have a spare bedroom, it is also likely that he did not want Charles to be exposed to his relationship with his wife and 13-year-old daughter. Daytime visits for meals would be far less problematic either in a public place or at Appleton's home when Vincenza and Minerva could be out of the house or perhaps viewed as family retainers. Still Charles and others must have been aware of the truth. Not long after Charles departed, Appleton's brother-in-law Thomas Perkins reported rumors of Appleton's situation having reached America. Appleton took care to correct the news of "my suppos'd marriage" in his next missive to Perkins. Could word of the "suppos'd marriage" have spread through the family grapevine in the wake of Charles's visit? It seems quite likely given that this appears to be the first and only mention of it that ever came from his family.[68]

The marriage and daughter were not Appleton's only secret, or perhaps the biggest. He also had converted to Catholicism early in the nineteenth century, most likely at his wife's insistence.[69] All of these details – the

---

[67] Argiero and Neri, *Bostoniani a Livorno*, 52–54; Appleton to G. Luciani, Nov. 28, [1812], GL; Appleton to William Shaler, Sept. 25, 1822, Shaler Papers.

[68] Entry for Jan. 20, 1823; Appleton to Perkins, May 16, [1823], both in GL.

[69] Argiero and Neri, *Bostoniani a Livorno*, 54.

conversion, the wife, the daughter – would have been truly scandalous news in Boston. Given the anti-Catholicism of that milieu it is almost unimaginable that Appleton could have shared this information. Had he done so, he quite likely would have been cut off entirely from his American family. Such a break certainly would take a personal toll, but perhaps even more importantly, it would have severed Appleton from his most important American business contacts, in particular his brothers-in-law, who handled his considerable American interests. Such honesty was probably unthinkable. Appleton's dilemma only underscores how extremely difficult it was for Protestant Anglo-Americans to mix with local populations. And yet, his willingness to cross that bridge and his increasing Italian and Catholic connections also demonstrate how members of the American community could, over time, become creolized.

By the end of the first decade of the eighteenth century, American consuls continued to be torn between the country they represented and the broader cosmopolitanism of the Mediterranean region and the world of trade. Yet, the rapidly growing American presence in the region Americanized their social circles to an extent. Increased US trade brought more ships, sailors, captains, and visiting merchants. By 1807, there may well have been seventy-five or more Americans residents in Alicante and Livorno combined, suggesting hundreds more throughout the region.[70] Trade also brought with it the establishment of a Mediterranean naval squadron, and naval officers, seamen, and ships to be provisioned. The consuls themselves contributed to the growth of the American community by establishing families, bringing over clerks and relatives, and attracting more American merchants. At the same time, to varying degrees, they also maintained deep family, personal, ethnic, and business connections outside of the world of American trade and diplomacy. While, initially, their ties to the United States may have appeared weak, particularly from the perspective of those living within the early republic's boundaries, over time the increasing size of the community and increasing intertwining of its members, created a more cohesive and more recognizably American community.

---

[70] Petition of Americans in Livorno, Oct. 1, 1807, GL; "Lista de los Individuos Americanos residentes en esta Plaza [1807]." More discussion of possible American populations in these places occurs in Chapters 3 and 4 above.

6

Business Networks and the Problem of Self Interest

The role of consuls was first and foremost to facilitate American trade. During the two decades after ratification of the Constitution, Americans had high hopes for business in the Mediterranean – hopes that were born out, as we have seen, by the rapidly increasing number of American ships in the region. These early expectations were the reason that the State Department began appointing so many consuls to the Mediterranean so quickly, and the expectations and eventual realization of profits were why so many were willing to serve. Since all consuls, with four exceptions, were unsalaried, they were motivated largely by the possibility of profits. Consulships could fulfill these hopes in a number of ways. For some, particularly those who were new to the region, being designated US consul conferred respectability that would make potential trading partners inclined to trust them despite a lack of personal acquaintance. For those conducting commerce, trust was a priceless commodity, and therefore a huge benefit of holding office. This was particularly true in a new nation that had much of its commercial infrastructure rearranged as a result of the American Revolution. For new consuls, too, the emergence of a national structure of consuls within the Mediterranean region provided a natural network of potential trading partners. Most merchants took many years to develop such a network, so the ready-made quality of consular relationships expedited this process and made it easier for young upstarts to gain a foothold in the difficult and risky world of Mediterranean commerce. Even for veteran US merchants like Robert Montgomery, consulship provided distinction among US traders and access to Americans at the highest levels of the State Department, as well as connections to others in the region.

To some extent at the time, and even more so in retrospect, the focus on personal profit may have seemed to conflict with consuls' role as public servants who were part of the new nation's commercial infrastructure. Yet, so long as American commerce was booming, private and public interest seemed to act in concert. Consuls worked to expand American commerce generally, because they knew it benefitted them personally. They helped to create a viable infrastructure and a dense network of people with interests in the American trade. This network, in turn, nurtured their businesses and their personal lives while creating more connections to the United States and a stronger American identity among its members. In this regard, consuls both contributed to the rise of the American nation in the Mediterranean and became some of the chief beneficiaries.

To understand the expansion of American commercial networks it might be helpful to move briefly away from the Mediterranean ports and go to sea. It is easier to visualize the numerous connections within the American network and how they facilitated trade from the vantage point of a ship. Each ship had an owner (or owners) of course, who had to make a number of decisions and plan for as many contingencies as possible based on fairly thin information before a voyage could begin. In this case, we will focus on the ship *Eliza*, owned by Brown and Ives of Providence, Rhode Island. Brown and Ives were among the most astute American merchants, and their records have been particularly well preserved. While better known for their role in the East India trade, they were also active in the Mediterranean and throughout Europe.[1]

In November 1803, Captain George A. Hallowell sat in Providence harbor awaiting orders, provisions, and cargo for the Brig *Eliza*. She was one of at least ten relatively small ships that the firm used to shuttle back and forth to European ports, reserving their larger ships for their Pacific trade.[2] This year the *Eliza* would be one of the 111 American ships to enter the Mediterranean by way of Gibraltar at a time when American commerce in the region was reaching its peak by taking advantage of neutral trade during the Napoleonic Wars.[3] Nearly two decades after the United States had started creating consulates in the Mediterranean, this

---

[1] James B. Hedges, *The Browns of Providence Plantation: The Nineteenth Century* (Providence: Brown University, 1968).

[2] *Ibid.* 118.

[3] Based on analysis of shipping news in the *Gibraltar Chronicle*. Of the 111 American ships touching at Gibraltar, 72 were heading into the Mediterranean and 38 heading out (with one not clear).

was also a period when American ships like the *Eliza* benefitted from a fairly well-developed infrastructure.

As relative newcomers to the Mediterranean, Brown and Ives pumped their neighboring firm, Lippitt and Rogers, for information. They recommended Brown and Ives contact the firm of Kuhn and Green in Gibraltar. This firm, formed about two years earlier, had strong American connections. The partners were brothers-in-law from Philadelphia. They had earlier been in business with Joseph Storm, son of a former Speaker of the New York State Assembly. In Tangier, James Simpson occasionally drew his State Department funds on their account.[4] The next year Kuhn would be appointed consul to Genoa where he would be in close contact with Thomas Appleton in nearby Livorno. Someone, possibly also Lippitt and Rogers, recommended John Rogers in Alicante, Robert Montgomery's son-in-law and competitor. Possibly the John Rogers of Providence was a relation. At any rate, Brown and Ives specifically instructed Captain Hallowell to avoid Montgomery's house, suggesting a bad past experience or less than sterling reports of his reputation.[5]

Throughout November they loaded up the *Eliza* with nearly $15,000 worth of goods, including West Indian coffee and cocoa, American beef, lard, flour, pork, and other products. In this way they were typical of Americans trading in the Mediterranean. More than two-thirds of American ships entering the Mediterranean by way of Gibraltar in 1803 carried flour.[6] To a lesser extent they also carried tobacco, fish, and West Indian reexports like coffee. Brown and Ives planned to send the shipment to Málaga and then possibly Alicante after consulting with Kuhn and Green in Gibraltar. This, too was typical of American voyages. Alicante, Livorno, and Málaga were the most popular destinations for American ships entering and exiting the Mediterranean and continuing via Gibraltar that year.[7]

[4] Brown and Ives to Kuhn and Green (a firm), Nov. 30, 1803, Box 10, Folder 7, B. & I.; Stephen Cathalan to Thomas Jefferson, n.d.; Peter Kuhn to [James Madison], Dec. 6, 1803; Peter Kuhn, Jr. to Jefferson, May 12, 1804; Aug. 2, 1804; Thomas Storm to Jefferson, Nov. 12, 1804, all in Peter Kuhn File, Jefferson Recs; James Simpson to Sec. State, June 14, 1804; Apr. 17, 1805, both in Tangier Despatches.

[5] Brown and Ives to Messrs. Grivegnée and Co., Dec. 1, 1803; to Capt. George A. Hallowell, Dec. 1, 1803, both in B10 F7, B. & I.

[6] Based on the *Gibraltar Chronicle* shipping reports, of the seventy-two US ships heading into the Mediterranean and touching at Gibraltar, forty-nine carried flour, fourteen tobacco, nine coffee, and six fish.

[7] The leading European destinations (for incoming and outgoing ships) were Gibraltar (fourteen), Alicante (ten), Livorno (ten), Málaga (nine), Barcelona (eight), and Naples (six). A large number of outgoing ships (thirty-five) only specified "market" as their destination, suggesting that the decision would be made after they entered the Mediterranean.

The *Eliza*'s voyage entailed a great deal of planning. Brown and Ives were flooded with information about Mediterranean markets from solicited and unsolicited price currents (showing current prices of imports and exports in specific ports) and letters from merchants interested in their trade.[8] All sorts of anticipated and unanticipated difficulties could cause disaster. Most obviously, the *Eliza* could encounter trouble at sea from the weather, resulting in the loss of the entire ship, cargo, and crew or portions thereof. Algerians or belligerent European powers could capture or detain the ship, resulting in loss of all or portions of the cargo and possibly of the ship itself. Even without these sorts of major disasters, all information received about conditions in Europe would be at least two months old when the *Eliza* arrived, and, due to the length of time it took to purchase and load a cargo, decisions would likely have to be made based on information that would be three or more months out of date. In that time, products that looked as though they might be profitable on the market could become unsalable, resulting in losses rather than profits. As a result, Brown and Ives realized that even the best-laid plans would have to be subject to change.

This led to yet another difficulty: finding trustworthy parties in Europe to guide the *Eliza* through unforeseen contingencies. Brown and Ives gave Captain Hallowell a good deal of discretion, but he needed the assistance of merchants with a better understanding of European conditions. Thus, it became crucial for Brown and Ives to have European contacts whom they could trust. In Gibraltar they hoped to use Kuhn and Green, but they gave Hallowell the option of using James Simpson's former partner, Robert Anderson, if he did not find Kuhn and Green "in good standing" on his arrival. They also advised Hallowell to sell whatever portion of the cargo Kuhn and Green or Anderson thought best to dispose of in Gibraltar before continuing, first to Málaga to dispose of the rest, and then to Alicante to purchase wine and brandy for the return voyage.[9] In Spain, Brown and Ives consigned Hallowell's cargo to the partnership of Grivegnée and Co. in Málaga, to whom they sent detailed directions on its disposition. Like Kuhn, Green, and Rogers, Grivegnée and Co. was well connected to American circles. One of their partners, William Kirkpatrick, had served as US consul to Málaga since 1800. Kirkpatrick was a Scottish merchant who married one of the Grivegnées' daughters. Their granddaughter would marry Louis Napoleon III and become

---

[8] They were also called "prices current," though the merchants I have studied in the Mediterranean at this time more frequently labeled them "price currents."

[9] Brown and Ives to Hallowell, Dec. 1, 1803, B531 F7, B. and I.

Eugenie, empress of France. It is extremely likely that Kirkpatrick handled all of Grivegnée and Co.'s correspondence with Brown and Ives, which was in perfect English.[10]

The choice of Grivegnée and Co. in Málaga was crucial to the success of *Eliza*'s voyage. Brown and Ives gave the firm control over all transactions in Europe. They instructed Kuhn and Green to send remittances to Grivegnée and Co. and empowered that firm to settle their accounts using proceeds from the sales. They also instructed Grivegnées to use discretion in choosing an Alicante agent if they were not satisfied of Rogers's standing – so long as they avoided Montgomery. Finally, they instructed Grivegnées on how to send the proceeds back to the United States.[11] Clearly the voyage would be disastrous if Grivegnée and Co. proved incompetent or untrustworthy. The importance of a reliable, known correspondent like Kirkpatrick within the Grivegnées firm could not be overestimated, and the fact that Brown and Ives also entrusted the cargo of a second ship, the *Polly* to his firm, demonstrated their continuing trust in Kirkpatrick and the firm and further raised the stakes of the relationship.

Unexpected occurrences further demonstrated how much even a large, well-run firm like Brown and Ives's relied on overseas assistance. After an uneventful month-long voyage, Captain Hallowell arrived in Gibraltar only to find three unexpected conditions: that a fever was raging in Málaga with the town under heavy quarantine; that the West Indian cocoa and coffee they carried was no longer being admitted into Spain on American ships; and that the price of beef was extremely low in Alicante. After consultation by post with the Grivegnées and in person with Kuhn and Green, Hallowell left the cocoa and coffee and a good deal of beef in Gibraltar and shipped some beef, pork, and lard to nearby Cádiz, where prices were reputed to be higher. Kuhn and Green were to handle all these sales. To avoid excessive quarantine time in Málaga, on the Grivegnées' advice, Hallowell decided to take the *Eliza* directly to Alicante rather than landing in Málaga as originally planned.[12]

When Hallowell brought the *Eliza* into Alicante harbor on January 26, 1804, he arrived at the height of the American trade. As already noted,

[10] Colin Carlin, *William Kirkpatrick of Malaga* (Glasgow: Colin Carlin, 2011). As we will see, Appleton similarly handled US business as American consul when he belonged to the Livornese firm of DuPouy and Brothers.

[11] Brown and Ives to Hallowell, Dec. 1, 1803; to Messrs. Grivegnée and Co., Dec. 1, 1803, B531 F7, B. & I.

[12] Kuhn and Green to Brown and Ives, Jan. 9, 1804; Hallowell to Brown and Ives, Jan 11, 1804; Grivegnée and Co. to Hallowell, Jan. 17, 1804, B531 F7, Brown and Ives.

forty-three American ships had arrived the previous year, and twenty-nine more would arrive in 1804. Two days before the *Eliza* landed, Rogers wrote his father, "[I] have had since last I wrote you eight vessels to my address ... [and] am also daily expecting another from Gibraltar," no doubt referring to the *Eliza*.[13] This was a period when merchants in America and those within the American network in the Mediterranean could make very healthy profits.

    Although the *Eliza*'s was by no means the most profitable Mediterranean voyage, nearly all associated with it profited. Hallowell received $45 per month, or over $200, plus shipping privileges for any merchandise he might sell on his own account. Kuhn and Green and Rogers received commissions on the trade they conducted, which they deducted from the returns they sent to Grivegnée and Co., though the exact amount is not clear. Robert Montgomery, though shunned by Brown and Ives, received his consular fees when he certified the outgoing cargo. Rogers received a total of $345.82 – a $66.89 commission and brokerage fee on the sales of the *Eliza*'s cargo and a $278.93 commission on the brandy he procured for the homeward voyage. Although they never saw the *Eliza* or its cargo, Grivegnée and Co. made $140.64 on commissions and brokerage fees for handling the financial aspects of the voyage, including transferring funds between all parties and back to Brown and Ives. As for Brown and Ives, they may have profited less than anyone. At the voyage's inception they valued the *Eliza*'s cargo at $14,884.90 and total known sales in Europe amounted to $13,981.70 – a 6 percent loss, at least on paper.[14] However, if the large load of brandy Hallowell brought from Alicante sold well, they may still have made a decent profit.[15]

***

From start to finish, then, Brown and Ives and many merchants like them relied on the information and services provided by merchants and officials

---

[13] John H. Rogers to John Rogers, Jr., Jan. 24, 1804, Rogers-Bridges Family Collection; Robert Montgomery to Sec. State, Sept. 26, 1803, Alicante Despatches.

[14] This calculation would depend on an accurate valuation of the cargo, which, considering the merchants' interest in keeping insurance valuations up and tariffs down is probably unrealistic.

[15] Draft of certificate for *Eliza*, n.d.; Brown and Ives to Hallowell, Dec. 1, 1803; US Consulate Certificate Brig *Eliza*, Feb. 21, 1804, B531 F10, all in B. & I.; Kuhn and Green to Brown and Ives, Apr. 2, 1804; Brown and Ives acct. current with John Rogers, Feb. 7, 1804; Brown and Ives acct. current with Grivegnées and Co., Mar. 7, 1804; Invoice of brandy from John Rogers, Feb. 20, 1804, all in B531 F7, B. & I. Recorded sales figures are: $9,430.79 in Gibraltar, $904.00 in Cádiz, and $3,646.91 in Alicante.

connected to the American network in the Mediterranean. It is not surprising that American consuls sat at the center of this network since they were the officials tasked with facilitating American trade and were themselves merchants. The appointment of US consuls in the region in the 1790s signaled the new republic's commitment to establishing the Mediterranean trade, and the new consuls were among the first to benefit from the growth in commerce. As a result of their centrality and the government's refusal to create a professional, salaried consular corps, these consuls continually faced issues that we today would consider conflicts of interest.

As already discussed, these networks were initially created by the State Department's ambitious program of appointing American consuls to the Mediterranean in the 1790s. To the extent that many of the first consuls had been merchants before the Revolution, the State Department built on older colonial trade networks. The intense consular involvement in protecting American trade from Barbary pirates and the belligerent powers during the Napoleonic Wars deepened the connections between the various Mediterranean consuls who were frequently writing each other and occasionally meeting in person to deal with the many concerns that fell into their laps as the most numerous representatives of the US government in the region. This interaction allowed them to deepen social ties and putative business connections while, at the same time, expanding American trade and providing additional support for regional commerce and especially for merchants like Brown and Ives.

Consuls also expanded the trading network and the services available by appointing vice-consuls who could deal with merchant and sailor concerns in ports without consuls. As American traffic in the region increased, these officials must have been useful to American ships. But there can be little doubt they also benefitted the consuls who appointed them. Montgomery's fourteen vice-consuls formed a sub-network stretching roughly 400 miles from Santander to Alicante composed of merchants who all owed Montgomery a debt for providing them with prestigious and potentially lucrative posts that, in effect, labeled them trustworthy and creditworthy. Most, if not all, maintained close connections to Montgomery. Thomas Vague, Montgomery's vice-consul in Valencia and an important wine merchant, had earlier been appointed British vice-consul by Montgomery's former partner, Daniel Budd, the British consul to Alicante. Montgomery and Budd gave him power of attorney to act as their agent in Valencia, as did Montgomery's solo firm later on. Such an appointment rested on a great deal of trust as Vague was empowered to represent Montgomery in court, to collect his debts, and perform other sensitive legal matters. As British vice-consul and a prominent merchant, Vague's access to capital and information was invaluable to Montgomery and, in turn, Vague could expect healthy commissions if he succeeded, further tying him to Montgomery. The whole relationship would undoubtedly deepen the business connections between the two merchant houses.[16] Montgomery also maintained or potentially maintained business and personal ties with other vice-consuls. He appointed his brother and business partner to be vice-consul in Barcelona. His daughter would later marry the brother of Roberto Ryan, the vice-consul in Benicarló. Other vice-consuls provided valuable mercantile connections. For example, Lewis M. O'Brien, of Santander was British vice-consul and had links to British and American merchants in the region.[17]

Some of Montgomery's contemporaries viewed these appointments with suspicion. Spanish officials thought they gave him too much power over too broad an area and bristled at his lifetime appointment of Ryan.[18] David Humphreys also looked askance at these appointments and an attempt by Montgomery to place a nephew in Algiers, ostensibly as a US agent but probably also to establish a branch of Montgomery's firm there. Humphreys wrote, "I question how far stress is to be laid upon the recommendations ... of consuls who happen to be mercantile men themselves, of other persons for consuls by whose appointment they may be

---

[16] Consulta sobre petición de Real Cédula de aprobación de Tomás Vague ... Estado, 628, Exp. 5; Consulta sobre petición de Real Cédula de aprobación del nombramento de Tomás Vague como Vicecónsul de Gran Bretaña, Estado 632 Exp. 17, both in Junta de las dependencias y Negocios de Extranjeros, Archivos Nacionales, Madrid. Montgomery and Co. poder (power of attorney) a Vague and Boneli, June 3, 1789, Protocolo Notarial de Vicente Izquierdo y Suredo; Dn. Roberto Montgomery, poder a Vague y Llano, June 6, 1805, Protocolo Notarial de Ramon Izquierdo, all in PN (Note: "Protocolo de Notariales" (notarial notebooks) are identified by name of the notary and date in the archives throughout this chapter).

[17] Consulta sobre petición de Real Cédula de aprobación del nombramiento de Roberto Ryan como Vicecónsul de los Estados Unidos de América en Benicarló, 1796, PARES; Dn. Roberto Montgomery land sale (*venta real*) to Ricardo Ryan, Nov. 19, 1819, Pedro Fuentes y Sanchez, PN. Margaret L. O'Brien to Mr. Bowdoin, May 2, 1806; Strange and Co. and others, petition, Nov. 5, 1806; John White and Sons to Samuel Welles, May 21, 1806, all in Lewis O'Brien File, Jefferson Recs.

[18] Estado, 632, Exp. 34, 4–5, 27–52, Consulta sobre petición de Real Cédula de aprobación del nombramiento de Roberto Montgomery como Cónsul de Estados Unidos de América en Alicante; Lewis M. O'Brien Expediente Personal 2, 8–15, all in Junta de las Dependencias y Negocios de Extranjeros, Archivo Nacionales, Madrid. David Humphreys to Timothy Pickering, Apr. 20, 1797, Humphreys-Marvis-Olmsted Collection, Box 1, Folder 20, David Humphreys Papers.

either directly or indirectly benefitted in their affairs" immediately after voicing concerns about Montgomery's nephew.[19]

Appleton and Simpson also attempted to appoint their friends and business connections to office, albeit on a smaller scale. Though Appleton's appointment was limited to Tuscany, and therefore to the maritime area around Livorno, he proposed expanding his power to the Papal Dominions and Naples, which would have allowed him to appoint consuls or vice-consuls to a number of other Italian ports.[20] Part of Simpson's job was to appoint and monitor a vice-consul for Mogadore (Essaouira), the only Moroccan port with a significant American trade and also a point where captives from shipwrecks were frequently redeemed. The Mogadore vice-consul received $1 for every certificate signed and 25 cents for each affidavit as well as unspecified consulage fees. Beyond that, the position conferred a level of respectability that could benefit a merchant vice-consul seeking commissions from American ships. Hence, when Simpson appointed James Renshaw, a British merchant, to the post he stirred up a hornet's nest. William Court, another British merchant, who had previously handled most American commissions was livid and tried to attack Renshaw's character to scuttle the appointment. Simpson stuck to his guns, arguing that Court's firm was "notoriously in a state of insolvency with heavy demands still unsatisfied hanging over their heads," and he feared their perilous financial position would cause problems for Americans if Court was reappointed. In choosing Renshaw, Simpson explained, he "looked for good result to the American merchants."[21]

Among the good results that consuls hoped would develop through their evolving information networks were the intensification and expansion of American trade. The State Department required consuls to submit annual reports on ship arrivals in their ports which, even today, are the best and practically only means of determining the flow of American exports and imports through the region. Although the State Department never seems to have distributed this information, in theory it could have been useful to merchants like Brown and Ives who needed to make

[19] Humphreys to Pickering, Apr. 20, 1797, Humphreys-Marvis-Olmsted Collection, David Humphreys Papers, Box 1, Folder 20.

[20] Thomas Appleton to Philip Mazzei, Oct. 25, 1801, GL; Thomas Appleton to Sec. State, Dec. 12, 1801, Leghorn Despatches.

[21] James Simpson to Peter Gwyn, Aug. 19, 1800; Aug. 25, 1800, both in NARA; James Simpson to Sec. State, Aug. 24, 1807; Vice-Consuls, petition, July 9, 1807, both in Tangier Despatches.

decisions about which goods to trade. All three consuls also sporadically sent more detailed descriptions of trade in their ports to the State Department.[22] Like the price currents that merchants regularly exchanged among themselves, these items would have been intended to encourage more trade of needed goods to the consuls' posts, which would, of course, also benefit the merchant-consuls.

Consuls also floated ideas for expanding the scope of the Mediterranean trade. Appleton spent a good deal of effort gathering data about the trade across the Black Sea from Turkey to Russia from his trading partner and kinsman, George Perkins of Smyrna. Appleton believed that the United States could exchange the same West Indian products that arrived in Livorno with the Russians across the Black Sea for valuable hemp, iron, and duck cloth. Opening this trade would likely have benefitted Appleton and Perkins as well as merchant houses like Brown and Ives, which already had some interest in the West Indies and the Balkans. Similarly, Montgomery volunteered to negotiate a commercial treaty with the Court of Naples which he believed would provide a good outlet for American rice, tobacco, naval stores, fish, and other goods. Simpson worked to educate Americans on the proper customs to follow in trading to Mogadore so as to avoid contravening Moroccan laws and customs, of which they were often ignorant, and to facilitate smoother trade with that up and coming port.[23] The consuls also worked to shorten the length of health department quarantines that delayed the movement of American goods during times of fever, and Appleton attempted to set up a ship's registry in Gibraltar that would provide information on regional hazards to American ships entering the Mediterranean.[24] All of these measures were aimed at expanding, deepening and quickening the trade that was the lifeblood of all Americans in the region, including, of course, the consuls.

***

[22] Appleton to Sec. State, Jan. 15, 1802; June 1, 1802; June 1, 1807, all in Leghorn Despatches; Simpson to Sec. State, Jan. 31, 1803; Mar. 2, 1804, both in Tangier Despatches; Montgomery to Sec. State, Sept. 26, 1803; Mar. 6, 1806, both in Alicante Despatches.

[23] Appleton to George Perkins, Dec. 2, 1803; May 4, 1804; to R. R. Livingston, May 10, 1804, all in GL; Appleton to Sec. State, May 26, 1804, Leghorn Despatches; Montgomery to Sec. State, Nov. 30, 1794, Alicante Despatches; Simpson to Sec State, Aug. 27, 1807, Tangier Despatches.

[24] Montgomery to George Erving, June 17, 1806, Alicante Despatches; Appleton to Sec. State, May 29, 1803; July 10, 1802, Leghorn Despatches; Appleton to Joel Barlow, Dec. 25, 1802, GL.

But, to what extent did consular activity benefit the consuls themselves? To get at this question it is necessary to attempt to examine the nature and extent of the consuls' personal business. This is not an easy task. While records relating to consuls' official duties are well preserved by the State Department, records of their private activities are scattered at best. Furthermore, even where records do exist, they may well understate the extent of consuls' commercial affairs. Fragmentary records may not show all aspects of consuls' personal business, and, since most consuls felt some pressure not to become entangled in business affairs that would compromise their ability to act in the public interest, those who did so had motive to underrepresent their business concerns. Nevertheless, a surprising amount of evidence can be uncovered to reveal consuls' active participation in the Mediterranean trade and the advantages that their official positions provided, particularly for Appleton and Montgomery, who clearly profited from their posts to varying degrees.

Montgomery viewed most consular trade as unproblematic. He disapproved of France, Spain, and Naples' governments' efforts to prevent consuls engaging in trade, arguing they resulted more from "the vanity of their monarch[s]" than from real policy concerns. In fact, he argued that mercantile trade on the part of consuls benefitted the public good insofar as it alerted consuls to various issues outside of their consular offices. However, he recognized that too much involvement in trade could interfere with consuls' ability to do their jobs and urged the State Department to find policies that would "make the service of his country an object of [a consul's] first consideration."[25]

Before his appointment as consul in 1794, Montgomery had been an active international merchant involved in several large, profitable ventures. From 1778 until about 1784, he worked closely with Jaime Fallo (probably James Falls) a merchant with connections to Ostend, Holland who usually resided in Alicante. The two formed a partnership by 1778 and exported barilla into Holland and possibly northern Ireland, where Montgomery was the firm's agent during a brief period away from Alicante. Barilla, or saltwort (not to be confused with barilla wheat) was used to create soda ash as a base for textile dyes among other things. This was an extremely lucrative trade, and Montgomery and Falls were among the largest barilla exporters in Alicante.[26] In the mid-1780s,

---

[25] Montgomery to Sec. State, Oct. 9, 1795, Alicante Despatches.
[26] Enrique Giménez López, *Alicante en el Siglo XVIII: Economice de una Cuidad Portuaria en el antiguo régimen* (Valencia: Institución Alfonso el Magnánimo, 1981), 397–98.

Montgomery worked on sporadic ventures with his brother John, who was then in Boston. They forged contacts throughout Spain and sold ships owned by Montgomery and other Bostonians in Spain. In at least one case the motive seems to have been to fly the ship under a Spanish flag, perhaps to protect it from Algerian cruisers or from customs officials. Robert was trusted enough by his fellow Alicante merchants by now that they gave him a role in organizing "Algerian companies" to protect local shipping.[27]

By 1789 Montgomery formed a new partnership with Daniel Budd, the British consul to Alicante. They imported shipments of *bacalao* (salted cod) from the North Atlantic, most likely with the assistance of John Montgomery, who served as their agent in Boston. In Alicante, they contracted with local merchants to sell the fish in nearby villages and provided them with credit, allowing the small merchants to pay for the fish with the sales profits. They also contracted with a nearby potter to procure some of the region's distinctive ceramics for export. Additionally, they no doubt exported the same brandy and wine that attracted Brown and Ives to Alicante a decade later.[28] Some of these exports went through Guernsey, a notorious "free port" located in the English Channel and accessible to French and British merchants who could illegally transship Spanish goods into British markets in order to avoid tariffs. This practice was frequent during the American Revolution according to Montgomery and Budd's Guernsey agent, John Guille. Their Barcelona and London

SS Montgomery y Falls a favor de Manuel Botella, Dec. 22, 1778, Francisco Aracil; Robert Montgomery poder a Dn. Jayme Fallo, Feb. 8, 1780, Francisco Aracil; Dn. Francisco Martinez Oblign a Robert Montgomery y co., Mar. 9, 1781, Francisco Perez y Romira; Jayme Falls poder a Robert Montgomery, Nov. 21, 1789, Vicente Izquierdo y Suredo, all in PN.

[27] La Compania de Montgomery poder a Dn. Luis Laborde, July 15, 1785, Vicente Izquierdo y Suredo; Dn. Alexandro Gonzoll Oblig a la Compa. Montgomery, Sept. 9, 1787, Vicente Izquierdo; Dn. Roberto y Juan Montgomery consignado a Juan Bautista Roman, Apr. 25, 1788, Nicolas Paredes; La Compa Montgomery Indemnización a Dn. Pedro Cabanus, May 24, 1788, Vicente Izquierdo y Suredo; La Compa. de Montgomery poder a la Sociedad de Turnbull, July 7, 1788, Vicente Izquierdo y Suredo, all in PN.

[28] Dn. Roberto Montgomery y Dn. Daniel Budd combenio, Mar. 2, 1789; Josef Molto Obligación a la Compa de Montgomery, Jan. 20, 1789; Francisco Pastor Obl. a la Compa Montgomery, Feb. 13, 1789; Dn. Clemente Dura Obl. a la Comp de Montgomery, Feb. 17, 1789; La Compa de Montgomery poder a Dn. Juan Montgomery, July 2, 1789; Mariano Fuentes Obl. a la Compa de Montgomery, Jan. 31, 1791; Mario Hueso Obl. a la Compa de Montgomery, Mar. 15, 1791; Josef Marco Obl. a la Compa de Montgomery, Apr. 19, 1791; Miguel Griffano Obl. a la Compa de Montgomery, Apr. 20, 1791; Roman García Obl. a la Compa de Montgomery, Apr. 20, 1791; Vicente Guifano, Apr. 28, 1791, all in Vicente Izquierdo y Suredo, PN.

agents were both Guernsey natives, suggesting that Montgomery and Budd were heavily invested in this quasi-illegal trade.[29]

In 1793 Montgomery and Budd dissolved their firm and Montgomery formed a new company with his brother John. The brothers pledged that they would "serve their friends" as commission merchants specializing in American produce. They touted their expertise in selling American ships and goods in the region and suggested that fish and flour would be appropriate imports.[30] It is not clear why Budd and Montgomery dissolved the business. Possibly on the eve of his consular appointment, Montgomery recognized that a partnership with an Englishman who was also British consul might be seen as a conflict of interests. It is also possible that Budd left Alicante or that the onset of the Anglo-French wars changed their calculations. The most probable explanation, though, is that Montgomery's appointment, the rise in American shipping, and the uncertainty posed by the war all pointed to American commissions as a profitable and relatively safer alternative to shipping under his own name. Additionally, it was also the norm for consuls to work as commission merchants, while very few shipped under their own names. This shift may well have reflected Montgomery's awareness of ethical concerns that consuls would tilt the field in favor of their own firms if they were directly involved in overseas shipping.

After his 1793 consular appointment and his new focus on commissions, Montgomery's footprint in Alicante's archive shrank significantly. In the eleven years from 1780 to 1791 he issued twenty-one powers of attorney to merchants acting as his agents throughout Europe, Britain or America. In the thirteen years from 1793 to 1806 he and John issued only eleven (some under John's name only), nearly all in Spain.[31] Now, as a commission merchant, his focus was primarily on nearby ports, where he could orchestrate the best sales for his clients, much as Grivegnée and Co. had directed the *Eliza* and her cargo to the most propitious Spanish ports. Much of the paperwork for ships consigned to the Montgomery brothers would have been filed in Boston, Salem, Providence, and other US ports, so that the

---

[29] La Compa de Montgomery poder a Dn. Juan Guille, Jan. 22, 1791; La Compa de Montgomery poder a Reserson y Tuper, Jan. 23, 1791; La Compa de Montgomery poder a F. Gregory, Mar. 4, 1790; Jan. 27, 1791, all in Vicente Izquierdo y Suredo, PN. Gregory Stevens Cox, *St. Peter Port 1680–1830: The History of an International Entrepot* (Suffolk: Boydell Press, 1999) 19–20, 26.

[30] John Montgomery to Caleb Davis, Mar. 28, 1793, Caleb Davis Papers, Massachusetts Historical Society, Boston, MA.

[31] The eleven were to the following ports: Alicante (three), Valencia (two), and one each to Madrid, Málaga, Cádiz, Cartagena, La Coruña, and Belfast.

Alicante archives do not yield much insight into the firm's daily activity, and the lack of notarial records in the United States makes any evidence very scattershot. One exception is a power of attorney from the prominent Boston firm of Caleb and Loring, which was made in Boston but had to be recopied by the local Spanish notary. In this document, Curtis and Loring granted the brothers Montgomery broad powers to handle the cargo of their 168-ton ship, the *Otter*, much as Brown and Ives had done for the Grivegnées with the *Eliza*. The Montgomery brothers had full power to sell the cargo and other effects of the ship, as well as to purchase any needed products and make any necessary contracts pertaining to the ship and to bring any necessary suits in local courts. Besides the commissions to be made from such transactions, earning the trust of a firm like Caleb and Loring was important. Not only could they provide much more business for the brothers, both directly and indirectly through referrals, but they also had influence with the State Department as authors of letters of recommendations for merchants such as Thomas Appleton and John Montgomery's son-in-law, Obadiah Rich, whom they supported for consular appointments.[32]

The change in focus to the commission trade did not insulate Montgomery from criticism. In 1798 David Humphreys, the American minister to Spain wrote that Montgomery was the consul of whom he had "heard more ill spoken than any others" and "that he is by many others looked upon as a very self-interested character, and by some as a man destitute of principle." In that same year, Henry Prince, captain of the Salem Ship, *Astrea*, penned a devastating sketch of Alicante's commission merchants, all of whom, he described as having "a very suspicious look after one another in business." The greatest competition was between the Montgomery brothers and the British firm De Mercier and Stemborg, the only companies to handle US commissions and whom Prince described as "at swords points" with each other. When an American ship that had not yet consigned its cargo arrived in port, according to Prince, "Montgomery, the American consul … with his clerk comes alongside to enquire 'who does your business' with the greatest pretensions of friendship – and the minute you land some clerks will attend you to his house . . . ." Word of this overly aggressive reputation may have reached Brown and Ives through European

---

[32] Roberto y Juan Montgomery substitution of power of attorney to Langsamer y Co., Feb. 8, 1802, Ramon Izquierdo y Suredo, PN; N. Appleton to John Adams, Oct. 16, 1797, Adams Recs.; Caleb Loring to James Madison, July 24, 1815, James Madison Papers, Founders Online.

correspondents such as Humphreys's in-laws, the Bulkeley family of Lisbon, who were powerful merchants and close allies to Brown and Ives.[33] Such aggressive efforts to make clients of American ship captains on the part of a consul could easily be seen as an ethically questionable effort to leverage public office into private profits, particularly when one considers that all ship captains had to meet with the consul and share information about their cargos.

Whatever the ethics, all evidence points to the commission business being very profitable for the Montgomery brothers. They remained the only American merchants at a port with from ten to forty annual American cargos until John Rogers arrived in 1802. Montgomery's position as consul provided him with respectability and prestige, and it gave him access to US captains who had to report to him to get their papers signed. Additionally, his vice-consular networks and connections to other US merchant-consuls throughout the region enabled him to sell his consignees' cargoes readily and also guaranteed more referrals. By 1800, the growing firm had begun leasing a warehouse on Alicante's beach. An early form of vertical integration practiced by large merchants in the region, having a warehouse would allow the Montgomerys to avoid storage fees for their consignees' cargoes and to profit further by charging fees to store other merchants' goods. When the firm dissolved in 1803, having reached the end of the ten-year term for which it was founded, Robert paid John a very healthy settlement of 10,000 pesos, roughly $10,000. Afterwards, all indications point to Robert continuing the commission trade under his own name, as well as shipping some cargoes throughout the region himself, such as the shipment of cod from Lisbon that the firm was anticipating at the time of its dissolution.[34]

At the height of the American trade, Montgomery's profits would have been very impressive. In a year with twenty ships consigned to him, he would have made $2,000–4,000 in commissions alone. He would also have received fees for signatures affixed to certify American ships – usually $2 per signature – plus other miscellaneous fees. In a year with forty ship

---

[33] Humphreys to Pickering, July 27, 1798, Box 1, Folder 21, David Humphreys Papers, Humphreys-Marvin-Olmsted; [Henry Prince] Log *Astrea*, 1798–99, Philips-Peabody-Essex Institute, Salem, MA; Hedges, *The Browns of Providence Plantation*, 101–2.

[34] Dn. Conde de Soto amendo arrendar a Dn. Roberto y Dn. Juan Montgomery, Nov. 6, 1800, Ramon Izquierdo; Dn. Roberto y Dn. Juan Montgomery combieno y disleuzon, July 4, 1803, Francisco Aracil, both in PN. The English merchants Webb and Holmes pursued a similar strategy in Livorno. See "Testimony of John Webb," July 26, 1796, Leghorn Despatches.

arrivals that could add perhaps $200 or more to his income. He would have received additional income from split commissions for cargoes he referred to other merchants and from goods he shipped under his own name, such as the cod he imported from Lisbon – although, conversely, he may have had to share some of the Alicante commissions with others. Montgomery once wrote that a consul should expect about $300 in fees and would need $3,000 annually to support himself, which seems to approximate his actual income in a good year. Over time the brothers were able to accumulate significant wealth. When John's daughter married in 1809, he provided her with a dowry of £5,000, or roughly $20,000. John asserted that this figure was one-tenth of his wealth. If so, his net worth of $200,000 would be as much as $10 million in today's money.[35] Robert likely was worth at least that much, considering that the brothers were partners and that later in life he complained of losing $200,000 after numerous setbacks, a sum that suggests considerable wealth before his reverses.[36]

***

Toward the end of his life, Thomas Appleton recalled that on first arriving in Livorno in 1798 he decided not to engage in trade. He wrote, "I observed the numerous obstacles which would attend the combining commercial views with my consular duties, thus I have altogether abstained from the former." Consuls, he explained, should be "impartial agents" in cases of disputes between captains and sailors and in the inspection and sales of damaged goods. Yet this impartiality was not possible when the cargo of a ship was consigned to a merchant-consul.[37]

Despite Appleton's recollections and advocacy of the ethical high ground, he was in fact actively engaged in the American trade almost

---

[35] I base this calculation on the fact that the typical unskilled laborer in the United States at the time made about $1 a day which, even with full employment, would equate to about 1/100th of today's minimum wage worker's annual income of up to $20,000 per year. Thus $200,000 could equate to as much as $10 million. Conversely, an online calculator based, presumably, on commodity prices, has it at $4 million, still a substantial sum (www.officialdata.org/us/inflation/1800?amount=200).

[36] Dna. Ana Montgomery y Dn. Obadiah Rich, recepción de dote, July 14, 1809, Francisco Aracil, PN; Montgomery to Sec. State, June 29, 1815, Alicante Despatches. On fees, see below and Appleton to Samuel Hodgdon, Feb. 5, 1799, GL. Until at least 1816 the standard value of a dollar or peso (piece of eight) was 4s 6d sterling for a ratio of roughly 4:1. See John J. McCusker, *Money and Exchange in Europe and America 1600–1795* (Chapel Hill: University of North Carolina Press, 1978) 7–8.

[37] Appleton to Robert Livingston, Oct. 23, 1833, Leghorn Despatches.

from the minute he arrived in Livorno. At that time, or possibly even slightly before, he agreed to join the local firm of DuPouy and Brothers as their agent for American commerce. The DuPouys would have been pleased to have the new American consul on board as a means of breaking into the growing business with American shipping. They were at a decided disadvantage against the two major firms that had dominated the market – the British house of Webb and Holmes and the house of the former US consul, Philip Felicchi. But, as Appleton explained to a Baltimore merchant, his own "neutrality" as an American citizen would allow the firm to avoid trouble with the belligerent powers. For his part, Appleton was happy to have the resources and reputation of a well-established firm behind him. In his first year in Livorno he wrote to dozens of merchants involved in the US trade, mostly in America, but some in the Mediterranean and Britain, soliciting their business and touting the respectability of the DuPouys.[38]

In addition to drumming up consignments for DuPouys, Appleton spent a great deal of effort referring consignees to his many contacts around the Mediterranean in return for a portion of the commission.[39] In theory this business promised easy profits, since all that was required was a strong recommendation to a captain. In practice, however, it was not always so easy. Very early on, Appleton forged an arrangement with his in-law George Perkins of Smyrna, to provide referrals by sending him an American captain who had originally been directed to do business in Livorno but had been disappointed with the prospects on arriving. At the time, Appleton wrote Perkins, "It is customary in Leghorn, indeed as well as in all the ports of Italy, that in consignments of a similar nature that the medium through whom the consignments are obtained should participate in the emoluments of the commission . . . ."[40]

---

[38] Appleton wrote eighteen solicitation letters from Dec. 29, 1798 to Sept. 13, 1800. Several were circulars addressed to multiple merchants. Appleton to David Pearce, Dec. 29, 1798; to George and Sam Perkins, Jan. 27, 1799; to Mr. Tailor, Apr. 17, 1799; to Black and Co., May 20, 1799; to Stephen Cathalan, June 27, 1799; to multiple merchants, [?] 1799; to Thomas Massey and others, June 30, 1799; to Thomas Bulkeley and others, Aug. 28, 1799; to William Eaton, Sept. 2, 1799; to E. H. Denby, Sept. 3, 1799; to M. Sartori, Sept. 12, 1799; to Tom Williams, Oct 1, 1799; to Nathaniel Amory, Nov. 14, 1799; to multiple recipients, Nov. 30, 1799; Mar. 1, 1800; to William Crafts, Mar. [?], 1800; to multiple recipients, Sept. 20, 1799 [1800]; to Mr. Wagner, Sept. 13, 1800; Quote from Appleton to Valck and Co., all in GL.

[39] In addition to Perkins, see Appleton to Mr. Tailor, Apr. 17, 1799; to Mr. Wagner, Feb. 18, 1801; to Mr. Woolaston, Mar. 25, 1801; June 12, 1801; to Mr. Degan, July 13, 1801, all in GL.

[40] Appleton to George and Samuel Perkins, Jan. 27, 1799, GL.

Perkins appears to have entered into a formal agreement with Appleton to split this and future commissions. It is unclear whether Appleton conducted this business as part of the DuPouy firm or on his own. Soon after entering the agreement Perkins refused to share a commission on an American cargo that had already been split once before. Perkins argued the cargo would have come to him anyway because he was American, and since it was already split with a third merchant, he would only receive one-quarter if he included Appleton. Appleton responded that full commissions were very rare, since "out of 20 American vessels in the Mediterranean 19 divide their commission with the merchant, and in every instance where the cargo is consigned by the captain," and that it was only due to "the warm manner" he spoke of Perkins's house that the captain agreed to the consignment. The dispute lingered more than a year and, even after Perkins settled with Appleton, he charged him so much interest on another item on his account that Appleton complained it nearly ate up the entire commission.[41]

Despite Appleton's initial enthusiasm, his efforts may not have paid as well as the DuPouys hoped. For example, despite receiving one of Appleton's circulars, Brown and Ives continued to prefer Webb and Co. and Felicchi. Furthermore, if Perkins's observations were correct, many of the commissions would have been quite miniscule once they were divided between all the merchants and then further divided with DuPouy, which no doubt would have been a disappointment for Appleton. Or, conversely, if Appleton was going rogue and splitting commissions without giving the DuPouys their due, they would likely have been dissatisfied with him. Whatever the cause, by 1803 Appleton and the DuPouys parted ways and he sent out feelers to various other Livorno houses. One of his selling points was that he had "the friendly assurances of every American consul in the Mediterranean," which implied that they would likely refer shipments to any firm with which he was connected. Nevertheless, he seems to have been unable to find a new partnership and, in 1808, he formed his own firm, Appleton and Co.[42]

It is hard to judge the exact profitability of Appleton's post. Based on his frequent complaints about fees and endless quest to get the more lucrative naval agency attached to his position, he seems far less successful than Montgomery. On the other hand, he once described Livorno as the "most

[41] Appleton to George Perkins, May 15, 1800; Mar. 16, 1801; Apr. 25, 1801; May 15, 1801; July 3, 1801; Aug. 21, 1801, all in GL.

[42] B533 F1, 532–34, B. & I.; Appleton to Anthony Dugan, Nov. 17, 1803; Appleton to Philip Jaume, Jan. 10, 1804; Appleton to Mr. Koster, Apr. 23, 1806, all in GL; Appleton to Brown and Ives, May 1, 1808, B109 F8, B. & I.

lucrative" consulate in the Mediterranean, based, presumably, on the number of US ship arrivals, which peaked near 100 during the heyday of the neutral trade – far more than in Alicante. Appleton generally charged between $2 and $2.50 per signature on ship certificates, drawback forms, passports, and other paperwork and usually averaged around $600 per year from these fees.[43]

His income from commissions, however, would have been much lower than Montgomery's. As an employee, he would have had to split a substantial portion of every commission with the DuPouys. And, despite the large number of US ships in Livorno harbor, his firm does not seem to have attracted that many consignees. Various injurious rumors about the firm, "unfounded" according to Appleton, were float-ing around the Mediterranean by 1800. To counter them, Appleton wrote a correspondent of the great interest American captains in Livorno were taking in the firm, with many pledging to use them on their next voyage and others regretting not having done so earlier. Yet, despite vaguely alluding to various consignments over the last year, Appleton was only able to name four specific cargoes – two from Philadelphia and two from Boston. Assuming perhaps six actual con-signments in that year, Appleton might have pocketed $500–1,000. If he were able to get split commissions for the same number of referrals to Perkins and others, that might have provided another $500–1,000 giving him a total income of $1,600–2,600 when his consular fees were included, which would have been right in the neighborhood of Simpson's salary in Morocco.[44] Appleton supplemented this income with small speculations buying and selling Mediterranean and West Indian goods. His usual partners were his wealthy American brothers-in-law, who could find space on their own ships or others for Appleton's goods and could manage purchases and sales in the United States. Appleton could draw on a good-sized inheritance from his father for capital. No doubt, when successful, these ventures made the difference between a good year and a bad one for Appleton.[45]

***

[43] Appleton to Robert Montgomery, May 19, 1802; to Mr. Storm, Dec. 3, 1805, both in GL; Appleton to Sec. State, Apr. 22, 1815; to Robert Livingston, Oct. 22, 1833, both in Leghorn Despatches.

[44] Appleton to Mr. Wills, Mar. 3, 1800, GL.

[45] Appleton to Samuel Emory and Thomas Perkins, Jan. 28, 1802; to Emory, Apr. 5, 1802; Aug. 11, 1802; to Emory and Perkins, Nov. 12, 1802; Mar. 4, 1804; Sept. 2, 1804; Feb. 7, 1805; Feb. 25, 1805; Sept. 25, 1805; Apr. 11, 1805; Dec. 19, 1805, all in GL.

If any of the three consuls avoided mixing private and public business, it was James Simpson in Tangier. He once stated that Barbary consuls "should be restrained from carrying on business in their own name, in order to prevent them making any commercial engagement with the governments, which seldom fail of being productive of bad consequences to their nations." Vice-consuls, however, he added, did customarily engage in trade. Simpson was the only of the three who actually received a salary from the United States (and one of only four in the entire consular service to do so) and this income should have provided him with a measure of independence.

However, Simpson experienced frustration, partly of his own making, with his consular salary. For some reason he had gained the false understanding that it would be $4,000. Before accepting the position, he stipulated to David Humphreys that even $4,000 would only be adequate were he also able to retain the Gibraltar consulate, which presumably produced more fees and allowed for more profitable private commercial adventures. It is unclear why Simpson believed he would get $4,000. Perhaps Humphreys gave him false hope on this account, as Congress was discussing raising consular salaries at this time, though in the end only the Algerian consul actually received the raise to $4,000. Whatever the reason, Simpson drew $4,000 a year for some time before learning of his error in 1798. This was possible because rather than receiving a paycheck, American consuls essentially drew on the State Department through nearby bankers who would advance them the money confident that any debts would be made good by the State Department.[46] Whatever the amount, Simpson usually had trouble collecting it, due to the difficulty in moving money into Morocco. In 1802 he unsuccessfully requested that instead of having to draw bank bills on the State Department, his account be "placed in the honor of the banker of the United States in London, to be held at my [dis]posal." In subsequent years Simpson mostly drew his account from merchants across the

---

[46] After claiming the accurate $2,000 salary in 1799, he took no more salary at all until 1802. At that point, he had drawn a total of $10,000 for five years, bringing his cumulative salary down to the correct figure. He then resumed drawing a regular salary, taking $2,000 in twice annual increments of $1,000 each. He attempted to draw $4,000 again in 1807 but appears to have reverted back to $2,000 in 1808. Simpson to Sec. State, July 17, 1798; "Extract of a letter to Col Humphreys dated Gibraltar 3 Jan. 1795"; Simpson to Sec State, Mar. 11, 1799; Jan. 8, 1802; Jan. 25, 1802; Aug. 3, 1802; Sept. 14, 1802; Oct. 6, 1803; Mar. 5, 1804; Nov. 24, 1804; Apr. 17, 1805; May 6, 1805; May 18, 1805; July 8, 1805; Jan. 20, 1806; Jan. 22, 1806; Oct. 23, 1806; Oct. 29, 1806; Aug. 19, 1807; July 18, 1808, all in Tangier Despatches.

Strait such as his friend and successor John Gavino in Gibraltar and Richard Meade, an American merchant and naval agent in Cádiz. These men were connected to the United States and could, presumably, more easily dispose of American bills than could Simpson. But this method, too, proved difficult in 1805 when the American house of Kuhn and Green in Gibraltar collapsed, just after Simpson drew a $500 bill on them in partial payment of his salary. Simpson had to return to Richard Meade to get a new bill and he continued to draw on Meade for his next payment despite continuing difficulties.[47]

Simpson complained that his salary barely covered the heavy contingent expenses that came with his job. These included the need to purchase gifts, usually textiles, tea, and sugar, for Moroccan officials, which could easily total hundreds of dollars annually. Additionally, Simpson had to pay about $200 annually for rent on the small consular townhouse in Tangier's old city, plus smaller sums for servants' quarters, stables, and wages for his interpreter and servants. Hiring boats to carry official letters, purchasing official seals for American agents in Morocco, and frequent repairs to the consular flags also required significant expenditures.[48] The combination of all these expenses meant that, despite providing a steady salary, the Moroccan consulate was not an economic windfall. Simpson frequently appealed to the State Department to recognize the hardship it caused his wife and children. When pushing for a larger salary he pleaded, "I hope it is not necessary for me to add more on this subject than barely to assure you, upon my honor, that I solicit nothing but what my duty to my children compels me." Another time he wrote of his family "being deprived of the property I have expended since I have resided in this country," and yet another time he threatened to go to Washington to discuss his accounts personally with officials. His position was not much worse than that of his British counterpart and friend James Matra, whose salary of £400 (roughly $1,600) was actually a bit lower than Simpson's, creating serious financial problems for Matra and his predecessors. In the end, Simpson argued that all of his spending and the concurrent debt were done out of a sense of duty. He wrote, "I have brought my private

---

[47] Simpson to Sec. State, Jan. 8, 1802 (quote); May 19, 1805; July 8, 1805, all Tangier Despatches. On Kuhn and Green see also James P. McClure, ed., *The Papers of Thomas Jefferson* (Princeton University Press, 2017) XXXVIII: 641.

[48] Simpson to Sec. State, Dec. 15, 1802; Dec. 24, 1802; June 14, 1804; Apr. 2, 1805; Apr. 17, 1805; July 5, 1805; July 13, 1805; Nov. 30, 1805; Jan. 20, 1806; Feb. 12, 1806; Oct. 15, 1806; Jan. 17, 1807; "An Account of Articles Provided for Public Service . . . From the First Day of January to . . . the Thirty First day of Dec. 1806," all in Tangier Despatches.

property during that time to the aid of what I have received from government to support the dignity of the office I have been entrusted with, and which I have the conscious satisfaction of knowing has been done to fullest effect."[49]

Considering these financial strains, it seems unlikely that Simpson completely abstained from trade after his appointment. Simpson was certainly engaged in trade before and during his term as consul to Gibraltar. During that time, he frequently solicited American business. Like most merchants in Gibraltar, Simpson and his partner were involved in the trade in provisions such as grain and poultry from Tangier which fed the British forces on the rock. Gibraltarians were surrounded by hostile Spaniards on a tiny outcropping. Without this trade it would have been extremely difficult to feed them and to maintain the British military presence.[50] He also made efforts to increase the American trade, urging Edward Church, US consul to Lisbon, and William Porter East, the vice-consul, to have ships heading to Spain stop in Gibraltar. Because Gibraltar was a free port, he wrote that goods from Málaga and other Spanish ports could easily be transferred without having to pay duties. No doubt this advantage had been on Brown and Ives's minds when they had the *Eliza* stop there on its voyage.[51]

However, there is little evidence of Simpson engaging in trade once he arrived in Tangier, though he could easily have done so. At the time of his departure, he wrote that his consular successor, John Gavino, had taken charge of his remaining private business in Gibraltar. Whether or not Simpson made any attempts to continue in the provisioning trade with or without Gavino is hard to say. Although there is no hard evidence, as one of the few Europeans able to live on the African side of the Strait and with many long-standing connections on both sides due to his long tenure in Gibraltar, it seems likely Simpson would have been tempted to attempt to keep a hand in that trade. His British counterpart and friend, consul James Matra, was deeply involved in it. Not only did the shipment of

[49] Simpson to Sec. State, July 17, 1798; Aug. 3, 1802; Apr. 20, 1805; Jan. 20, 1806, all in Tangier Despatches; Alan Frost, *The Precarious Life of James Mario Matra* (Melbourne University Press, 1995) 124–26.

[50] Governor Charles O'Hara to J. Ross and James Simpson, Nov. 2, 1789; to Robert Anderson, Oct. 27, 1790; to James Matra, Oct. 23, 1789, all in Consular Correspondence, 1780–1830 Box 1, Gibraltar National Archive.

[51] James Simpson to Edward Church, Nov. 17, 1804; to William Short, Dec. 18, 1794; to William Porter East, Feb. 22, 1796; to David Humphreys, Oct. 29, 1796, all in Simpson Letterbook.

provisions to Gibraltar occupy a good deal of his official duties, Matra's father-in-law and housemate was the agent for the contractors for vict-ualling the Army in Gibraltar. Matra also maintained close relations with the Gibraltar provisioning merchant J. H. Ross, with whom Simpson had also been connected. Matra sent provisions on his own account to Ross as late as 1804. British and Moroccan regulations would have made it more difficult for Simpson to participate in this trade, but there is no reason why he might not have pooled items of his own with Matra's shipments or others. Income from this sort of venture would help to explain how Simpson could have afforded to purchase and maintain the extensive Mount Washington estate. On the other hand, Simpson's frequent and seemingly genuine complaints about his financial position throughout his entire tenure in Tangier and the fact that he was heavily indebted to Gibraltar merchants at the time of his death suggest that any such ventures were not particularly successful over the long run.[52]

***

An unintended consequence of creating the consular infrastructure for US trade was that, in so doing, the State Department promoted a new net-work of American merchants. Consuls relied heavily on each other for advice, commissions, capital, and occasional partnerships in trading ven-tures. These connections were of great importance to consuls, many of whom were relatively small traders with relatively shallow roots in the Mediterranean without long-standing relationships with the larger European and American houses. Appointment as consul in itself implied a certain trustworthiness to potential trading partners since it involved a sort of vetting process in the form of letters of recommendation from American merchants to the State Department. Since all consuls could be assumed to have passed this vetting process, they could be assumed to be potentially reliable trading partners by other consuls and by merchants in the United States. Over time, as more consuls were appointed to the region and consuls became ever more accustomed to reaching out to each other, these trading connections expanded and deepened.

   This emerging network allowed the consuls and their American contacts to function almost as a far-flung commercial partnership at times. The extent to which they traded and solicited trade with each other and with

---

[52] Frost, *The Precarious Life of James Mario Matra*, 137, 179, 193, 211, 239–40; Simpson to Sec. State, Oct. 31, 1795; John Mullowney to Sec. State, Feb. 7, 1824, both in Tangier Despatches.

merchants in the United States is truly remarkable. Brown and Ives, for example, were flooded with letters, prices current, and solicitations from consuls and their associates throughout the Mediterranean. In addition to Appleton and Montgomery, they heard frequently from consul Kirkpatrick of the Grivegnée house in Málaga; from Robert Montgomery's son-in-law, John Rogers; from John Montgomery's son-in-law, Obadiah Rich, who was consul in Valencia; and from Montgomery's former clerk, Asa Fitch, in Marseille. They were also in close contact with the house of Lisbon consul, Thomas Bulkeley, and with Appleton's rival, Charles Degan, the naval agent in Livorno.[53]

Consuls, of course, were already well connected through their official correspondence, particularly the frequent circular letters warning of various dangers that worked their way around the shores of the Mediterranean. But they also kept up a stream of personal, business correspondence along these same channels, mostly involving continual efforts to direct new consignments their way and to split commissions for consignments sent to others. A good example is William Jarvis, Bulkeley's successor as Lisbon consul, who began his career as a captain trading in the Mediterranean. This experience introduced him to Joseph Chiappi, Simpson's agent at Mogadore and, presumably, to other Americans in the region. Once appointed consul, Jarvis received frequent "offers of services" from the Minorca consul J. M. Baker, who wrote, "I will cheerfully divide with you the commissions resulting from sale of any consignment you may influence in my favor – and make no doubt of you, as ready concurrence to the same on your part on commissions resulting from the sale of such cargoes etc. as my recommendations may waft your way." He received a similar but less explicit offer of services from Tobias Lear, the Algerian consul. From north of the Mediterranean, John M. Forbes, another Massachusetts merchant and US consul to Hamburg wrote, "[I]f anything can be done with advantage between this and your place, I shall be willing to enter into it either for my own or for joint account with you and should it be in your power to influence any consignments into my hands shall readily account with you for one third or even half commissions." Forbes suspected that such an arrangement might not be

---

[53] Bulkeleys: B108 F7, B108 F10, B108 F11, B109; Grivegnées: B100 F4, F11; Obadiah Rich: B110 F11; Montgomerys Fitch/Fitch: B110 F11, B112 F5, F10; B113 F1, F3, F4, F5, F6, F7, F8, F9; B116 F4, F6, F7, F8, F9, F10; B117 F1, F2, F3, F4, F5, F6, F7, F8, F9, F10; Rogers: B111, F1, F9; B112 F4, F10; B113 F1; B114 F9, F10; B115 F1, F4; B116 F4, F6, F7, F9; Degan: B114 F5, all in B. & I.

"practicab[le] consistently with strict probity," but admitted that he needed the help from his fellow consul in order to get his business started. "You must know as well as I that the great difficulty of getting into business in the midst of the all-powerful competition of wealth obliges young men to make these sacrifices and justifies them," he confided.[54]

Simpson, Montgomery, and Appleton all made use of this network. While still in Gibraltar, Simpson solicited business from the US consul and vice-consul in Lisbon and he left his business concerns with his successor as Gibraltar consul on leaving for Tangier. The Montgomerys did business with the US consuls to La Coruña, Málaga, and London, and Robert sought advice on consular fees from Appleton.[55] Of the three, Appleton made by far the most use of the consular network. He seems to have made a practice of contacting new consuls in the region as soon as he learned of their appointments in order to get them to agree to splitting commissions. The large number of letters may be due to more of his business correspondence having been preserved, but even so, his reliance on other consuls was quite notable. Of twenty-nine solicitation letters Appleton sent between 1798 and 1807, thirteen were to American consuls (including one to someone he mistakenly thought had been appointed).[56]

In a typical letter, Appleton congratulated Peter Kuhn (formerly of Kuhn and Green of Gibraltar) on his appointment as consul to Genoa and proposed an exchange of commercial information between the two. Usually this sort of exchange was a precursor to a formal agreement to split commissions. Not all consuls were keen to take this step with Appleton. Some, like Forbes, may have had a sense that such arrangements were not entirely ethical. Frederick Degan of Naples, for example, initially resisted but eventually acceded, after which Appleton promised

[54] Manifest for Port of Mogadore, July 19, 1799; John M. Forbes to William Jarvis, June 14, 1803; J. M. Baker to Jarvis, Jan. 1, 1804; Apr. 2, 1804; Oct. 20, 1804; Tobias Lear to Jarvis, Mar. 16, 1804, all in William Jarvis Papers, Massachusetts Historical Society, Boston, MA.

[55] Simpson to Church, Nov. 17, 1794; to Short, Dec. 18, 1794; to East, Feb. 22, 1796; to Humphreys, Oct. 29, 1796, all in Simpson Letterbook. Dn. Juan Montgomery poder a Dn. Josef Beccera, June 26, 1799 Josef Michel de Champonsin; Dn. Roberto y Juan Montgomery poder a Grivegnées y Co., Dec. 1, 1800, Ramon Izquierdo; Dn. Juan Montgomery poder a Dn. Samuel Williams, Oct, 25, 1810, Francisco Aracil, all in PN.

[56] The consuls include Stephen Cathalan, June 27, 1799; Thomas Bulkeley, Aug. 28, 1799; William Eaton, Sept. 2, 1799; M. Sartori, Sept. 12, 1799; Samuel Williams, Oct. 1, 1799; Conrad F. Wagner, Sept. 13, 1800; Frederick Woolaston, Feb. 6, 1801; M. Lee, May 7, 1801; Frederick Degan, July 13, 1801; John Broadbent, Aug. 3 1801; W. Kirkpatrick, Sept. 25, 1801; John Lamson, Jan. 15, 1802; Tobias Lear, Nov. 18, 1803; Francisco Navaro, Feb. 15, 1801, all in GL.

"ere long to be able to throw something in your way for I cannot but doubt that many vessels will arrive from America ... ." In other cases, Appleton suggested that American merchants in the area apply for consular posts. For example, he wrote Joseph Barnes that he should apply for the Naples consulate since it offered "great commercial advantage" and the current consul could easily be replaced as he was not an American. No doubt Appleton also realized he had a better chance of conducting business with Barnes, who was a good friend and business contact for Appleton while living in Messina.[57]

***

This consular network was particularly beneficial to small traders who would not otherwise have had the capital, access to information, and contacts necessary to engage in overseas trade. So long as the Mediterranean boom continued, becoming a consul gave them access to all the tools needed to profit from it. A good example is William Eaton, American consul to Tunis, and the voyage of his ship, *Anna Maria*, in 1801. *Anna Maria*'s voyage provides a sharp contrast to that of Brown and Ives's *Eliza* with which this chapter opened. While Brown and Ives stood at the top of the mercantile food chain, the people for whom the consular network and related trading infrastructure were created, Eaton and the *Anna Maria* represent the new possibilities created by the consular network for those with fewer resources.

A native of the interior of Connecticut and a military man, Eaton had no experience whatsoever in overseas commerce. He was one of the rare consuls who was not a merchant, and he never went overseas until his appointment in 1798.[58] Tunis was one of the four salaried Barbary consulates, so in theory it was not necessary for him to engage in trade. At first Eaton was hesitant to enter into the world of Mediterranean commerce. Almost immediately upon his arrival in Tunis, he received a note from Thomas Appleton informing him that Tunisian wheat

[57] Appleton to J Barnes, May 17, 1801; to Peter Kuhn, June 5, 1805; to Frederick Degan, July 13, 1801; Aug. 31, 1801, all in GL.

[58] On Eaton, see Charles Prentiss, *The Life of the Late General William Eaton* (Brookfield, MA: E. Merrian and Co., 1813); Cornelius C. Felton, *Life of William Eaton* in Jared Sparks, ed., *Library of American Biography* (New York: Harper and Bros., 1848) IX: 163–358; Richard Zacks, *The Pirate Coast: Thomas Jefferson, The First Marine, and the Secret Mission of 1805* (New York: Hyperion, 2005); Lawrence A. Peskin, "American Exception? William Eaton and Early National Antisemitism," *American Jewish History* 100 (July 2016) 299–317.

would sell well in Livorno and assuring him, "Should you point any plan of commerce we have amply the means to fund them." Despite at least two subsequent reminders from Appleton, Eaton resisted the call to trade for well over a year. He appears to have had ethical concerns over engaging in trade, or at least he voiced them to Appleton when he wrote, "In ordinary situations I am against the idea of a consul entering into commerce here, and am fully persuaded it should be forbidden by law of the United States." Nevertheless, he warmed to the idea of shipping wheat to Livorno. Despite his ethical concerns, he wrote, "the position I now hold induces a confidence that I may do something for myself here without danger of compromising the interest of the United States," and, he added, "my pittance of a salary compels the measure, and if the laws do not sanction it, they do not forbid it." Despite having pressed Eaton into trade, Appleton agreed, responding, "There is no law that forbids a consul being interested in trade though I see a thousand reasons (from dayly experience) why they should be prohibited."[59]

After overcoming this, possibly pro-forma, concern, the two went back and forth on various trading plans. Eaton ultimately did not trade to Livorno, but, by the next spring, he had acquired his ship and was planning to send the *Anna Maria* to Marseille, with a cargo of olive oil and barilla, which the captain would trade for some brandy before heading to New York. Because of the difficulties of moving money from Marseille to Tunis, Eaton asked Appleton to finance the voyage from Livorno. Appleton, drawing on DuPouy Brothers' credit, would act as an intermediary, sending a letter of credit to Marseille in return for bills that he could then easily send to Tunis or wherever Eaton directed. As financier of the voyage, Appleton's firm would receive brokerage fees and he, no doubt, would also hope to gain future business from Eaton.[60]

Unfortunately for Appleton and Eaton, the Marseille merchants refused a portion of the bill of credit Appleton had drawn up to fund the voyage. The unexplained refusal was upsetting for Eaton, both because it meant he would receive less profit than anticipated and could be

---

[59] Thomas Appleton to William Eaton, Feb. 28, 1799; Sept. 2, 1799; July 16, 1800; July 23, 1800; n.d. [1800]; Aug. 5, 1800; Aug. 30, 1800, all in GL; William Eaton to Thomas Appleton, July 3, 1800, Letterbook 1801–2, Eaton Papers.

[60] Eaton to Messrs. Chapelle, Neveau, and Moulton, Mar. 18, 1801, Letterbook 1800–1801; to Eliza Eaton, Apr. 14, 1801, Letterbook 1799–1802; to Appleton, June 27, 1801, Letterbook 1800–1801, all in Eaton Papers; "Copy of a letter of credit in my favor from William Eaton Consul for the USA at Tunis," June 27, 1801, GL.

potentially embarrassing should it indicate that he was not entirely credit-worthy. Appleton eventually learned that the cause was relatively benign. The *Anna Maria's* captain, George Coffin, had brought a good deal more brandy to ship from Marseille to New York than Eaton had instructed him to. As this purchase of more than $50,000 had come from the Marseille profits, the merchants had essentially deducted it from the letter of credit Appleton had drawn up at the start of the voyage. Eaton was not entirely satisfied with this explanation and suspected the French firm was overcharging him. He gave Appleton power of attorney to adjust any errors after failing to convince his friend, James Cathcart, the former US consul to Tripoli, to do so. Appleton in turn charged his friend Stephen Cathalan, the US consul to Marseille, to look into the matter. In the end they were able to recover a small sum for Eaton (from which they no doubt deducted a small commission).[61]

Despite this unpleasantness, Eaton must have been relatively happy with the voyage. In addition to any profits returned to him in Tunis, he was able to put away $5,000 in the US which he had transferred to his wife to be used for their children's education. Certainly, Eaton was not discouraged from business. By the fall of 1801 he had two ships sailing in the Mediterranean with wheat consigned to Cathcart, who was tempor-arily in Livorno, and the next year saw him importing West Indian produce into the Mediterranean. He also consigned goods to Degan and Purviance, the American naval agents in Livorno, though Cathcart warned him against them, and he drew some bills on William Wills, the US consul to Barcelona. Appleton tried, without success, to get Eaton to consign a shipment to his in-law and frequent correspondent George Perkins in Smyrna which, no doubt would have provided him with a split commission.[62]

In the end, Eaton appears to have profited from this activity. He bragged that his two ships, which, combined, carried over 500 tons

[61] James Cathcart to Eaton, Aug. 11, 1801, Box 5; Eaton to Cathcart, Aug. 17, 1801, Letterbook 1801–2; "Sales, Brandy and Wine, by order of Capt. George C. Coffin," Oct. 22, 1801, Box 5, all in Eaton Papers; Appleton to Eaton, Aug. 30, 1801; Sept. 24, 1801; to Cathalan, Oct. 11, 1801; to Eaton, Nov. 11, 1801; to Messrs. Chapelie Neveu et Moulton, Nov. 17, 1801, all in GL.

[62] Eaton to Eliza Eaton, Apr. 14, 1801, Letterbook 1799–1802; Stephen Pynchon to George Coffin, Nov. 25, 1801, Box 5; Eaton to Eliza Eaton, Feb. 15, 1802, Letterbook 1799–1802; Degan and Purviance to Eaton, Jan. 18, 1803, Box 6; Cathcart to Eaton, Mar. 12, 1802, Box 5; Cathcart to Eaton, May 5, 1802, Box 6, all in Eaton Papers; Appleton to Eaton, Apr. 7, 1802; Appleton to [?], Feb. 27, 1802; Appleton to Eaton, [May 19, 1802]; to George Perkins, May 20, 1802, all in GL.

burthen, were "as valuable and as handsome as any on the ocean of their size." By 1802, as he was preparing to return to New England, he wrote his wife, "If with the success I have already had I should succeed to increase my capital to $30,000 I think we may live decently with it in a country town." Still, potential disaster lurked around every corner in the risky world of overseas commerce, particularly for a poorly capitalized newcomer like Eaton. "But [do] not let our calculations be too sanguine," he warned, " – a gale at sea, or a superior enemy may defeat all these prospects."[63]

***

All things considered, it would seem that the consular system served American merchants well. As one of the largest departments in the federal government, it provided an infrastructure that, along with the Navy, served to assist and protect American merchants like Brown and Ives and their fleets within the Mediterranean. That it also created a new class of smaller merchants like Eaton and Appleton living in the Mediterranean and serving as consuls may not have been intended, but it nevertheless helped achieve the goal of establishing American trade more firmly in the region.

Nevertheless, the role of consuls within this network could appear unseemly then and now. The criticisms and distrust of Montgomery, in particular, and the consuls' efforts (particularly Appleton's) to downplay the extent of their participation in trade under their own names, all suggests some level of contemporary concern with potential conflicts of interest. From our modern perspective, it certainly appears as though the consuls' aggressive pursuit of personal profit at times must have undermined their commitment to assisting all American merchants. If the consuls were trading under their own name, they could be competitors to the very merchants who needed their assistance. Even as commission merchants to other Americans, they would have strong reasons to favor some merchants and vessels over others – particularly those that consigned their cargos to them. Beyond all this, there was the constant temptation to use their positions to their own advantage, often in quasi-legal or even illegal ways. So long as Mediterranean trade was booming these issues could frequently be overlooked. There was plenty of profit for everyone during the Napoleonic Wars, and the growth of American commerce and

---

[63] Eaton to Eliza Eaton, Feb. 15, 1802, Letterbook 1799–1802, Eaton Papers.

traders in the region that the consular network facilitated was a positive development for a new republic looking to solidify its postcolonial economy.

More fundamentally, though, the question of consular self-interest versus public interest is poorly framed and anachronistic. The very structure of the early consular service linked consular self-interest to national interest and, by doing so, to modern eyes, blurred the line between public and private, though in actuality public and private were never so opposed as they are considered to be today. So long as consuls were viewed as merchants' representatives, they and the consular service stood in a broad gray area between government and private enterprise, much like customs house officials, who were also compensated with fees and able to use their discretion on government regulations to assist local merchants during this same period. And, so long as consuls were unsalaried, they were expected to be merchants themselves, involved in trade and all of the conflicts and potential ethical issues that it entailed, even more so than customs house officials. In effect, by refusing to pay consuls, the State Department was expecting private actors (the merchant consuls) to fund a public good (the consular infrastructure). Cash-strapped American governments also employed this strategy domestically when they issued corporate charters and provided other incentives to private companies willing to fund internal improvements or build factories within the expanding territory of the United States.[64] This approach, and the lack of clear government guidelines on consular trade, guaranteed that consuls would follow their economic self-interest and attempt to profit from the booming Mediterranean market, indeed it encouraged such profit seeking. From the consular perspective, following their own self-interest could plausibly be viewed as assisting the American community as a whole, since what was good for merchant consuls was, in their view, and, arguably, in the eyes of government, also good for the development of American merchant capitalism.

---

[64] Gautham Rao, *National Duties: Custom Houses and the Making of the American* State (University of Chicago Press, 2016); Brian Murphy, *Building the Empire State: Political Economy in the Early Republic* (Philadelphia: University of Pennsylvania Press, 2015); Andrew Schocket, *Founding Corporate Power in Early National Philadelphia* (DeKalb, IL: Northern Illinois University Press, 2007); John Lauritz Larson, *Internal Improvement: National Public Works and the Promise of Popular Government in the Early United States* (Chapel Hill: University of North Carolina Press, 2001); Sean P. Adams, *Old Dominion, Industrial Commonwealth: Coal, Politics, and Economy in Antebellum America* (Baltimore: Johns Hopkins University Press, 2004); Lawrence Peskin, *Manufacturing Revolution* (Baltimore: Johns Hopkins University Press, 2003) 181–87.

7

Contact with "Others"

Race, Chauvinism, and the Notion of Empire

At the same time that the Mediterranean region promised new markets for American traders, it also provided a new cultural mosaic. Americans arriving in the region encountered large numbers of Catholics, Muslims, and Jews – groups that they would rarely if ever have encountered in the United States or the more familiar territory of Northwestern Europe. The Mediterranean, as a region, had been defined by the interaction between these three groups for centuries. Appleton's port of Livorno was well-known as a Jewish city, with Jews making up perhaps one-third of its population and strongly influencing the merchant class to which Appleton belonged. Because of trade with North Africa, Muslims also were common there, and, of course, most of the rest of the population was Catholic. Catholic Alicante was, perhaps, less cosmopolitan, but nonetheless it maintained strong connections with the nearby Islamic port of Algiers, and its harbor was still dominated by the massive Santa Barbara fortification originally constructed by Muslims in the ninth century. Tangier was a major crossroads for Catholic Spain, Protestant Gibraltar, and Islamic North Africa, and home to a sizable contingent of Jewish merchants, many of whom lived in Simpson's neighborhood. All told, life in this region would have seemed novel and exotic to Protestant North Americans and their British allies within the American trading network.

Americans abroad were not, however, always charmed by the exposure to new sorts of people. As Daniel Kilbride has noted, they were less virulently anti-Catholic during this period than they would become by the 1840s, even experiencing a degree of "Catholic envy" when contemplating European art and architecture. Nevertheless, both Appleton and

Montgomery exhibited some distaste for Catholics, who probably shared the same sentiments toward them. Appleton, in particular, clearly articulated his discomfort with the priesthood and what he perceived as the superstitious, disordered state the Italians had fallen into, which, he believed, marked a striking decline from the glories of Rome in its heyday. Similarly, Americans and their allies in North Africa, including Simpson, viewed contemporary Islam as in decline from the glory days of Carthage. Although none of the three consuls frequently discussed Jews, American representations of them at this time also perpetuated a number of negative stereotypes.[1]

While these types of condescending representations of others, particularly of Muslims, have often been labeled as orientalism and assumed to be a precursor to imperial conquest, the Americans do not seem to have had empire on their minds quite yet. Rather, they were practicing a sort of defensive chauvinism rooted more in fear that these seemingly unreliable, yet at times disturbingly powerful people, might be able to impede American trade in the region – the very trade that bound together the American network and which consuls were pledged to protect.

***

One of the best indicators of Americans' discomfort with Catholics is the uniform absence of intermarriages during the first decades of the Mediterranean network. As noted above, there is no evidence of a single marriage to native Catholics by the Americans in Alicante or Livorno during this period. There is also a good deal of evidence of delayed marriages, suggesting the need to wait for a suitable Protestant spouse. While Catholics were never particularly welcoming of unions with Protestants, such marriages were possible, and certainly did occur in later decades as longtime residents of the Mediterranean became less uncomfortable with Catholics. The fact that the Montgomerys' roots were in northern Ireland where Catholics and Protestants were in constant contact may have heightened their resistance to intermarriage. Appleton's

---

[1] Daniel Kilbride, *Being American in Europe, 1750–1860* (Baltimore: Johns Hopkins University Press, 2013); Christine Heyrman, *American Apostles: When Evangelicals Entered the World of Islam* (New York; Hill and Wang, 2015); Emily Conroy-Krutz, *Christian Imperialism: Converting the World in the Early American Republic* (Ithaca: Cornell University Press, 2015); Karine V. Walther, *Sacred Interests: The United States and the Islamic World, 1821–1921* (Chapel Hill: University of North Carolina Press, 2015); Lawrence Peskin, "From Shylocks to Unbelievers: Early National Views of 'Oriental' Jews," *Journal of the Early Republic* 39 (Summer, 2019) 267–98.

Puritan Massachusetts origins would have led to similarly strong prejudices. The fact that Appleton's brother, John, returned to New England from France to find a second wife after his first died rather than consider a French spouse, provides further evidence of the Appletons' discomfort with intermarriage. But even more telling is Appleton's apparent refusal to inform his own family of his eventual union with a Catholic woman years later.

Nevertheless, Americans who lived in the Catholic Mediterranean made Catholic friends, although such friendships sometimes took on an air of condescension. This was particularly evident in the fairly common occurrences of Americans attempting to ship European acquaintances off to the United States for their betterment. Montgomery's son-in-law John Rogers sent Anthony Minguillis, a young Spaniard whom Rogers seems to have adopted as a protégé, to America to be educated so that he could be "of use to himself and his friends." He may have done the same for John Morand of Denia, a nearby coastal town. Young Morand, like Minguillis, went to the United States to obtain an education at an academy near Newburyport, Massachusetts. The proximity to Rogers' American family suggests that, as with Minguillis, the young American may have played a part in sending Morand to the United States. Montgomery hoped to send a local farmer to America to provide information on Spanish farming secrets (perhaps sheep) but discovered that "from ignorance of his own" the Spaniard "made the matter so publick" that the authorities would no longer let him go.[2]

Consuls also frequently made enemies, often as a result of their contempt for local Catholic officials. Montgomery, who claimed to be friendly with all the leading men in Alicante, had a long-running feud with the governor, Don Josef Betegon. A number of policy issues initially sparked the animosity, which erupted into full flame during a chance encounter on the street in the summer of 1808 when Montgomery determined the governor's "looks were unusually insulting." As a result, the consul "could not help smiling with contempt," prompting the governor to turn and "violently [call] out, 'What sort of breeding have you that does not pull off your hat to the governor?'" to which Montgomery replied,

---

[2] Robert Montgomery to Thomas Pinckney, Feb. 18, 1796, Alicante Despatches; John B. Morand to John Rogers, Jr., June 22, 1806; John H. Rogers to John Rogers, Jr., Nov. 1, 1805; Feb. 20, 1806; Jan. 20, 1808; May 15, 1808, all in Rogers-Bridges Family Collection. Despite their Irish name, the Morands were from France, suggesting they were probably Irish Catholic merchants doing business in Spain.

"My breeding is as good as yours, the governor did not pull off his hat too, so must I pull off my hat first?" At this point the governor ordered Montgomery arrested, to which he replied, "You have no power to arrest me and I shall not go without an armed force."[3]

William and Samuel Purviance, the naval agents in Livorno, showed similar contempt for local authorities they deemed inferior to themselves, much to Appleton's distress. According to Appleton they "outrageously insulted" the town's health officers repeatedly, and William once barged into the governor's chamber and "spoke in an unbecoming manner," and, as noted in Chapter 4, later threatened him physical harm. Such apparent contempt for local officials no doubt went with the territory in an age of prickly honor codes and in a place where multiple cultures, each with their own codes, came into contact. American officers seem to have been particularly tied to honor codes, and duels between them were generally seen to be acceptable expressions of conflict. Nevertheless, the ferocity and undiplomatic reactions of these American diplomats and officials suggests that these particular Catholic governors and officials, at least, may have been deemed less worthy of respect and less equal than some others.[4]

It is unlikely that Appleton would have viewed himself as anti-Catholic, even before his conversion, but, like many elite Catholics, he was certainly anticlerical. His time as a young man in Paris was formative. While in Paris, he had many French friends with whom he remained in contact for years and about whom he frequently expressed concern while living in Livorno. Some were Catholic and some were Protestant, but what nearly all had in common was that they ran in scientific and pro-Revolution circles. Paris represented the epitome of enlightenment to Appleton. He once wrote a business partner, "Paris to my mind contains whatever constitutes human happiness . . . . The man who is in pursuit of sciences or the man of pleasure will there find abundant [*sic*] to gratify his desires."[5] In Livorno, too, he had Catholic friends of a similar stripe. Most notable was the French consul Mathieu de Lesseps who was married to Catherine Grivegnée of Málaga. He was a prominent Napoleonic loyalist and ran in scientific circles. His son, Ferdinand, would become

---

[3] Montgomery to Sec. State, Oct. 15, 1808; Mar. 1, 1809, both in Alicante Despatches.

[4] Entries for Sept. 9, 1802; May 25, 1805; Aug. 4, 1805, Register of Events; James E. Valle, *Rocks and Shoals: Naval Discipline in the Age of Fighting Sail* (Annapolis: Naval Institute Press, 1980) 137.

[5] Thomas Appleton to Louis DuPouy, June 26, 1801, GL.

famous for developing the Suez Canal.[6] Appleton also admired Philip Mazzei, the prominent Tuscan surgeon and revolutionist who was a good friend to Thomas Jefferson, and he was fond of a number of skilled Italian artisans, including some sculptors, a harpist, and a scientist who wanted to translate Jefferson's *Notes on Virginia*.[7] Appleton liked these Italians because he valued scientific and artistic knowledge. In this regard he viewed himself as what we might call an Enlightenment figure. He passed on the latest and best geographical and economic information on the Black Sea region to Washington. He presented a copy of his correspondent Thomas Jefferson's *Notes on Virginia* to the Florentine Academy of Agriculture and supported its translation into Italian. He frequently exchanged books on subjects such as the Greek archipelago, physiognomy, Etruscan vases, proper diet, and the works of the dramatist Alexis Piron.[8]

In contrast to France, Italy for Appleton was a country in deep decline, nothing like it had been during the glory days of the Roman Empire. "Italy," he wrote to Barlow, "offers few of the charms we have pictured to ourselves from history." The cause was not only the fall of Rome but the rise of the Catholic Church. "When one sees the columns of Trajan and of Antonin surmounted by saints," he continued in his letter to Barlow, "and the tomb of Adrian converted into a prison for the inquisition, the Pantheon melted down to decorate Gothick churches, or what is in my mind something worse, those of more modern architecture, when you find the inquisition taking the place of the Roman senate, and popes holding power without possessing the virtues of the Roman consuls: I say I am sure you will join me in a sentiment that, although it may excite a laudable curiosity, it nevertheless fills the mind with the utmost indignation."[9]

As that screed makes clear, Appleton's problem with Italy and Catholic Italians was rooted in Enlightenment distrust of organized religion generally, and with the pope specifically. In this respect he was very similar to his boss and correspondent, Thomas Jefferson, who wrote that "the degrading ignorance into which their priests and kings have sunk them"

[6] Colin Carlin, *William Kirkpatrick of Malaga* (Glasgow: Colin Carlin, 2011) 33–35.

[7] Appleton to Robert Fagan, [Jan. 1804]; to Mr. Fabroni, Mar. 21, 1805; Apr. 12, 1807; to Mr. Hammersley, May 5, 1805; to M de la Trobe, Nov. 18, 1805; to Robert Purviance, Nov. 17, 1805, all in GL.

[8] Appleton to J. Biddulph, July 10, 1801; to Mr. Partridge, Nov. 16, 1801; to Rvd. Parson Hall, Apr. 10, 1805; to Mdm. Deguis, June 30, 1806; to Biddulph, July 7, 1806, all in GL.

[9] Appleton to Joel Barlow, Apr. 22, 1801, GL.

had "disqualified" Latin Americans "from the maintenance or even knowledge of their rights."[10] Appleton's letters and his reports were suffused with anticlericalism and swipes at the pope. He articulated his concerns largely in republican terms arguing that the Church essentially supported a corrupt, tyrannical establishment. He wrote in despair to Joseph Pitcairn, US consul to Hamburg, that "It is difficult to see the future destiny of this wretched country, where the violence and avarice of its conquerors have been less destructive than the pernicious influence of its priests."[11]

He also seethed at the 1801 concordant between Napoleon and the Church, complaining of its secrecy and suggesting that Napoleon ceded too much to the pope. The treaty, he reported to the secretary of state, "could not have been more effectually concealed had it ever been fabricated in the inquisitorial tribunal of Rome," and he speculated that "it may arise only from that general desire of the Church of Rome to envelop all their proceedings under the veil of mystery." He approved of the king of Tuscany's efforts to deprive priests of the ability to censure the press and to make them "amenable for their crimes in common with the rest of his subjects." Hence, he was disappointed when he perceived the new king was reestablishing clerical prerogatives including, "the right of censure on the press, tribunals of inquisition with all the train of church priviledge." This was "an act which though it may forfeit him the esteem of one part of the community, has nevertheless acquired him powerful advocates in another."[12] In short, the roots of Appleton's anticlericalism were visible in what he saw as the secrecy, "inquisitorial" intolerance, and tyranny of the Church and the contrast to the Enlightenment ideals he had imbibed in France and to the positive view of the ancient Roman Republic he, like many Americans, carried with him.

Like many followers of the Enlightenment, Appleton also had a hypersexualized view of the Catholic Church based, in part, on popular views of nuns and convents. When giving his American friend Joseph Grant advice for touring Florence, Appleton opened with a dirty story about a young nun who died due to infection from a needle in her genitals. He recommended Grant view the needle and petrified flesh while in Florence. He then went on to recommend a Florentine acquaintance

---

[10] Jay Sexton, *The Monroe Doctrine: Empire and Nation in Nineteenth-Century America* (New York: Hill and Wang, 2012) 38.

[11] Appleton to Joseph Pitcairn, Nov. 2, 1801, GL.

[12] Thomas Appleton to Sec. State, June 1, 1802, Leghorn Despatches.

who was familiar with "the most secret and scandalous anecdotes of every man and woman in Florence" and who "will initiate you in one hour in the important love matters of Florence, more than all the books of [Tirso de] Molina in a year."[13] Appleton made no mention of any other worthwhile attractions in Florence, probably because the sites we favor today – cathedrals, Renaissance museums, and so forth – were associated with the Church. In short, Catholic Florence (as opposed to remnants of ancient Rome) held few attractions other than the possibility of novel sexual adventures.

***

American attitudes toward Islam and Muslims have received a great deal of scholarly treatment in recent years due to contemporary concerns with the Islamic world and interest in the Barbary Wars. Most scholars understand Americans to have been quite hostile to supposedly "barbaric" Muslims, though recently Christine Heyrman has argued that Protestant American missionaries may have found more to admire in North African Muslims than in Catholics.[14] Appleton, Montgomery, and Simpson all interacted frequently with Muslims as would just about anyone in the Mediterranean region. For all three, but most notably Appleton and Montgomery, the primary context for interaction with Muslims was their efforts to prevent or redeem ship captures. Clearly this context was not one that produced kindly feelings of brotherhood.

Appleton, who was not thrilled that Livorno's population included many "Turks," spent a good deal of his time warning American captains and the State Department of potential attacks from North African corsairs. Hence it is not surprising that he frequently referred to North Africans as "barbarians." At one point during the Barbary Wars, he accused Commodore Edward Preble of naivety when he assumed that

---

[13] Appleton to John Grant, May 30, 1805, GL. Molina was author of the racy Don Juan play, "The Trickster of Seville."

[14] Christine Leigh Heyrman, *American Apostles: When Evangelicals Entered the World of Islam* (New York: Hill and Wang, 2015); Emily Conroy-Krutz, *Christian Imperialism: Converting the World in the Early American Republic* (Ithaca: Cornell University Press, 2015); Karine V. Walther, *Sacred Interests: The United States and the Islamic World, 1821–1921* (Chapel Hill: University of North Carolina Press, 2015); Fuad Sha'ban, *For Zion's Sake: The Judeo-Christian Tradition in American Culture* (Ann Arbor: Pluto Press, 2005); Timothy Marr, *The Cultural Roots of American Islamicism* (Cambridge University Press, 2006); Jeffrey Einboden, *Jefferson's Muslim Fugitives* (Oxford University Press, 2020); Denise A. Spellberg, *Thomas Jefferson's Qur'an: Islam and the Founders* (New York: Vantage Books, 2013).

"barbarians" from Tripoli would provide good treatment to American prisoners so long as the United States acted reciprocally with their Tripolitan prisoners. Appleton explained, "I am inclined to think our commander has not been apprised of a maxim of the Bey, to wit, that if a Musselman surrenders himself to a Christian, he merits every species of inhumanity that the latter may please to inflict upon him." Yet, more frequently, he saved his ire for the Catholic European powers – for example, when he wrote that the vexations against US vessels by Spanish ships were "really more despicable than the barbarians inasmuch as they have not the frankness to avow their infamous intentions."[15]

Unlike Appleton, both Montgomery and Simpson dealt directly with Islamic North African officials, and, to varying degrees, staked their professional reputations on their ability to negotiate with them. As a result of this personal interaction and the need to persuade often-powerful Islamic officials to come to agreements with them, both consuls tended to be more conciliatory toward and less condemnatory of Muslims. Alicante was particularly close to Algeria via Mediterranean shipping routes, and, consequently, Montgomery had a good deal of experience with that country. He was involved in efforts to protect the city's shipping from Algerian cruisers in 1783. When seeking an appointment as envoy to Algiers in the early 1790s he claimed to have many contacts in Algiers, including men "of importance and of good influence [with the] Divan so that I can be well introduced to the minister." When the old Dey died in 1791, he again pursued the appointment noting that the new ruler was an old friend. In short, while he was not above labelling the Africans "pirates," Montgomery did not vilify them as a group, nor would it have been easy to do so while at the same time touting his connections and ability to work with them.[16]

Much the same could be said of Simpson. From his home in Gibraltar, he had constant contact with Moroccan officials located across the Strait. He based his reputation on his knowledge of and ability to negotiate with

[15] Appleton to Marquise de Chastellux, Mar. 17, 1802; to J. Barnes, n.d. [Aug. 1804]; to Pitcairn, Nov. 2, 1801; n.d.; to Livingston, Apr. 18, 1804, all in GL.
[16] Dn. Roberto Montgomery Fiansa por Dn. Alejandro Gozpoll y otros May 6, 1783; May 12, 1783; Salvador Blanes fianza a favor de Roberto Montgomery, July 22, 1783, all in Protocolo Notarial de Antonio Espinoza, PN (Note: "Protocolo de Notariales" (notarial notebooks) are identified by name of the notary and date in the archives throughout this chapter); Robert Montgomery to John Jay, Aug. 5, 1788, Jefferson Papers; Robert Montgomery to Sec. State, July 24, 1791; July 26, 1791, both in Alicante Despatches.

these Muslim elites, and his appointment to the consulate in Tangier
reflected the US government's faith in these abilities. He rarely denigrated
Muslims in Tangier, never using the standard "barbarian" or "savage"
appellations to describe his neighbors that Appleton and others further
from the scene employed. Even when he was forcibly detained by
Tangier's governor during a period of delicate negotiations, he termed
the detention "a gross insult, which none but a person of [the governor's]
rude manners would have been guilty of," but fell well short of applying
the usual derogatory racialized epithets.[17]

However, when it came to Moroccans living in the interior portion of
the country, Simpson and others were far less polite. Although Simpson
had little personal experience with these Moroccans, often referred to as
Arabs, his role as consul put him at the center of the Arab–American
encounter, eventually making him a minor print celebrity as a character
in James Riley's best-selling captivity narrative. While Simpson was
consul, six well-publicized shipwrecks (five American ships, including
Riley's, and one Spanish ship with American crew members) occurred on
the Atlantic coast along a portion of the Sahara Desert, which lay along
a dangerous and poorly mapped passage between mainland Africa and
the Cape Verde islands. The captains of these ships, like others before
them, assumed that they were passing to the west of the islands, when in
fact they were on the east and dangerously close to the mainland. All
told, at least fifty-three American seamen were involved in these unfortunate events spanning the years from 1800 to 1816, and all were held
for a time as captives by Moroccan Arabs.[18] Simpson's writings do not
reveal as much about his attitudes toward these interior Moroccans as
one might like, but the three published narratives and a number of letters
written about these incidents by American captives provide a wealth of
material from which to tease out American attitudes. Simpson was
closely tied to all of these authors. He was ultimately responsible for
ransoming them and returning them to the United States. He interacted
with all of them, was mentioned in the two narratives published during
his lifetime and undoubtedly read them. Taken together, then, these
accounts can also be understood to amplify Simpson's rare statements

---

[17] James Simpson to Sec. State, Sept. 5, 1803, Tangier Despatches.
[18] The wrecks were *Oswego* (June 1800), *Betsy* (June 1802), *Indefatigable* (Mar. 1806),
Charles (Oct. 1811), and *Commerce* (Nov. 1815). The Spanish ship was wrecked in Sept.
1816. All are detailed in Tangier Despatches.

on the subject and to provide a reflection not only of American attitudes toward Moroccan Muslims but of Simpson's as well.[19]

Ever diplomatic, Simpson did not often vent his emotions, even during these captivity crises. His ire only rarely became apparent, and even at his most exercised he was careful to delineate between the Islamic residents of the port cities whom he generally referred to as Moors and the so-called Arabs in the desert who captured the American sailors. Simpson made the distinction between supposedly barbarous Arabs and coastal Moors most explicitly when reporting that one of the captives had been punished severely for striking a Muslim, an offense "which even in this more civilized country of Barbarism [i.e., Tangier] is held to be a most heinous crime in any Christian." Though it is important to note here that Simpson was actually siding with the Muslim against the Christian receiving the punishment, Simpson's description of Tangier as a more civilized yet still barbarous country offers rare insight into how he seems to have viewed Moroccans on a sliding scale of barbarity/civilization. At other times, he described the desert nomads as "merciless savages" living in a "barbarous" country. Unlike their more civilized brethren they were "banditti" living in "a state of total insubordination" who could not even be relied on to return wrecked Christian seamen through the usual sorts of diplomatic arrangements.[20]

The accounts written by the American captives all read like Conrad's *Heart of Darkness* in reverse as they follow a voyage from savagery and barbarism to Simpson's house in the "more civilized country of Barbarism." The very landscape they described marked this progression. All the authors expressed fear and despair at being forced to leave the ocean, which for them represented safety and a clear connection to their world of commerce and navigation. The desert land on which they wrecked was "dreadful" – rocky, perpendicular, sweltering and bone dry. The earlier portions of the narratives all deal with the horrible "suffering" as they attempt to march across this desert. As they come nearer to "civilized" society, the land becomes softer and literally more cultivated, providing, at first, scattered signs of settled agriculture and then, around Wadenoon (modern day Port of Tan Tan in Guelmin-Oued

---

[19] The three published accounts are Judah Paddock, *A Narrative of the Shipwreck of the* Oswego (London, 1818); James Riley, *An Authentic Narrative of the Loss of the American Brig* Commerce (Hartford, 1817); and Archibald Robbins, *A Journal Concerning an Account of the Loss of the Brig* Comerce (Hartford, 1849).

[20] Simpson to Messrs. Wm. Court etc., June 24, 1800, Simpson NARA; Simpson to Sec State, Jan. 22, 1815; Mar. 27, 1806, both in Tangier Despatches.

Noun) they saw irrigated gardens. Finally, as they near the southern cities of Santa Cruz (Agadir) and Mogador (Essaouira) they see more impressive and greener settled fields with fruit trees and abundant livestock. They know that Santa Cruz marks the beginning of the king of Morocco's dominion, and all are relieved that they are leaving what they view as the lawless Arab territories for the relatively more civilized rule of law. At Mogador, they know they have reached the gateway to civilization when they view large numbers of modern sailing ships. The joy at the first sight of shipping nearly "produced delirium" among Archibald Robbins's companions and caused Judah Paddock to lose his power of speech.[21]

In all accounts, the people of the desert matched the savagery of the landscape. All the sailors were clearly amazed and intrigued by the variety and exotic nature of the inhabitants. Details of race and color occupied a good deal of their thought and their accounts often read like amateur anthropology. All were terrified by their initial encounters with the people that they usually described as "wandering Arabs." It did not help that these first encounters generally involved the Arabs flashing sharp knives at their captives, who initially feared they were to be stabbed to death – though the knives were used more for intimidation and to cut off the prisoners' clothing. Paddock described these people as "savage barbarians" and suspected that they had murdered a group of Europeans based on his early discovery of human skeletons in the desert. James Riley thought his captor's face "resembled that of an ourang-outang more than a human being." Robbins, the most anthropologically minded of the three, discerned "something of humanity" in them but nevertheless described his captors in animalistic terms, noting "gnashing teeth," "opened mouths," "red flashing eyes," and the "terrible appearance of their ferocious brood."[22]

Their anthropological ruminations led the captives to consider the origins of their captors. Robbins assumed they were descendants of Ishmael, though he also compared some of their behavior to "American savages." Riley also was reminded of Indians, noting his captor's complexion was "between that of an American Indian and Negro." Rather than Ishmaelites, the wandering Arabs reminded him of the biblical Jewish patriarchs "who also lived in tents, and wandered about from place to place [and] ... owned slaves." Paddock described their posture as

---

[21] Robbins, *A Journal*, 105, 248; Paddock, *A Narrative*, 292.
[22] Paddock, *A Narrative*, 65; Riley, *An Authentic Narrative*, 33; Robbins, *A Journal*, 68, 25–26.

"straight as any American Indian."[23] All of these observations were similar to American reactions to the natives of their recently acquired trans-Mississippi desert territory and to depictions of Native Americans as noble savages and possible descendants of the lost tribes of Israel. It is easy to see how the Americans mapped a desert with which they were a bit more familiar onto the strange place where they had landed.

Even when, as in Robbins's case, these Americans saw signs of humanity in the wandering Arabs, they understood them to be savages. This understanding accorded with the view that Anglo-Americans had often taken of Native Americans. They might be noble; they might be descendants of ancient Jews and have once had a great civilization, but they were most definitely *not* Christian, and therefore neither modern nor civilized. In turn, encounters in North Africa were a factor in shaping the racialized rhetoric of manifest destiny that justified expelling Native Americans from the trans-Mississippi West.[24] These encounters also brought out generalized condemnations of Islam on the part of the captives. Robbins contrasted the "imposter" Mohammed to the "religion introduced" by Jesus which taught "peace on earth, and good will to men . . . [and] to check the operation of passion and depraved nature." By contrast, he wrote Islam's "Paradise is a region of gluttony, drunkenness and debauchery." While, according to Robbins, Christianity teaches its followers "to feed the hungry and clothe the naked," Islam taught the Arabs "to tear from the unfortunate being in their power, the last piece of raiment that guards him from inclemency of the seasons." He also viewed Islam as hypocritical, noting that the Arabs and all other Muslims prostrate themselves to God three or four times a day "lest their violations of common justice be ever so enormous" and "the next moment after this ceremony is ended" the slave cannot feel safe "from a stroke of the scimitar, the spear, the club."[25]

As the Americans moved toward the more cultivated lands around the area they knew as Wadenoon they also found the residents to be more cultivated. At Wadenoon, Robbins noted, "the ingenuity of laying out gardens here must excite the admiration of every beholder." Nearby, he expressed some admiration for the "Shilluh" (Shilka) people whom he described as exhibiting "great superiority" over "all the other races of

---

[23] Riley, *An Authentic Narrative*, 373, 33; Paddock, *A Narrative*, 70.
[24] On the connection between overseas encounters and manifest destiny, see Brian Rouleau, *With Sails Whitening Every Sea: Mariners and the Making of an American Maritime Empire* (Ithaca: Cornell University Press, 2015) 74–101.
[25] Robbins, *A Journal*, 81–82, 87.

Mahometans in Africa." He noted that they were "lighter in complexion than the Arabs and speak a language so different, that they cannot understand each other." Like other Muslims though, they practiced a defective religion in his view. "They seem to want nothing but the benign influence of Christianity, to render them a most esteemable race of men," he wrote. Riley, too, expressed admiration for these light-skinned ("tawny colored") people, who are descended from Berbers, the early settlers of Morocco and the broader Maghreb. He described them as "very industrious," particularly in their clever agricultural methods.[26]

As they approached Santa Cruz and the Moroccan kingdom, the Americans began to encounter people they described as "Moors." Robbins conflated Arabs and Moors, describing the latter as "Mahometan Arabs." But, generally, Moors seemed to represent a higher degree of civilization for them, as they did for Simpson. Both Riley and Paddock described them as relatively fair skinned – "olive" or "light copper" colored. Riley sometimes differentiated between "Moorish Arabs" who appeared fairly similar to "wandering Arabs" and their more urban counterparts. He described one of the latter as a "very respectable looking man" who bade the captives "to sit down in a shade formed by his wall and rest ourselves." Paddock was very grateful for assistance from the governor of Santa Cruz, a Moor whose "pleasing, manly look prepossessed me in his favour." These Moors' facility with European languages such as English and Spanish, combined with the power they wielded in Morocco differentiated them from the other Islamic denizens of the region in the eyes of the Americans.[27]

Much of this anthropological approach calls to mind Edward Said's discussion of orientalism among European intellectuals. No doubt the American writers also were influenced by that discourse on some level, whether by reading orientalist accounts of the region in preparing their own work or just gaining the viewpoint through discussions with other westerners. This perspective also accorded well with their knowledge of American Indians and the western frontier in their own country. But in other ways – particularly the relatively kind view of Moors and especially elite Moors – their viewpoint also aligns with David Cannadine's description of "Ornamentalism," which posits a Western class-based response to Middle Eastern and other non-Western people in which the elite are

---

[26] *Ibid.* 201, 238–39; Riley, *An Authentic Narrative*, 325.
[27] Robbins, *A Journal*, 39; Paddock, *A Narrative*, 248–49; Riley, *An Authentic Narrative*, 159–60, 176.

seen as far more equal to Westerners than the masses.[28] This notion certainly seems to accord with Simpson's efforts to distinguish between varying levels of "barbarism" within the diverse Islamic world of North Africa, and helps explain Simpson's and other consuls' general acceptance of powerful Muslims.

The captivity crises also provided a rare view of Americans of color in the broader Mediterranean. No doubt a number of American merchants and diplomats, like Thomas Jefferson, brought slaves with them when they traveled into the Mediterranean, and it is well known that African-Americans were well represented on the ships that entered into foreign ports, but by and large these individuals remain the invisible people of the American Mediterranean community. The Americans' heightened sensitivity toward race in Morocco briefly brought a few of these usually invisible men into the historic record. There were at least six Black American crew members among the captives. Additionally, the Americans met and mentioned other Western people of color along their route, as well as free and enslaved sub-Saharan Africans. Robbins viewed North Africans and sub-Saharan Africans as all of the same race and marveled that North Africans had Black slaves. "It is singular," he observed, "that the Negros, although Africans like the Arabs, should even by their own countrymen, although of a different tribe, be used with such barbarity." He added, "This miserable race of beings seems to be left by their creator to the cruelty of the whole human race." At another point he observed that, "Africans, of every name and feature and complexion, take delight in enslaving each other."[29]

These observations led to antislavery discussions. The Americans, who tended to oppose slavery, assumed that their Black companions would be treated worse than white sailors in captivity. Americans often noticed that Black captives were singled out for particularly harsh treatment by their Arab captors. Paddock tried to intercede when the Arabs refused to send two of the Black crew members to Mogadore for redemption by insisting the consul would redeem them, but the Arabs, who may well have understood Western racism, refused to believe him, and the group was separated, never to be reunited. "The poor negroes wept bitterly, and for our own part we were sorely afflicted with the parting," Paddock wrote. Paddock's companion and possible servant, Dick, was also separated

[28] Edward Said, *Orientalism* (New York: Vintage, 1979); David Cannadine, *Ornamentalism: How the British Saw Their Empire* (New York: Oxford, 2002).
[29] Robbins, *A Journal*, 119, 91.

from the group but not before promising he should hold onto some valuable cloth for Paddock's wife. When, much later, Paddock discovered the cloth, but no sign of Dick, he was so powerfully affected by his remembrance of Dick's assistance and probable death, that he "could not refrain from turning aside, and giving vent to my anguish in a flood of tears." At first Robbins thought a different Dick, the *Commerce*'s Black cook, was receiving better treatment from the Arabs than his white counterparts, but witnessing an episode in which his master administered a savage beating to Dick had Robbins so angry that he had never "more ardently pant[ed] to revenge the injury of a shipmate." In the end, though, he was unable to help and later learned that Dick had likely been left to die.[30]

On the other hand, the Americans, who were all familiar with racial inequality, often suspected that, despite receiving harsh treatment, Black seamen might prefer staying in Morocco rather than returning home to a land of slavery. Paddock and his companions had met three Black "boys" – former English seamen – who served as translators. Paddock would have liked to rescue them, but apparently their captors anticipated "through despair of being ransomed [they] might at last embrace the faith of those Mahometans and spend their remaining days with them." At least one of the three, Jack, did just that. When given the opportunity to recant in Mogadore, he refused and explained, "He did it because he believed the condition of the Mahometans to be preferable to that of Christians; that if he should continue in the religion he had adopted he should see God and be saved; whereas the Christians were all to be damned." Robbins thought this speech had been coached by the Arabs but, given the life prospects for Black men in the British Caribbean or in a British ship, Jack may have chosen the safer course.[31]

In Tangier, Simpson also suspected that African-Americans might be tempted to remain behind. While Paddock's crew waited for two of their Black shipmates to be redeemed, he wrote, "Perhaps the two negroes remained at the place Captain Paddock describes, may wish to continue with the Arabs; at all events there can be no need to detain in this country those we may be able to release until the others can be recovered." His attitude toward these two men certainly differs sharply from his own and other Americans' usual conviction that all Americans must be rescued as expeditiously as possible from captivity. The fact that none of the

[30] Paddock, *A Narrative*, 115, 264; Robbins, *A Journal*, 115, 118–19.
[31] Paddock, *A Narrative*, 313, 335–37.

American officials or officers seems to have made more of an effort to locate them and ascertain whether they were safe also points to a double standard. On the other hand, Simpson and other Americans may not have been wrong to assume that their African-American companions might prefer to take their chances in Morocco rather than return to the antebellum United States. Two years later, Simpson wrote that "by every account I have been able to trace of them," the two men "voluntarily remained with the Arabs and got married." Whether true or just a rationalization for failing to free these two, the fact that it seemed logical to Simpson that they might wish to remain behind powerfully reflects the duality of African-American identity in the Mediterranean community.[32]

***

The third exotic group with which Americans in the Mediterranean frequently had contact was Jews. While there were large populations of Jews in North Africa and Italy, Americans most often came into contact with the small merchant class. These wealthier individuals often served as financial and cultural intermediaries between the Europeans on the Mediterranean's northern shore and the Africans on the southern littoral. Americans became particularly familiar with them during the various captivity crises from 1784 to 1815 when state- sponsored North African cruisers held American crews and their ships for ransom. Typically, Jewish merchants, most famously Algeria's Bacri family, served as financial go-betweens as Americans negotiated with the North African governments. As such they were generally despised and often viewed within the context of age-old Shylock stereotypes.[33]

Two of the most vociferous critics of North African Jews were Appleton's associates and fellow consuls, James Cathcart and William Eaton. Their discussions of Jews dealt in frequently nasty Shylock analogies as well as occasional references to "Christ killers." Living in Livorno, Appleton had contact with the many Jewish merchants there, including members of the originally Livornese Bacri family, and they were also his business competitors and occasional associates. Despite, or perhaps because of, this proximity, he did not share his companions' extreme

---

[32] Simpson to Messrs. Wm. Court etc., June 24, 1800, Simpson NARA; Simpson to Sec. State, Sept. 3, 1802, Tangier Despatches.

[33] Lawrence Peskin, "From Shylocks to Unbelievers: Early National Views of 'Oriental' Jews," *Journal of the Early Republic* (Summer, 2019) 267–98; Morton Rosenstock, "The House of Bacri and Busnach: A Chapter from Algeria's Commercial History," *Jewish Social Studies* 14 (Oct. 1952) 343–64.

hostility. At most he displayed a genteel disdain toward them. When complaining about Livornese social life to his friend Madame Chastellux, he explained, "I pass the life of a hermit without the tranquility, for [Livorno] is composed of Jews, Turks, and what is still more unsupportable than either, by Jewish Christians." While many critics, including Eaton and Cathcart, viewed Jewish merchants as overly aggressive, at one point Appleton complained of their passivity, noting that "their fears in commerce equals their hope of the coming of the messiah, and we believe, my friend, neither will be realized." He also joked with a potential business partner that he was hoping for him to agree to a deal with Appleton, but if he should decide to work with others it would not bother him, "for even if they should be Jews, I shall not (be assured) be jealous of the preference."[34]

The city of Tangier and specifically Simpson's immediate neighborhood, had a very sizable Jewish population. There is no record of Simpson's opinions about these neighbors, but his interactions appear to have been friendly. Because the American house was so tiny, Simpson could not keep many guests there. He had no compunctions against renting rooms for his visiting son from a Jewish neighbor.[35] He also had a long-time Jewish servant. Her marriage was noted by Simpson's neighbor, Wyk, suggesting that she was well-liked by the consular community.[36]

Simpson also encountered Jews, frequently in conjunction with the shipwrecked Americans. Once again Jews served as intermediaries, this time between the Arab captors and those redeeming the captives, including Simpson, his vice-consul, and merchants in Mogadore. Simpson could be condescending, sometimes referring to these intermediaries as "my" Jews. He felt that they drove the price of redemption up, noting that "Fifty dollars a man would satisfy the Arabs, but if the business of Jews and others purchasing Christians be not checked, some of us will one day be thrown into a very unpleasant predicament." These concerns culminated with an order from the Moroccan emperor to execute a Jew who had been recalcitrant in giving up two members of the *Indefatigable*'s crew. This man, Simpson was told, was arrested and lay in chains in a Mogadore jail for some time until "the governor received an order from the emperor . . . to convey him to the waterside and there cut off his head as a warning for

[34] Appleton to Marquise de Chastellux, Mar. 17, 1802; to Alan Melville, Nov. 17, 1801; to Anthony Dugan [Jan. 1815], all in GL.
[35] Riley, *An Authentic Narrative*, 517.
[36] Entry for Jan. 10, 1809, Konsulatarkiv.

the Jews not to buy Christians." Simpson averred that, "This was a severe punishment," but added, "[I]t will, I trust, be followed by happy consequences to those Christians who may at a future day have the misfortune to be shipwrecked on the coast of Wednon."[37]

Although some of the American captives developed negative feelings for Jews, by and large they were happy to see them. From Simpson's perspective, safely ensconced in his consular house in Tangier, Jewish mediators may have seemed like grasping opportunists representing the "savage" Arabs, but in the harsh, uncultivated desert the captives saw them as welcome representatives of civilization. For one thing, unlike their captors and most of the Muslims they met, many Jews could speak European languages, including English. The first helpful person Paddock met in Mogadore was an English-speaking Jew. Riley was assisted by an English-speaking interpreter, whom he once approvingly described as a "cunning Jew," as well as a Russian Jewish doctor who "spoke Spanish fluently." He was also assisted by the Livornese-born British consul in Rabat, who, "though a Jew, was nevertheless a man of feeling and much of a gentleman."[38]

Unlike Simpson, the American seamen often came face to face with poor Jews living in impoverished, isolated communities. They felt a good deal of sympathy for these Jews, both because of their poverty and because they seemed to be fellow victims of Arab "savagery." At Wadenoon Robbins noted, "A Jew is esteemed but little higher than a Christian, although they are never enslaved." Jews there "stood in awe of both Moors and Arabs." Similarly, in a nearby village he noted, "there were many of these children of Israel in this place, as in all others, despised and abused." Riley also included an extended description of the "miserable dirty" Jews in the smallish community of Safi. Robbins echoed the theme of fallen glory that characterized Appleton's view of the current Italians when he reported being particularly touched that the "once favored people of Heaven should humble themselves before the descendants of Ishmael, the most despised and degraded of all the ancient children of Abraham."[39]

The most evident example of the Jews' fallen state was the oppression that the Americans viewed them suffering from Muslims. All three authors

---

[37] Simpson to Messrs. Wm. Court etc., June 24, 1800; to Peter Gwyn, Aug. 19, 1800, both in Simpson NARA; Simpson to Sec. State, Apr. 17, 1808, Tangier Despatches.

[38] Paddock, *A Narrative*, 303; Riley, *An Authentic Narrative*, 255, 257, 351–52, 419–20.

[39] Riley, *An Authentic Narrative*, 391; Robbins, *A Journal*, 215–16, 237–38.

related stories demonstrating this oppression ranging from laws requiring Jews to remove their shoes in certain places and other regulations regarding dress to disturbing physical violence against Jews in Mogadore as they were forced to pay tribute to Muslim overlords. Considering the captives' position, these passages should be read as much for their condemnation of Muslim tyranny as for any sympathy with the Jews. Riley noted, "the Jews in West Barbary are as completely under the control of the Moors as if they were slaves."[40]

For all the Americans' sympathy for the "enslaved" Jews, gratitude to Europeanized Jews and anthropological interest in Jewish rites and customs, Riley also presented an undertone of distrust of Jews based on Western tropes of the perfidious Jews emerging from Christianity and English literature, most obviously the Shylock narrative. This may be because Riley spent the most time in Morocco of any of the authors, and he spent a good deal of it travelling with Jews and in the various Jewish quarters of Moroccan towns. By the latter stages of his journey, he had become quite disenchanted with Jews in general and his specific Jewish traveling companions. As he neared Simpson's consulate in Tangier, he determined "to proceed without my Jew's company, whom I had found out to be deceitful and dishonest, having already manoevered me out of most of my money." Nevertheless, on leaving Tangier for home he once again had Jewish fellow passengers, this time European Jews who had been expelled by the emperor for refusing to pay tribute and conform to Moroccan dress codes. Their friends who came out to wish them farewell were beaten by Moors with sticks "with such singular dexterity peculiar to the Moors, as to lay many decent looking Jewish females, as well as males, prostrate upon the beach." His final thoughts while setting sail from Morocco forever were, "to thank my God again that I was not a Jew, and that I was once more free from a country inhabited by the worst of barbarians."[41]

***

Disdain for their neighbors in the Mediterranean had consequences for Americans. On a personal level, it created social separation between Americans and the people who surrounded them, though it is unlikely that Catholics, Jews, or Muslims would have interacted more closely with these Protestants even if they had expressed more toleration or anything short of conversion. The Americans' attitudes also had consequences on a geopolitical

---

[40] Paddock, *A Narrative*, 335; Riley, *An Authentic Narrative*, 241–42, 332–34, 344.
[41] Riley, *An Authentic Narrative*, 380–81, 387, 415, 439–40.

level. Condescension toward "barbarians," Catholics, and Jews – or to put it differently, toward "others" – was part and parcel of the nineteenth-century movement toward colonization and imperialism. The Mediterranean was the seedbed of the nineteenth-century "orientalist" notions described by Edward Said as an important step in the process of conquering the supposedly inferior, decadent inhabitants of the region. Closer to home, American condescension toward Native Americans and Catholic Hispanics was already starting to emerge as the handmaiden to conquest of the West. Americans' occasional comparisons between North Africans and Native Americans gains further significance when viewed in light of these developments and might be seen as the base of a racialized imperialist rhetoric.

The most evident way in which the consuls and their community translated their unease with the denizens of the Mediterranean into policy was in their continual calls for an increased US naval presence in the region. Considering all of the three consuls' near-constant concern with the capture of American ships by North Africans and by the warring European powers, the call for naval protection is very understandable and, in fact, this was a policy embraced by many other consuls. Montgomery, who was active in US–Algerian negotiations from the 1780s onward wrote that the US needed at least ten "fast sailing frigates" with forty guns in the region. While still consul to Gibraltar, Simpson got wind of the US effort to build six frigates in the 1790s and wrote approvingly, "I am firmly of opinion you never will have security to your trade without such." As consul to Tangier, he continually asked for more naval presence, and seven years later he recollected his earlier letters, noting, "I have often since summer 1795 had the honor of stating in my dispatches, there is not anything has such weight, as showing the Moor that naval force is at hand, to act against them in case of need." Appleton made similar points in official despatches and personal correspondence, for example when he discussed the "deplorable" French blockade and North African aggression. He wrote, "It is long since my opinion, instead of regalias and tribute, we should send three frigates, and on my word they would be forced . . . to purchase a peace of us."[42] The extent to which such persistent calls influenced US policy is hard to judge. Consuls often felt as

---

[42] Montgomery to Sec. State, Jan. 16, 1795, Alicante Despatches; James Simpson to Sec. State, July 25, 1795, Gibraltar Despatches; Simpson to Sec. State, July 3, 1802, Tangier Despatches; Thomas Appleton to Frederick Woolaston, May 6, 1801, GL. For Americans in the Mediterranean and the call for a navy, see Lawrence Peskin, *Captives and Countrymen: Barbary Slavery and the American Public, 1785–1816* (Baltimore: Johns Hopkins University Press, 2009) 112–15.

though their letters were ignored, and the State Department rarely responded to them. But their frequent and uniform support for naval expansion could not have hurt those in Washington who supported increased naval power.

While couched in imperialistic or protoimperialistic language, the consuls' belligerent demands for naval assistance had nothing to do with militant expansion. At this time, as far as can be discerned, there was not a single discussion of the possibility of conquest. There are two compelling reasons for the absence. First, the consuls were all too aware of the weakness of the US military and specifically its inability to protect US interests in the region. Their concern was protection of shipping. Conquest, even if desirable, would have seemed laughably improbable given the inability to protect shipping. But, second, conquest was not particularly desirable. The goal of the consular service, and therefore of the State Department which it numerically dominated, was to protect American commerce. Consuls were merchants and they represented other merchants and the seamen who worked on the ground (or on the water) to keep American commerce flowing. Territorial acquisition simply was not a part of the equation.

What the consuls most wanted for the US and its ships was respect and access. Appleton wanted the United States to make "our commerce and our flag respected in those seas and having the double advantage of proving to the world, that our councils are not governed by the same vile intrigues which have animated the courts of Europe." He hoped the United States could "establish our national dignity." Montgomery hoped the Navy could "check" the "insolence" of the Algerian "pirates." Simpson saw the "grand necessity" of a naval force that would "command respect" for the American flag in the Mediterranean. The fact that they looked down on the Mediterranean people surrounding them made their lack of respect for Americans that much more insulting. Appleton complained bitterly of detentions of American ships by the Spaniards who had been in military decline for centuries. "How long we are with impunity to suffer these insults from so contemptible a nation while we hold the means of revenge, God only knows," he wrote, referring to the Navy.[43]

To summarize, Americans in the Mediterranean exhibited a good deal of chauvinism toward the people they met there. They used language typically associated with efforts to rationalize imperial conquest, yet at this stage they

[43] Appleton to M. Rose, May 8, 1801; to J. Barnes, [Aug. 1801], both in GL; Montgomery to Sec. State, Jan. 16, 1795, Alicante Despatches; Simpson to Sec. State, July 25, 1795, Gibraltar Despatches; Appleton to Pitcairn, Nov. 2, 1801, GL.

had little interest in conquest, which did not seem particularly feasible or desirable. Instead, they wanted to protect American honor which they believed was being sullied by the lack of respect local "barbarians" and Catholics displayed for the American flag. On a policy level, they hoped to protect and expand American commerce in the region, which was the purpose of the consular service, and so long as the American population in the region continued to be dominated by merchants and seamen, the goal of the American community. In short, rather than a new empire, American denizens of the Mediterranean saw themselves as a rising trading nation.

Even if it did not signal an immediate turn to empire, American chauvinism in the Mediterranean was significant. It presaged racialized notions of manifest destiny that would develop over the course of the coming century and suggests that at the turn of the nineteenth century these attitudes were neither new nor directed only at Native Americans and Latinos. The naval chauvinism expressed by Americans also comports well with current notions of the development of the defensive anticolonial basis of American imperialism – specifically the ambivalence toward conquest outside of North America.[44] While usually associated with the Monroe Doctrine of 1823, it is fair to conclude that Americans in the Mediterranean shared this defensive, ambivalent attitude a good deal earlier. Perhaps, then, it should not be a surprise that John Quincy Adams, author of the Monroe Doctrine, spent most of his early years in Europe in the midst of this very same American trading nation that Appleton, Montgomery, Simpson, and their associates were cultivating.

[44] Sexton, *The Monroe Doctrine*.

PART III

COLLAPSE

8

The Long Decline

After reaching its peak in the period from roughly 1803 to 1807, America's Mediterranean trade collapsed. Americans within the region remained hopeful. But over the subsequent years and decades it would slowly become apparent that neither their commerce nor their community would ever recover from the shock of these years.

While the US government did not keep separate statistics for Mediterranean imports and exports, the aggregate value of imports from all sources (including the Mediterranean) dropped from a high of $144 million in 1807 to $58 million in 1808. The general trend continued downward until imports reached a low of $13 million in 1814. Similarly, the reexport trade which was so important to the Mediterranean dropped from a high of roughly $198 million in 1807 to $40 million in 1808 and down all the way to $248,000 in 1814.[1]

Other evidence specifically from the Mediterranean also shows a sharp decline. Any ships trading between the United States and Mediterranean ports had to go through the Strait of Gibraltar. Many, if not most, would stop at Gibraltar before continuing into the Mediterranean. Like Captain Hallowell of the *Eliza*, discussed in Chapter 6, many American captains took advantage of banking facilities and easy trading in James Simpson's former home, which was well connected to the London banking system and was also a free port. Gibraltar was also a good place to stop for supplies and repairs. In 1803 well over a hundred American ships stopped

---

[1] Douglass C. North, *The Economic Growth of the United States 1790–1860* (New York: Norton, 1966) 228, 230. I have combined North's statistics for cocoa, coffee, pepper, and sugar for my reexport totals.

there. By contrast in 1808, virtually none arrived, a startling drop reflecting the precipitous decline of American shipping to the region.[2]

The rapid decline was also very obvious from the vantage point of specific Mediterranean ports. By 1807, Livorno had become the biggest destination for US shipping in Italy if not the entire Mediterranean with 152 arrivals. In 1808 that figure dropped to nineteen. By the end of 1808 American business in Livorno was completely dead and the largest American merchant house was facing bankruptcy. The same was true in Spain where business dropped precipitously in 1808 and over the next several years both Montgomery and John Rogers would flee Alicante temporarily for other ports due to the Peninsular War that ravaged Spain from 1808 onward. This period also saw the collapse of the influential Grivegnée merchant house in Málaga which did a great deal of American business, with which Montgomery had connections, and into which the American consul William Kirkpatrick was married.[3] By 1811 the American scientist John Maclure travelling through Trieste said of that recently flourishing port, "At present the favorable union of circumstances is changed and the port become what it was originally intended to be, a fishing town." He added that, "Most of the merchants have left it, and their fine town and country houses are empty."[4]

Typically, US historians discussing the economic downturn during these years have focused on a series of American actions taken in response to European outrages against US ships. The major events in the sequence are the implementation of the 1806 Nonimportation Act and the 1807 embargo, followed by the 1809 Nonintercourse Act and Macon's Bill Number 2 of 1810, which modified the latter. All of these Republican bills forbade US trade to Europe to a greater or lesser degree. Nonimportation and nonintercourse basically targeted the French and British while the embargo stopped all incoming and outgoing trade. These acts were designed to force belligerent powers to respect American shipping without actually plunging the United States into war. When they failed, the War of 1812 is understood by historians to have put an effective end to American overseas trade until 1815.

[2] *Gibraltar Chronicle*, Jan.–Dec. 1808.

[3] Charles A. Keene, "American Shipping and Trade, 1798–1820: The Evidence from Leghorn," *Journal of Economic History* 38 (Sept. 1978) 681–700, Table 1; Colin Carlin, *William Kirkpatrick of Malaga* (Glasgow: Colin Carlin, 2011) 126.

[4] John S. Doskey, ed., *The European Journals of William Maclure* (Philadelphia: American Philosophical Society, 1988) 416.

But from the perspective of Americans in the Mediterranean, developments in Europe were more immediately detrimental to American trade than anything done in Washington. While denizens of the American community rarely mentioned Jefferson's embargo, they were constantly concerned about port closures within Europe. French and British ship confiscations were also a constant concern, as was the rising threat of captures by North African cruisers. As the wars intensified, Americans also worried about the movement of troops and wartime devastation. The expense and devastation of war prompted local governments to try to extract taxes and other payments from Americans in the region. Finally, wartime alliances and realignments could, and did, lead to duties that discriminated against American shipping. So, while the embargo, nonintercourse, and the War of 1812 certainly played a role in the devastation of American commerce, events within Europe and North Africa usually were a greater concern for the American community in the Mediterranean.

***

The year 1807 marked the end of the bonanza in the Mediterranean. In Alicante, according to Montgomery, the previous year, 1806, produced "an image of our navigation at this port beyond anything we have yet had." His son-in-law and competitor, John Rogers, reported ninety-nine American vessels arriving there between April 1806 and May 1807. In Livorno, 152 American ships arrived in port, more than ever before and probably after.[5] Yet it also became very evident that all of this commerce was facing a great deal of risk due to European and North African captures. After all, 1807 was the year in which both the British Orders in Council and the French Berlin and Milan Decrees signaled the intention of the belligerent powers to crack down on neutral shipping. While Americans in the Mediterranean rarely discussed these decrees, they quickly saw their effects.

As the new year dawned, French privateers began capturing American ships throughout the region. On December 26, 1806, the French privateer and former smuggler, the *Serpent*, captured a Massachusetts ship, *Cyrus*, captained by Samuel Earvin, off the coast of Alicante. Montgomery immediately protested to Spanish officials and notified Commodore Campbell of

---

[5] Robert Montgomery to Sec. State, Oct. 10, 1806, Alicante Despatches; John Rogers to Brown and Ives, May 1, 1807; "List of Vessels And their Cargoes Arrival at Valencia Consigned to PC Tupper and Co.," both in B111 F1, B. & I. In the first half of 1807 at least twenty-two ships bearing sugar arrived in the Valencia and Barcelona regions, according to the Brown and Ives documents.

the Mediterranean fleet in hopes of naval protection. Nevertheless, the French captured a second Massachusetts ship, the *Azores*. In both cases, Montgomery reported, the "pretext" was that the cargoes contained English fish, which would have been prohibited by the Berlin Decree.[6]

In Livorno, with its heavy American traffic, French privateers found even better hunting. They captured the Boston ship *Hibernia* captained by Oliver Appleton (a cousin of the consul) on December 28, 1806, two days after the first capture in Alicante. In January and February 1807 they captured seven more American ships. As in Spain, the pretext in all cases was that they carried British goods. Privateers stood to benefit from these captures or "prizes" as they were called, and Appleton implied that the pretext of British goods was often flimsy. "Indeed," he complained, "there is a sort of unaccountable caprice which seems to direct them in the choice of those they capture, for in several instances, the corsair has suffered American vessels direct from England to enter the roads unmolested, while at the same time, they arrest others, which have touched at no port since their departure from the United States."[7]

Both Appleton and Montgomery spent most of the year dealing with this situation. As Appleton noted, with the boom in American trade "it becomes therefore of much importance to [remove] as far as possible any obstacle which will impede its free course."[8] By late March, Montgomery had reached the point where he expected at least one of the two detained ships would soon be freed, and he planned to sue for damages in both cases in order to "prevent or check" future detentions.[9] In Livorno Appleton tracked the American cases as they worked their way through the Paris prize court. Despite his allegations of capriciousness, there was some logic to the French actions. Six of the eight American ships had landed in England before arriving in Livorno, and the other two carried reexported West Indian merchandise which may well have been suspected to be the product of British colonies. (See Table 8.1.) In the end the court entirely liberated two of the eight American ships and allowed four others to sail on bond pending a final decision, while the fate of two others is not known. Despite these relatively favorable rulings, the ships' owners would

---

[6] Montgomery to Sec. State, Jan. 2, 1807; Mar. 25, 1807, both in Alicante Despatches.

[7] Entries for Dec. 28, 1806; Jan. 8, 1807; Jan. 19, 1807; Feb. 5, 1807; Feb. 26, 1807, Register of Events; Thomas Appleton to John Armstrong, Jan. 18, 1807; to American Captains, Feb. 13, 1807; to Armstrong, Feb. 13, 1807; Feb. 19, 1807; Mar. 6, 1807, all in GL. Quote from Appleton to Armstrong, Feb. 13, 1807.

[8] Appleton to Armstrong, Feb. 19, 1807, GL.

[9] Montgomery to Sec. State, Mar. 25, 1807, Alicante Despatches.

TABLE 8.1 *Livorno ship captures 1807*

Date captured	Ship	Captain	From	Cargo	Disposition
Dec. 28, 1806	Brig *Hibernia*	O. Appleton	Boston	Colonial merch.	Liberated
Jan. 8, 1807	Ship *Massachusetts*	Benting	Liverpool, Eng.	Fish	Bond
Jan. 16, 1807	Ship *Anna*	Bradford	Falmouth, Eng.	Pitchers	Liberated
Jan. 18, 1807	Brig *Henry*	Groves	Salem	Fish, colonial merch.	Liberated
Feb. 5, 1807	Ship *Aurora*	L. Hill	Pool, Eng.	Fish	Bond
Feb. 5, 1807	Ship *Kitty*	J. Day	Falmouth, Eng.	Pitchers	?
Feb. ?, 1807	Brig *June*	Rutherford	England	?	Bond
Feb. 26, 1807	Brig *Alexander*	Langthon	Yarmouth, Eng.	Herring	?

have suffered financial loss while their ships were stuck in port for several months, as would, presumably, the sailors who were left out of work.[10] While these ships were a small percentage of the American arrivals at Livorno, the fact that nearly all American ships in the region either carried West Indian reexports or fish that could be plausibly accused of being English products, made the potential threat to American shipping in the region very great.

While American shipping continued at its peak, the threats escalated in the second half of the year. As summer arrived, the British began a campaign to capture American ships deemed in violation of the Orders in Council forbidding neutral shipping between ports closed to the British. In submitting his list of American arrivals in July, Montgomery noted the large numbers were pleasing but, "from the practice of the English in capturing or detaining our vessels from one enemy's port to another, our trade has been lately very much obstructed, and it is to be apprehended must suffer considerable towards autumn . . . ."[11]

By Autumn, the British had captured at least thirty American ships and hauled them to a prize court in Malta. Eleven of these had either left from Livorno or intended sailing there, including one that had just been released after being captured by the French. (See Table 8.2.) Appleton was initially suspected of malfeasance in providing papers to American ships in contravention of the Orders in Council, but, according to him, the court cleared his name and instead blamed British officials for failing to provide him with the orders. However, Frederick Degan, the American consul to Naples, was caught red-handed sending a letter to an American captain explaining that Degan was providing him with papers to travel to Lisbon (a legal journey) when in fact he was planning to head to Marseille illegally. Interestingly, more than half of the Livorno captures were traveling to or from either Gallipoli (in the Italian boot heel) or Smyrna, suggesting that the trade to the eastern Mediterranean that Appleton had been promoting was beginning to take off.[12]

Appleton's bigger problem, however, was with the French. On August 29 a French division led by General Sextus Alexandre François de Miollis took possession of Livorno and immediately embargoed all

---

[10] Appleton to Fulwar Skipwith, Apr. 18, 1807; Apr. 28, 1807, both in GL; Thomas Appleton to Sec. State, May 27, 1807, Leghorn Despatches.

[11] Montgomery to Sec. State, July 21, 1807, Alicante Despatches.

[12] Appleton to Sec. State, Dec. 17, 1807; Samuel Field to Appleton, Dec. 9, 1807; "Observations on the Trial and Decision of American Vessels . . .," all in Leghorn Despatches.

TABLE 8.2 *Livorno captures in 1807 Malta Court*

	Ship and Captain	Destinations
1	[*Reborn*] Capt. Henson	Livorno-Gallipoli-Livorno
2	*Nymph* Capt. Henson	Gallipoli to Livorno
3	*Georgetown* Capt. Prince	Livorno to Gallipoli
4	*Massachusetts* Capt. Buntin	Livorno to Monfredonia
5	*Glory* Capt. Moore	Smyrna to Livorno
6	*Fortune* Capt. Johnson	Smyrna to Messina (orig. Livorno)
7	*Cleopatra* Capt. Logan	Smyrna to Messina (orig. Livorno)
8	*Aurora* Capt. Stall [Hill?]	Livorno to Santos
9	*Hibernia* Capt. Appleton	Livorno-Sante-Bristol
10	*Two Brother* Capt. Candler	Tunis to Livorno
11	*Amazon* Capt. Page	Alicante to Livorno

ships in the port, including a number of Americans. Appleton consulted with his friend, the French consul, Mathieu de Lesseps and met with the general. American ships were relatively quickly freed, but the French confiscated their cargo. Appleton was hopeful that Miollis, who had served heroically on the American side at the Battle of Yorktown and seemed amenable, would soon get the merchandise released once it was confirmed that it was not from Great Britain.[13]

Unfortunately, that seemingly simple task stretched out through most of the rest of the year. American merchants in Livorno, and there were a lot of them by now, were unhappy and probably giving Appleton a lot of grief. They proposed sending a petition to the Etruscan queen, something Appleton, with de Lesseps's advice, discouraged on the grounds that after the French troops' arrival, she no longer had enough power. Instead, he pushed them to petition John Armstrong, the American minister in Paris, who could use their complaint as leverage in dealing with the imperial authorities. In early October the committee of merchants also sent a petition to General Miollis.[14]

[13] Entry for Aug. 29, 1807, Register of Events; Appleton to Sec. State, Sept. 25, 1807, Leghorn Despatches.

[14] Entries for Sept. 20, 1807; Sept. 28, 1807, both in Register of Events; Petition to Gen. Miollis, Oct. 10, 1807; Appleton to Armstrong, Oct. 2, 1807, both in GL; Appleton to Sec. State, Sept. 25, 1807; Oct. 6, 1807, both in Leghorn Despatches.

Unfortunately for the Americans, the next week General Miollis announced that all sequestered merchandise – not just from the Americans – would be held until Livorno's merchants paid him 2.5 million livres. This order appears to have come from his superiors in France, presumably as a way to finance the war effort. After another month had passed in negotiations, the Livornese and General Miollis reached an agreement that the property would be liberated in exchange for a payment of 1.2 million livres. To raise the funds all the sequestered property was to be sold off. Appleton valued the American share at about $300,000. The Livornese committee then assessed the American merchants 45 percent of their property's value as their share of the 1.2 million livres. The Americans were incensed, but since this was a decision by the local authorities, they were unable to protest to the general or other French officials. Nonetheless, Appleton wrote that, due to rapidly rising prices for their goods, the Americans may well have come out ahead.[15]

***

At the same time, a number of troubling developments occurred on the African side of the Mediterranean that further contributed to the sense of menace. In mid-January, Appleton, and presumably other consuls, received copies of a circular sent by the commander of the Mediterranean squadron warning of a possible war with Tunis. Like all wars with the so-called Barbary states, this one would carry the threat of further ship captures. A month later Commodore Campbell wrote that the problem had been resolved, and Appleton passed the news on to Americans in the region. Then, in November, the American consul in Naples learned of a new threat of war from the Algerians, which he passed on to Appleton, Montgomery, and others. By late November, while still dealing with the forced levy on American merchants, Appleton wrote that the Algerian news "has so alarmed the masters of our vessels here that none has left the port from the time this intelligence reached me until the last two days." Almost exactly a month later, in mid-December, the American consul in Algiers informed the community that he had taken care of the issue and the threat had abated.[16]

---

[15] Entries for Oct. 9, 1807; Nov. 19, 1807; Nov. 30, 1807, all in Register of Events; Appleton to Armstrong, Oct. 16, 1807; Nov. 20, 1807; Nov. 24, 1807, all in GL; Appleton to Sec. State, Oct. 20, 1807; Nov. 26, 1807; Jan. 4, 1808, all in Leghorn Despatches.

[16] Entries for Jan. 19, 1807; Mar. 2, 1807; Nov. 14, 1807, all in Register of Events; Appleton to Armstrong, Mar. 6, 1807; Nov. 16, 1807; quote from Appleton to Armstrong, Nov. 20, 1807, all in GL; Appleton to Sec. State, Nov. 26, 1807; J. B. Ducouster to Appleton, Sept. 9, 1807; Tobias Lear to Appleton, Dec. 16, 1807; Appleton to Sec. State, Dec. 17, 1807, all

In Morocco, Simpson also faced restrictions on American shipping. The relatively flourishing American trade at Mogadore (Essaouira) had consisted primarily of American ships with their cargo holds mostly empty after trading in the Mediterranean and returning home. These ships used some of the money they had received in Europe to invest in Moroccan items, primarily animal skins. In May Emperor Muley Soliman forbade this trade, writing that "whoever does not import goods to the benefit of the country and employment of the port, but brings only ballast and empty ships" would be turned away. Simpson was hopeful these restrictions would be short-lived, but he admitted there was nothing he could do to ease them.[17]

At the end of 1807, Congress passed the Embargo Act cutting off all trade into and out of the United States. While most histories of the United States during this period devote a good deal of attention to this audacious and controversial experiment, it was of less importance to the American community in the Mediterranean. All three consuls were certainly aware of it, but only Appleton seems to have written about it at length, and none complained about it. Indeed, Appleton strongly supported it. He lamented Britain's Orders in Council as an "unexampled [code] of maritime commerce" and believed the embargo was a popular measure to destroy it. At the onset he predicted that Britain would probably see it as a "declaration of war on the part of the United States." He viewed this as a good thing. Always a strong Francophile, he saw Britain in a weak position, further predicting that "if Great Britain does not make a peace with France and Russia before the expiration of the present year [1808], that she will not hold an inch of territory in India." Presumably this weakness would give the United States the advantage in any prospective warfare. Less politically outspoken and less of a Francophile, Montgomery nevertheless likely would have agreed that the embargo was a positive measure considering that he had called for a naval response to French captures of American ships the previous year.[18]

The embargo certainly had an impact on Mediterranean merchants. By 1809 Simpson blamed the complete absence of American shipping in

---

in Leghorn Despatches; Charles D. Cose to John Leonard, Nov. 5, 1807; Montgomery to Sec. State, Dec. 8, 1807, both in Alicante Despatches.
[17] "To All the Merchants in Mogadore ...," May 9, 1807; James Simpson to Sec. State, June 12, 1807; "Instructions for the Information of Masters ...," n.d., all in Tangier Despatches.
[18] Appleton to Tobias Lear, Feb. 20, 1808; Mar. 18, 1808, GL; Montgomery to Sec. State, Jan. 2, 1807, Alicante Despatches.

Morocco on it. But in 1808 activities within the Mediterranean seemed more important and more menacing. As early as late autumn of 1807, rumors of war with Great Britain and increasingly worrisome French actions had already prompted Appleton to urge all American ships in the region to return home. Some of his fears were realized in January 1808 when the Emperor Napoleon laid an embargo on all ships in French ports, including Livorno. Appleton described the extreme anxiety of the roughly 200 seamen aboard fourteen American ships. Most of the captains had no merchandise and wanted to get home due to the threat of war with Britain. Appleton, perhaps colored by his Francophilia, wrote that many of the captains would be willing to become armed privateers against the British as soon as war commenced. Neither this possibility nor the lack of cargo immediately swayed the French from their determination to continue to detain these vessels, and they remained stuck in port until late March.[19]

The French also began a campaign of capturing American ships alleged to be violating the Milan Decree in the Mediterranean in 1808. They captured two off Livorno in February, two off Málaga, and ten off Alicante between March 18 and 20. (See Table 8.3.) In nearly all cases the French claimed that these ships had touched at British ports or carried British goods. Montgomery agreed that they had done so, writing that, "There is no doubt they have all come from England at the last from Tangier where they called only for the purpose of changing their papers." Faced with having to maintain more than 130 stranded seamen, Montgomery contemplated bribing local officials to allow the ships to leave, but he was unsuccessful at freeing them until Spain revolted against the French later in the year.[20]

Because so many of the captured ships sailed from Tangier, Simpson also became involved in efforts to address the problem of these captures. He reported that the British were actually soliciting American ships to bring cargos from Spain back to the Strait of Gibraltar, presumably to help provision British troops on the Rock. The British provided these

[19] Simpson to Sec. State, July 8, 1808, Tangier Despatches; Entries for Jan. 19, 1807; Mar. 22, 1808, both in Register of Events; Appleton to Armstrong, Jan. 29, 1808; to Skipwith, Feb. 9, 1808; to captains of American vessels in the port of Leghorn, Mar. 22, 1808, all in GL; Appleton to Sec. State, Mar. 23, 1808; "List of Americans Left at Leghorn Feb. 19, 1808," both in Leghorn Despatches; Log Book Brig *Eliza* 1806–1808, B712 F2, B. & I.

[20] Appleton to Skipwith, Feb. 9, 1808; to Degan Guebhardt and Co., Mar. 25, 1808, both in GL; Entries for Feb. 12, 1808; Mar. 18, 1808, both in Register of Events; Montgomery to Sec. State, Mar. 20, 1808; June 19, 1808, both in Alicante Despatches.

TABLE 8.3 *1808 French ship captures near Alicante, 18–19 March*

Vessel	Belonging to	Capt.	From Where
Ship *Neptune*	Portland	Joshua B. Osgood	Tangier
Ship *Ranger*	Baltimore	Saml. Sherburn	Ditto
Ship *Hannah*	Newbury Port	John Cottle	Ditto
Ship *Ann*	Alexandria	Charles Bradford	Ditto
Brig *May Flower*	Newbury Port	Joseph Buntin	Ditto
Brig *Reward*	Portsmouth, NH	John Thompson	Ditto
Ship *Minerva*	Charleston	William Lud	Rotterdam
Ship *Diana*	Boston	Francis Noble	Tangier

ships, seventeen of which had been docked at Tangier, with licenses to protect them from capture by British privateers. Montgomery understood that, after these no doubt lucrative runs into Spain, the American ships returned to Tangier "for the purpose of changing their papers" so it would not be evident they had been in contact with the English. This was clearly a risky violation of neutrality, and neither consul condoned it. Simpson attempted to legalize the situation by convincing the emperor to allow Tangier to become a free depot for goods that could be deposited by American ships whatever previous ports they had visited, whether French or British, and purchased in Tangier by ships from other countries in order to avoid the hazards of sailing between the various ports. The emperor seeing the possibility of taxing these transactions initially agreed, and at least one American ship took advantage of it, but as the British gained influence in Morocco and blockaded Tangier, the idea became impracticable.[21]

***

Despite all of these setbacks and impositions, Americans in the Mediterranean remained fairly optimistic. In March 1808, Montgomery took in two new partners, former clerk George Clark and Asa Fitch, a 19-year-old Connecticut native who had already spent three years in Europe but was still too young to be allowed to sign documents as a full partner. At the same time, Appleton announced that he was reentering the

[21] Montgomery to Sec. State, Mar. 20, 1808, Alicante Despatches; Simpson to Sec. State, Apr. 14, 1808; Apr. 26, 1808, both in Tangier Despatches.

American trade under his own name, as his time with DuPouy Brothers had expired. While both Montgomery and Appleton knew as well as anyone how badly US shipping had tailed off during 1808, clearly they did not anticipate the slow down to last long, and they intended to profit by being present when commerce resumed.[22]

Appleton, Montgomery, and others like them had reason for optimism. They had managed to make big profits for much of the last decade or so despite continual (though lesser) concerns about captures. While an increase in captures heightened risk, it also promised greater rewards for those willing to accept it, particularly in the case of commission merchants whose position was much safer than that of the merchants who owned the ships and cargo. As for the US embargo, far from seeming to be an existential threat, to Appleton at least it seemed a promising development insofar as it could ameliorate impositions on US ships, and, whatever the outcome, it was unlikely to be permanent.

Even more important, though far less visible from across the Atlantic, was the fact that over the last decade American ships in the Mediterranean had increasingly focused on what was known as the carrying trade. The historian Silvia Marzagalli has found that half of all American ships arriving in Marseille in 1807 sailed on to another Mediterranean port before returning home. Furthermore, the percentage of American ships sailing to other Mediterranean ports from Livorno rose from 32 to 42 percent between 1804 and 1807. The figures compiled by Appleton for American shipping to Livorno in the second half of 1807 show that only 45 percent for whom information is available made no other stops. The vast majority stopped at other Mediterranean ports, though small numbers stopped at Denmark, England, and India. By 1808, according to Appleton, shipping documents for US ships usually just stated that they planned to sail "to one or more ports in the Mediterranean, to Leghorn and a market," and some ships remained abroad for two or three years before returning home.[23]

---

[22] Montgomery to Brown and Ives, Mar. 1, 1808, B110 F11; Appleton to Brown and Ives, May 1, 1808, B110 F8, both in B. & I.; Appleton to Lear, May 18, 1808, GL; D. Hamilton Hurd, *History of New London County, CT* (Philadelphia: J. W. Lewis, 1882) 379.

[23] Silvia Marzagalli, "American Shipping into the Mediterranean during the French Wars: A First Approach" in Silvia Marzagalli, James R. Sofka, and John J. McCusker, eds., *Rough Waters: American Involvement with the Mediterranean in the Eighteenth and Nineteenth Centuries* (Newfoundland: International Maritime Economic History Association, 2010) 55–59; "List of Vessels Sailed for the Port of Leghorn in the year 1807 from 1st July to 31st December"; Appleton to Sec. State, May 27, 1807, both in Leghorn Despatches.

The sad story of Captain Oliver Appleton of the ship *Hibernia* illustrates the dangers that these profit-seekers faced. Appleton, a native of Ipswich, Massachusetts and cousin of the consul, arrived in Livorno in December 1806, meaning he would have most likely left Boston sometime around October 1806. He brought with him "colonial merchandise," meaning reexported goods which he or someone else would have purchased in the West Indies and brought to Boston as a means of avoiding prohibitions by Britain and France against exporting them directly from their colonies. French authorities seized the ship when it entered Livorno harbor on December 28, claiming these goods were British. Appleton, the consul, maintained they were not and were all consigned to Livornese merchants, possibly including himself considering the familial connection. Nevertheless, authorities detained the *Hibernia*, sending its papers to Paris for further examination. The ship was freed by May 1807. Captain Appleton then sailed from Livorno to Santé, France (Villefrance-Sur-Mer) from whence he had intended to continue to Bristol, England. But learning the Berlin Decree prohibited that journey, he rechartered the *Hibernia* to sail to Copenhagen.[24]

Unfortunately, the *Hibernia* was once again captured, this time by a British privateer which found the new papers suspicious and hauled Captain Appleton into the prize court at Malta. After being cleared by the British court, Captain Appleton successfully sailed to Copenhagen and Tonningen in Denmark. From Tonningen, Appleton piloted the *Hibernia* back into the Spanish Mediterranean where he was captured a third time, in March 1808, by a French privateer off the port of Alicante for allegedly having "spoken in her passage" to a British ship at Gibraltar, a particularly suspicious activity since the British had been enrolling American ships there to buy provisions for them in Spain. At Alicante, Montgomery paid to send the *Hibernia*'s crew back to America but did not record if or when the ship itself returned. In total, the *Hibernia* was away from Boston from at least October 1806 to March 1808 and probably longer, and she stopped at no less than five European ports inside and outside the Mediterranean. None of these activities would have been affected by the Embargo Act, which applied only to ships

---

[24] Duane H. Hurd, *History of Essex Country, Massachusetts* (Philadelphia: J. W. Lewis and Co., 1888) II: 1176; W. S. Appleton, *A Rough Sketch of the Appleton Genealogy* (Boston: T. R. Marvin and Co., 1873) 11; Entry for Dec. 28, 1806, Register of Events; Appleton to Armstrong, Jan. 18, 1807, GL; Appleton to Sec. State, May 27, 1807; "Observations on the Trial and Decision on American Vessels …," Dec. 9, 1807, both in Leghorn Despatches.

entering and exiting American ports. Clearly there was a good deal of money to be made in this carrying trade even under the embargo, but just as clearly, as the *Hibernia* demonstrates, it was becoming extremely risky due to French and British actions.[25]

Masters of American ships in the carrying trade took a wide array of measures to avoid capture. Breaking a voyage at a legal port long enough to get new papers was a quasi-legal method. A more efficient ploy was simply to carry false papers. In some cases, as with Frederick Degan of Naples, such documentation might actually be provided by a consul. More often it came from the ship's owners or consignors. For example, the *Ann*, captained by Charles Bradford of Alexandria, DC (now Virginia), had a false bill of lading on board when captured off Alicante indicating it was bound for New York when it had actually been chartered by London merchants to carry its cargo of Spanish wine to England. Similarly, at this time John Rogers of Alicante and Thomas B. Harris, captain of the American brig *Sally*, agreed that Harris would carry $768-worth of Spanish almonds, raisins, and other items to the United States for Rogers under a phony bill of lading that would not show that the *Sally* had stopped in Alicante. This was clearly a ploy to avoid capture by the British at a time when they were swarming the Spanish coast. Robert Montgomery played a role in the deception by certifying that despite the fake paperwork, the property did indeed belong to Rogers, documentation which would presumably be useful once the ship arrived in the United States.[26] Such ruses, as well as licenses from the British (as with the ships sailing from Tangier), insurance policies, and financial incentives from merchants all helped to mitigate the risk.[27]

The consul to Hamburg, John M. Forbes, was particularly explicit in describing to his brother Ralph Bennet Forbes how to navigate around the British and American authorities. Bennet, as he was known to his family, appears to have been one of the many Americans to have had his ship seized by British authorities in 1808. John advised him that if the capture had not been publicized, he still might be able to use his original papers, providing they showed no evidence of stopping in an English port, to continue the voyage either with the original cargo, if possible, or with one "of similar

[25] Montgomery to Sec. State, Mar. 20, 1808 Alicante Despatches.

[26] "Observations on the Trials and Decision on American Vessels ...," GL; Montgomery to Sec. State, July 3, 1808, Alicante Despatches; Deposition of Thomas B. Harris, Mar. 21, 1808, Rogers-Bridges Family Collection.

[27] For an example of a financial incentive see the case of P. Bradford in "Observations on the Trial and Decision on American Vessels ...," GL.

description" purchased in Europe. Assuming the crew "could be totally depended on and totally concealing your call in [i.e., the stop in British territory]," John wrote his brother he might "make immense prices" by proceeding to Hamburg. However, John noted, "every chance of gain is surrounded by so many chances of loss that one knows not what to advise." He concluded that the safer course was probably to "come without goods" and to trade on a joint account with a local merchant house in Hamburg that would, presumably, hide the fact that goods had been purchased by Americans. John suggested selling linens and had already gone about collecting 250 tons of them for the next season on the expectation that neutral ships from Hamburg would be able to navigate safely in the coming spring. In this way, Americans would be able to continue to carry on an active trade in the region with far less likelihood of capture and without needing to worry about the restrictive Embargo Act.[28]

There is also evidence of complete and outright defiance of the embargo in the case of the ship *John*, skippered by Captain Chaytor, which had the audacity to sneak out of Baltimore on May 8, 1808. That date was five months into the embargo, and everyone associated with the ship well knew it was in force. The *John* was owned by prominent Baltimore merchant John Donnel who had consigned it to the Purviances in Livorno and was in contact with them by letter. Captain Chaytor got the *John* past Baltimore's Fort McHenry early in the morning with the collusion of Major John Sterrett. The Sterretts and Purviances had long been associated with each other and members of both families had held prominent positions in the administration of Baltimore's port over the years. They were also connected to prominent Baltimore Republican Congressman Samuel Smith. Chaytor admitted he was guilty of violating the embargo but refused to give a deposition because it would implicate "persons of high station in Baltimore," most likely Sterrett and the Purviances, if not Smith.[29]

After escaping Baltimore, the *John* sailed to La Guaia, Venezuela, where it arrived on May 20. The ship was then loaded up with the sort of West

---

[28] J. M. Forbes to R. B. Forbes, Nov. 30, 1808, Ralph Bennet Forbes Correspondence, Massachusetts Historical Society, Boston, MA.

[29] Most of the information on the *John* comes from Appleton's depositions of the crew conducted on Nov. 15, 1808 and found in Leghorn Despatches. Appleton to Sec. State, Sept. 6, 1808; to Armstrong, Sept. 6, 1808, both in Leghorn Despatches; Entries for Nov. 5, 1808; Nov. 9, 1808, both in Register of Events. On the Sterretts and Purviances, see Brantz Mayer, *Baltimore Past and Present* (Baltimore: Richardson and Bennett, 1871) 41; Purviance Papers, "Descriptive Summary," MS 1394, Maryland Historical Society, Baltimore, MD.

Indian products typically reexported to Livorno, including coffee and indigo. The ship was equipped with a Swedish flag, presumably to be used to show neutrality if stopped by British or French privateers, as well as with false papers giving Denmark, another neutral country, as its destination. Captain Chaytor and the others hoped that the schooner's unusual quickness would also help to avoid captures, which it was able to do when two British war ships attempted to stop it near Majorca. Originally Donnel had instructed Chaytor to unload the cargo at Livorno and return to Hampton Roads in Virginia to await further instructions, thereby avoiding Baltimore officials. However, after Chaytor departed Baltimore, Donnel wrote the Purviances in Livorno to instruct Chaytor that plans had changed and he should instead proceed to Barcelona for a load of brandy to be sold in Vera Cruz, Mexico.[30]

Instead, the *John*, Chaytor, his twenty-six-man crew, and his entire cargo ended up sequestered in Livorno by the French authorities. The reason was that the ship's papers – or lack of papers – raised suspicions. Chaytor did not have the requisite Mediterranean pass, role of equipage, property certificate, or, according to Appleton, "any permission under whatever shape from any authority in the United States to depart from [Baltimore]." At the same time, friendly French authorities allowed Appleton to begin investigating the *John*'s probable violation of American laws.[31]

All of this raises a number of questions, most crucially: How did Donnel and Chaytor think they could get away with this deception? Early on, Chaytor told Appleton he expected that once he arrived in Livorno he would be out of danger. How is that possible? For one thing, when they concocted their scheme, Chaytor and Donnely were unaware that the French had dissolved the Kingdom of Etruria's control over Livorno and instituted direct governance. Chaytor confessed to Appleton that, had he known of this development he would not have landed in Livorno. Why not? Probably because he knew the French had been hypervigilant about ships' papers since the Berlin and Milan Decrees and that the *John*'s lack of papers would raise alarms. If so, this also suggests that he might not have been detained in ports that were still not directly controlled by the French.[32]

---

[30] John Donnell to S. and W. Purviance, July 15, 1808, certified Dec. 15, 1808; Appleton to Armstrong, Sept. 6, 1808; Health Office Entry for Schooner *John*, Aug. 19, 1809; Appleton to Armstrong, Aug. 23, 1808, all Leghorn Despatches.
[31] Appleton to Sec. State, Sept. 6, 1808, Leghorn Despatches.
[32] Appleton to Armstrong, Sept. 6, 1808; Nov. 11, 1808, both in Leghorn Despatches.

But one also must wonder how Chaytor expected to get around American authorities in such a blatant violation of the Embargo Act. In fact, according to Appleton, Chaytor had raised this concern with Donnel, but the merchant reassured him that Appleton would not be so exacting about the law. Donnell was in regular communication with the Purviances who must have been all too aware of Appleton's resentment of them. So, why would Donnel possibly believe Appleton would let the matter slide? Perhaps it was common practice for consuls to look the other way. Perhaps Appleton himself had done so in the past, and perhaps the Purviances had even made some sort of arrangement with him which he could no longer abide by once the French came on the scene and started investigating the ship. Interestingly, Chaytor once told Appleton that two other ships similar to the *John* had left Baltimore in the same manner as he had, at the same time, also bound for the West Indies and Livorno. Since there is no evidence of their arrival, they likely were either captured en route or learned of the enhanced danger in Livorno and changed course.[33]

This raises perhaps the largest question: How many other ships attempted to evade the embargo this way, and how many succeeded? Certainly, the incentive was very high. The *John* could have made $200,000 in profit, Appleton estimated. If three ships had been tempted by the opportunity for these enormous profits, probably many others made the attempt and have escaped the historical record because they were not caught and exposed. Between these outright lawbreakers and others who skirted the gray areas around commercial regulations, American ships found many ways to continue profiting from the Mediterranean trade despite the embargo.[34]

***

With the end of the embargo both European and American commercial policy became somewhat less restrictive, but the mercantile future remained hazy. The 1809 Nonintercourse Act allowed American ships to leave and enter the United States but forbade direct trade with France or Britain. Thus, only trade with neutral powers could legally resume, and it would be easy enough for devious American captains to get around the restrictions, particularly with the assistance of corrupt or lax consuls Nevertheless, during this period, American trade remained depressed

[33] Appleton to Armstrong, Nov. 11, 1808; Donnell to Purviance, July 15, 1808; Appleton to Armstrong, Aug. 23, 1808, all Leghorn Despatches.
[34] Appleton to Armstrong, Aug. 23, 1808, Leghorn Despatches.

due to European conditions which included the continued threat of ship captures, local embargoes as in Livorno, active harassment by local officials, and massive wartime disruptions and hostilities as the Napoleonic Wars intensified. Finally, the advent of the War of 1812 between the United States and Great Britain strongly punctuated the decline in trade. Nevertheless, throughout these years many in the American Mediterranean community maintained a guarded optimism that conditions would improve and were occasionally able to make opportunistic profits.

Things were so bad in Livorno after the French and American embargoes that Appleton left town for about a year. Sometime around September 1809, he departed for Naples to investigate the bankruptcy claims against Degan and Purviance. The Livornese firm, which had been longtime naval agents for the United States, owed a good deal of money to the federal government, which Appleton had been charged to collect. This job would have provided him with some subsistence as he expected to have expenses paid and to gain a commission for money collected. The fact that he was willing and able to take on a long-term task like this away from Livorno clearly indicates the complete lack of business for a merchant and consul at what had formerly been Italy's busiest port.[35]

On his return, Appleton did evince some optimism that France's revocation of the Berlin and Milan decrees would revive business. Three days after learning of these developments, he again began writing his American correspondents seeking commissions. With the resumption of commerce in 1810–11 came the resumption of occasional American ships, though neither appears to have been anywhere near the scale of previous years. No data exists for American shipping in the years from 1808 to 1815, which along with the lack of discussion from Appleton suggests it was probably quite slow. Appleton only had to deal with two ship captures in 1810–1811, which probably reflects the lack of American shipping rather than French and English cooperation.[36]

In Livorno, at least Americans' persons and property were relatively safe. Not so in Alicante, where the war had begun to cause anxiety in the

---

[35] There are large gaps between 1808 and roughly 1811 in all of Appleton's private letterbooks and in his state department despatches, further indicating the lack of business. The gap in the letterbooks runs from Mar. 1809 to July 3, 1812, while that in the despatches goes from Sept. 1, 1809 to July 10, 1810.

[36] Appleton to Brown and Ives, Aug. 20, 1810, B111 F5, B. & I.; Appleton to Sec. State, Sept. 3, 1811, Leghorn Despatches; Appleton to M. de la Grange, Aug. 13, 1812; to D. B. Warden, Aug. 23, 1812, both in GL; Keene, "American Shipping and Trade," 687–90.

foreign community as early as 1808 when French troops arrived in Valencia. On May 1808, the French "liberation" of Spain had sparked the so-called Second of May Riot in Madrid, and anti-French feeling was high. That month, John Rogers wrote that his French friends, the Morands, who lived in a castle in nearby Denia, had half their property confiscated by the Spanish government. The next month anti-French Spanish revolutionaries confiscated the property of eight naturalized Frenchmen whom they arrested and tore from their families. Montgomery feared that American merchants might suffer the same fate and worried that he could do little to assist them. The next spring, Montgomery's frequent antagonist, Alicante's governor Josef Betegon, began to insist the Americans in the region should pay a pro-rata portion of the forced loan demanded by the Spanish government to fight off the French. Montgomery protested that these forced payments violated America's treaty with Spain, but to no avail, as the governor threatened to expel Americans who refused to pay. By May, Betegon had been removed as governor and both Robert and John Montgomery's sons-in-law – John Rogers in Alicante and Obadiah Rich in Valencia – expressed optimism about the fish trade for the coming year.[37]

While the British fish trade did indeed revive, America's did not. With the Spanish government relying on Britain to help it fend off the French, they dropped duties on British fish imports while leaving the duties for all others at the higher rate. American ships sailing into Alicante to take advantage of the improved market were forced to sell their product at a loss due to the differential tariff. Montgomery protested, without success, that the tariff modification violated the US–Spanish treaty. To add insult to injury, in February 1810, the governor of Valencia announced that American citizens living in the province must enroll in the militia or face steep fines and imprisonment. Montgomery's protests were again ineffectual, and he reported that, as a result, a number of Americans had left the region. Montgomery also urged the secretary of state to push for a bounty on imported fish to offset the Spanish duty, again without success. Dejected, after the earlier optimism, he wrote, "Our fish trade and many of our merchants in it have been ruined this year by the diminished duties on English fish." By July, with no improvement in

---

[37] John H. Rogers to John Rogers, Jr., May 15, 1808, Rogers-Bridges Family Collection; Montgomery to Sec. State, June 19, 1808; Mar. 1, 1809; May 26, 1809, all in Alicante Despatches; Rogers to Brown and Ives, Apr. 26, 1809, B111 F1; Rich to Brown and Ives, May 1, 1809, B110 F11, both in B. & I.

sight, Montgomery wrote, "The commerce is or may be considered as nearly extinguished here."[38]

Moroccan trade, too, mostly suffered during this period. Very few, if any American ships appear to have arrived in 1809, and at least one had forged paper work suggesting it may have been landing in Tangier as part of a plan to conduct prohibited trade. That year Asa Fitch, Robert Montgomery's young business partner, hatched a plan to have American ships offload their produce at Oran, Algeria onto Algerian ships which could then cross over into Alicante with the cargoes in about a day. Presumably the Algerians ran much less of a risk of capture than American ships. It seems likely that other Americans were practicing similar strategies in places like Tangier. In the first half of 1811, an unusually large number of Americans, nine, landed there. All but two continued with all of their cargo, and the other two likely retained most of it since it consisted of West Indian pepper that was in demand in Spain. All of these ships were either heading to or coming from Spanish ports or Gibraltar where they were exposed to French and British seizures. It is possible that Simpson somehow colluded with them to evade restrictions as is obliquely suggested by Fitch's speculation that Americans evading the Spanish first stop in Tangier for "information" from Simpson.[39]

Like his European counterparts, the emperor of Morocco demanded American contributions to his military efforts – in the form of armaments that the United States had earlier promised but not yet shipped. These were needed because the emperor was once again engaged in trying to control rebellious provinces. At about the same time, he also raised duties on most imports. It is unclear whether this, too, was connected to his military funding or was part of his push toward economic independence. The new duties affected the goods that the few American ships to Mogadore had been purchasing, causing Simpson to fear further damage to the American trade.[40]

From 1812 onward, with the beginning of the War of 1812, the so-called Second Barbary War with Algiers, and continued European depredations, the situation became even bleaker. By 1812, Appleton was considering leaving Livorno for Paris to rejoin his old friends. He wrote one of them,

---

[38] Montgomery to Sec. State, June 17, 1809; Jan. 13, 1810; Feb. 1, 1810; Feb. 19, 1810; Apr. 14, 1810; July 4, 1810, all in Alicante Despatches.
[39] Simpson to sec. State, Jan. 2, 1809; Jan. 4, 1809; July 8, 1809; July 1, 1812, all in Tangier Despatches; Asa Fitch to Brown and Ives, Nov. 6, 1809, B110 F11, B. and I.
[40] Simpson to Sec. State, Apr. 13, 1811; Mar. 2, 1812; Apr. 29, 1812, all in Tangier Despatches.

"[Y]ou know equally well with myself, that our commerce is totally at an end, and must remain so in the Mediterranean as long as the war continues; and even should peace return it never could return to its former greatness."[41]

In Alicante, by December 1811 it was becoming evident that the region was no longer safe, and many merchants in the general area began fleeing to the relative safety of Cádiz. The following month, Montgomery reported 1,600 English and Sicilian troops in Alicante along with perhaps 25,000 Spanish troops in the region, while as many as 18,000 invading French troops were in nearby Valencia and La Font de la Figuera. On January 9 and 10, the French captured Valencia and began attacking Alicante. Montgomery wrote, "under those circumstances, and finding I can be of no real service to the United States during the present contest, I have decided to retire with my family." They fled to Gibraltar, leaving Robert Jr. behind to manage any business that might arise.[42]

During this dangerous period a number of people within the American community also had to dodge accusations of espionage and partisanship that endangered their persons and property. In 1810 a London newspaper ran a report that letters from Alicante revealed "a treasonous correspondence between the French and certain Americans resident in that city." As Montgomery was by far the most prominent member of the city's small American community, he would have been the person most likely to have been associated with the rumor by knowledgeable readers. Montgomery claimed it was all "a falsehood of a weak and foolish invention written by some of the English tories here in order, I suppose, to throw a temporary odium on their competitors: the Americans." Given Montgomery's previously friendly ties with Britain and subsequent attacks on him by the French, this explanation is believable. In Madrid, Thomas Gough, an interpreter and informal vice-consul at the American legation, was arrested and accused of spying for the Spanish republican forces opposing Napoleon. Gough was a clergyman later described by the American minister as "an honest sincere man and a true Irishman [who] has been in prison as often as St. Paul but he fears nothing." Gough allegedly corresponded with Spanish forces and was caught with detailed information about the recent Battle of Talavera. Despite Gough's claim that he was under the protection of the American flag, French officials who were occupying Madrid confiscated his papers and hauled him off to prison. A survivor,

---

[41] Appleton to Daniel Parker, Dec. 8, 1812; to Mdm. de Brancas, Feb. 8, 1813, both in GL.
[42] Montgomery to Sec. State, Dec. 30, 1811; Jan. 14, 1812; Jan. 20, 1812; Feb. 29, 1812, all in Alicante Despatches.

he was still hale and hearty when Washington Irving met him in Madrid in
1826 and described him as a "violent ultra" who had been imprisoned
thirty-five times. In Málaga, the American consul William Kirkpatrick had
apparently actively supported the French during the invasion of that port.
Nevertheless, Montgomery wrote, he had "paid very dear for it" when
French authorities threw him and his partners into prison after he insisted
on collecting a debt from the French consul.[43]

Montgomery returned to Alicante at the end of February to find wheat
prices very high as Spaniards began to panic about the possibility of
a famine due to wartime destruction. In May, as French forces again
threatened Alicante, both Montgomery and John Rogers again fled, to
Gibraltar and London respectively. Robert Jr. remained behind and
reported that the French had plundered the fertile orchard region where
Montgomery had his country home. They massacred forty "old infirm
men" in the streets of nearby San Juan, leaving them in the street "mangled
with the most savage cruelty." They entered and pillaged Montgomery's
house, despite being aware it belonged to the American consul, and they
"dragged out and butchered in cold blood" Montgomery's overseer.
Nevertheless, the price of flour continued to rise, and by autumn
Montgomery had returned. Unfortunately for potential profiteers, but
fortunately for the Spaniards, by 1813 a good European wheat crop was
anticipated and prices for imports sunk due to the growing supply. "Spain
at all events is become a skeleton," Montgomery wrote, "The source of all
its production and even its industry has been destroyed by the war." The
only potential bright spot was Montgomery's hope that Spain's economy
would improve under the new constitutional government that had been
promulgated in 1812.[44]

Besides putting Americans in personal and financial danger, these
developments also frayed the cords that held the American community
in the Mediterranean together. With so many residents evacuating (and
sometimes returning to) their usual homes, it became difficult to remain in

[43] Montgomery to Sec. State, May 17, 1810; June 23, 1812, both in Alicante Despatches;
"Expediente relativo al arresto de Tomás Gogg …," Estado 2952, EXP4, Archivos
Nacionales; George Erving to William Maclure, July 1, 1821, New Harmony
Manuscripts; William P. Trent and George S. Hellman, eds., *The Journals of Washington
Irving (hitherto unpublished)* (Boston: The Bibliophile Society, 1919), www.loc.gov, II: 8;
Carlin, *William Kirkpatrick*, 120–22.

[44] Montgomery to Sec. State, Mar. 15, 1812; Apr. 28, 1812; May 21, 1812; June 23, 1812;
Oct. 14, 1812; July 11, 1813; Dec. 10, 1813, all in Alicante Despatches; John H. Rogers to
Brown and Ives, May 25, 1812, B111 F9, B. & I.

contact or plan for future business. More importantly, the lack of shipping between the Mediterranean and the United States created problems beyond the decline of commerce. Credit networks became very strained as Americans had great difficulty redeeming (i.e., cashing) bills on the United States. This was a particular problem for Simpson who drew $2,000 annually on the United States for his salary. Usually, he sent the bills to merchants in Gibraltar or Cádiz, who provided him credit and would eventually ship them back to the United States as payment for debts, where they would be redeemed by the government and taken out of circulation. Americans faced similar problems in Italy, where Appleton complained that "to negotiate [US] bills here was utterly impossible, considering the total annihilation of trade in this place." Finally, the dearth of shipping also made it more difficult for Americans in the Mediterranean to communicate with each other and with their correspondents in the United States. A large gap between Simpson's October 1809 despatch (#149) and that of February 1811 (#166) in the State Department files suggests that seventeen missing despatches probably did not make it through the various Mediterranean blockades and captures to Washington. Appleton, too had mail problems. In April 1813 he wrote that he had not received a single line in sixteen months from his brother-in-law Thomas Perkins in Boston, who was usually one of his most frequent correspondents. When Appleton finally did hear from him in April, Perkins explained that a number of Appleton's letters had simply never arrived in Boston.[45]

Finally, in late 1812, the Dey of Algiers declared war on the United States. Not only did this declaration cut off the possibility of sending US ships to North African ports to avoid capture, it also made the entire Mediterranean far more dangerous. Like the Moroccan emperor, the Dey of Algiers had begun pressing the United States to make long overdue payments in cash and military goods which, in this case, had been stipulated by the US–Algerian treaty negotiated in 1797. The Dey may have been stimulated to take action by the War of 1812, which promised to further delay payments and left the United States vulnerable and at war with his putative ally, Great Britain. Also, because of the war and other disruptions, communications were not good, so that Appleton, a friend and close correspondent of Tobias Lear, the Algerian consul, did not learn

---

[45] Appleton to Thomas Perkins, Apr. 13, 1813; Apr. 29, 1813; to C. D. Coxe, Apr. 5, 1813; to R. B. Jones, May 29, 1813, all in GL. For a detailed example of one of Simpson's bills, see Samuel Larned to Brown and Ives, Dec. 26, 1812, B111 F10, B. & I.

of the disturbing news until October 1812, three months after Lear had been forced to flee Algiers. At that time the rumor was that an American ship, the *Allegany*, had been captured by Algerine cruisers. In fact, the Algerians had captured the American ship *Edwin* on August 25 off the coast of Spain and enslaved its nine-man crew. This was bad news for American shipping, and the fate of the crew members deeply concerned Americans in the region who raised $2,000 for their relief in Gibraltar and Cádiz.[46]

Although, in the end, the *Edwin* would be the only ship captured by the Algerines, fears of further captures persisted in the Mediterranean until the war concluded in 1815. Simpson, in particular, well remembered how an Algerine–Portuguese truce that some believed had been negotiated by Britain had led to the capture of eleven American ships and a major crisis in 1793. After the British consul to Morocco lost his job due to allegations of malfeasance in the provisioning trade, Simpson was concerned about the appointment of a new "English Minister to the barbary States." Not only was this man supposedly providing Muley Solimon's government with anti-American propaganda, but Simpson also suspected he was trying to influence all of the North African governments to act against the United States as Britain had allegedly done with Algiers in 1793.[47]

***

The cumulative effect of all these developments on individual members of the American community who remained in the Mediterranean was devastating. Merchants could no longer count on profiting from direct trade with America, the Mediterranean trade, or on commissions as they had before. And if merchants were unable to trade, then captains, seamen, diplomats, and all the people associated with the Mediterranean economy suffered. Some prominent merchant houses completely collapsed under the financial strain, losing what would be millions of dollars in today's money. All merchants, even those who remained solvent, had to struggle to find new sources of income during this difficult period.

---

[46] Lawrence Peskin, *Captives and Countrymen: Barbary Slavery and the American Public, 1785–1816* (Baltimore: Johns Hopkins University Press, 2009) 192–94; Frank Lambert, *The Barbary Wars: American Independence in the Atlantic World* (New York: Hill and Wang, 2005) 183–84; Frederick C. Leiner, *The End of Barbary Terror: America's 1815 War against the Pirates of North Africa* (Oxford University Press, 2007) 5–15; Appleton to Joel Barlow, Oct. 1, 1812; Notation for Oct. 1, 1812, both in GL.

[47] Simpson to Sec. State, May 14, 1813; June 9, 1813; July 6, 1813; July 7, 1813, all in Tangier Despatches.

One of the most spectacular bankruptcies was that of Appleton's rivals and frequent antagonists, the Purviances of Livorno. Appleton was closely tied to their demise and partly responsible. The Purviances dissolved their long partnership with Charles F. Degan in 1807. Degan went to Switzerland and formed a new partnership, while the Purviances reorganized as "Samuel and William Y Purviance" in Livorno. Perhaps the first sign of real trouble came in April 1808, when Joseph Barnes, former consul to Sicily and a friend of Appleton, unsuccessfully attempted to recover payment on bills of exchange issued by the Purviances. Barnes recounted to Appleton that one of the partners told him the firm had many debts in America, that if Barnes pursued the matter they would declare bankruptcy and he would never recover the debts, and, finally, after more recrimination, that "Barnes might wipe his [ass] with the bills."[48]

Appleton was already monitoring the firm's condition. He would have certainly done so in any event, but at this time he was also giving advice (probably with a power of attorney) to Tobias Lear, the American consul to Algiers. Lear frequently sent bills for America toward Livorno, including those drawn on the United States, presumably for his salary and all the multitude of expenses that he, like James Simpson, faced as a North African consul. In May, just shortly after Barnes's run in with Purviance, Appleton consulted with his friend, the powerful Algerian Jewish broker Moses Bacri, on the status of Lear's notes with the Purviances and found that at least one had been refused, meaning that the recipient did not trust that he could receive payment from the Purviances if he cashed it. In response, Lear sent Appleton power of attorney and other documents that would allow him to pursue the matter as vigorously as possible. It would be customary for Appleton to receive a commission on anything he collected and have his expenses refunded. After investigating, Appleton reported that the Purviances looked to be in very bad shape. It appeared as though they had sold $40,000-worth of bills they received from Lear in a suspicious fashion, and they blamed any putative malfeasance on their former partner, Degan. According to Appleton, a Purviance brother who had come in from Baltimore to investigate matters "found the utmost confusion in [Degan's] affairs and ... very far from any emoluments since [Degan's] departure from the country."[49]

[48] Entry for [June 1808], Register of Events; Appleton to Lear, May 18, 1808, GL.
[49] Entry for Jan. 13, 1808, Register of Events; Appleton to Lear, May 18, 1808; Aug. 22, 1808, both in GL.

Captain Chaytor and the schooner *John* arrived in Livorno at almost
the exact same time Appleton received Lear's documents. The Purviances
would have been very glad to see it. Despite the French seizure, they must
have calculated they had a decent chance to get their hands on the cargo
which had been consigned to them, considering the ship had broken no
French provisions other than not having all of the proper papers. Once
they were able to gain control of the cargo, valued at about $250,000, they
would be in a far better position with their creditors, including Lear.
Appleton, however, was determined not to let that happen. He vigorously
fought against their recovering the cargo for months. Part of his motivation, perhaps all of it, was outrage at the flagrant violation of the
embargo. There was also likely at least some profit motive: Appleton
read the Embargo Act of 1807 as promising him a portion of the sales of
the seized cargo, although John Armstrong, the American minister to
France believed this was a misinterpretation. Considering Appleton's
long-term rivalry with the Purviances, he must also have felt some personal satisfaction at their plight. His reports of the situation frequently
were followed by allusions to slights he had suffered and to renewed
requests for the naval agency which he presumed would be taken away
from the Purviances if their house collapsed.[50]

At this delicate moment, Appleton pressed hard to recover Lear's
losses. In a two-hour-long meeting with Robert Purviance, he learned
that the firm was $300,000 in debt (at least $5 million–6 million in today's
dollars) with virtually no assets. The debt included $60,000 to the secre-
tary of the navy, Robert Smith. Purviance repeatedly blamed Degan for
the firm's troubles, alleging he had run off with $100,000 of the firm's
property and owed them another $50,000. Appleton suspected Degan's
actions may have been sanctioned by the firm. As he wrote Lear, "There
may possibly be some small difference in common life, between doing and
suffering to be done, but in a legal view, I believe there is none." All of this
information, plus what he saw as a good deal of evasiveness on
Purviance's part, convinced Appleton that "an amicable adjustment is
impossible," and he began to pursue legal action. He also attempted
some overtures to Degan in hopes of playing one end against the other.
By October, William Purviance had fled to Paris after leaving Livorno "in

[50] Appleton to Armstrong, Aug. 23, 1808; to Armstrong, Sept. 21, 1808; to Warden,
   Oct. 10, 1808; to Armstrong, Nov. 8, 1808, all in GL; Appleton to Sec. State, Nov. 26,
   1808; Dec. 20, 1808; to Armstrong, Dec. 24, 1808; Feb. 14, 1809; to Sec. State, Mar. 22,
   1809, all in Leghorn Despatches; Entry for Aug. 19, 1808, Register of Events.

secrecy." Pursuing the case was made more difficult by the transition from Italian law to the Napoleonic Code in Livorno, but on November 9 Appleton finally obtained a judgment against Samuel Purviance. When the court demanded payment on December 2, Purviance declared bankruptcy. His destruction seemed complete as the sheriff arrived at his house to carry out an inventory of his furniture. Appleton wrote that Purviance would never have "desired the disgrace for so small a sum" as Lear demanded if he had not "speculated wildly in colonial produce which will not now bring more than one half what it cost him." Appleton concluded that Lear would never recover his losses.[51]

Once the Purviances declared bankruptcy, the newly adopted Napoleonic code mandated that syndics be appointed to oversee the examination of the failed company. Appleton managed to get the Livornese authorities to appoint him to that position through his friendship with the president of Livorno's Tribunal of Commerce. He claimed to have done so "solely with a view to have a clearer insight to [Degan and Purviance's] concerns while acting as navy agents" and to try to ensure that any debt due the United States would be considered privileged and more easily retrievable. However, syndics also received compensation for their time, which in Appleton's case meant months poring over the convoluted books of the various Purviance and Degan companies.[52]

To some extent Appleton's work was fruitful. Although unable to recover any funds, he discovered while going through the books that Degan Purviance had been in a partnership with two other firms: one in Marseille and one in Naples. The Neapolitan firm was run by Frederick Degan, former US consul to Naples and son of Charles F. Degan, the Degan Purviance partner. Appleton had already been authorized by the US government to institute a suit against Degan Purviance to recover the lost governmental funds, and so, in 1811, apparently with the permission of the French minister, John Armstrong, he relocated to Naples to pursue a case against Frederick Degan who was still in business and

[51] Appleton to Lear, Sept. 15, 1808; to Stephen Cathalan, Oct. 5/7, 1808; to Charles F. Degan, Oct. 7, 1808; to Warden, Oct. 10, 1808; to Lear, Nov. [Dec.] 2, 1808, all in GL; to Sec. State, Mar. 25, 1808, Leghorn Despatches; Entry for Dec. 1, 1808, Register of Events.

[52] Appleton to Sec. State, Sept. 1, 1809; Oct. 10, 1813, both in Leghorn Despatches; James Beardsley, "The New French Bankruptcy Statute," *The International Lawyer* 19 (Summer, 1985) 974–75; Pierre-Cyrille Hautcocar and Nadine Levratto, "Bankruptcy Law and Practice in 19th Century France," PSE Working Papers (2007), https://core.ac .uk/download/pdf/47764465.pdf.

presumably solvent. Unfortunately for the United States, Degan was close friends with the Naples chief justice, was willing and able to spend $20,000 on his case, and, according to Appleton, had "in such a manner arranged his books, that there will appear a loss in their trade instead of a benefit." For these and other reasons, Appleton and three clerks were unable to recover a penny despite an investigation lasting more than a year and the perusal of 200 volumes of accounts and twenty chests of papers.[53]

The investigation did, however, have some political impact. Appleton called the Degan Purviance bankruptcy "the most scandalous act of fraud and infamy ever committed in this place" and "no small discredit to our national mercantile character." In Washington, the secretary of the navy, Robert Smith, already in trouble, would be badly damaged by events in Italy. Smith was the brother of the powerful Republican congressman Samuel Smith who was one of Baltimore's political bosses and aligned with the Purviance family there. As secretary of the navy, Robert also was technically their boss when they were naval agents in Livorno. Degan Purviance owed Smith $60,000 in notes, and there were rumors that, back in Baltimore, Smith had been cashing bills that he knew the firm could never pay. The treasury department released a report on the matter on March 12, 1811. Smith resigned the next day.[54]

Appleton himself was also nearly ruined by the economic turndown and quite possibly would have been entirely destroyed without the income provided from his service to Italy and the United States. Before 1808 his personal letterbook is filled with efforts to find commissions (as discussed in Chapter 7). With the cessation of trade after 1808 he never mentions the possibility of commissions to his correspondents, and he more-or-less stopped writing to many of the merchants, such as Samuel Perkins in Smyrna, with whom he had been in close contact before. He attempted, instead, to begin selling Italian marble and marble busts of famous Americans to the United States. Having lived in Livorno for twenty years, he had developed artistic and mercantile contacts who had access to the excellent marble found in Tuscany, and he eventually became

[53] Appleton to Sec. State, Sept. 1, 1809; July 10, 1810; to Albert Gallatin, Aug. 1, 1812, all in Leghorn Despatches; Luca Codignola, *Blurred Nationalities Across the Atlantic: Traders, Priests, and Their Kin Travelling between North America and the Italian Peninsula, 1763–1846* (University of Toronto Press, 2019) 62.

[54] Appleton to Gallatin, Aug. 1, 1812, Leghorn Despatches; Robert Smith, *Address to the People of the United States* (London: J. Hatchard, 1811); Frank A. Cassell, *Merchant Congressman in the Young Republic: Samuel Smith of Maryland* (Madison: University of Wisconsin Press, 1971) 148, 171; *Geneva Gazette* (NY), Jan. 16, 1811.

a partner in a quarry in nearby Carrara. He hoped to use his American connections, particularly his brothers-in-law Thomas Perkins and Samuel Emery, to help distribute the products to elite American purchasers.[55]

Increasingly, however, Appleton saw little prospect of business success in Livorno. No evidence is more damning than the fact that in the five years from 1810 to 1815 he was away from that port for roughly two years and four months – thirteen months in Naples auditing Degan's books and fifteen months on vacation visiting friends in Paris.[56] The latter trip was probably partially prompted by his financial reverses; he declared bankruptcy twice, once shortly before departing and once while still in France. The first bankruptcy apparently was connected to Appleton's efforts to assist Lear, or so Appleton claimed. No doubt a majority of Appleton's income, such as it was, now came from noncommercial sources. He asked his brother-in-law to invest his savings in American governmental stocks which would prove a good long-term strategy. In the interim he would have received some income as syndic for the Purviance bankruptcy in Livorno and in his fees from Armstrong and Lear for pursuing the case. While in Naples auditing Degan's books, he charged the United States $6 per day for his expenses over the course of more than a year. On an annual basis this slightly exceeded Simpson's $2,000 salary, but Appleton would have a good deal of difficulty getting reimbursed. Shortly thereafter, he also instigated a lawsuit against his Philadelphia brother-in-law, Samuel Emery, who had long owed him over $2,000. Appleton no doubt calculated that all these funds would allow him to get through this difficult financial stretch. He also continued to push for the lucrative naval agency that the Purviances had held before their collapse.[57]

The Montgomerys and others in the Spanish Mediterranean suffered through similar economic difficulties. By 1808 Robert Montgomery was near the height of his economic power. He was able to offer to cash $35,000 in American bills of exchange without any problem. In 1809, John Montgomery offered a huge dowry to his new son-in-law Obadiah Rich and, no doubt, staged an elaborate wedding for him and Ana

[55] Appleton to N. and C. Appleton, Feb. 15, 1809; to Samuel Emery, Mar. 1, 1809; to Parker, Aug. 21, 1812; Nov. 13, 1812; to William Lee, Nov. 16, 1812; to Parker, Dec. 8, 1812; to Perkins, Apr. 29, 1813, all in GL.

[56] The gap in letters during his time in Naples is from July 1810 to Sept. 1811, and for Paris it is Oct. 1813 to Jan. 1815.

[57] Appleton to Gallatin, Aug. 1, 1812; to Perkins, Aug. 1, 1812; Jan. 3, 1813; Apr. 20, 1812; to Coxe, Nov. 16, 1815, all in GL.

Montgomery Rich. Although no records survive, it would not be surprising if Robert offered a similar dowry to John Rogers when he married his daughter Isabella in 1808 and staged a similarly splendid wedding.[58]

Those weddings would mark the beginning of the end of the family's heyday. Within two or three years, Obadiah and Ana Montgomery Rich had fled to America, where they settled for a time in Georgetown, DC. By Christmas of 1812, Rich wrote William Shaw that he had lost most of his fortune and would "probably be obliged to return to Europe again." During the sojourn in the United States, he applied for consular positions in Valencia and Málaga. Similarly, by 1812 John Rogers and Isabella Montgomery Rogers had fled Alicante for London "in consequence of the critical situation of Spain," and Rogers planned to form a new merchant house in British-controlled Malta.[59]

Meanwhile, back in Alicante, Robert Montgomery began to shift his financial strategy away from the commission business. Much like Appleton in Livorno, he turned toward his local connections and away from American merchants. Alicante was an important wine and brandy producing region, and as Brown and Ives's *Eliza* voyage demonstrates, those products had been in demand in the US during the boom years. Montgomery had owned a home and land in the fertile Huerta district outside Alicante near the present San Juan beach for many years. After 1808, with the decline in the commission business, he began a concerted effort to purchase more land. Between 1809 and 1814, he made five recorded purchases of land with vineyards and fruit trees, at least four of which were connected to his original property. These purchases brought him an additional ten acres of valuable land in a region where land parcels tended to be small. The new property would allow Montgomery to produce and sell grapes and fruit, and likely wine and brandy to local consumers and producers as well as to other merchants in the region. There is no evidence that he or his brother engaged in much, if any, overseas trade during these years. Nor could he have received any commissions from American shipping, but sales within the region may

[58] Montgomery to Sec. State, Dec. 15, 1807; July 18, 1816, both in Alicante Despatches; Dna. Ana Montgomery recepción de dote, July 11, 1809, Protocolo Notarial de Francisco Aracil, PN (Note: "Protocolo de Notariales" (notarial notebooks) are identified by name of the notary and date in the archives throughout this chapter).

[59] Norman Paul Tucker, "Obadiah Rich, 1783–1850: Early American Hispanist," PhD dissertation (Harvard University, 1973) 15–32, quote at 18; John H. Rogers to John Rogers, Jr., July 6, 1812; Apr. 20, 1813; Mar. 2, 1814, all in Rogers-Bridges Family Collection.

well have been possible, and Montgomery probably calculated investment in these vineyards would pay off once the wars ended. As with Appleton, this turn toward local production as opposed to international shipping, could also have resulted in Montgomery disconnecting from the American community to some extent.[60]

The extraordinary financial strain and efforts to move away from reliance on overseas trade were even more pronounced with the house of Grivegnée and Co. in Málaga. Located about 300 miles to the south of Alicante, Málaga was a common stopping point for ships heading up the coast toward Alicante, Valencia, and Barcelona (as with Brown and Ives's *Eliza*). Montgomery was well acquainted with the Grivegnées and particularly their son-in-law and partner, William Kirkpatrick, the long-term American consul. Like Montgomery, who could well have modelled his smaller empire on theirs, the Grivegnées turned toward local production after 1809. In 1810, Kirkpatrick applied for a license to manufacture chemical products in association with a Spanish partner. He also established a cotton textile manufactory in that year with Grivegnée and Co. and a Spanish partner using, no doubt, raw materials from the cotton plantation he owned in nearby Churriana. The Grivegnées also owned a sugar plantation and other smaller projects in the area. The combination of wartime disruptions and this inward turn also separated Kirkpatrick from the US network. The secretary of state did not receive a single letter from him between November 1809 and October 1812.[61]

Despite these efforts, the Grivegnées and Kirkpatrick suffered financially during the war. The family certainly sympathized with the French occupiers, but, as has already been noted, Kirkpatrick himself was arrested by French authorities for pursuing debts they owed him. There are also indications that financial desperation pushed him to flout French regulations. After the French withdrawal, Kirkpatrick appears to have been imprisoned by Spanish officials who would have viewed him as a French collaborator despite his earlier legal problems. Soon

---

[60] The sales were as follows: Juan Selles de Rocque venta real a Dn. Roberto Montgomery, Apr. 7, 1809, Francisco Aracil (6.25 tahullas); Dn. Josef Morant venta real a Dn. Roberto Montgomery, Jan. 26, 1811, Francisco Aracil (6.75 tahullas); Bautista Garcia venta real a Dn. Roberto Montgomery, Feb. 13, 1811, Francisco Aracil (4.75 tahullas); Josef Lopez de Antonio venta real a Dn. Roberto Montgomery, Oct. 30, 1812, Francisco Aracil (2.87 tahullas); Dn. Joaquin Linares venta real a Dn. Roberto Montgomery, Jan. 16, 1814, Pedro Fuentes y Sanchez (26 tahullas), all in PN. I am converting 1 tahulla to 0.276 acres.
[61] Dn. Roberto Montgomery poder (power of attorney) a Grivegnée y Co., Dec. 1, 1800, Ramon Izquierdo, PN; Carlin, *William Kirkpatrick*, 111–23.

Kirkpatrick, his wife and daughter fled Málaga for Paris. The disruptions to trade and the unsympathetic Spanish government were too much for the Grivegnée firm, which finally declared bankruptcy in 1815.[62]

***

Many in the Mediterranean hoped or expected the year 1815 would mark a turnaround, and that the decline of the previous half decade would prove to have been temporary. Their hopes were buoyed by the end of the Napoleonic Wars, the US triumph over Algeria, and treaties with the other Barbary powers following the Second Barbary War. In Alicante, Montgomery exulted over the end of the hated discriminatory Spanish fish duties, writing that the repeal "again places our fisheries on a footing with [Britain's] and in due time will render the utility much greater than we at present can calculate." He also continued to support the new family firm in Marseille led by his sons and former clerk, Asa Fitch. In the midst of setting up a new commission business in Naples, John Rogers also continued to seek business for his Alicante house, now run by his brother Josiah, on the basis of the tariff repeal. Montgomery's chief rivals in Alicante, Stemborg and Roselt, wrote that "prosperous time[s] will, we hope, make amends for the late impropitious period." New hope sprang up in Livorno as well. For the first time in years, Appleton returned to the commission trade with a new partner, Edward Swords, an Irish merchant.[63]

Certainly, the year 1815 marked a period of triumph and optimism for all Americans, or at least all Americans of means, with the end of overseas wars and the acquisition of vast new quantities of territory in the Mississippi Valley. Unfortunately, Americans in the Mediterranean would discover over the coming years that their hopes for a positive turning point had been false.

---

[62] Carlin, *William Kirkpatrick*, 121–38.

[63] Montgomery to Sec. State, Dec. 16, 1814, Alicante Despatches; Rogers Bros. to Brown and Ives, Jan. 1, 1815. B112 F3; Jan. 1816, B113 F1; Dec. 16, 1815, B112 F10; Stemborg and [Roselt] to Brown and Ives, Mar. 20, 1815, B112 F4; Montgomerys Fitch and Co. to Brown and Ives, May 9, 1815, B112 F5; Appleton to Brown and Ives, Aug. 1, 1815, B112 F7, all in B. & I.; Appleton to Sec. State, Oct. 1, 1815, Leghorn Despatches; Codignola, *Blurred Nationalities*, 119.

9

Selling Empire

After 1815 Americans could realistically begin to contemplate becoming an empire. While they had not exactly defeated Britain in the War of 1812, they had managed to hold off the world's greatest superpower and maintain the *status quo ante bellum*. This quasi-victory demonstrated (in their minds at least) that they could successfully engage the great powers. In the Mediterranean the easy victory over Algiers and favorable treaties with the other Barbary states exorcised the sense of weakness that earlier ship captures had produced in the region. The acquisition of the Louisiana Territory in the West and successful efforts to settle it (and remove Native Americans) and, most importantly, the emergence of the Monroe Doctrine, all cheered Americans in the Mediterranean and confirmed the new republic as a rising power.

Ironically, however, in the Mediterranean, where so many of the new republic's earliest performances on the international stage had occurred, the United States appeared to have little interest in or ability to project power, imperial or otherwise. Despite having been the birthplace of American orientalism and the site of the new nation's first overseas military adventures with the Barbary powers, not to mention the destination of the first US naval squadron, after 1815 the Mediterranean receded in importance due to the economic decline and instability discussed in the previous chapter. Far from championing conquest or even an extension of American naval power as they had before, consuls and other Americans in the region now found themselves cut off from the mainstream of American economic and military developments which were increasingly directed toward continental expansion.

Those who remained in the region scrambled to find new ways to support themselves. As the Mediterranean became more peripheral to the US economy, it became more of a cultural destination. The end of the Napoleonic Wars marked the beginning of the tradition of the European grand tour for young Englishmen and women of means. Young Americans began to travel to Europe more frequently after 1820, though initially the numbers were only in the hundreds. Still, Appleton began writing about a surge of American travelers in Tuscany as early as 1816 and by 1819 he observed, "The number now travelling in Italy, has made it indispensably requisite to appoint a person of responsibility at Florence." Consequently, he appointed James (or Giacomo) Ombrosi as a vice-consul there to deal with these tourists.[1] The rise of tourism (and, arguably, the evolving American view of the entire region) was based on the Mediterranean's cultural heritage. Both sides of the sea – Carthage, Grenada, Rome, and the places in between – were the seats of ancient empires, cultures which Americans increasingly wished to experience and emulate. To facilitate and profit from those desires, Americans in the Mediterranean now became cultural brokers, connecting the citizens of the rising American empire to the memory of the ancient Mediterranean empires.

***

To an observer in the first decade of the nineteenth century, the actual Mediterranean as well as the memory of the ancient Mediterranean might have seemed like a logical seedbed for a rising American empire of a commercial stripe. The growing number of American residents there, the increase in trade, and, above all else, the emerging American Navy, all could be viewed as potential ingredients for an American trading empire along the lines of eighteenth-century Great Britain or the Dutch empire. Nearly all these residents agreed that the new nation needed to exhibit military might in the region through a naval presence, due to the large number of ship seizures by European and North African powers. The creation of the Mediterranean Squadron in 1794 answered American consuls' and others' prayers, and as a result Americans in the region

---

[1] Daniel Kilbride, *Being American in Europe 1750–1860* (Baltimore: Johns Hopkins University Press, 2013) 2–3; Will B. Mackintosh, *Selling the Sights: The Invention of the Tourist in American Culture* (New York University Press, 2019) 8–9; Thomas Appleton to Sec. State, Apr. 2, 1819, Leghorn Despatches; Thomas Appleton to Henry Jackson, May 20, 1816, GL.

were the only ones to have regular contact with naval ships and officers. This development reflected the unique importance of the Mediterranean at the time. While the squadron benefitted the public interest by supporting US trade, it also benefitted the private interests of the American Mediterranean community in two ways. First, it protected their trade from capture at a very minimal cost. Absent the Navy, the risk of loss would have been far higher as would have been the cost of purchasing insurance to mitigate that risk. Second, because the hundreds of crew members in the squadron had to be fed and their ships maintained, the presence of the Navy in the region produced numerous opportunities for lucrative government contracts. Appleton's constant efforts to become Livorno's naval agent reflect how desirable these contracts could be.[2]

The consuls' push for naval power may have had some influence in Washington, considering that weakness in the Mediterranean prompted the reestablishment and growth of the US Navy following the Revolution. Yet, for all their insistence on the need for naval power, Americans in the Mediterranean never seem to have viewed it as an avenue for conquest in the region. Rather, at least until 1815, they viewed the United States as a weak power that desperately needed to find means to protect its vital commerce from greater and even lesser powers with well-funded navies.

After 1815, at least some Americans in the region did begin to call for a more aggressive use of US power than merely as a defensive means of protection. When they did so, however, they had the American continent in mind rather than the Mediterranean. Specifically, they hoped to free Latin American colonies from their Mediterranean masters, and to do so forcibly if necessary. These hopes stemmed in part from the enlightenment republican ideology of the American Revolution, which led Americans to associate Latin American independence with their own independence from Britain. But commercial motives also played a major role. Latin American colonies often were difficult trading partners for US merchants due to colonial regulations which might well disappear with independence. These colonial goods had, until recently, been the most profitable cargoes in the Mediterranean. Independence could well revive the indirect reexport trade between the colonial ports and the Mediterranean from

---

[2] See Lawrence Peskin, *Captives and Countrymen: Barbary Slavery and the American Public, 1785–1816* (Baltimore: Johns Hopkins University Press, 2009) 110–33; Kenneth J. Hogan, *This Peoples Navy: The Making of American Sea Power* (New York: Free Press, 1991) 21–24; Marshall Smelser, *The Congress Founds the Navy, 1787–1798* (South Bend: University of Notre Dame Press, 1959); Craig L. Symonds, *Navalists and Antinavalists: The Naval Policy Debate in the United States 1785–1827* (Newark: Delaware, 1980).

which Americans in the region had profited before the Napoleonic Wars brought a stop to it.

Robert Montgomery, who often seemed more Spanish than American in earlier decades, now became the leading American victim of the Peninsular War and a vocal advocate of a muscular approach to Spain. In 1816, he wrote then-Secretary of State James Monroe that the United States must push Spain as hard as possible to receive restitution for Americans whose property had been seized during the wars. This matter was personal for Montgomery, who claimed that he had lost $200,000 to the Spanish, an enormous sum at the time, and that his struggle against the Spanish "threw me into a disorder which injured my constitution and nearly cost me my life." He was aware that his friend, America's Spanish minister, George Erving, had been appointed to address the issue, and Montgomery probably had been in contact with him about potential negotiations. Montgomery urged Monroe to take a very hard line by seizing the Spanish colonies of Florida and Puerto Rico and perhaps others, and to use these territories to secure funds for repayments to the injured parties, the "honest industrious merchants who with their inno-cent families have been reduced to bankruptcy and every state of misery by [Spain's] nefarious proceedings."[3]

Two years after Montgomery wrote Monroe, at the dawn of the Seminole War in which the United States would take Florida from Spain, Andrew Jackson made almost the same argument. He wrote now-President Monroe that "the whole of East Florida [should be] seized and held as an indemnity for the outrages of Spain upon the property of our citizens." Monroe never responded, but he did not prevent Jackson from taking Florida, a position that historian Daniel Walker Howe sees as crea-ting plausible deniability for the president. After the war, Erving himself played a small role in the negotiations that would bring Florida into the new republic when he shared with the Spanish government an aggressive memorandum from John Q. Adams, Monroe's secretary of state.[4] The extent to which Montgomery's early letter influenced Monroe's actions on Florida is difficult to say, and judging from the frequent lack of response to consular dispatches should not be overestimated. But it is clear that the collective voices of Americans in the Mediterranean were heard in

---

[3] Robert Montgomery to Sec. State, July 18, 1816, Alicante Despatches.

[4] Daniel Walker Howe, *What Hath God Wrought: The Transformation of America, 1815–1848* (Oxford University Press, 2007) 97, 107.

Washington even if they were not the only ones calling for the Florida annexation.

Anger and contempt for Spain continued after the cession of Florida. Reacting to Spain's recalcitrance in agreeing to the cession, Montgomery's former clerk, Asa Fitch, described the king of Spain as "savage" and "blind to his own interest." Montgomery saw Latin American independence as a way around the onerous tariffs Spain had been placing on imports for years. Writing on Latin America, he observed, "that vast and fertile country which is forever severed from the metropolis offers great hope for enterprise." Montgomery envisioned a day when America's growing manufacturing sector would allow the new republic to monopolize trade with the former Spanish colonies and push France and England out of those markets. In the meantime, he hoped that Spanish tariff revisions would allow American ships to gain some ground, particularly in the fish trade. He also chafed at strict Spanish control of the profitable colonial tobacco trade but was cheered that "the [Spanish] public opinion with respect to the South American possessions is gradually tempered with indifference" since independence would make Spanish strictures irrelevant.[5]

With Spain's impending collapse in America, members of the Mediterranean community also scented the possibility of new land speculations. Thomas Appleton's wealthy and somewhat shady friend, Daniel Parker in Paris, began importuning him to join in a scheme to profit from Spanish lands. Though not entirely clear, the plot involved Parker and George Erving, both of whom had been involved in Florida speculation for more than a decade and both of whom had deep pockets. The two were attempting to enlist Appleton to make overtures to Manuel Godoy, aka the "Prince of Peace," who had formerly served as the Spanish minister involved in American land negotiations and now lived in exile in Rome. Parker and Erving apparently hoped Godoy would cede them a great deal of American land that could then be surveyed and sold for speculation. It is unclear where exactly this land was, though most likely either in Florida or modern-day Texas, and even to Appleton it was not entirely clear whether Godoy had legal title. Appleton eventually concluded that the scheme was too risky, and there is no evidence that Parker and Erving went ahead without him, but their willingness to consider such a plan underlines the opportunities that Spain's problems presented to

---

[5] Asa Fitch to William Shaler, Sept. 9, 1819, Shaler Papers; Montgomery to Sec. State, Jan. 1, 1822; June 1, 1822, both in Alicante Despatches.

Americans who were well versed in Spanish affairs and well connected in the Mediterranean.[6]

Certainly, many Americans in the Mediterranean community took part in US efforts at expansion into Spanish territories during this period. In addition to Parker, Appleton, and Erving, Appleton's friend, John Armstrong, the American minister to Paris from 1804 to 1810, was also involved in the early Florida negotiations. Appleton and Fitch's mutual friend, William Shaler, had a long history in Latin America before arriving in Algiers in 1815 to become American consul. Beginning in about 1803 he had traveled to Chile, Mexico, California, Cuba, and New Orleans in various capacities where he often was involved in American plots, official and unofficial, to gain influence, while, at the same time, pursuing his own business interests. Robert Montgomery's son, Frederick, journeyed to New Orleans about 1817. Though the nature of his trip is unclear, he could have little reason to go there at that time other than to pursue land speculation and other trading opportunities. At about the same time, Appleton's occasional Livorno neighbor and former US consul to Tripoli, James Cathcart, also arrived in the Spanish-speaking Louisiana territories as part of a government surveying party laying the groundwork for land speculation. No doubt these individuals decided to follow this course based on the lure of potentially large profits in areas where they could use their knowledge of Spanish to advantage and by the concomitant lack of opportunity in the Mediterranean.[7]

***

The Monroe Doctrine of 1823, the most famous and arguably most influential foreign policy pronouncement in American history, further energized the interests of the Mediterranean community in Latin America. By proclaiming American hegemony on the American continent,

---

[6] Appleton to Daniel Parker, Oct. 3, 1822; Oct. 5, 1822, both in GL. On Parker, Gody, and Erving's experience in America see Clifford L. Egan, "The United States, France and West Florida 1803–1807," *Florida Historical Quarterly* 47 (Jan. 1969) 227–52; [Jabez L. M. Curry] "Diplomatic Services of George W. Erving," *Proceedings of the Massachusetts Historical Society* (Oct. 1889) 7–27; Henry Adams, *History of the United States of America during the Second Administration of Thomas Jefferson* (Cambridge University Press, 2011) III: 371–91.

[7] Egan, "US France and West Florida"; Roy F. Nichols, "William Shaler: New England Apostle of Rational Liberty," *New England Quarterly* 9 (Mar. 1936) 71–96; Montgomery to Sec. State, July 26, 1817 [1818?] Alicante Despatches; Brett Goodin, "Opportunities of Empire: Three Barbary Captives and American nation-building, 1700–1840" PhD dissertation (Australian National University, 2015) 190–94.

it brought American traders a step closer towards being able to capture commerce in the former Spanish colonies. As such, it was welcomed by American Mediterranean traders who had been pushing for this outcome for years. Nevertheless, because it also renounced American ambitions overseas, it proved a double-edged sword for the Mediterranean community. The renunciation of ambitions beyond the American continent undermined any hope that the United States might exhibit more muscle in the Mediterranean region.

Nevertheless, Americans in the Mediterranean applauded the Monroe Doctrine when they learned of it in 1824. In Italy Appleton wrote, "The speech of the President is read with great admiration and has given a deadly blow to the projects of the Holy Alliance."[8] Asa Fitch wrote William Shaler that he would be pleased with the doctrine, which was one of the "most important state documents that has appeared for ages and must give great umbrage to the crowned heads in this quarter." He noted that it would not only check the "holy allies" in helping Spain "recover her colonies" but would also deter the British crown from interfering in Spanish America. Fitch's former boss, Robert Montgomery had worried that the United States and Europe might get pulled into war "from the anti-social system pursued by the Holy Alliance, and the obstinate perseverance of this country [Spain] not to recognize the independence of South America." He hoped the new doctrine would prevent European powers from "crush[ing] the principles of liberty and civilization disseminated in the new world."[9] Montgomery viewed the American position in ideological terms. He wrote of the contrast between the blessings the United States received from its "political institutions" and the "grinding oppression," famine and revolution produced by European despotism. He affirmed, "It is a source of inward satisfaction that we [the United States] are animated by no selfish feelings, and that we are always desirous to assist those who having long groaned under the yoke of despotism claim our efforts to procure for them similar advantages." He added that "Columbia, Mexico, Peru, forever severed from the dominion of this imbecile [Spanish] government attest the sincerity of our well wishes and the moral influence which their cause has derived from our countenance."[10]

---

[8] Appleton to Thomas Perkins, Feb. 21, 1824, GL.
[9] Fitch to Shaler, Jan. 12, 1824, Shaler Papers; Montgomery to Sec. State, Aug. 15, 1824, Alicante Despatches.
[10] Montgomery to Sec. State, Apr. 2, 1825, Alicante Despatches.

But given the context of these Americans' earlier comments about Florida, it is clear that their approval also stemmed from personal interests. In addition to potentially opening up Latin American markets to US traders, by portraying the United States as a hegemonic empire in the West, the Monroe Doctrine gave notice to European powers, particularly Spain, that Americans and their concerns must be respected – a message that Montgomery in particular could embrace given the way the Spanish government had trampled over his property. Thomas Appleton, always an Anglophobe, even gained some hope that the newly aggressive United States, and Andrew Jackson in particular, might drive Great Britain from North America. "Old Hickory," he wrote in 1826, "can neither be coaxed nor bullied … Should we ever, during his presidency, have a war with England, Canada and Nova Scotia will form new states."[11]

But, unfortunately for Appleton's and Montgomery's interests and those of their circle, the Monroe Doctrine never really delivered for them. It foreclosed naval action in the Mediterranean, and trade with former Spanish colonies, the hoped-for pay-off, never quite came through to the extent that Americans in the Mediterranean and at home hoped. What the Monroe doctrine indubitably succeeded in doing was to raise America's profile among world powers and to put the United States on the road to implementing what one historian has termed "imperial anti-colonialism."[12] In the end, Americans in the Mediterranean were able to profit from and even nurture this turn toward imperialism by capitalizing on American aspirations to be connected to the ancient and early modern empires of the Mediterranean world.

***

The collapse of the Mediterranean trade, the turn toward empire, and the growth of tourism all provided opportunities for consuls and other Americans to sell the trappings of empire to their countrymen. They cleverly nurtured and benefitted from American nostalgia for the ancient Mediterranean empires that accompanied the Monroe Doctrine and the rise of Manifest Destiny in the West. A remarkable aspect of the interest in Mediterranean empires which these consuls stoked, is that Americans, whose origin story involved defeating the British Empire, now collected remnants of the great empires and bought books romanticizing them.

---

[11] Thomas Appleton to Shaler, Feb. 3, 1825, Shaler Papers.
[12] Jay Sexton, *The Monroe Doctrine: Empire and Nation in Nineteenth-Century America* (New York: Hill and Wang, 2012) 5–8.

A nation that little more than a generation earlier had fought the first successful colonial war was now beginning to identify with emperors rather than the colonized.

More than any other place, the Mediterranean region represented the corruption and decline of empire to the new republic. Due to their interest in political philosophy and the rhetoric of their own revolution, Americans were well versed in Roman history. During the American Revolution they self-consciously modeled themselves on the Roman republic, a pose that continued well into the early republic with its emphasis on neoclassicism. If the Roman republic was a source of emulation, the Roman empire served as a cautionary tale about the threat of corruption faced by republics.[13] Yet, by the nineteenth century, Americans, including those in the Mediterranean, were beginning to see the notion of empire, particularly an "empire of liberty," in a more favorable light. As early as 1794, the three consuls' friend and nominal superior, David Humphreys, was praising the new republic in verse as a rising empire, albeit more "chaste" and more industrious than corrupt, slothful predecessors. In glorifying the new, industrious, empire, he articulated the standard view within the Mediterranean of the decline of its lazy, corrupt predecessors when he asked, "Where art thou, Athens! Thy high spirit lost! ... And where (in dust her mould'ring trophies hurl'd) / Imperial Rome, the mistress of the world!" Spain prompted the same sort of reflections when he wrote, "And will not grave Iberia learn, at length, / In toil, not gold, consists a nation's strength?"[14]

With the rising power of the new republic after 1815, fear of imperial corruption began to fade, and Rome may have become as much a model of grandeur as a cautionary tale. Appleton and other Mediterranean cultural brokers profited from and stoked this interest. They were more than willing to connect Americans to the glories and decline of the Mediterranean empires through tangible goods or cultural experiences. Italy was ground-zero for imperial fascinations, and Appleton certainly profited from Americans' heightened interest. As more Americans began

---

[13] Gordon Wood, *Empire of Liberty: A History of the Early Republic, 1789–1815* (Oxford University Press, 2009) 557–59; Bernard Bailyn, *The Ideological Origins of the American Revolution* (Cambridge, MA: Belknap Press, 1967); Eran Shalev, *Rome Reborn on Western Shores: Historical Imagination and the Creation of the American* Republic (Charlottesville: University of Virginia Press, 2009); Carl J. Richard, *The Founders and the Classics: Greece, Rome, and the American Enlightenment* (Cambridge, MA: Harvard University Press, 1995).

[14] David Humphreys, "A Poem on the Industry of the United States of America."

to take grand tours to see the Roman ruins, he became a frequent tour guide, advisor, and marketer of Italian products. He even seems to have warmed a bit to the charms of Renaissance Florence for which Livorno served as the primary port.

Appleton's interest in cultural products began early in his term in Livorno. Always fond of citing classical philosophers, especially Cicero, he clearly had an intellectual interest in the ancient world, as did many of his contemporaries.[15] As early as the summer of 1802 he made a connection with Giuseppe Luciano, a marble dealer in Carrara, the center of Italian marble production, located about 50 miles from Livorno. At that time, he bought twenty-six marble chimney pieces and a sizable assortment of marble paving stones from Luciano which he then sent to his brother-in-law Samuel Emery in Philadelphia. Presumably Emery would then sell them to wealthy Philadelphians on commission. At about the same time he also made contact with a vase dealer, Settimo Guadaroli e Cil in the Tuscan alabaster center of Volterra, also about 50 miles from Livorno. Appleton bought fifty pairs of 10–12-inch vases from Guadaroli and shipped them to Emery, also presumably to be sold on commission.[16]

For Appleton, Italy's ruins, antiquities, and artistic legacy were more than a matter of intellectual interest. Over time they became his business. In a sense, all merchants are cultural brokers, introducing potential customers to new sorts of goods and educating them on their provenance and utility. Wine is a good example. Like Montgomery, Appleton frequently sold it to Americans, though he never grew it himself. His most famous client was Thomas Jefferson, for whom he procured sizable quantities of Italian wines for decades. The process was not based merely on a cash nexus. It involved the exchange of educational information which both informed Jefferson and other clients and, presumably, made Appleton's products more attractive to the consumer. Jefferson was interested in the culture of vines, and Appleton was happy to send him cuttings from Italian vineyards. He also informed Jefferson and other clients of the differences in quality and taste between various vintages and types of Italian wines. When Montepulciano, which Jefferson favored, was having

---

[15] For some of his references to Cicero see Appleton to Marquise de Chastellux, Mar. 17, 1802; to Joel Barlow, Mar. 25, 1804; to Stephen Cathalan, Aug. 24, 1804; to William Shaler, Sept. 18, 1815, all in GL.

[16] Philipp Fehl, "The Account Book of Thomas Appleton of Livorno: A Document in the History of American Art, 1802–1825," *Winterthur Portfolio* 9 (1974) 136; Appleton to Samuel Emery, Aug. 11, 1802, GL.

a bad year, Appleton recommended other types of wine, such as Carmignano, that Jefferson may not have known of. When Captain William Bainbridge expressed an interest in wine, Appleton wrote him a long description of all the types available in Italy and France.[17]

Appleton's greatest love was sculpture, a medium that would be particularly suited for America's imperial aspirations. He admired the sculptor Giuseppe Ceracchi's work at least as early 1804, only a few years after the Florentine master died. Ceracchi had visited the United States twice in the 1790s and sculpted busts of leading Americans including George Washington. In January 1804, Appleton began searching for Ceracchi's widow to see if she would be willing to sell him the originals of these busts. His friend Joseph Barnes, the American consul to Genoa, introduced Appleton to Robert Fagan, who lived in Rome and agreed to serve as an intermediary. After a long wait (Mrs. Ceracchi apparently was out of town), Fagan finally located her, and Appleton directed him to purchase the Washington bust for £20 sterling or have a copy made in gesso. It is unclear whether Mrs. Ceracchi ever agreed to this offer. Appleton had asked Guadaroli to make several alabaster busts of Washington, one of which he sold to Stephen Cathalan, the American consul in Marseille. These busts, though, were produced in 1803, so it is unlikely they were based on Ceracchi's work, unless Appleton had access to another copy.[18]

Appleton also developed an interest in grand-master paintings. In the summer of 1804, he bought four from Fagan – one by Guio Reni, one by Rubens, and two Titians, one of which may have been an imitation by Giovanni Sassoferrato. Appleton paid roughly $500 for this lot. It is unclear whether he intended to sell them or was collecting them for himself. At about the same time Appleton began what would be a continuing effort to send Italian craftsmen to America. In 1805 he funded the emigration of five sculptors to the United States to work on the construction of the new Capitol Building in Washington DC. He received a commission of roughly $40 for his part, in addition to reimbursement of his expenses. In 1807 he sent two skilled engravers to New York who, though German speakers, had presumably lived in Italy for some time. One of the two, Moritz Furst later sued the US government,

---

[17] Appleton to Charles Pinckney, May 19, 1802; to David Gelston, Mar. 17, 1804; May 1, 1805; to Gabriel Christian, Mar. 20, 1807; to Thomas Jefferson, Mar. 20, 1816; May 10, 1816; July 30, 1816, all in GL.

[18] Philipp Fehl, "The Account Book of Thomas Appleton of Livorno: A Document in the History of American Art, 1802–1825," *Winterthur Portfolio* 9 (1974) 137.

claiming Appleton had led him to New York with the false promise that he could become an engraver at the US Mint with an annual salary of $2,000.[19]

When business began to collapse after 1807, Appleton built on many of the cultural enterprises in which he had previously dabbled. His continuing contacts with the State Department and, increasingly, the steady stream of well-to-do Americans visiting Italy assisted in these efforts. By 1816, Appleton reported, "Crowds of Americans have arrived in Italy since the peace, exploring the dreary mansions of the catacombs of Herculaneum ... ." Some, who were attached to the State Department and Navy, served as professional contacts. Others, travelling privately, served as new business contacts. Most important for Appleton were Mr. and Mrs. John J. Astor, with whom he spent a good deal of time in 1819 and 1820, and who purchased a pair of busts of themselves sculpted by Appleton's brother-in-law, Raimondo Trentanove. Later, John Astor's company helped Appleton move money between the United States and Europe, and Appleton hoped to partner with them to procure furs to sell in Italy. Even young American men taking the grand tour gave Appleton access to valuable American contacts. After meeting a Mr. McClelland of New York, Appleton wrote to Ezra Weeks, apparently a relative or connection of the young man, to discuss his plans to study art. Weeks later served as Appleton's principal contact in an effort to get a sculpture commission in New York. Similarly, young John J. Ambler's father in Richmond would serve the same purpose when that city was considering erecting an Italian-made statue.[20]

Appleton took another stab at selling old master paintings to Americans in 1817. He may have been prompted by a new association with Luigi Cajano, an art dealer in Florence with whom he entered into two ventures, along with his brother-in-law Thomas Perkins. Together these two shipments contained seventy-three paintings of various sizes, fifteen of which Appleton had previously purchased, and the rest from

[19] Appleton to Robert Fagan, July 5, 1804; to Gordon Mumford, June 10, 1807, both in GL. Fehl, "The Account Book of Thomas Appleton of Livorno," 128–29, 137–38. Appleton's account book noted these sums in sequins, which he valued at a little more than $2. See *ibid.* 133.

[20] Appleton to Jackson, May 20, 1816; to J. Astor, Nov. 14, 1819; Dec. 1, 1819; to J. J. Astor and Son, Jan. 3, 1820; Mar. 15, 1820; Oct. 3, 1820; Oct. 12, 1820; to Ezra Weeks, Mar. 31, 1823; to William H. Eliot, June 9, 1824; to Perkins, June 9, 1824; to John J. Ambler, Oct. 8, [1824]; to Col. John Ambler, Oct. 20, 1824, all in GL; Appleton to Sec. State, Apr. 2, 1819, Leghorn Despatches,

Cajano. Most were old-master products, including some attributed to Caravaggio, Veronese, Tintoretto, and Van Dyke. Others were by students of prominent painters, and others were likely skilled copies. Appleton paid Cajano roughly $225 for the second group of paintings which he valued at $306, including several paintings Appleton added to the bunch. At a little less than $10 per painting this was quite a bargain and no doubt offered the possibility of easy profits. That same year Appleton also shipped twenty seascapes and battle scenes to Buenos Aires, which he hoped to trade for Argentine merchandise. There is no evidence of whether these shipments succeeded, but the fact that Appleton never again attempted to sell paintings suggests that they did not.[21]

At any rate, Appleton's real passion turned out to be Italian marble with its connection to classical sculpture, rather than canvas and more "modern" old-master paintings. He continued to pursue a copy of Ceracchi's bust of Washington, suggesting he had no luck with the sculptor's widow. Finally, in 1808 he located one in Bourdeaux with the help of William Lee, the American consul there. Planning on making marble copies to sell in the United States, Appleton offered Lee one-half of future sales. This arrangement must have been agreeable to Lee, as he shipped the bust to Appleton via their mutual friend, Stephen Cathalan, American consul to Marseille, and it arrived safely in Livorno in July 1809.[22] At the same time, Appleton was searching for similar busts of Christopher Columbus and Amerigo Vespucci. He eventually acquired some "copied from the original paintings in the gallery of Florence and of the size of life."[23]

Appleton's plan was to sell these Italian marbles in the United States and, perhaps, Europe. He offered a dozen to William Lee, though it is unclear whether Lee accepted them or even if they were ever made. He definitely had his contacts at Carrara produce three – one each of Washington, Columbus, and Vespucci, which he sent to Daniel Parker in Paris in 1813, and another half dozen (two Washingtons, two Columbuses, and two Vespuccis), which he sent to his Baltimore cousins, Nathaniel and Charles Appleton in 1815 on consignment. He paid Luciani in Carrara about $46 each to make these busts and valued them at $80 each on the invoice to the Appletons. He instructed the cousins to

[21] Fehl, "The Account Book of Thomas Appleton of Livorno," 141–42.
[22] *Ibid.* 139; Appleton to William Lee, Sept. 9, 1808; Oct. 10, 1808, both in GL.
[23] Appleton to John Grant, May 30, 1805; to Parker, Aug. 21, 1812; to Lee, Nov. 16, 1812, all in GL.

sell them at $100 each, which would have provided Appleton a healthy profit even after shipping costs and the cousins' commission. However, the busts apparently did not sell well, as Appleton expressed willingness to lower the price by 20 percent a few months later. After this uninspiring effort, he stuck to busts of Washington, producing several life-sized figures and sending them to his contacts in the United States to sell on commission in 1817 and 1818.[24]

Appleton's efforts paid off unexpectedly when, in 1815, North Carolina's legislature voted to erect a full-size statue of George Washington inside their state house. The governor solicited advice on whether such a statue could be made in America or if it was necessary to import one. Most respondents favored importing from Italy, and several mentioned the Italian sculptor Antonio Canova as best suited to the job. Both William Thornton, the architect of the US capital, and Thomas Jefferson suggested that Ceracchi's bust could serve as a model. Jefferson was aware that Appleton owned the Ceracchi bust and had connections to Canova. Describing the consul as a "man of worth and taste," he recommended that the state use him as their agent in acquiring a statue by Canova. (See Figure 9.1.) Governor William Miller agreed and asked William R. King, who was travelling to Italy on his way to become secretary to the American Legation in Russia, to discuss the matter with Appleton.[25]

The commission occupied a good deal of Appleton's time over the next few years. He was able to get Canova to agree to take the job relatively easily. He and Canova concurred that, due to the low height of North Carolina's senate chamber, the statue should be of a seated president. Appleton also commissioned his brother-in-law Raimondo Trentanove to sculpt an ornamental pedestal. Along the way he had to deal with a recalcitrant partner in Carrara who attempted to seize the Cerrachi bust, and a wayward nephew who made off with part of the funds from the state of North Carolina. Appleton told Jefferson that he did not request compensation from North Carolina, but doubtless he took some sort of commission from Canova. Considering that the statue cost $10,000, the customary 2 percent commission would have brought him

---

[24] Appleton to Lee, Mar. 4, 1813; to G. Luciani, June 14, 1813; Sept. 2, 1813; to Massimo Ravenna, Sept. 2, 1813; to N. and C. Appleton, July 25, 1815; Aug. 8, 1815; Sept. 1, 1815; to Daniel Parker, Aug. 21, 1812, all in GL. Fehl, "The Account Book of Thomas Appleton of Livorno," 140–42.

[25] R. D. W. Connor, *Canova's Statue of Washington* (Raleigh: NC Historical Commission, 1910) 5–7, 13–28; Appleton to William R. King, Aug. 21, 1816, GL.

FIGURE 9.1 Antonio Canova statue of George Washington (North Carolina Historic Commission, *Canova's Statue of Washington* [1910])

the considerable sum of $200. He certainly would also have received some sort of commission from Trentanove, who was paid $210 for his work on the pedestal. Still, he wrote Jefferson of his disappointment that North Carolina had not offered him any token of gratitude even after the successful delivery of the statue and its very positive reception. Once again Jefferson came through, and finally, in 1823, the state legislature offered Appleton a vote of thanks along with a $500 payment.[26]

His experience with the North Carolina statue prompted Appleton to search for other, similar commissions, suggesting that he saw a good deal of interest in Roman-style sculpture of the founding father, and, concurrently, much potential for profit. At first, as Canova was beginning work on the seated Washington, Appleton contacted merchant connections in

---

[26] Appleton to King, Aug. 25, 1816; to Marquis Canova, Sept. 8, 1816; to King, Sept. 12, 1816; Sept. 20, 1816; to William Miller, Sept. 20, 1816; Oct. 1, 1816; to Luciani, Oct. 18, 1816; to Bald Casmi, May 5, 1820; to Perkins, June 21, 1820; Nov. 20, 1820; to William Bainbridge, Mar. 7, 1821; Mar. 15, 1821; to Jefferson, Apr. 2, 1823; June 10, 1824, all in GL; Fehl, "The Account Book of Thomas Appleton of Livorno," 144.

Boston, Rhode Island, and Charleston describing his work on the North
Carolina statue and soliciting similar projects from them. None of these
efforts panned out, but in the early 1820s, with the Canova statue having
received acclaim, Appleton sensed the time was again ripe. In 1822, he
learned from State Department contacts and Americans in Italy that both
New York City and the federal government were considering erecting
statues, and he began a vigorous campaign for those commissions, particularly the New York one. That same year he learned that a monumental
statue of Napoleon was for sale and made an offer for it in the hopes of
selling it to an American municipality. In 1824, he got wind of the news
that the Boston Athenaeum was considering erecting a Washington statue
and made a pitch to them. That same year, an American visitor from
Richmond mentioned the Virginia capital was considering a similar idea,
and Appleton read in the *National Gazette* that Philadelphia had put
together a committee to consider erecting a Washington statue there.
Appleton wrote to the Richmond visitor's father, Col. John Ambler, and
to the head of the Philadelphia committee offering his services.[27]

In making his pitch, Appleton stressed both his experience gained from
the North Carolina commission and his familiarity with Italian culture.
Writing to a New Yorker he had met in Italy, Appleton suggested several
classical sculptures in Rome that could serve as models. Most notably, he
discussed at length the famous statue of Marcus Aurelius located on the
Capitoline Hill (and now in the Capitoline Museum), suggesting that
New York would likely want a slightly larger, but similar work. In
doing so, he subtly suggested connections between the Roman republic
and the American republic, while allowing Washington to overshadow
Marcus Aurelius slightly in size.[28]

He also suggested that only a sculptor working in Italy could have
access to a proper model. That sculptor clearly would be Appleton's
protégé and brother-in-law, Raimondo Trentanove, whom Appleton end-
lessly touted to his American correspondents as the true successor to
Canova, who had died in 1822 after a period of illness. The stakes were
high, particularly for the New York project, which Appleton estimated

[27] Appleton to Perkins, Oct. 8, 1816; to Thomas Halsey, Oct. 9, 1816; to William Crafts,
Oct. 20, [1816]; to Dewit Clinton, June 29, 1822; to L. Brandish, Aug. 2, 1822; to
Ravenna, Oct. 24, [1822]; to Weeks, Mar. 27, 1823; to Perkins, Aug. 8, 1824; to
Jefferson, Oct. 8, 1824; to Col. Ambler, Oct. 20, 1824; to John Sergeant, Dec. 3, 1824,
all in GL; Appleton to Sec. State, Aug. 29, 1822, Leghorn Despatches.

[28] Appleton to Weeks, Mar. 17, 1823, GL; Appleton to Sec. State, Aug. 29, 1822, Leghorn
Despatches.

might cost $50,000 to $70,000 and would have provided him a hefty income as chief contractor, agent for Trentanove, and partner in the marble quarry that no doubt would have supplied the stones for Trentanove's model on which the brass would have been based. Even after the New Yorkers seemed to be losing interest, Appleton remained hopeful. He suggested that Trentanove might sculpt a marble statue at a quarter the cost of a brass one. Unfortunately for Appleton, in the end neither the New Yorkers nor any of the other possible commissions came through.[29]

But the new republic's attachment to neoclassical architecture and Appleton's Jefferson connection paid off one more time. Beginning sometime in 1820, Jefferson and Appleton began discussing the possibility of creating monumental capitals for the massive pillars of the Rotunda building being constructed at the new University of Virginia. (See Figure 9.2.) Jefferson's architectural masterwork was very much in the Roman style. At one point Appleton even supplied him with a sketch of Rome's Pantheon, on which the Rotunda was certainly based. Hence, capitals made by Italian sculptors from Carrara marble seemed particularly appropriate for the college's most important structure. Appleton initially planned to send Jefferson ten large capitals and eight slightly smaller at a cost of $8,500. He offered the job of sculpting to Trentanove, but in the end it was done by Massimo Ravenna of Carrara who frequently collaborated with Appleton in marble projects. Appleton delivered the capitals in 1823 in custom-made cases. Jefferson then ordered ten more Corinthian capitals at a cost of $6,140. Appleton delivered these items and marble paving stones for the campus grounds in 1825. Although his accounts do not show how much profit accrued to Appleton, it must have been substantial. As part-owner of the marble works that supplied the marble, he would have received a fair amount of profit from an order well in excess of $10,000 and which required more than 10,000 pounds of marble. Additionally, Appleton no doubt would have extracted the usual commission for his services as chief contractor.[30]

---

[29] Appleton to Cole Trumbull, Sept. 28, 1822; to J. J. Astor, Mar. 4, 1823; to Weeks, Mar. 27, 1823; Dec. 20, 1823; to Robert Greenhose, Jr., Feb. 15, 1824; to Weeks, Feb. 16, 1824; Sept. 12, 1824, GL.

[30] Appleton to R. Trentanove, June 18, [1824]; to Jefferson, July 7, 1821; to Ravenna, Aug. 7, 1821; to Jefferson, Aug. 15, 1821; to Ravenna, Aug. 23, [1821]; to Jefferson, Oct. 17, 1822; Apr. 2, 1823; Feb. 8, 1824; July 28, 1824, all in GL; Fehl, "The Account Book of Thomas Appleton of Livorno," 148–49.

FIGURE 9.2 The capitals and columns of the Rotunda, University of Virginia (author's photo)

Finally, Appleton also turned himself into an expert advisor on Tuscan and Italian agriculture. During a period when Americans were forming numerous gentlemen's societies to promote scientific agriculture, there was a good deal of curiosity about methods used in Europe. Appleton saw it as his patriotic duty to inform Americans, and from early in his appointment he had occasionally sent Jefferson and other governmental contacts clippings of olive trees, vines, and grasses. But in the 1820s he encountered renewed interest in such matters both from Americans abroad, such as Commodore Jacob Jones, and from various American societies that contacted him with questions. For a time, he became Italy's Giovanni Appleseed, sending large packets of seeds and samples as well as long agricultural discourses to various individuals as well as agricultural societies in Massachusetts, Pennsylvania, and New York. The Philadelphia Society awarded him an elegant silver medal, and the American Academy of Arts and Sciences made him an honorary member, presumably for his agricultural work. While this activity, unlike his marble work, did not provide Appleton with immediate profits, promoting Tuscan agriculture was potentially good for business. For example, his lauding of wheat and vegetables to naval officers could only aid his efforts to provision American ships, and samples of Tuscan straw no doubt would promote his trade in straw hats, at least until Americans began growing it in large enough quantities to compete with him.[31]

***

The chivalrous Spanish Empire also served as a useful model for imperial-minded Americans due to the romance of Spain's westward expansion into the Americas in the age of the conquistadors. After the Louisiana Purchase, Americans could readily identify with the Christian Spaniards' successful crusade against "noble savages" and contrast it (and American expansion) to what they perceived as modern Spain's deep decline or somnolence.[32] Columbus's discovery now represented the transit of civilization from Spain to the New World, and Spain's more recent decline made it all the more imperative that the United States take up its former role as overseer of Latin America, a development that was explicitly supported by the Monroe Doctrine.

The extended Montgomery clan became acquainted with a surprisingly large number of American intellectuals most of whom were intrigued by romantic notions of the Spanish Empire and appalled at the reality of modern-day Spain. They served the visiting Americans as landlords, business agents, intellectual mentors, translators, and land agents. Their most important connection was with Washington Irving, one of the early republic's best-known author/celebrities. The Montgomerys came to know Irving as a result of the bibliographic expertise of John Montgomery's son-in-law, Obadiah Rich. As a young man, Rich developed an interest in natural history that brought him first into the Massachusetts Historical Society and then the Boston Athenaeum. Even

---

[31] Entry for July 20, 1821, Leghorn Despatches; Appleton to Samuel Dana, Sept. 15, 1821; to James Mease, Sept. 15, 1822; to William H. Crawford, Sept. 16, 1822; to Walcott Chauncy, Nov. 23, [1822]; to Pres. Agricultural Society of New York, Feb. 17, 1823; to James Mease, Feb. 1, 1823; Feb. 15, 1824; June 10, 1824; to Jefferson, Oct. 8, 1824; to Crawford, Oct. 25, 1824; to James Robertson, Nov. 1, 1824, all in GL. On agricultural societies see Ariel Ron, *Grassroots Leviathan* (Baltimore: Johns Hopkins University Press, 2020).

[32] It is no accident that two of America's first great historians, Francis Parkman and William Prescott, addressed these themes. The most useful discussion of early American views of Spain comes from the essays in Richard L. Kagan, ed., *Spain in America* (Urbana: University of Illinois Press, 2002), particularly those of Kagan, Rolena Adorno, Thomas R. Hart, Jr., and James D. Fernandez.

before marrying Ana Montgomery, as a young merchant in France, he had begun collecting and selling European books to American clients. On his return to the United States with his family in 1812, the Athenaeum asked him to create their Cabinet of Natural History specimens. He had been periodically furnishing the Athenaeum with books since becoming a charter member, eventually becoming their official book agent. At some point his interest seems to have shifted from natural history to Spanish and particularly Spanish-American history. Due to the disruptions of the Peninsular War, a number of excellent libraries with valuable finds such as early editions of Las Casas's *Historia de los Indias* fell into his hands.[33]

Rich's growing reputation as a bibliophile served him well during the post-1815 downturn. After returning to Spain as consul to Valencia in 1816, Rich could not have been sustained financially by the meagre shipping in the region. Luckily the American minister in Spain, Alexander Everett, needed assistance to preserve the archive at the American legation and had called Rich to Madrid for that purpose. Rich moved his entire family to the capital, no doubt glad to escape the chaos from which Robert Montgomery and family were suffering on the coast. There is no evidence that he ever returned to his post despite retaining the title of consul for some time.[34]

Rich's book collecting activities drew attention from knowledgeable Americans. George Ticknor, a Harvard scholar and America's leading Hispanist, was a client as early as 1818. Ticknor later wrote that Rich "offered me many kind services." Rich's most famous contact, though, was Irving, who came to Madrid in 1826 with the idea of translating some of the material on Columbus that Rich and others had turned up. Alexander Everett wrote Irving of the possibility of a translation, though Rich claimed to have given Irving the idea. It is also possible that Ticknor or his associates at Harvard had informed him of the material.[35] Irving arrived in Madrid at 10 a.m. on Wednesday, February 15. Unable to locate Everett, he spent a "cold shivering day" in a hotel. The next day he found Everett, who brought him to meet Rich. Rich immediately showed him several manuscripts including a Lope de Vega play, a letter of Cortez, and a handwritten copy of Las Casas's *Journal of Columbus*. Irving returned to Rich's house

[33] Norman Paul Tucker, "Obadiah Rich, 1783–1850: Early American Hispanist," PhD dissertation (Harvard University, 1973) 1–17.

[34] *Ibid.* 42–43.

[35] Adrian W. Knepper, "Obadiah Rich: Bibliophile," *Papers of the Bibliographical Society of America* 49 (Second Quarter, 1955) 119, 124–25; William P. Trent and George S. Hellman, eds., *The Journals of Washington Irving (hitherto unpublished)* (Boston: The Bibliophile Society, 1919), www.loc.gov, II: 247–48.

the following day to look at more Spanish manuscripts, and he agreed to rent a room there for $5 a week. Irving soon described himself as "buried in the very depths of a great rambling Spanish house." His room looked out on a small garden, the view of which was enhanced by floor-to-ceiling windows "with iron gates . . . through one of which we have a wicket by which we can enter the garden." Altogether, he wrote, "We have the stillness of a cloister, with now and then the bell of a neighbouring convent to help the illusion." Irving was pleased to be "surrounded by [Rich's] curious library entirely at my command." He referred to his host as a "most obliging and good hearted man" and as "excellent and amiable."[36]

For the next fourteen months Irving would see Rich nearly every day when both were in town. Rich and his Montgomery kin acted as cultural ambassadors for Irving, particularly early on. Beyond allowing Irving the run of his library, Rich introduced him to other bibliophiles. Members of the family also introduced Irving to a wide range of Spanish culture that would prove valuable as he mined the country's heritage for material to use in the books he was writing. The family occasionally accompanied him to the Spanish theater, where Irving saw plays ranging from those of de Vega to ephemeral works of poor quality. Rich took him to see museums and private art collections. His daughters accompanied Irving to the armory where he was able to view suits of armor and clothing worn by Cortes, Ferdinand and Isabella, and others. Even the entertainment the Riches occasionally brought home in the evening – musicians, dancers, and ventriloquists – no doubt provided local color for the author. In return, Irving's praise of Rich to his London correspondents likely helped his landlord's book sales in England and America.[37]

Irving was not the only literary figure to visit the Riches. Nineteen-year-old Henry Wadsworth Longfellow, engaged on a grand tour of Europe, arrived in Madrid in March 1827. The future poet would spend a good deal of time with Irving and the Riches during his stay. Both Irving and Longfellow documented their visits, and their journals and letters offer a rare glimpse into the Montgomery family circle during this period. Longfellow noted that American society at this time in Madrid was really limited to the Everetts and Riches, as well as Washington Irving, his brother

---

[36] *Journals of Washington Irving*, II: 5–7 (Feb. 15–18, 1826); Charles Robert Leslie, *Autobiographical Reflections* (Boston: Ticknor and Fields, 1860) 271–72.

[37] *Journals of Washington Irving*; Irving to Henry Brevort, in Pierre M. Irving, ed., *The Life and Letters of Washington Irving* (London: Richard Bentley, 1862) I: 260; Leslie, *Autobiographical Reflections*, 271.

Peter, and the naval Lieutenant Alexander Slidell, who would also become a minor literary celebrity among other things. Irving described the Rich family circle as a "very agreeable one" and he certainly seems to have been pleased to spend time with them. In addition to his admiration of Rich, Irving appears to have been very fond of the two unmarried Montgomery girls who frequently spent time in the Rich household, and he reported himself as miserable when they departed in November 1826.[38] Irving also spent a good deal of time with Robert Montgomery's daughter and son-in-law, Luisa and Ricardo Ryan, who had departed Alicante for Madrid some time earlier. Irving initially met the Ryans during their frequent visits to the Rich household but soon developed an independent friendship with them, particularly with Ricardo.[39] He also became friendly with Henry and Isabel Montgomery O'Shea, the sister and brother-in-law of Ana Montgomery Rich, whom, like the Ryans, he first met at Rich's home.[40] Importantly, he spent a good deal of time with Ana and Isabel's brother, George Washington Montgomery, another aspiring writer. He also briefly met Robert Montgomery, Jr., who was in from Alicante to visit his Madrid kin.[41] All told, the Montgomerys presented a cohesive group that, perhaps like many other Spanish families then and now, felt most comfortable socializing among themselves when possible.

Amidst all the socializing and gathering of historical sources and cultural lore, Irving was engaged in a flurry of writing. During his incredibly productive stay with the Riches, he completed his *History of the Life and Voyages of Christopher Columbus* and wrote a good deal of the *Chronicle of the Conquest of Granada*. Lessons learned in Madrid no doubt also contributed to *Tales of the Alhambra* which he wrote after moving on to Granada. These books, which would become very popular, further established Irving as one of America's most

---

[38] Samuel Longfellow, ed., *Life of Henry Wadsworth Longfellow With Extracts from His Journal and Correspondence* (Boston: Houghton Mifflin, 1891) I: 108; *Journals of Washington Irving*, II: 44 (Nov. 13, 1826). It is unclear whether these were John's daughters, Robert's, or a combination.

[39] Ryan had given up the house he bought from Montgomery in Alicante in 1820, probably in order to move to Madrid.

[40] I am presuming O'Shea was married to John Montgomery's eldest daughter as family genealogists believe she was born in Baltimore, and only John – not Robert – was in the United States at this time (Guilermo O'Shea y Montgomery entry in myheritage.com). The Robert Montgomery File in the Archivo Nacionales includes a request from a Spanish family member named Guillermo O'Shea y Montgomery, son of Henry and Isabel. See Roberto Montgomery File, Estado Lag. 3554, Roll 2215, Archivos Nacionales, Madrid.

[41] *Journals of Washington Irving*, II: 35 (July 31, 1826).

influential writers. They also helped to promote a fascination with the Spanish empire and Columbus in the new republic. This interest on the part of Irving and his American readers seems odd in some ways. There is no history of Americans ever admiring or wishing to emulate Spain. In fact, quite the opposite was true considering that Spain was not only Catholic but historically the enemy of Great Britain, two points against it in a country that, despite the American Revolution remained Protestant and culturally British.

Yet Irving's focus on fifteenth-century Spain was in fact relevant to issues within the United States. All three of his Spanish books dealt with the late fifteenth century which saw simultaneously the defeat of the Muslim Empire, the birth of the unified Spanish Empire under Ferdinand and Isabella, and the "discovery" of America. All were tinged with sadness at the decline of the Moors, who were portrayed as worthy opponents, and triumph at the rise of the virtuous Christian knights. But even this triumph would have been tinged with sadness for American readers, who shared the widespread perception of the decline of Catholic Spain both in Europe and Latin America by the nineteenth century. Most importantly, these tales, and particularly the focus on Columbus, foretold a transit of imperial might from Spain to the New World.

In a later work, Irving explicitly discussed the connection between the conquest of Granada and Columbus's voyages. Columbus's agreement with the Spanish sovereign was "in a manner, signed with the same pen that had subscribed the capitulation of the Moorish capital, and his first expedition may almost be said to have departed from beneath the walls of Grenada." And the conquest of America, therefore, was a continuation of the war against the Moors, as "Many of the youthful cavaliers who had fleshed their swords' in that memorable war, crowded the ships of the discoverers thinking a new career of arms was to be opened to them – a kind of crusade into splendid and unknown regions of infidels." In other words, the Americans were now following in the footsteps of the chivalric Spaniards in their own Christian war of conquest against the natives. This was an interpretation that could bring great comfort to a nation on the verge of embarking on imperial action in the Indian territories of North America and the former Spanish territories to the south.[42]

[42] Washington Irving, *Voyages and Discoveries of the Companions of Columbus* (Philadelphia: Carey, Lea and Blanchard, 1835) 5. For a more detailed discussion, see Iván Jaksić, *The Hispanic World and American Intellectual Life, 1820–1880* (New York: Palgrave Macmillan, 2007).

Irving's visit to Madrid made a tremendous impression on John Montgomery's son George Washington Montgomery. Montgomery, 22 years old at the time of Irving's arrival, was already on his way to becoming a cultural broker. Educated in England and speaking perfect Spanish, he served as a translator for the American legation. He spent a good deal of time with Irving and must have been very impressed by the young American literary figure. Shortly after Irving's departure he published his first short-story volume, written in the romantic style that Irving was also adopting for his Spanish works. In 1831, he published the first translation of Irving's *Conquest of Granada* into Spanish. In doing so he completed the circle. The Montgomerys had introduced Spain to Irving, and now George was introducing Irving (or Irving's Spain) to Spain.[43]

Shortly thereafter, Montgomery published his most important work, *Bernardo del Carpio (El Bastardo de Castilla)*. Like *The Conquest of Granada* and Irving's other Spanish works, *Bernardo del Carpio* portrayed a rising, chivalrous Spain defined by deeds of derring-do by Christian knights and their worthy Muslim opponents and occasional allies. Montgomery's story was, however, at its core a romance of hidden identities and multiple, predictable *deux ex machina*. The book does not appear to have received much attention in Spain, but it did achieve modest popularity in the United States, where a translated version appeared in 1843. Appropriately enough, considering Montgomery's career as a translator, the Spanish version was used to teach Spanish at Harvard College, perhaps with the recommendation of Rich's friend, George Ticknor. Certainly, Montgomery's later career, in which he continued his role as a bridge between the United States and the Spanish-speaking world, would owe much to his youthful acquaintance with Irving and Irving's subsequent patronage.[44]

The Montgomerys also benefitted from a long-term relationship with William Maclure, the well-known American geologist. When he first came to Alicante in 1808, the Scottish-born Maclure was retired from a very successful mercantile career spent in New York and Virginia. He had recently begun a series of domestic and European scientific expeditions that would make him the most important American geologist of the period. That year, an

[43] *Journals of Washington Irving*, II: 20 (Apr. 13, 1826), 22 (May 6, 1826), 28 (June 26, 1826), 31 (July 12, 1826), 39 (Oct. 1, 1826); Salvador García Castañada, "Acerca de George Washington Montgomery, Washington Irving y Otros Hispanistas Norteamericanos de la Epoca Fernandina," in *Ideas en Sus Pacoajes Homenaje al Profesor Russell P. Sebold* (Universidad de Alicante, 1969) 195–201.

[44] Castañada, "Acerca de George Washington Montgomery," 195–201; G. W. Montgomery, *Bernardo del Carpio* (Boston: Brainard and Co., 1843).

acquaintance described the 45-year-old Maclure as in perfect health, "robust and vigorous" with a ruddy complexion and "winning and attractive" manners. He entered Alicante on March 8 and immediately began an informal geographical survey of the mineral springs in the area. During his week-long stay he found Alicante's human society "pleasant and well-informed" consisting "mostly of foreigners who enjoy the privileges of a social intercourse with the nobles." Towards the end of his stay, he "attended a large party" which more than likely would have been held to honor the presence of such an unusual and distinguished visitor. There can be little doubt that Maclure would have met Robert Montgomery during his trip since, as the American consul and leading member of the American community, Montgomery was interested in all American visitors, particularly in rich merchants such as Maclure.[45]

Maclure returned to Spain fourteen years later, on a dual mission. Both parts involved the Montgomery clan. First, he continued on his long-term geologic project, collecting mineral specimens in Spanish soil and sending them back to the new world. Obadiah Rich provided assistance in making these shipments, as he had done for years. Typically, merchants providing this sort of service, at a minimum, received reimbursement for their expenses, and there is no reason to believe Rich would have eschewed this source of income. Mineralogical collections like Maclure's literally brought the soil of the Old World into the New, and from that perspective could be seen as part of the transfer of wealth and cultural authority from what Maclure clearly viewed as a badly declined empire into the rising western empire across the Atlantic. Maclure often voiced concerns about what he viewed as Spanish decline, and he saw the advancement of mining in Spain as a way of building an industrial base there along with other measures to advance Spanish industry, such as his investments in a silk factory in Valencia.[46]

Maclure's second, more ambitious project, was to create an educational foundation for Spain in the neighborhood of Alicante. Maclure envisioned two schools, one based on the most cutting-edge liberal methods developed by Joseph Lancaster and Johann Pestalozzi as well as an agrarian institute based on American farming methods. Although at

---

[45] John S. Doskey, ed., *The European Journals of William Maclure* (American Philosophical Society Press, 1988), 138–41. Before arriving in Alicante, Maclure had met Montgomery's acquaintances Vague and Llamos in Valencia, who also would no doubt have recommended he see Montgomery in Alicante.

[46] Alberto Gil Novales, "The Spain William Maclure Knew," *Indiana Magazine of History* 94 (June 1998) 99–109; Obadiah Rich to William Maclure, June 8, 1821, New Harmony Manuscripts.

first glance this educational project seems widely divergent from Maclure's mineralogical activity, there is a common thread. Both projects attempted to advance what Maclure viewed as a terribly backward, declining society into modernity. Maclure and other liberals were hopeful during a short period in the early 1820s that the new constitutional government could finally mold what they viewed as a chaotic, dangerous, and often ignorant country into an enlightened republic. Maclure himself rued that in Spain "anarchy occupies the place of reason" and "the wealthy classes have no knowledge, only indolence and imbecility." Building a modern educational and economic base could, he hoped, eradicate these problems. In this regard Maclure anticipated later nineteenth-century civilizing projects in the West Indies and Asia that have been seen as the handmaiden of American imperialism.[47]

Maclure planned to locate this ambitious project on a huge tract of land in Alicante, where he hoped to spend his retirement. He thought the climate would be healthy for him, certainly better than Madrid which might do in the summer but not during its notoriously frigid winters. Robert Montgomery may also have played a role in this decision. In 1822 the constitutional government was in the process of confiscating and selling church lands. In September, the Montgomerys, in apparent partnership with Maclure, purchased a large tract known as the San Gines farm which consisted of nearly 10,000 acres, a convent, and as many as twelve houses. It was planted with vineyards and olive groves. Maclure arrived in Alicante in November to take possession of it and other land he had purchased in the vicinity, including a 100-acre tract near town that he planned to use as a summer residence. Montgomery, who was collecting vineyard lands himself, must have acted as Maclure's agent in this purchase. He and his sons obtained a third of San Gines via a mortgage on Maclure. Most likely they received very good terms as reimbursement for their efforts on Maclure's behalf. Montgomery's sons Robert Jr. and Frederick, went to work rebuilding the convent and other houses at San Gines before Maclure arrived.[48] Maclure remained in Alicante for six months, departing for Ireland on May 2, 1823. During this period, he would have been in almost daily contact with the Montgomerys while making plans for his educational project and his new properties. Sadly, the

---

[47] Novales, "The Spain William Maclure Knew," 103–4; Doskey, ed., *European Journals*, 677–79.

[48] Doskey, ed., *European Journals*, 681–83; Deposition of Frederick and Robert Montgomery, Sept. 6, 1823, Alicante Despatches.

project would be doomed by France's invasion of the Valencia region the following summer, an event that would have tragic consequences for American trade in the region generally, and specifically for Maclure and the Montgomerys when the French seized former church lands, including San Gines. Maclure unsuccessfully attempted to regain the property for the rest of his life, claiming to have lost at least $30,000–40,000 on it.[49]

***

The Roman Empire, as well as the Phoenicians and early Islam, existed on the south side of the Mediterranean as well as the north. It was not uncommon for European writers to contrast the glory of those early empires with the perceived backwardness of modern-day North Africans. Tangier specifically had been an important port in Phoenician and Roman times. Simpson was certainly aware of that history. He was interested in and knowledgeable about some of the mysterious local monuments apparently created by ancient people, as demonstrated by a long conversation he had with the French envoy Captain Antoine Burel.[50] Unlike his colleagues in Italy and Spain, however, Simpson does not appear to have attempted to profit from Moroccan culture or even to have acted as an expert in any sort of public way.

In Livorno, however, Appleton was also interested in North African antiquities. Having bought up a number of Roman coins in Italy, it occurred to him that they may be easier to procure in North Africa, where there were numerous Roman sites and, presumably, less interest in antiquities. In 1821 he wrote to his friends Thomas Anderson and Townshend Stith, respectively the consuls to Tripoli and Tunis, requesting that they keep an eye open for Roman coins. In doing so Appleton revealed a deep knowledge both of numismatics and of the market for coins. He offered Anderson a detailed overview of the various types of coins and their value, requesting specific types of coins (e.g., those with Britannica, Penitence, Psearis Negro, or Octavia on the front or with "Col" for colony on the rear). He also quoted prices and expressed the hope that since Tripoli "does not furnish any first rate erudites in the numismatic science," he would be able to acquire large quantities at rock-bottom prices. While Appleton did not elaborate on his plans for

---

[49] Novales, "The Spain William Maclure Knew," 99–109. The Montgomerys likely lost in the neighborhood of $20,000 as a result of the confiscation.

[50] Jacques Caillé, *La Mission du Capitaine Burel au Maroc en 1808* (Paris: Arts et Métiers Graphiques, 1953) 114.

disposing of such large quantities of coins, it seems likely that he had a client in mind who was interested in purchasing them.[51]

Stith's predecessor as consul to Tunis, Mordecai M. Noah, exhibited deep interest in ancient ruins. In fact, he wrote that Tunis's proximity to the ancient Phoenician and Roman ruins of Carthage was an important factor in his decision to accept the consulate. Echoing the common trope of North Africa's decline into barbarity, he wrote that he feared he might not be able to visit the region as a private citizen since "travelers in those regions, now inhabited by barbarians, must be strongly protected," adding that, "The simple merchant in the eyes of Musselmen have no right to contemplate the site of ancient cities, or view the mouldering columns and broken shafts of antiquity." Therefore, in order to facilitate a safe visit to Carthage, he applied to the US government for a consulship in the region. Although there is no evidence that once in Tunis Noah bought and sold antiquities, he did act as a cultural broker through the publication of his book *Travels in England, France, Spain, and the Barbary States*. His rapturous description of Carthage's ancient ruins and the "illustrious characters" and "great events" it brought to mind, was tempered by his horror at its current state under Islamic rule. He hoped that "a change of masters, or the adoption of a new political system may place that country into hands less barbarous; and while Rome is stripped of its splendour and power without a Regulus or a Scipio, Carthage, its fallen rival, may once more rear its head, and if the Barbary States become a province of a civilized power, Carthage, from its commanding position and great commercial advantages, will once more become the first city in Africa."[52]

***

All of these new consular hustles provided income for the American community and stoked the new republic's growing imperial fascination, but they hardly offered the sort of path toward sustainable riches that the shipping boom of previous decades had provided. Nevertheless, for a time, at least, they brought Americans in the Mediterranean into the center of American culture. Historians have usually emphasized the role of Anglo-Saxon identity in the formulation of early American imperialism. This racial conception justified Manifest Destiny generally and, more

---

[51] Appleton to Thomas Anderson, May 18, 1821; to Townshend Stith, May 21, 1821, both in GL.
[52] Mordecai Manuel Noah, *Travels in England, France, Spain, and the Barbary States in the Years 1813–1814 and 15* (New York: Kirk and Mercein, 1819) 1, 269.

specifically, the displacement of supposedly inferior Latino and Native American people in the territories conquered by the new republic. However, the idealization of the Roman and Spanish empires in which Americans in the Mediterranean were involved also reveals a less frequently observed Mediterranean model for the American imperial project. The Mediterranean community's embrace of the Monroe Doctrine, support of naval power, and condescending, often chauvinistic views of Catholics and Muslims suggest that they were ideologically predisposed to an American empire. But beyond that, stoking America's affinity for the trappings of empire was also good business, since they were the people best positioned to sell those trappings to their countrymen. Not only did they provide cultural products to feed America's interest in empire, but they also helped to fuel that interest through their publications and through their correspondence with Americans whom they hoped would buy their products. In this sense Americans in the Mediterranean acting as cultural brokers could also be viewed as impresarios of empire.

IO

Death and Dismemberment

Buoyed by the end of the Napoleonic Wars and the prospect of a rising American empire after 1815, Americans in the Mediterranean retained some optimism that their decade of misery might soon end. Unfortunately for them, the post-1815 decades would be just as miserable as the preceding years, and they would mark the end of the American community in the Mediterranean as it had existed for the previous generation. With few exceptions, commerce failed to return to anything like its postwar peak, forcing Americans in the region to realize that there would be no return to the prewar prosperity. The downturn in business and changing domestic priorities made the region much less central to the US economy than before. As a result, in addition to grappling with age and declining abilities, the three consuls struggled with personal hardship and anger at a State Department that now seemed to offer even less support than ever during increasingly desperate times. One of their biggest fears was that the ensuing generation would be unable to support itself within the American community. As they reached the end of their lives, the consuls' fears about their own positions and their children's futures would be realized.

***

In Alicante, Robert Montgomery's reports mostly illustrated the "dullness" of business. In 1816, prices in Alicante offered "no encouragement" for American shipping. Poor wine harvests raised the price of the main export those ships could carry home and presumably also hurt the Montgomerys personally, since they had invested heavily in wine production. By 1817, Montgomery wrote "scarcely any business is going on

TABLE 10.1 *US shipping to Livorno 1815–33*[1]

Year		1815	1816	1817	1818	1819	1820	1821	1822	1823
US ships		8	46	28	25	35	29	N/A	N/A	N/A
Year	1824	1825	1826	1827	1828	1829	1830	1831	1832	1833
US ships	Est. 36[2]	N/A	N/A	N/A	N/A	28	22	31	21	30

[1] Charles A. Keene, "American Shipping and Trade, 1798–1820: The Evidence from Leghorn," *Journal of Economic History* 38 (Sept. 1978) 687; Thomas Appleton to Sec. State, Dec. 31, 1829; Dec. 31, 1830; Dec. 31, 1831; Dec. 31, 1832; Dec. 31, 1833, all in Leghorn Despatches.

[2] Twelve reported by April would lead to thirty-six through extrapolation, but the real number was probably lower.

between America and this country."[1] Yet 1818 brought some hope as Alicante became a port deposit where goods could be deposited free of duties, a designation that presumably would benefit American shippers who often faced stiffer duties than their British competitors. One of Montgomery's local rivals predicted that the decree would be particularly beneficial to merchants moving West Indian colonial produce, which would include many Americans.[2]

In Livorno, forty-six American ships arrived in 1816. This was a respectable number, far less than the peak of 152 in 1807, but within the usual range of the prosperous years of neutral trade. Nevertheless, this commerce appears to have been less profitable than Americans might have hoped. Appleton wrote that a number of American ships carried goods that would not sell well in Livorno and that, overall, American trade was not very profitable there or in the Mediterranean generally due to "the universal high prices of colonial produce in America," which made it difficult for shippers to recoup their expenditures with European sales. As a result, US shipping to Livorno dropped precipitously for the rest of the decade, with the number of annual arrivals averaging in the high twenties.[3] (See Table 10.1.)

[1] Robert Montgomery to Sec. State, Dec. 31, 1815, Alicante Despatches; Rogers to Brown and Ives, Jan. 15, 1816, B113 F1, B. & I.; Montgomery to Sec. State, July 15, 1816; Apr. 11, 1817, both in Alicante Despatches.

[2] Westzynthius and Co. to Brown and Ives, Aug. 15, 1818, B114 F7, B. & I.

[3] Charles A. Keene, "American Shipping and Trade, 1798–1820: The Evidence from Leghorn," *Journal of Economic History* 38 (Sept. 1978) 687; Thomas Appleton to Brown and Ives, Jan. 24, 1816, B113 F1, B. & I.; Thomas Appleton to William Shaler, May 8, 1816; to Thomas Jefferson, May 1816, both in GL.

Strong American exports may have made prospects seem brighter in 1817 as the formerly bankrupt Charles Degan resumed business under his wife's name (presumably to avoid problems with his previous firm's creditors). But the hope was a false one and by the next year trade was "miserably low." Degan's new firm failed, and the venerable Felicchi house was also suffering. Appleton, who had been focusing on his domestic marble business, presumably was more insulated from this downturn, though, at a minimum, it would have had a marked effect on his consular fees.[4]

Tangier and Morocco, never centers of US trade, nonetheless suffered with the rest of the Mediterranean. James Simpson found it nearly impossible to cash American bills in the region, which prevented him from receiving his annual salary, and, more importantly, from paying for official expenses. This was a particularly troublesome development at a time when several American crew members of wrecked ships had to be redeemed at considerable cost. Simpson reported that those merchants willing to cash American bills were charging "discounts" (actually fees) of 20 percent or more. He made inquiries to a number of merchants, including his cousins in Gibraltar, the Duguids, all of whom cited the lack of demand for American notes as the reason for the steep discounts. The root causes seem to have been a combination of irregularities by some American creditors and the poor balance of American trade in the region, which cut down on the circulation of American notes, making them unattractive to merchants who would not readily find means of selling them. More than just a problem for Simpson, then, the problem seems to have reflected the declining significance of the United States in the Mediterranean.[5]

As in Livorno and Alicante, trading prospects briefly improved in Morocco after 1816. At the end of the year, the American consul to Algiers, William Shaler, solved Simpson's credit crunch by physically bringing $2,000 to him in Tangier. By 1817, a trickle of American shipping was arriving at Mogadore and Simpson was finding it easier to move money from Gibraltar. Morocco's government now appeared ready to

---

[4] Thomas Appleton to William Shaler, Jan. 7, 1818, Shaler Papers; C. F. Degan to Brown and Ives, May 11, 1818, B114 F5, B. & I.; Appleton to D. Parker, Nov. 20, [1819]; to H. Preble, Dec. 25, 1819, all in GL.

[5] James Simpson to Sec. State, Apr. 7, 1816; to Sec. Treasury, Jan. 1, 1816; Apr. 8, 1816; to James Monroe, Apr. 1, 1816; John and Wm. Duguid and Co. to Simpson, Feb. 1, 1816; Bernard Henry to Simpson, Feb. 1, 1816; Horatio Sprague to Simpson, Feb. 2, 1816; Charles H. Hall and Co. to Simpson, Feb. 26, 1816; Augn. Bearley to Simpson, Mar. 1, 1816; Ch. Des Fontaine to Simpson, Mar. 1, 1816; Simpson to Monroe, May 10, 1816; to Alex Dallas, May 29, 1816; to Monroe, Aug. 10, 1816, all in Tangier Despatches.

create a fairer tariff system and to open up the grain trade to some extent. Both developments could be beneficial to American traders. Simpson's associates in Mogadore saw the possibility for an uptick in American business and began to solicit merchants in the United States with the assistance of Simpson's Duguid cousins.[6]

Any hopes for further liberalization of trade were dashed by two new crises in Morocco. The first was the arrival of the plague, which came to Tangier by June 1818 and intensified by September, when eight to thirteen people were dying of it daily in that city. A shipwrecked Frenchman visiting Tangier toward the end of the outbreak wrote that, "The plague had carried off a great part of [Tangier's] population, and the return of the scourge was still dreaded." Most of the European consuls had remained shut up in their houses for nearly a year, while others had fled the city. Only the French consul, Edouard Sourdeau, overwhelmed by "the idea of the misery which he could experience by living in his own house as a prisoner" decided to brave the dangers of the contagion and continue to roam the city and interact with local people.[7]

The plague virtually cut off Simpson and his fellow consuls from Europe, severely disrupting trade and communications. "The sight of the Spanish coast [visible across the Strait of Gibraltar] had become indifferent to them, and that of the numerous vessels which were continually crossing the Straits of Gibraltar, and avoiding the African coast, brought no relief to their ranks." The only connection to the outside world was a boat that arrived from Gibraltar twice monthly. Simpson once again faced great difficulty receiving his salary and necessary funds from Spain and in sending reports back to the United States.[8]

The second crisis was political in nature. Various factions began to revolt against the emperor, Muley Solimon, beginning in Fez and spreading into the mountains, and to the north. By October 1819, rebels had disrupted communications sufficiently that Simpson was having difficulty getting information about their activities. Attempting to gain control of northern ports,

---

[6] Simpson to Monroe, Nov. 13, 1816; Dec. 23, 1816; Jan. 10, 1817; Jan. 20, 1817; Feb. 10, 1817; May 19, 1817; "Report of Arrival and Departure of Trading Vessels ...," June 30, 1817; to J. Q. Adams, July 18, 1817; Mar. 30, 1817, all in Tangier Despatches. James Renshaw and William Wilshire to Brown and Ives, Mar. 30, 1818, B114 F4, B. & I.

[7] Simpson to Adams, June 22, 1818; Sept. 4, 1818, both in Tangier Despatches; Charles Cochelet, *Narrative of the Shipwreck of the Sophia on the 30th of May, 1819 ...* (London: Richard Phillips, 1822) 114–15.

[8] Cochelet, *Narrative of the Shipwreck*, 115–16; Simpson to Adams, Sept. 4, 1818, Tangier Despatches.

rebels, termed "hordes of barbarians" by Simpson, unsuccessfully attacked Tangier and Larache, and had more success in the nearby port of Tétouan. By December Simpson was reporting on public disorder and frequent robberies in Tangier. These disturbances, combined with the continuing ravages of the plague and some apparent efforts by the emperor to crack down on illicit importations at Mogadore further paralyzed what was left of Moroccan–American trade.[9]

On the northern shore of the Mediterranean, new problems stemmed from disruptions during the conservative Bourbon restoration that followed Napoleon's ouster. By the late 1810s there was considerable conflict between royalists and liberal constitutionalists in Spain. Trade with the United States continued to suffer, and in March 1819 Montgomery's son-in-law John Rogers finally shut down what was left of his firm in Alicante. In 1820 constitutionalists regained power, offering some hope that the hated duty on American fish might be lowered. Montgomery also saw some prospects for importation of American tobacco, albeit mostly by illicit means.[10] The constitutional government soon collapsed, however, as the French Bourbons sent a large army into Spain to support King Ferdinand and his followers who were taking vengeance on the liberals. In the spring of 1823, 6,000 French troops took control of nearby Valencia and French privateers captured two American ships and brought them into the port of Torrevieja, about 30 miles from Alicante. Turmoil, disruptions, and dismal trading prospects would continue for the rest of the decade, putting the nail in the coffin of US trade with Alicante.[11]

The Montgomerys suffered grievously during this civil war. Like most Americans in the region, they preferred liberal regimes. Moreover, they had benefitted materially from the constitutionalist government which had dissolved church property, allowing the Montgomerys and their friend, the American geologist and educator William Maclure, to purchase a large church estate known as Dehuse of San Gines near Alicante in 1822. This purchase of church lands no doubt marked the family as enemies of the conservatives, and liberal soldiers deposited ammunition there in the middle of the French invasion, presumably to hide it from the

---

[9] James A. O. C. Brown, *Crossing the Strait: Morocco, Gibraltar and Great Britain in the 18th and 19th Centuries* (Leiden: Brill, 2012) 79–84; William Wilshire to Sec. State, Apr. 17, 1819; Simpson to Sec. State, June 24, 1819; Oct. 18, 1819; Nov. 1, 1819; Dec. 13, 1819, all in Tangier Despatches.

[10] John H. Rogers to Brown and Ives, Mar. 1, 1819, B114 F9, B. & I.; Montgomery to Sec. State, Jan. 18, 1821; July 1, 1821; Jan. 1, 1822; June 1, 1822, all in Alicante Despatches.

[11] Montgomery to Sec. State, June 19, 1823, Alicante Despatches.

Bourbon forces. On July 11 French troops arrived at Montgomery's house, unsuccessfully searched for the ammunition at the nearby St. Gines property, arrested Frederick and Robert Montgomery, Jr., and stole many of their possessions. The royalists and their supporters unsuccessfully tried to get the brothers to join in "their execrable songs" and their cries of "death to the constitution." They insulted the recalcitrant Montgomery brothers "in the most gross manner, by, 'of what religion are you, Jews, Protestants, heretics, etc. to possess yourselves of Friars' property.'" They carried the brothers to the "common jail" and thrust each of them into a "separate dungeon" where they remained for four days during which royalists pillaged their estate. The brothers then briefly regained control of the property, but in August the royalist authorities returned it to the Church, stripping the Montgomerys of the valuable property without compensation and taking the barilla crop, barley, figs, and what remained of the family's personal possessions. The Montgomerys' losses likely totaled around $20,000.[12]

Italy, and specifically Tuscany, underwent similar disruptions at the same time, mirroring the constitutionalist–royalist conflict in Spain.[13] Like Montgomery, Appleton supported the liberal constitutionalists. He had been a true believer in French liberal ideals since his youth in Paris, and he also benefitted from the free trade ideals of the liberals, as did American merchants in the Mediterranean generally. By 1820, Appleton began to report that the Austrian emperor, Francis I, was readying a force of 100,000 men to secure northern Italy at a time when liberal revolutions in Spain and Portugal created fears of similar events there. Rebellions in Turin and Naples looked likely, and Appleton predicted war would soon break out. He noted that Milan's trade had sunk since Francis's restoration in 1814. He recalled that when he had visited Milan in 1815 he saw 222 "large wagons of merchandize from France destined for that place in short space of five hours," but "this immense trade is now extinct." The decline, he believed, was an object lesson in the difference "between a free and unlimited trade, and one shackled with all the chains of despotism."[14]

[12] Fred. Montgomery to Sec. State, Sept. 6, 1823; Statement of Fred. and Robt. Montgomery, Sept. 6, 1823, both in Alicante Despatches; Alberto Gil Novales, "The Spain William Maclure Knew," *Indiana Magazine of History* 94 (June 1998) 104–6.
[13] Axel Korner, *America in Italy: The United States in the Political Thought and Imagination of the Risorgimento, 1763–1865* (Princeton University Press, 2017) 114–15.
[14] Appleton to Shaler, Sept. 27, 1820; Jan. 22, 1821, both in Shaler Papers; Appleton to S. Bradish, Aug. 7, 1822, GL. Francis I was also known as Francis II, Emperor of the Holy Roman Empire.

The turmoil in the region no doubt contributed to the continuing decline of American commerce. In Livorno, Appleton's careful records told the story of commercial collapse. Unlike in Alicante, the American trade hobbled along into the 1830s, though at the same low levels as the 1820s, with an average of just 26 US ships annually (and never more than 33) between 1829 and 1838, compared to annual arrivals ranging from 24 to 152 in the salad days of the neutral trade. By 1830 even veteran US traders to Livorno were redirecting their ships elsewhere in the Mediterranean or toward the Orient.[15]

In 1834, Appleton noted that, "The commerce [in Livorno] had been progressively decreasing for more than ten years." Much of that trade had shifted roughly 110 miles to the northeast to the port of Genoa. Livorno, according to Appleton, had "declined to a state, which alarms both the government and the people" and had prompted the Chamber of Commerce to enter into an agreement with the government in which local merchants rather than incoming ships would pay commercial duties. This arrangement did little to stem the decline. By 1835, the venerable Livorno merchant Antonio Felicchi wrote that the dearth of American shipping had reduced his commissions to "naught." In the summer of 1836 Appleton reported the complete absence of American ships from April to July of that year, an absence, he wrote, that was "unexampled during thirty-eight years I have resided here." Appleton blamed this remarkable decline on the high prices of the West Indian goods typically reexported to Livorno as well as the rapid rise of beet sugar grown in France and Germany which, he predicted, could destroy American importation of West Indian cane sugar "in the course of a very few years."[16]

Having left the commission business to concentrate on marble and occasionally provisioning the US Navy, Appleton personally would not have suffered quite as dramatic reversals as Felicchi or Montgomery. Nevertheless, Appleton continued to envy the Paris consul, Isaac Cox Barnet, who "reposes on a bed of down" while Appleton suffered the Livornese downturn. He was also concerned that interest on his considerable investment in US treasury notes had fallen from a high initial yield to only 4½ percent, and he began to move that money into European notes.

[15] Appleton to D. Parker, Nov. 20, [1819]; to H. Preble, Dec. 25, 1819; to J. J. Astor and Son, Mar. 15, 1820; to ___ May, Apr. 25, [1821], all in GL; Appleton to Shaler, May 14, 1823; Shaler to ____ Barnet, May 16, [1824], both in Shaler Papers.
[16] Luca Codignola, *Blurred Nationalities Across the Atlantic: Traders, Priests, and Their Kin Travelling between North America and the Italian Peninsula, 1763–1846* (University of Toronto Press, 2019) 188–89; Appleton to Sec. State, July 28, 1834; July 6, 1836, both in Leghorn Despatches.

TABLE 10.2 *Thomas Appleton's annual income from consular fees*[1]

1834	$349
1835	$337.50
1836	$306.50
1837	$162
1838	$200

[1] Leghorn Despatches.

His intake from consular fees dropped precipitously. After 1834, when the US government began to require that consuls report their annual fees, Appleton averaged about $10 per arriving ship, and the actual intake ranged from a miserable $162 in 1837 to $349 in 1834. During the height of the neutral trade in the first decade of the century, he likely made five to ten times these figures. Considering that typical wages for a manual laborer averaged $1 per day during this period, it is quite clear that Appleton could not possibly have survived as consul to Livorno had he relied solely on these fees for income.[17] (See Table 10.2.)

***

Consuls tended to blame developments within the Mediterranean for the decline in trade, citing political and military disruptions and shifts in local prices. But shifting economic currents within the United States also had an impact. After 1815, the most important was the new focus on western settlement and the rise of the cotton kingdom. Movement into the new territories of the trans-Appalachian west redirected a good deal of commercial activity toward the internal trade envisioned by the Whig Party's American System with its three pillars of internal improvements, domestic manufacturing, and high tariffs, all of which redirected energy away from overseas trade. At the same time, increased interest in South America, announced by the Monroe Doctrine in 1823, pushed some ambitious Mediterranean merchants to move their attention toward that region. Finally, after the War of 1812, cotton increasingly dominated the US export trade. During the boom years of the neutral trade in the early

---

[17] On naval provisioning, see Register of Events; Appleton to Thomas Perkins, Sept. 10, 1824; Appleton to ___ May, Apr. 25, [1821] both in GL.

1800s, cotton's share of US exports hovered around 10 percent, but by the late 1820s it pushed close to 40 percent. Because the US cotton trade was primarily with Great Britain, Mediterranean ports mostly did not benefit from it but continued to receive the same mix of fish, flour, and reexported West Indian goods after 1815 as they had before.

US exports as a whole in the decades after 1815 never quite returned to the prewar peak of $108 million attained in 1809, but they did push past $80 million a few times in the 1810s and 1820s. However, since cotton made up 30 percent or more of the total exports in these years, the numbers for the non-cotton exports heading to Mediterranean ports would actually have been considerably lower. Take the peak year of 1825, during which $90.7 million in US goods were exported. Only three years during the prewar neutral trade produced more exports – 1805 ($95.6 million), 1806 ($101.5 million), and 1807 ($108.3 million). Yet, when cotton is excluded, the 1825 figure drops to $53.9 million, which is far below the earlier peak years when cotton is similarly excluded – $86 million, $93 million, and $94 million. In short, despite the overall growth in the US economy, exports failed to regain their peaks, and the situation was far worse for most of the Mediterranean ports which did not benefit from the one bright spot – the exportation of cotton. (See Table 10.3.)

Americans in the Mediterranean held out some hope that the port of Marseille might buck the general declining fortunes of the area. It seemed to be in the best situation to handle American cotton, as it was in the midst of the region of heavy French textile manufacturing. Because of the industry in the region, it was also a good market for dye stuffs that were increasingly being imported from the Latin American markets by Yankee shippers. Additionally, it offered a fairly low tariff environment for the typical American and West Indian goods that had been imported into the region since the American Revolution. This promise lured much of Alicante's American community to Marseille in the 1810s. Robert Montgomery set up a new firm there named Montgomery, Fitch and Co. in 1814. It was headed by his sons, Frederick and Robert Jr., as well as his former clerk, Asa Fitch, Jr. In 1819, Montgomery's son-in-law John H. Rogers also moved his Alicante firm to Marseille, thereby reuniting his wife Isabella with her brothers. By the early 1820s, Fitch described Marseille as the most important port in Europe after London and Liverpool. A few years later he bragged that Marseille had not "in the slightest degree" suffered from the many business failures plaguing Europe "but on the contrary still abounds with capitalists, who are eager to employ their funds in the purchase of colonial goods . . . ." Montgomery, Fitch and Co. also bragged about the

TABLE 10.3 *US exports 1805–29*

Year	All exports A[1] (millions $)	Cotton exports C[2] (millions $)	Non-cotton exports A – C (millions $)	Cotton as % of total
1805	95.566	9.445	86.121	9.9
1806	101.537	8.332	93.205	8.2
1807	108.343	14.232	94.111	13.1
1808	22.431	2.221	20.210	9.9
1809	52.203	8.515	43.688	16.3
1810	66.748	15.108	51.650	22.6
1811	61.317	9.652	51.665	15.7
1812	38.527	3.090	35.443	8.0
1813	27.856	2.324	25.532	8.3
1814	6.927	2.683	4.244	38.7
1815	52.557	17.529	35.028	33.4
1816	81.920	24.106	57.814	29.4
1817	87.671	22.627	65.043	25.8
1818	93.281	31.334	61.946	33.6
1819	70.142	21.081	49.060	30.0
1820	69.692	22.308	47.383	32.0
1821	54.596	20.157	34.438	36.9
1822	61.350	24.035	37.314	39.2
1823	68.326	20.445	47.880	29.9
1824	68.972	21.947	47.024	31.8
1825	90.738	36.846	53.891	40.6
1826	72.891	25.025	47.865	34.3
1827	74.310	29.360	44.950	40.0
1828	64.021	22.487	41.536	35.0
1829	67.435	26.575	40.860	39.0

[1] 1804–14 export figures from Timothy Pitkin, *A Statistical View of the Commerce of the United States of America* (Hartford: Charles Hosmer, 1816) 36; 1815–29, Douglass C. North, *The Economic Growth of the United States 1790–1860* (New York: Norton, 1966) 23.
[2] North, *The Economic Growth of the United States 1790–1860*, 231, 233.

port's proximity to textile manufacturing as a circumstance "eminently calculated to make this a large cotton market."[18]

[18] Montgomery, Fitch and Co. printed announcement, Sept. 1, 1814, Alicante Despatches; John H. Rogers to Brown and Ives, Mar. 1, 1819, B114 F9; Fitch Bros. and Co. to Brown and Ives, Jan. 5, 1821, B115 F2; June 19, 1821, B115 F4, all in B. & I.

TABLE 10.4 *US shipping to Livorno and Marseille compared*[1]

Year	1817	1819	1820	1825
Livorno	28	35	29	12 by April
Marseille	34	32	32	14 by March

[1] Montgomery Fitch to Brown and Ives, Mar. 18, 1818, B113 F4; Fitch Bros. to Brown and Ives, Jan. 5, 1821, B115 F2; Fitch Bros., Circular, May 8, 1825, B117 F1, all in B. & I.; Thomas Appleton to Sec. State, in Leghorn Despatches; Charles A. Keene, "American Shipping and Trade, 1798–1820: The Evidence from Leghorn," *Journal of Economic History* 38 (Sept. 1978) 687.

While Montgomery, Fitch and Co. appears to have been quite successful, Marseille did not escape the downturn in the Mediterranean to the extent that they hoped. When war in Spain broke out in 1823, Fitch made a rare call to Americans to stop shipments into the area. Through the late 1810s, the number of American arrivals closely tracked those in Livorno, as did shipments in early 1825, the one period in the 1820s for which we have comparable data. (See Table 10.4.) Though American cotton did occasionally appear profitable there, it never quite matched Americans' hopes. Lured by reports from Marseille, the Providence firm of Brown and Ives lost a good deal of money on a shipment of New Orleans cotton that they consigned to Fitch in late 1826, just after prices had dropped significantly in the region. By early 1827 Fitch was again predicting an upturn in the market for US cotton noting that American importations so far had been "disproportionately small." Despite some arrivals in the late 1820s, by 1829 they reported that, as in other European ports, Marseille's cotton market was "not brisk" and the price of American cotton had fallen again.[19]

***

As their fortunes in the Mediterranean declined, the American consuls became increasingly dissatisfied with the State Department. There had always been tensions. Consuls rarely received replies to their letters to their superiors in Washington or Philadelphia, and never in a timely fashion. Reimbursements for frequent official expenditures came slowly,

[19] Fitch Bros. to Brown and Ives, June 28, 1823, B115 F8; Apr. 2, 1825, B117 F1; Apr. 13, 1825, B117 F1; Brown and Ives to Fitch Bros., Oct. 7, 1826, B117 F8; Jan. 1, 1827, B117 F8; Fitch Bros. to Brown and Ives, Jan. 8, 1827, B117 F9; Jan. 23, 1827, B117 F9; Printed Circular, Feb. 19, 1827, B117 F9; Fitch Bros. to Brown and Ives, Mar. 28, 1829, B117 F10, all in B. & I.

if at all, and bills on the State Department could be hard to cash. The lack of salaries (or, in the case of Simpson, low salaries), lack of power to enforce regulations, and lack of clear directives on consular fees and other issues had all created tensions since the beginning of the consular service. But so long as the consuls were young, vigorous, and prosperous in a booming Mediterranean economy, these irritations had been minor. As the economy tanked and the consuls reached old age in a society without any sort of protections for the elderly, these problems became far more important. At the same time, as the Mediterranean became less crucial to American concerns, so too did the concerns of the consuls in the region become less important to the federal government.

One relatively new issue that threatened both Montgomery and Simpson was that of citizenship. When they had been first appointed in the 1790s most Mediterranean consuls had not been US citizens because few lived in the region, and a cosmopolitan view of the American trading nation as a community of interests and ideals minimized the importance of territorial notions of citizenship as defined by geographical boundaries. By the time of the Jefferson administration, the territorial notion of citizenship began to gain ascendancy as the United States acquired more land and began to look more to the American continent rather than Europe. While few applicants for consular positions in the John Adams administration had stressed the citizenship issue, during Jefferson's two terms a good number of applicants not only stressed their citizenship but actively sought to replace noncitizen consuls. For example, when applying for Italian consulates, Appleton's friend Joseph Barnes highlighted his own citizenship and the fact that the consul at Naples was "neither a man of business nor a native" noting he was "aware of the great evils which result from foreigners filling the offices of consuls of the United States in various parts of Europe, who possessing neither common feelings or interests with the citizens of the United States, instead of protecting often conspire to defraud our citizens of their property." A petition in his favor signed by American citizens at Messina used almost identical language. Similarly, the friends of Appleton's acquaintance Frederick Degan attacked the noncitizen consul at Naples and requested that, since there were no US citizens residents there, Degan, as the man "possessing those qualifies most nearly allied to one," be appointed to replace him.[20]

---

[20] Joseph Barnes to Thomas Jefferson, Sept. 27, 1800; Petition of Robert Rose and others, Mar. 11, 1801; both in Joseph Barnes File, Jefferson Recs.; Memorial of Frederick Degan,

Ironically, Robert Montgomery, who had so carefully acquired a certificate of citizenship in 1778 from Benjamin Franklin, was one of the targeted "noncitizen" consuls. John R. Fenwick, member of a wealthy South Carolina planter family and Revolutionary War general who had been educated in Europe and developed an intellectual interest in the Mediterranean region, managed to receive an appointment to replace Montgomery in the spring of 1815. Obadiah Rich, who was living in the District of Columbia at the time, got wind of the appointment shortly after it had been confirmed and wrote to the State Department to complain. Rich stressed that Montgomery was an American citizen and hinted that perhaps some vaguely defined and unfair charges had been levelled against him.[21]

In Alicante, Montgomery learned of the development a couple months later, likely having been notified by Rich. In complaining to the State Department, Montgomery again stressed his citizenship as well as his long service to the United States, and he added, "I think it a little hard to be disgraced in my old age and not know that I have ever given cause for it." Though Fenwick decided to refuse the appointment – perhaps because, as Montgomery noted, as a nonmerchant he would not be able to support himself on the small income it provided – Montgomery was still afraid that the State Department would find some other American to take the job. After the Fenwick scare, Montgomery or one of his friends dug up his original 1793 appointment and discovered that rather than being listed as an American citizen, Montgomery had been described as "Robert Montgomery of Spain," a formulation that implied noncitizenship. As a result, Montgomery wrote to the State Department requesting that the error be corrected and that he receive a new commission, not only for himself but "to secure the right of citizens to his children born in Spain."[22]

In Tangier, James Simpson, of course, was not a citizen and was likely defensive about that fact, particularly with the enhanced emphasis on citizenship. Mordecai Noah, an American citizen and consul to Tunis, had complained about noncitizens generally and about Simpson

---

May 1 / Sept. 1, 1803, Frederick Degan File, Jefferson Recs. For another example, see File of Isaac Coxe Barnet, *ibid.*

[21] Obadiah Rich to James Madison, Apr. 22, 1815, Letters of Application and Recommendation during the Administration of James Madison 1809–17 M438RG59, General Records of the Department of State, NARA; John R. Fenwick to Thomas Jefferson, Aug. 16, 1810, Jefferson Papers.

[22] Montgomery to Sec. State, June 22, 1815; June 29, 1815; Memorial of Robert Montgomery, Mar. 17, 1816, all in Alicante Despatches.

specifically when he passed through Morocco in the 1810s, and those complaints found their way into his well-read 1819 book. In 1817, Simpson was concerned to learn that John O'Sullivan, a New York merchant, was appointed consul to Mogadore (Essaouiria) without his knowledge. In the context of the purge of noncitizens and the structure of Moroccan consulates, Simpson would have viewed this appointment as a real threat not only to his authority but potentially to his position. Hitherto Simpson had always appointed a vice-consul or agent to Mogadore. The current one, to be replaced by O'Sullivan, was William Wilshire, a British citizen who seems to have been very helpful to Americans and even beloved by the shipwrecked crew members he redeemed. To make the situation worse, two years earlier, Simpson had briefly appointed O'Sullivan his agent to Mogadore until the implementation of the Treaty of Ghent would bring peace between the United States and Great Britain, thereby allowing Wilshire to resume his position as US agent. During that short period, Simpson caught O'Sullivan in the highly irregular proceeding of charging the high sum of $50 to certify affidavits relating to a captured American ship.[23]

As if this context did not make O'Sullivan's appointment ominous enough, Simpson also had questions about who would be subservient to whom and even how two consuls could operate simultaneously in Morocco, particularly since Simpson's title was "consul of the United States for the Empire of Morocco." The State Department responded that O'Sullivan's appointment was not intended to "supersede" Simpson but that the two should operate simultaneously as would consuls in different European ports. Nevertheless, Simpson feared the emperor would not recognize such an arrangement, as he was used to dealing only with consuls at Tangier (and in fact Morocco had isolated European consuls there to keep them from the rest of the country). When O'Sullivan arrived, the emperor did, in fact, refuse to recognize him as a consul. O'Sullivan's commission was finally revoked in 1818 on the grounds that it manifestly violated the act of 1810 establishing salaries for minister and consuls in Barbary, which stipulated there should only be one US consul in each of those states. Restored to his previous authority, and

---

[23] Mordecai Manuel Noah, *Travels in England, France, Spain, and the Barbary States in the Years 1813–1814 and 15* (New York: Kirk and Mercein, 1819) 217–18; Simpson to Sec. State, Aug. 17, 1815; Affidavit of John Foxcroft, July 31, 1815; Simpson to Adams, July 22, 1812, all in Tangier Despatches.

with O'Sullivan back in the United States, Simpson then reappointed Wilshire as his Mogadore agent.[24]

The other issue that distressed the consuls and created tensions with the State Department was the problem of reimbursements. As with citizenship, it became an increasing concern after the end of the Napoleonic Wars, both because of the consuls' reduced economic positions and because the State Department appears to have made some active efforts to settle claims. In 1817 Montgomery filed a claim for $4,484.90, which he described as covering all of his "pending accounts." This was a very large sum – equivalent to perhaps $100,000 today, and it included expenses going back decades.[25] An auditor for the State Department explained the reimbursement process to Montgomery, who claimed to be unsure of it – suggesting he either had never heard from the State Department about it before or that it was new. Montgomery complied with the procedure, hoping to see the money soon. Instead, to his "disgust and pain," the authorities refused his claims "for compensation of my unremitted services of forty years." Over the next year or two he continued to push his claims as well as those for his late nephew, George Clark, who had run up expenses while assisting the American captives in Algiers. At one point he delegated his son, Frederick Montgomery, who was visiting New Orleans, to go to Washington to pursue the matter. There is no evidence that Montgomery ever received payment for any of these claims, and by this time he badly needed money due to the spoliations of the Peninsular War.[26]

At the same time, Appleton was making efforts to get reimbursed for expenses incurred back in 1809 when he was working on tracking down Degan Purviance's accounts in Naples during their bankruptcy. Appleton had charged the United States $6 per day for his expenses, amounting to nearly a year's work, and he also recorded over $2,000 in "disbursements" including bribes to Italian officials. Unfortunately, despite his efforts, the government does not appear to have recouped any of the

---

[24] Simpson to Adams, Aug. 11, 1812; Aug 20, 1812; Jan. 24, 1818; Aug. 8, 1818, all in Tangier Despatches; J. Q. Adams Digital Diary, Mar. 10, 1818, www.Masshist.org; "An Act Fixing the compensation of Public Minister, and of Consuls Residing on the Coast of Barbary . . . ," Acts of the 11th Congress Chap. XLIV, www.loc.gov.

[25] www.officialdata.org values it at $74,000 based on consumer prices. Based on a minimum wage of $300 or so at the time ($1 per day), it would amount to roughly $200,000 in today's money.

[26] Montgomery to Sec. State, Sept. 7, 1817; Nov. 17, 1817; July 26, 1817 [1818], all in Alicante Despatches.

money that Degan Purviance owed it. Nevertheless, Appleton still needed to be reimbursed, and in 1816 he authorized his brother-in-law Thomas Perkins to negotiate with the government, instructing him to accept a partial settlement if necessary. Appleton insisted, "The whole claim is just before Gad and man," yet, reflecting his exasperation with the government, he added, "considering they are who I have to deal with, you will receive from them such a portion as they will pay merely because they have the power to say 'we will pay no more.'" Still Appleton held out hope he might receive half his claim at least. Instead, his entire claim of $1,934.62 was denied. By the early 1820s he was unable to hide his bitterness. Citing his long record of service, he noted that in Italy such a "faithful servant who has served his country or his master" could expect to retire "on a proportionate pension," but "neither length of years, nor the most important services, have any claim on our government." He added, "To suffer an old and faithful dog to starve, would disgrace even a bad man; it is only governments, who can do with impunity, what is dishonorable to the worst of men."[27]

More than any of the three, James Simpson suffered from slow communication and lack of repayment from the State Department. From the beginning of his term, he believed he had been promised twice the salary he received, and his position in Morocco demanded a high level of expensive gift-giving to local officials and pricey housing. He complained of heavy expenses in the postwar years, including having to pay rent on his small consulate, which he calculated cost him $1,152 between 1810 and 1816. In 1814, at the age of 67, he asked permission to leave his post and travel to Washington to argue his case, but it was denied. When the recently released captive, James Riley, arrived in Tangier in 1816, Simpson complained to him about the consular rent and his personal expenditures on a plot of land suitable for a new consulate. Riley found Simpson in a very "embarrassed" situation and reported that, as a consequence of spending his entire private fortune of $80,000 on consular affairs, he now lived in penury, dependent on his friends in Gibraltar and elsewhere for financial assistance and no longer able to maintain his country house, Mount Washington.[28]

---

[27] Appleton to Thomas Perkins, May 16, 1816; July 8, 1816; Aug. 14, 1816, all in GL; US Treasury Dept., *An Account of the Receipts and Expenditures of the United States* (1817) 185, www.Hathitrust.org; Appleton to Shaler, May 17, 1821, Shaler Papers.

[28] Simpson to Sec. State, July 21, 1814; to Alexander Dallas, July 1, 1816; to Monroe, Dec. 20, 1816; to Adams, July 22, 1817; to David Humphreys, Aug. 20, 1818, all in

Simpson now had the clever idea of commissioning Riley as his agent to lobby Congress for reimbursement. Once in Washington, Riley was able to gain two meetings with Secretary of State John Quincy Adams, probably because of his celebrity as a redeemed captive, a status which would grow during his time lobbying for Simpson due to the publication of his very popular narrative. Burdened with a great deal of paperwork from Simpson and making use of letters from David Humphreys, Adams prepared a report. In the meantime, Riley portrayed Simpson as a worthy charity case who deserved pity due to his penury in the service of the United States. Simpson, Riley wrote, "has expended, besides his salary, all his private property in the public service; and has been forced to the humiliating necessity of appealing to Congress in order to enable him to pay debts he has been obliged to contract for his ordinary subsistence." Despite Riley's piteous language and his celebrity, he and Simpson had little success. Congress refused to act on the memorial, although it held out some hope of future reimbursements with the proper vouchers and of raising the salaries of Barbary consuls by 25 percent to $2,500 per year.[29]

***

Despite the consuls' disenchantment with the State Department and their economic decline, and in some cases because of it, they and other Americans continued to form a close community in the region through the 1820s. They were knit together by the developing US Navy, whose high-ranking officers landed frequently in Livorno and other major Mediterranean ports, bringing with them news and gossip about community members, and sometimes physically transporting Americans from one port to another.[30] As they always had, members of the community mixed mercantile trade, their professional duties, and personal friendships in their relationships. The papers of William Shaler, consul to Algiers from 1815 to 1828, offer particularly strong insight into a portion of this

---

Tangier Despatches; James Riley, *Sequel to Riley's Narrative* (Columbus: George Brewster, 1851) 331, 341.

[29] J. Q. Adams Digital Diary, vol. 30, Mar. 16, 1818; July 14, 1820, www.Masshist.org; Brett Goodin, *From Captives to Consuls: Three Sailors in Barbary and Their Self-Making across the Early American Republic, 1770–1840* (Baltimore: Johns Hopkins University Press, 2020) 144–45; Riley, *Sequel to Riley's Narrative*, 339–41.

[30] In the 1820s these included Como. Isaac Chauncey, Como. Charles Stewart, Capt. Charles Ridgley, Capt. William Crane (later a Commodore), Capt. John Rodgers (later a commodore), Capt. Henry Ballard.

community. Shaler was very sociable and very mobile, and he knew and kept track of many Americans. As the "consul general" to Algiers, other Barbary consuls were nominally supposed to report to him. He was certainly in fairly regular contact with James Simpson. He also spent time in other Mediterranean ports as well as traveling to the United States at least once during his tenure.[31]

Shaler spent at least two winters in Marseille during the late 1810s and later was there during the summer of 1825. He made himself part of the social circle surrounding Richard Montgomery's former clerk Asa Fitch, who was a partner with the two Montgomery sons in Montgomery, Fitch and Co. until it dissolved. This group consisted mostly of youngish single men, some American merchants, and some of the usual English and Irishmen who made up British trading circles throughout the Mediterranean. Included in the circle, but probably a bit removed, at least before they left Marseille around 1824, were the Montgomery brothers – Frederick and Robert Jr. – whom Fitch described as the "royal family." Two unmarried Montgomery daughters, probably the same two who would charm Washington Irving in Madrid in 1826, also visited Marseille, as did numerous other American merchants and sea captains. Shaler and Fitch also socialized with the British consul Alexander Turnbull and an Irish couple, Doctor and Mrs. Luby, who seem to have had connections with the radical United Irishmen. Oddly, they do not appear to have been friendly with Joshua Dodge, who served as American consul from 1819 onward, perhaps because Dodge and Fitch were rivals.[32]

At the very center of Fitch's circle were three men – John Ledyard Hodge, John Higginson Cabot, and a Mr. Bowles. All three were playing cards with Fitch when a letter from Shaler arrived one day in January 1823 and were pleased to find that they were mentioned in it and "borne in [Shaler's] embrace." Born in Philadelphia, at the time Hodge was 39 and unmarried. It appears he would spend most of his long life in Europe,

---

[31] James Simpson to Shaler, Feb. 28, 1817; Richard B. Jones to Shaler, Sept. 21, 1821, both in Shaler Papers.

[32] Fitch to Shaler, Jan. 7, 1818; Sept. 9, 1819; Jan. 31, 1820; Jan. 1, 1823; Jan. 2, 1824; Feb. 27, 1824; Jan. 12, 1824; Sept. 13, 1827, all in Shaler Papers; Richard Robert Madden, *The Memoirs* (London: Ward and Downey, 1891) 15; Andrew Boyd, "The Life and Times of RR Madden," in *Seanchas Ardmacha: Journal of the Armagh Diocesan Historical Society* 20 (2005) 133–54; *The New York Genealogical and Biographical Record* VII (1876) 13; Harrison Ellery, *The Pickering Genealogy* (John Wilson and Son, 1897) II: 408.

eventually becoming consul to Marseille in 1851. Hodge's brother and sister-in-law also visited and may have known Shaler. Cabot, age 40 and also unmarried, belonged to a famous Boston family and was a merchant who moved to Marseille for his health. He would spend the rest of his life there. Little is known about Bowles, although he had a sister (or possibly a daughter) who was quite popular with the men in Fitch's circle.[33]

Shaler also was well connected to the American circle in Livorno, where he had visited at least twice, in 1818 and 1821.[34] In frequent correspondence, Appleton often passed on news about and greetings from numerous mutual friends there. These included the strange duo of the American merchant and consul to Sicily, Joseph Barnes and his close friend and business partner E. I. Newton, as well as the British parson Thomas Hale (or Hall). Shaler also was acquainted with the occasional vice-consul to Florence, James Ombrosi, and a couple of other Italians in the American circle, including a shipbuilder named Bastiani.[35] But Shaler's closest contacts in Livorno were the numerous Americans with business in North Africa who seem to have viewed the Italian port as a sort of European respite, a perception reaching back at least to 1801 when James Cathcart landed there after being ejected from Tripoli. Thomas Anderson, consul to Tripoli from 1816 to 1819 often served as a liaison between Shaler and Appleton. In 1819, after contracting cholera, he moved to Livorno for treatment, where he encountered Shaler on one of his visits. Four years later, after being appointed consul to Tripoli, Anderson returned to get treatment for a painful ocular condition which nearly blinded him and kept him there for at least two years. Similarly, Townshend Stith, Anderson's successor as consul to Tunis and another Shaler acquaintance, showed up in Livorno in 1822 to have an eye extracted by the same doctor who treated Anderson.[36] Perhaps Shaler's closest friend in Livorno was Dr. Samuel D. Heap. Brother-in-law to Captain David Porter, Heap had been appointed as a doctor in the Navy, but he seems to have lost the position and encountered serious money problems. He and his fellow

---

[33] Fitch to Shaler, Jan. 31, 1823; July 7, 1823; Jan. 12, 1824; Sept. 13, 1827; Jan. 12, 1824; Oct. 20, 1831, all in Shaler Papers; "John Ledyard Hodge," in Seward Family Digital Archive, https://sewardproject.org/person-public-fields/74215.

[34] Appleton to Shaler, Mar. 2, 1818; October 16, 1819; Jan. 22, 1821, all in Shaler Papers.

[35] Appleton to Shaler, Dec. 1, 1818; May 8, 1821; Sept. 27, 1820; May 14, 1823, all in Shaler Papers. On Barnes and Newton, see Miriam Allen DeFord, "An American Murder Mystery," *Prairie Schooner* 22 (Fall 1948) 284–87.

[36] Appleton to Shaler, Oct. 16, 1819; May 14, 1823; Dec. 18, 1824; Feb. 3, 1825; Aug. 2, 1825; Sept. 25, 1822, all in Shaler Papers.

naval physician, Dr. Reese, traveled around Italy together while waiting for some sort of monetary settlement. Ombrosi appears to have helped Heap and his family find a place to live in Florence for a time. He was finally appointed acting consul to Tunis in 1824 and became the permanent consul in 1825, but he left the post and returned to New York with his family by the end of the year. Shaler feared that Heap somehow blamed him for whatever was behind this rapid withdrawal, but Appleton assured him the doctor bore him "the least ill will."[37]

The members of this group, like all communities, enjoyed gossiping among and about each other. Besides providing information, this practice also served to strengthen personal ties among the Americans. They often talked about their own and others' families. Appleton frequently wrote about his nephews' progress. He even mentioned his Italian wife and daughter to Shaler, a topic he rarely ever broached with anyone and apparently never with his own family in America. Everyone discussed an unfortunate incident when Shaler's nephew attempted to fill in for him in his consular position while the uncle was away. Fitch wrote about his brother in Marseille and gossiped about the Montgomery clan.[38] They also complained about their professional and financial problems and those of their friends, thereby bonding over the community's decline.

Often they gossiped about love, sex, and flirtations. When Stephen Cathalan, the foreign-born American consul to Marseille died, Fitch described the domestic scene in detail. Cathalan, Fitch wrote, died "after a very short illness occasioned, it is said, by the ill-treatment [of] his infamous wife. They got into a violent dispute respecting some repairs in his estate in the country, when she followed him out and countermanded in his presence the orders he had given to his workmen; from words it is said they came to blows or kicks the results of which bringing on what the Spaniards call a *suffoco* and a fever." Five years later, apparently with a bit of snark, he informed Shaler that the new consul, Joshua Dodge had

---

[37] Appleton to Shaler, May 8, 1824; Feb. 3, 1825; Apr. 22, 1825; Aug. 2, 1825, all in Shaler Papers. There is also a separate correspondence with Heap in the Shaler Papers. Appleton to Como. Stewart, Oct. 10, 1819; to Charles Shaw, May 22, 1820; to D. Hambleton, Oct. 6, 1820; to William Bainbridge, Oct. 9, 1820; to Samuel D. Heap, Jan. 7, 1821; Feb. 23, 1821; to Shaler, July 2, 1824, all in GL. Hunter Miller, ed., *Treaties and Other International Acts of the USA* (Washington DC: GPO, 1933) III: 143; Grace Overmyer, *America's First Hamlet* (New York University Press, 1957) 350.
[38] Appleton to Shaler, Sept. 25, 1822; Fitch to Shaler, Jan. 12, 1824; Appleton to Shaler, Feb. 5, 1825; Sept. 25, 1822; Fitch to Shaler, Jan. 31, 1823, all in Shaler Papers.

"married a daughter of James De Woold, a girl of 17 who no doubt you are acquainted with."[39]

Marseille offered the Americans numerous opportunities for socializing, amorous or otherwise, particularly during Carnival season. At the end of January 1823, Fitch wrote that he had been "constantly engaged at balls and parties for the last three weeks excepting my own nights which have been attended by ladies . . . ." Within the American group, he added, Miss Bowles was "still the hand of discord" and was particularly admired by Hodge as well as Cabot and a Captain B. G. Another time, he wrote that Cabot had spent fifteen or twenty days with the "Irish nymph" under the roof of her father's mansion, but "from his returning to Paris single handed it is to be presumed he has given up all hopes of consummating the happy union." Describing to Shaler the suffering of their mutual friend Daniel Parker, Appleton wrote that he "remains as quiet, as the feeling of most indignant action, can allow him in the arms of that old viper at Versailles." He later explained that one of the causes of Parker's troubles was "certain female connections that no one else would have accepted [that] directly and indirectly, cost him millions of francs."[40]

Chatter about events in America, particularly politics, also strengthened the Americans' bond to each other and to their homeland. European political news was easy to come by, and Americans constantly shared it, glorying in the triumph of republican principles and, usually, cheering British setbacks. American news was much harder to gather, and correspondents frequently shared scarce American gazettes with each other through the mails. Sometimes they wrote about less political events, such as the Great Match Race of 1823 that pitted a northern horse (Eclipse) against a southern horse (Henry) for a $400,000 purse on Long Island.[41]

Most frequently, though, their interest was politics, which affected them vocationally as well as personally. Appleton and Shaler were particularly drawn to republican and specifically Jeffersonian rhetoric. Appleton approvingly wrote to Shaler of an address by Connecticut Republicans as "in the true spirit of '76" and "couch'd in terms which, if followed, will insure the most lasting liberty and happiness to our country." Both Fitch and Appleton were excited by the cession of

---

[39] Fitch to Shaler, May 27, 1819; Feb. 27, 1824, both in Shaler Papers.

[40] Fitch to Shaler, Jan. 31, 1820; Jan. 31, 1823; Jan. 12, 1824; Appleton to Shaler, Feb. 3, 1825; Aug. 2, 1825, all in Shaler Papers.

[41] Fitch to Shaler, July 7, 1823, Shaler Papers. For examples of sharing gazettes, see Appleton to Shaler, Jan. 7, 1818; Jan. 29, 1823; Feb. 23, 1823, all in Shaler Papers.

Florida to the United States by Spain. Fitch was outraged when it appeared as though the Spanish king would refuse the treaty, suspecting that England was responsible, for "otherwise would the savage King of Spain be so stupidly blind to his own interests?" Finally, all Americans seem to have taken a great deal of interest in the lengthy saga of the contested 1824 presidential election. Both Appleton and Shaler admired Andrew Jackson, whom Shaler had started calling "Old Hickory." As the political machinations continued, Appleton wrote approvingly, "'Old Hickory' as you call him has gained much ground of late, and very much to the displeasure of John Bull, as the latter thinks he can neither be coax'd nor bullied, and so I think myself." In addition to spreading news, such exchanges of similar political sentiments helped to define the Americans to themselves, at least, as forward-thinking men, and to distinguish themselves from their apparently less enlightened neighbors in the region.[42]

***

Despite these continued connections, the American community was badly fragmented in the 1820s by the death of the earliest settlers and by the lack of opportunity for the next generation. All parents worry about their children's futures, but the concern in the declining American community at this time was particularly wrenching. Montgomery's actions give real insight into those worries. When he discovered his US citizenship had not been properly documented by the State Department, one of his stated concerns was that if he was not considered a US citizen then neither would his children. Without citizenship they would have a much more difficult time within the American Mediterranean community or within the United States itself. Judging from Frederick's trip to New Orleans in 1817 or 1818, it seemed possible they may have considered returning to the United States at least to participate in the growing cotton business there. The amount of effort Montgomery put into setting up his sons in business in Marseille and attempting to get a consulship there for them or himself as well as his efforts to set up his daughter and son-in-law on a good parcel of vineyard land in Alicante also speaks to his hopes and concerns for his progeny.[43]

---

[42] Appleton to Shaler, Jan. 7, 1818; Fitch to Shaler, Sept. 9, 1819; Appleton to Shaler, Apr. 25, 1821; Appleton to Shaler, Dec. 18, 1824; Feb. 3, 1825, all in Shaler Papers.

[43] Montgomery, 1817, Petition, Alicante Despatches. Note: This petition is inserted at the end of the microfilm reel.

Most importantly, time was running out for all the consuls, and their families' situations, rather than improving, were becoming progressively worse. Simpson was the first to go. He awoke at Mt. Washington on the morning of March 8, 1820, having fled the plague and political turmoil in the city. Feeling healthy and energetic, he took a morning walk through the gardens surrounding the deteriorating house, had a sudden "attack of apoplexy" (likely a stroke), and died almost immediately. He was 73 years old and had served the United States for nearly twenty-six years, twenty-four of them in Tangier.[44] For the Simpson family the financial timing could not have been worse, coming as the consul was still contending with the State Department for back-pay and reimbursements. His son John Simpson wrote that his father's death left his own young family as well as his brother and sister "without so much as even one cent." They estimated their father's debts at $7,000 and Simpson's successor, John Mullowney, a more impartial observer, guessed they were even higher, though he also estimated the family might recoup $1,500 in real estate sales, presumably referring to the declining Mt. Washington estate. Creditors seemed to be coming out of the woodwork demanding payments, including a Jew from Gibraltar who claimed that Simpson owed him $3,000.[45]

Noting that the elder Simpson had spent nearly twenty-four years in service to the United States "in a most barbarous country, almost totally excluded from civilized society, and shut up from all intercourse with friends," the Simpsons bemoaned the unhappy fact that he "departed this life leaving the [junior] part of his family in the extremes of poverty, and his estate encumbered, with serious and heavy dependencies." They referred once again to Simpson's understanding on taking the Tangier consulship that his salary would be $4,000 rather than the $2,000 he actually received and requested retroactive reimbursement of the difference up to 1810 at least. Finally, noting that Simpson had spent an enormous amount of his own money on official expenditures over his decades of service, but that it still fell $18,000 short of the maximum allowed by law, they again begged for reimbursement. The new consul, John Mullowney duly submitted the six packets of Simpson's accounts compiled by his sons to the State Department. There is no record that the

---

[44] John Simpson to Sec. State, Mar. 15, 1820, Tangier Despatches; *Scots Magazine* 95 (July 1820).

[45] John Simpson to Sec. State, July 20, 1821; Petition on the part of John Simpson, July 20, 1821; John Mullowney to Sec. State, Feb. 7, 1824, all in Tangier Despatches.

family was ever reimbursed for the father's expenses nor that they received the disputed portions of his salary.[46]

Robert Montgomery died three years after Simpson, on August 31 1823 in the midst of a severe family crisis. The royalist counterattack on Spain's liberal constitutionalists and their allies as well as dire personal and national economic problems had been a source of anxiety for some time. The royalists' confiscation of the family's Dehuse property, culminating in his sons' imprisonment, no doubt added a great deal to the already heavy load of stress borne by the 69-year-old man. Shortly after the Montgomerys' release from prison, local authorities ordered the family off its land and on August 7 returned it to the Church. Montgomery took ill twelve days later, on the 19th, and he died twelve days after that.[47]

Like the Simpsons, the Montgomery family attempted to gain some sort of recompense from the State Department after their patriarch died. In the same packet in which they sent news of their father's death, the younger Montgomerys also sent a detailed "state of the unparalleled atrocities, insults and robberies" inflicted on them by the royalists, thereby emphasizing the impact of these events on the senior Montgomery's health as well as the family's finances. Elizabeth Montgomery wrote that her husband's death and recent "unfortunate commercial transactions" left her "utterly destitute of means of subsistence." She noted that her late husband's "services to the United States and in favor of distressed citizens have always been approved by government and in particular by his Excellency James Monroe," who had been Montgomery's correspondent as secretary of state and was then president. She enclosed a copy of a petition Montgomery had submitted in 1819 detailing his long service to the United States and asking that Robert Jr. be appointed consul in his place. She somewhat optimistically noted that it had "ever been the policy" of the United States to reward "those officers that have faithfully and scrupulously fulfilled the posts with which they have been honored," an assertion which she probably knew was most certainly not the case.[48]

At the same time, the family resubmitted Montgomery's petition from 1819 in which he had requested that Congress ratify his citizenship and, in consideration of his years of service, "decree him a salary competent

---

[46] John Simpson to Sec. State, Mar. 15, 1820; June 12, 1820; Mullowney to Sec. State, June 26, 1821; John Simpson to Sec. State, Jan. 9, 1821; Mar. 4, 1821; July 20, 1821; Mar. 3, 1822; July 12, 1822; Jan. 24, 1824, all in Tangier Despatches.

[47] Frederick Montgomery to Sec. State, Sept. 6, 1823, Alicante Despatches.

[48] *Ibid.*

thereto, or such other compensation as the wisdom of this august assembly may approve." In the petition he had also requested that Congress appoint Robert Jr. to replace him in the Alicante consulate. Along with the two petitions, Frederick enclosed a letter to the State Department's auditor of accounts claiming that the department owed his father $941.91 in reimbursements for expenses incurred since the 1790s. Admitting he could no longer document all of these old debts, Frederick wrote, "I can now only appeal to your generous feelings and consideration on this long standing affair . . . ." Probably realizing that none of the family's monetary claims – neither the pension nor the reimbursements – were likely to be approved, Elizabeth Montgomery suggested that providing Robert Jr. with the consular position would at least partially compensate her for these claims. Referring to the prospective appointment as an "act of beneficence," she wrote that "it would be providing for a destitute widow and not burthening a nation for which the petitioner must ever entertain sentiments of the most sincere attachment . . . ." However, she added, should Robert Jr. not be appointed, she hoped the secretary of state would provide her with a pension "such as His Excellency's beneficent mind may think sufficient for her subsistence." In short, the consular appointment could serve as a cost-free method of reimbursing the family for their patriarch's service.[49]

Appleton, the youngest by a decade, was also the last to die. While he was never a prolific correspondent to the State Department, Appleton's correspondence notably tapered off further during his last years. No doubt old age, declining American commerce to Livorno, disenchantment with the State Department, and his own local business interests made the consulate less of a priority in later years. An event in 1836 suggests that Appleton may have appeared to Americans to be too old, too Italian, or too indifferent to be very effective any longer. In February, a number of Americans, including a prominent Philadelphia church minister, William H. DeLancey, arrived in Livorno aboard a French steamboat on what they believed was the first leg of a journey to Marseille. Unfortunately, the ship was badly damaged and could not immediately continue. The steamship company attempted to keep the passengers' passports in an effort to force them to continue on the original ship once it was repaired, but the Americans demanded the return of their papers so they could continue on a different ship. The steamship company apparently convinced local police to detain Reverend DeLancey, who complained of being arrested and, embarrassingly, marched through the street by

[49] Petition of Elizabeth Montgomery, Sept. 6, 1823, Alicante Despatches.

police. Appleton claimed that he acted quickly to free DeLancey and the others and to have the steamship company punished, but the Americans believed that he had not shown enough vigor in protecting them from this insult. They wrote a petition to the State Department complaining of Appleton's "dilatoriness ... in vindicating the rights and character of an American citizen" and of their mortification at seeing "an authority of America insulted in the presence of Englishmen, Italians and Frenchmen without any prompt effort to vindicate it." Consequently, they urged the State Department to institute "such a change in the consular office at Leghorn as shall secure to the many American citizens passing through the city an active, efficient and respected consul."[50]

Appleton fended off this attack, but he would not live much longer. He died on April 27, 1840 at the age of 76 or 77. He had been sick for at least a couple of years before that, and his successor reported that due to his "feeble health" Appleton left the documents at the consulate in a disordered state. Despite Livorno's declining trade, he left his wife a comfortable annual pension of over 1,000 florins (perhaps $290 at the time or about the annual wage of manual laborers in the United States). This pension would require at least $7,000 in capital to be sustainable, and, since it apparently only represented a portion of the estate he left to his daughter, it seems likely that Appleton's estate was relatively substantial, likely well over $10,000 or in the neighborhood of $250,000 today. Unlike Simpson, Appleton's heirs did not hope to continue receiving his consular salary, due at least in part to the lack of male descendants. However, Appleton's successor, John Sartori appears to have attempted to reimburse his daughter, Minerva Appleton, money due to Appleton out of State Department funds only to have the transaction refused by the Department, which no doubt further exacerbated the Appletons' irritation with the State Department's accounting system and further distanced them from the United States.[51]

***

---

[50] Appleton to John Forsyth, Mar. 13, 1836; to Rev. Dr. DeLancey, Mar. 5, 1836; Isaac H. Townsend to Forsyth, June 13, 1836, all in Leghorn Despatches.

[51] Maria Argiero and Algerina Neri, *Bostoniani a Livorno: il Console Thomas Appleton e I suoi conerranei* (University of Pisa, 2012) 54–55; John B. Sartori to Forsyth, Apr. 30, 1840; Victor A. Sartori to Sec. State, Mar. 10, 1841, both in Leghorn Despatches. In 1851, a Tuscan florin was valued at about 29 cents in J. Thompson, *The Coin Chart Manual* (New York: Wm. W. Lee, 1851) 29; The Coin Chart Manual Second Series (www.wiki media.org).

The Simpson and Montgomery families continued negotiating with the State Department for years after their patriarchs died. While the younger generation continued to feel some connection to the United States or at least to their fathers' years of service to the republic, the cash nexus determined their relations to the State Department. Considering that both Simpson and Montgomery died at a time when the Mediterranean business generally was in steep decline and their personal finances and the condition of their home ports perilous, it is understandable that their children looked to the United States for support and became frustrated when they did not receive much.

John S. Simpson, also known as James, was living in Tangier when his father died on March 8, 1820, and he was the first to report the event to the State Department. He pledged to "[take] charge of the affairs of the consulate until such time as the arrangements of government be known." In the next sentence, he requested that he be granted the position of consul permanently in consideration of his father's "long and faithful services" which began in the administration of "the immortal Washington, by whom his commission is signed." More immediately, Simpson needed to support his growing family, likely including his unmarried sister, Helen, as well as his wife and children, all of whom, he wrote, were left destitute by Simpson's death and feared starvation if John could not acquire the consular position with its annual salary.[52]

Morocco and Tangier were going through an extremely turbulent period, with the plague continuing to rage at the same time as something like a civil war ensued. Considering the distance from the United States – and with communications slowed by the political and epidemiological disturbances – it made sense for the younger Simpson to hold down the consular fort until he could get directions from Washington. Doing so required money. In the year after his father's death, John Simpson drew over $8,000 on the State Department. Much of the sum – roughly $6,000 – went for the presents that European consuls were expected to give local authorities from time to time. A number of events conspired to drive the sum up, including Emperor Muley Solimon's visit to Tangier, the appointment of a new governor of Tangier, the visit of Muley Ibrahim Ben Yazid who deposed Muley Solimon, and then another gift for Muley Solimon when he regained power following Muley Ibrahim's sudden death. In order to cover all these expenses, Simpson would have had to provide his own funds and

[52] John S. Simpson to Sec. State, Mar. 15, 1820 (2), Tangier Despatches.

then request reimbursement, usually from the American consul in Gibraltar, who had better access to State Department accounts. Presumably, Simpson would also have charged the customary 2 percent commission for his services. All of this expense was justified as necessary to insure that "the offices and flag of the US continue to be respected," a serious concern in a place where the rulers occasionally expelled diplomats who did not follow protocol and even occasionally declared war on the countries they represented.[53]

Young Simpson also continued to take his father's salary, drawing $2,000 for that purpose on the State Department via Gibraltar in the year he took it on himself to act as consul. Apparently desperate for money, and no doubt having realized the near impossibility of obtaining retroactive compensation from the State Department, he simply drew the money from friendly Gibraltar merchants in the name of the State Department and begged the secretary of state not to refuse payment. Three years later he similarly drew $2,000 in the name of the State Department to settle his father's debts based only on his "utmost and pressing want" and a professed belief in "the justice and humanity for which [the US] is so remarkable." Whether or not the State Department allowed any of these payments is not clear, although Simpson's repeated use of the tactic over several years suggests that he may have had some success.[54]

But ultimately Simpson failed in his main goal: to be appointed as consul and obtain the annual salary that went with it. In fact, Congress acted unusually quickly. Despite Simpson's pleas of poverty and family loyalty, and despite receiving support for his appointment from Emperor Muley Solimon, Congress appointed John Mullowney of Pennsylvania to fill the position in June 1820, only three months after the elder Simpson's death and likely less than a month after the news of it reached Washington. Simpson did not complain. It would not have done much good and, considering the rapid turnover in consular posts and numerous cases where appointees failed to arrive at their posts, it would make no sense to burn his bridges. Even after Mullowney arrived in Europe, Simpson remained cooperative. He also continued to plead with the State Department for reimbursement for expenses

---

[53] John S. Simpson to Sec. State, Apr. 14, 1820; Apr. 29, 1820; June 12, 1820; July 9, 1820; Mar. 9, 1821, all in Tangier Despatches.

[54] John S. Simpson to Sec. State, July 9, 1820; Jan. 9, 1821; Jan. 24, 1824, all in Tangier Despatches.

incurred during his father's term. But Mullowney's installation would effectively mark the end of the Simpson family's long connection to the United States.[55]

With Mullowney firmly established in Tangier and busily planning a new consular house for the United States, Simpson looked elsewhere for work. In late 1821 or early 1822 he managed to get himself appointed consul for Sardinia, a small neutral power not all that different from the United States. It was a move James Simpson no doubt would have understood, having served both the United States and Russia in Gibraltar. Shortly thereafter, young Simpson and his entire family – probably including his unmarried sister – received orders from the Moroccan government to leave the empire immediately. They soon found themselves packed into a ship in Tangier harbor together with the Swedish consul and his family, all headed across the Strait to Gibraltar and out of Morocco forever. While the Swedish consul apparently wrote a pamphlet critical of the Moors, Simpson's offense was not entirely clear. Mullowney believed he had angered the government by failing to produce the customary gifts when appointed Sardinian consul, negligence that may have stemmed from his money problems. Once in Gibraltar, Simpson continued his efforts to gain reimbursement for his father's claims on the United States. He left the Rock within a year and continued to persevere, making one last attempt to draw $2,000 from the United States as partial settlement while living on the island of Lissa in the Adriatic. This was the last communication between a Simpson and the State Department, and, perhaps, the last surviving letter from John. Where he went from Lissa and how he survived is not entirely clear, but what is clear is that his family's long association with both the United States and Tangier was over.[56]

***

Unlike the Simpsons, the Montgomerys managed to secure a consular appointment for the next generation. Robert Montgomery, Jr. succeeded his father as consul to Alicante, despite competition from George Adams, a well-connected American merchant also living in Alicante. Adams's brother, Thomas, credited the letter from Montgomery's widow,

---

[55] Petition of John James Simpson, July 20, 1821; John Mullowney to Sec. State, June 20, 1820; June 26, 1821; Sept. 17, 1821, all in Tangier Despatches.

[56] Mullowney to Sec. State, Jan. 30, 1822; May 15, 1822; John S. Simpson to Sec. State, Jan. 24, 1824, all in Tangier Despatches.

Elizabeth, with doing the trick.[57] In a sense, however, the Montgomerys won the battle but lost the war. Retaining the consular post did not guarantee success or even survival. Far from it in Alicante in the 1820s. Violence between royalists and liberals continued to rage and to effect American interests. Robert Jr. reported that royalist police continued to be ominously active around the region. In September 1824, they opened the private letters of American citizens which they took from a US ship suspected of touching on the British port of Gibraltar. Because the officials ultimately did not read or translate the letters, Montgomery refrained from making an official protest. At about the same time, police twice broke into the American merchant George Adams's house, presumably searching for liberals as they had at the Montgomery estate. They arrested Adams and his clerk, Samuel Hale, on the pretext that they were searching for a person "they *pretended* was secreted there," according to Adams. Adams insisted this person had never been in his house and had not been seen in Alicante for at least six months previously. The king now also began to insist that foreign merchants established in Spain make "contributions" to the sovereign, presumably because of the royalist government's precarious financial position. Montgomery protested that any contributions beyond the usual taxation would be arbitrary and violate America's treaties with Spain. Still worse, in March 1826, French troops under the command of General Antonio Bezan arrived in Alicante and began persecuting liberals, executing thirty-three suspects.[58]

Even more disturbing to American commerce were the government's repeated efforts to control trade through tariffs and monopolies. The duties on fish continued to be a bone of contention. In 1824, Robert Jr. wrote, "The duty of nearly four cents per pound, in addition to what is formerly paid, laid on *bacalao* [salted cod] amounts nearly to a prohibition of this article." Later in the year he complained that Henry O'Shea, who had purchased the exclusive contract to manage the local *bacalao* trade was purposely slowing the sale of fish because, due to a miscalculation in his contract with the government, he was actually losing money whenever he allowed sales to proceed. Montgomery

---

[57] *The Papers of Henry Clay*, VI: *Secretary of State, 1827* (Lexington: University Press of Kentucky, 1981) 995–96; Petition of Elizabeth Montgomery, Sept. 6, 1823, Alicante Despatches.

[58] Samuel Hale and George Adams to R. Montgomery Jr., Sept. 21, 1824; Montgomery Jr. to Sec. State, Sept. 25, 1824; Sept. 29, 1824; to Hugh Nelson, Oct 5, 1824; Mar. 4, 1826, all in Alicante Despatches. *The Papers of Henry Clay*, V: *Secretary of State, 1826* (Lexington: University Press of Kentucky, 1973), 144.

reported an uproar among the local merchants and predicted that O'Shea's "host of enemies" would "certainly effect his ruin." Despite O'Shea eventually losing the contract and a slight easing of the tariff, Montgomery continued to report that high duties were killing the *bacalao* trade. Evidently possessed of deep pockets, O'Shea managed to regain his footing, getting appointed as the government's contractor for the tobacco trade, a position similar to his earlier role as fish contractor. In return for paying $4 million dollars annually, he gained the "exclusive privilege of introducing, manufacturing and selling all the tobacco that is consumed on the peninsula for the space of ten years." Montgomery predicted that O'Shea would lower the price of tobacco to prevent smuggling, thereby further harming American merchants. As a result of all these developments, Montgomery reported, not a single American vessel had arrived in Alicante between February and November 1826.[59]

These events sapped what enthusiasm Robert Jr. might have had for the consular position his family had secured for him. Like his father before him, he came to doubt whether he could make a living in Alicante. But, unlike his father, he viewed the situation within a very political framework. Somehow Robert Jr. had acquired a strong republican orientation, which no doubt was further confirmed by the atrocities committed against his family and others by royalists in and around Alicante. His experience also led him to consider the royalists as generally corrupt and incompetent, as reflected by their administration of the hated tariffs and their handling of the tax farming exemplified by Henry O'Shea. Furthermore, he bristled at Spanish plans to subdue the new republics emerging in South America. When it appeared as though Spain, together with the Holy Alliance, was contemplating sending troops there, Montgomery comforted himself with "our revered president's last message [i.e., The Monroe Doctrine] and the notes passed by British ministers at foreign courts relative to the only species of interference in the affairs of [Latin] America." He also worried about the Spanish king's rumored unwillingness to ratify the cession of Florida to the United States. He breathed a sigh of relief when he learned that the king's Latin American project had been "exploded" and that "nothing now remains but the rage of impotence." He suspected that this lingering rage was part of the motivation for the "onerous" tariffs and impositions

---

[59] Montgomery Jr. to Sec. State, July 19, 1824; Nov. 12, 1824; Aug. 1, 1825; Sept. 3, 1825; Aug. 21, 1826; Nov. 1, 1826, all in Alicante Despatches.

since the king "considers the US and England as the fomenters of the revolution in [Spain's] late colonies."[60]

By the end of 1826 Montgomery reached his limit. He left Spain for the more republican air of South America, arriving in St. Thomas (now the US Virgin Islands) by Christmas on his way to Santa Marta, Colombia. He wrote the secretary of state that he planned to return to Alicante after taking care of some personal business in Colombia, although, somewhat contradictorily, he also offered to take over the American consulate in Santa Marta. Back in Alicante, George Adams, now serving as acting consul, doubted Montgomery would return, believing he intended to set himself up permanently as a merchant in South America. Adams was right. Montgomery never returned to Spain, and his family's long ties with Alicante and the Mediterranean coast were permanently sundered, though a number of relatives remained in Madrid, some 265 miles inland.[61]

By 1827, then, two families that had represented the United States literally and metaphorically for a combined total of close to eighty years were gone. Their departure was part of a vicious Mediterranean cycle. The decline in shipping made it hard for merchants to make a living. Political and economic turbulence in the region pushed long-timers out. The departure of long-term mercantile representatives meant that US merchants lost their contacts in the region and were consequently even less inclined to risk shipping their cargoes in that direction. The continuing decline in shipping meant that there was little incentive for new families to attempt to take the place of the old. All of these factors resulted in a double displacement for families like the Simpsons and Montgomerys. They cut ties with the United States because they felt deserted by the State Department, and they left their Mediterranean ports because they saw no opportunities there. By the 1830s, the remaining American community in the region would be very different and much diminished compared to what it had been for the previous fifty years.

---

[60] Montgomery, Jr. to Sec. State, Aug. 15, 1824; Sept. 29, 1824; Apr. 2, 1825; Mar. 4, 1826, all in Alicante Despatches.

[61] Montgomery, Jr. to Sec. State, Dec. 24, 1826; George Adams to Sec. State, Dec. 31, 1826, both in Alicante Despatches.

EPILOGUE

Latin America and the Turn toward Empire

Many of the developments of the 1820s continued into the 1830s and beyond. The old consular families continued to distance themselves figuratively from the United States and physically from the Mediterranean littoral. Subsequent generations in the cases of the Montgomerys and Appletons crossed the line into the Catholic world, while the Simpsons rejoined the British Empire in the antipodes. Many in the second and third generations also found their way to Latin America for a variety of reasons. Their particular choices mirrored the general trend in which the Mediterranean lost its luster to an emerging American empire that increasingly faced south and west rather than eastward.

The extended Montgomery clan was most affected by the political and economic instability of the postwar years due to their location in Alicante. As we have seen, their property and persons came under attack during the ongoing conflict between royalists and constitutionalists in the region. These circumstances pushed them away from the Mediterranean coast. At the same time, the collapse of Spain's overseas empire created new opportunities particularly in Latin America. As experts in the Spanish language and Spanish commercial practices with good connections in the Atlantic as well as the Mediterranean, they no doubt hoped to continue their mercantile activities and fill the vacuum left by the end of the old Spanish mercantile monopoly in the former American colonies. They also had some interest in returning to the United States, but in the end their attenuated connection to their homeland, declining interest in the Mediterranean, and intense competition from men already in the United States who were interested in the Latin American trade blocked that pathway.

By the 1830s every one of the Montgomery boys had left Spain. Robert Montgomery's sons Frederick and Robert Jr. had moved to Marseille by 1814 to set up Montgomery, Fitch and Co. with former clerk Asa Fitch, and at that time their father held some hope of being appointed consul there. They returned to Alicante in 1823 to help their aging father during the constitutionalist crisis. Frederick appears to have left shortly after his father's death in 1823, while Robert stayed on through most of 1826, when he finally departed for Santa Marta, Colombia, where he believed "there is more scope for activity and ordinary talents ... than in Spain where commerce is dwindling away to a shadow and where knowledge is in much opposition with the avowed principles of its government." With his consular experience, French and Spanish skills, and familiarity "with all the different shades of the Spanish character," he hoped to fill the empty US consular post at Santa Marta. His application was not successful and the job went instead to a Bostonian named William J. Stewart. Robert appears to have spent most of the rest of his life in Santa Marta. He retained his connection to Ireland but, after the rebuke from the State Department, does not seem to have had further contact with the United States. Late in life, he returned to Alicante, where he died in 1859 at the age of 67 or 68.[1] (See Figure E.1.)

Frederick, the younger Montgomery brother, had at least some interest in the United States. He visited New Orleans and the northern states in 1817 while still a merchant in Marseille. He was doing business with New Orleans merchants subsequently, probably as part of the cotton trade between Louisiana and France. Perhaps he had thoughts of settling in the United States before returning to Alicante along with his brother. After their father died, he found his way to Mexico City where he began a very successful mercantile career. He became a member of a group of merchants who were financing Mexico's debt and making outsized profits for themselves in doing so. His firm, Montgomery, Nicoud and Company joined with a consortium in 1840 that raised a 2 million peso loan for the government in return for 17 percent of Mexico's customs duties, and later, they floated a 2.2 million peso loan in exchange for a 6 percent premium. Despite an unfortunate bankruptcy, he died a rich man in 1843, approximately 51 years old and with a fortune estimated to be over $150,000.[2]

[1] Robert Montgomery, Jr. to Sec. State, Dec. 24, 1826, Alicante Despatches; List of US Consular Officers, 1789–1939 M 587, General Records of the Department of State RG59, NARA; Testimony of Mary Anna Montgomery, Mar. 30, 1872, Cartagena de Indias, in author's possession; author's correspondence with Luis R Dunoyer.

[2] Robert Montgomery to Sec. State, July 26, 1817, Alicante Despatches; *James McLanahan v. John S Ellery*, 1st Circuit Court, 1828; Barbara A. Tenenbaum,

FIGURE E.1 Robert Montgomery, Jr. (in author's possession courtesy of the Dunoyer family)

Frederick and Robert seem to have dropped all identification with the United States in Latin America. Frederick's mercantile firm was described as English or Irish. He benefitted from assistance from the British minister in negotiating one of his Mexican loans and his descendants described him as a "British subject." He moved in the highest circles of Mexican politics and was a strong supporter of President Antonio López de Santa Ana even when he was fighting the United States. Descendants understand that when Santa Ana was in exile he once stayed with Robert Montgomery's descendants in Colombia. Robert Montgomery was also described as a British subject shortly before his death. He married a Mexican woman, Evarista Vargas, and their descendants were Catholics. Later generations did not recall that the family had ever been American or Protestant.[3]

Like his cousins, George Washington Montgomery, John Montgomery's only son, spent most of his remaining life in Latin America. The budding

"Mexico's Money Market and the Internal Debt 1821–1855," https://core.ac.uk/down load/pdf/304707984.pdf; William H. Wynne, *State Insolvency and Foreign Bondholders* (New Haven: Yale University Press, 1951 [2000 reprint]) II: 15; Testimony of Mary Anna Montgomery.

[3] Tenenbaum, "Mexico's Money Market," 281, 289ff; Author's correspondence with R. L. Dunoyer; Testimony of Bentick M. Doyle, British Consul to the Judicial Circuit Court, Santa Marta, Colombia, July 18, 1815, extract in author's possession.

author served for a time as translator to the American legation in Madrid. His patron, Washington Irving, unsuccessfully recommended him for the US consul position in Oporto, Portugal and then, in 1835 succeeded in getting him the Puerto Rican consulship. Unfortunately, like so many other consuls without a good mercantile business, Montgomery was unable to make the position pay. He soon left and traveled to Guatemala. His published narrative of this trip reflects his dissatisfaction with the consular service when it describes one long-time resident as shocked to learn than a "Mr. P" was the American consul and added, "I wonder if your government knows it." He later spent time in Tampico working for the State Department and was appointed secretary of the US legation in Mexico before he took ill and returned to Washington DC, where he died at the age of 37 in 1841.[4]

The families of the two Montgomery daughters married to native-born Americans remained mostly in Europe and well away from Alicante. Robert Montgomery's daughter Isabella and son-in-law John Rogers spent most of their lives in Marseille, the one Mediterranean port that still remained viable for the American trade. Although Isabella was buried as a Protestant, they assimilated into the culture well enough that, when he died in 1856 at age 84, John H. Rogers was listed as "Jean Henri Rogers." Their children mostly married Catholic spouses and lived in Marseille or Naples.[5] John Montgomery's daughter Ana and son-in-law Obadiah Rich spent most of their lives in London after Rich was pushed out of Spain in 1828 due to slow business and conflicts with the royalist government. For a time, he split his year between London and Mahon where he served as US consul from 1834 to 1844, though he appears to have spent the majority of his time in London. After his death in 1850, his widow, Ana, left London for the United States, presumably to be with her daughter, Julia and son-in-law, Charles W. Morgan, a commodore in the US Navy who may have met the Riches while touring the

[4] Salvador García Castañada, "Acera de George Washington Montgomery, Washington Irving y Otros Hispanistas Norteamericanos de la Epoca Fernandina," in *Ideas en Sus Paisajes, Homenaje al Profesor Russell P. Sebold* (Universidad de Alicante, 1999) 195–201; "Biography of Mr. Montgomery," in G. W. Montgomery, *Bernardo del Carpio* (Boston: Brainard and Co., 1843); George Washington Montgomery to John Forsyth, Nov. 1, 1836, Puerto Rico Despatches; George Washington Montgomery, *Narrative of a Journey to Guatemala in Central America in 1838* (New York: Wiley and Putnam, 1839) 100–101.

[5] Information primarily based on family tree provided by R. L. Dunoyer and genealogy websites geni.com and genea.net. "Jean Henri Rogers Family Tree," https://gw.geneanet .org/pierfit?lang=en&n=rogers&oc=o&p=jean+henri.

Mediterranean. When both Julia and Charles died in 1853, she stayed on to care for their two sons.[6]

There is no evidence that any other lines of Montgomery descendants ever came to the United States or maintained American identities. Robert's daughter Louisa and her husband, Ricardo Ryan, moved to Madrid well before their father's death and apparently remained there. Another Montgomery daughter married the hated tax farmer, Henry O'Shea, and also resided in Madrid. At least one of their children married into the Spanish aristocracy and the family seems to have remained firmly Irish and Spanish with no visible sense of American identity, and little connection to the Mediterranean coast.[7]

The Simpson family broke even more cleanly with both the United States and the Mediterranean after the 1820s. After leaving Tangier for Lissa in 1822, John James Simpson's trail runs cold for a time. The 1834 Gibraltar census has him living there with a wife and daughter, but family documents have him dying in Greece in 1833, shortly before the census was published. He had at least one son, Juan Diego (i.e., John James), who had migrated to Brazil by 1850 before settling his family in Uruguay, where he died in 1868. Like the Montgomery descendants, the Simpsons intermarried with local Catholics in South America, though they proudly maintained elements of their British identity. Helen Simpson had emigrated to New Zealand in 1840 with her surgeon husband. There they became prominent settlers, always eager to discuss Gibraltar, Morocco, and the family and friends they had left behind in the Mediterranean world, but with no apparent interest in or connection to the United States. In 1854 Helen helped her younger brother, Thomas Sebright, and his family to emigrate to New Zealand. He had been "very unfortunate in business" and sadly died before the ship's departure, but

[6] Norman Paul Tucker, "Obadiah Rich, 1783–1850: Early American Hispanist," PhD dissertation (Harvard University, 1973) 74–88, 154–55; Thomas Harrison Montgomery, *A Genealogical History of the Family of Montgomery* (Philadelphia: Printed for Private Circulation, 1863) 149. Much information on his descendants is pieced together from various genealogy websites and therefore should be considered somewhat speculative. See www.richfamilyassociation.org; www.findagrave.com (Julia Morgan, Anna Montgomery Rich).

[7] It is unclear which daughter married into the O'Shea family, though I suspect it was one of John's. Genealogy websites list her as Isabella, and on one site her birthplace is listed as Baltimore, which, if true, would rule out Robert as her father. On the other hand, descendants requested a copy of Robert's consular appointment which might suggest more of a connection to him than to John. See Robert Montgomery File, Consules Estranjeros, Estados Unidos. See genea.net for Guillermo Henry O'Shea, who is also the man who requested Robert's consular appointment.

his wife and two children, Emily and Willie, arrived in New Zealand the following year. They appear to have settled there permanently, and the daughter married a local man named Towgood.[8]

As for the Appletons, this most American family became the least American in just one generation. In addition to his secret marriage and daughter, Appleton himself had converted to Catholicism by the time he wrote his will in 1837, and this document explicitly requested that he be buried as a Catholic. His daughter Minerva remained alive in Livorno until at least 1880. She married into an aristocratic local family and had three sons and a daughter. The name of one, Amerigo Poggesi, gave a nod to his American heritage in perhaps the most Italian way possible, but there is no evidence that any family members ever returned to America, and, in fact, there are still Poggesis, including at least one Amerigo, in Livorno today. Appleton's nephew, John James Appleton, who probably did know of his uncle's secret family, remained in the service of the State Department for many years, posting briefly in Brazil as well as Madrid and Stockholm. He died at the family estate in France in 1864. His daughter married the mayor of Rennes, suggesting she, too, converted to Catholicism, and there is no evidence that any of his descendants returned to the United States.[9]

***

The choices made by these individuals to leave the Mediterranean coast reflected a larger trend. By the 1830s, the Mediterranean was clearly becoming peripheral to the State Department. In 1830, the department asked Daniel Strobel, former consul to Bordeaux and Nantes to report on possible changes to the consular system. He suggested a completely

---

[8] Rootschat.com; Helen Ann Wilson to Donald Maclean, May 1, 1854; May 19, 1854; June 13, 1854; Aug. 31, 1856; Sept. 26, 1857; Sept. 2, [1854 or 1855]; n.d. [1854]; n.d., [1854 or 1855], all in McLean Letters; List of Inhabitants 1834, 1868, Gibraltar Inhabitants 1704–1914. I am grateful to Diego Hernandez of Bethesda, MD for providing me with genealogical information on John James Simpson's descendants. His information lists only one son, Juan Diego, who was born in 1816 and died in Uruguay in 1868. Helen Simpson, in a letter dated May 19, 1854, refers to a son of John James who was 34 years old at the time and considering emigrating to New Zealand. I am assuming this is also Juan Diego. However, the family documents date his birth to approximately 1816 (38 years old) which leaves open the possibility of a second son.

[9] Maria Argiero and Algerina Neri, *Bostoniani a Livorno: il Console Thomas Appleton e I suoi conterranei* (Pisa University Press, 2012) 53–55; "John James Appleton," www.history.state.gov; John James Appleton obituary, *Gold Hill Daily News*, May 6, 1864, www.chroniclingamerica.loc.gov.

overhauled, smaller consular network that would eliminate unnecessary posts and thereby allow the reduced number of consuls to be salaried. He recommended that the number of consuls in Europe be reduced to twelve, with only three in Mediterranean ports (Marseille, Cádiz, and either Alicante or Barcelona). This proposal, though never implemented, suggested a marked decline in the importance of the Mediterranean considering that one in three of all US consular positions in the 1790s had been Mediterranean ports while Strobel dropped that ratio in Europe alone to one in four.[10]

When Congress finally reformed the consular service in 1856, the shift away from the Mediterranean was evident. Only 14 percent (16 of 116) of the revised list of consular posts were in the Mediterranean. Many formerly important Mediterranean region posts such as Alicante, Algiers, and Lisbon were completely eliminated. Salaries in the Mediterranean were among the lowest anywhere, further reflecting the lack of importance. Since consuls were now forbidden to engage in trade, they would not be able to augment these salaries. Formerly important Mediterranean ports including Cádiz, Livorno, Genoa, and Messina only paid $1,500 a year, less than Simpson made in Tangier sixty years earlier. Even Marseille paid only $2,500; and the Barbary State positions, $3,000. By contrast, Le Havre, on the Channel coast, paid $6,000, Liverpool and London paid $7,500, and formerly obscure ports such as Melbourne, Australia and Hong Kong paid, respectively, $4,000 and $3,500. Clearly, staffing consular positions in the Mediterranean was no longer a high priority.[11]

On the other hand, in Latin America, the trajectory was in the opposite direction. During the two Washington administrations, there were only nine American consulates in Latin America and the Caribbean, and only one of these (Demerara) was on the mainland.[12] By contrast there were seventeen Mediterranean consulates at that time. By 1856 the proportion had reversed, with twenty-seven Latin American/Caribbean consulates

[10] "Mr. Strobel's Report to the Secretary of State Relative to Consular Fees etc. etc.," in *Public Documents Printed by Order of the United States* (Washington DC: Duff Green, 1831) II: 4–13.

[11] "An Act to Regulate the Diplomatic and Consular Systems of the United States," 34th Congress Sess. I, Chap. 127 (Aug. 18, 1856). High salaries might also reflect the expense of living in certain distant ports, such as Melbourne, but the relatively higher salaries in Latin American ports discussed below could not reflect distance or high expenses. So, while higher salaries should not be seen as correlating perfectly with higher importance, it nevertheless seems evident that relatively inferior Mediterranean salaries reflect a relative drop in importance of that region.

[12] The others were Hispaniola, St. Eustasius, Santa Cruz, Falmouth, Cape François, Curaçao, Martinique, and Santa Cruz.

(23 percent of the total) and sixteen in the Mediterranean (14 percent of the total). Furthermore, the Latin American and Caribbean consulates paid far more than those in the Mediterranean, with nine paying more than $2,000 per year, including $4,000 for St. Thomas and $3,500 each for Panama and Callao. By contrast, the only Mediterranean ports paying more than $2,000 were the three Barbary consulates ($3,000 each) and Marseille ($2,500). These relatively high salaries and numerous consulates reflected the increasing importance of an independent Latin America free of the old Spanish trade monopolies. American exports to the region nearly doubled between 1816 and 1836, until they become roughly one-third of all US exports by the 1830s.[13]

The Montgomerys, James Simpson, and John James Appleton were not the only members of the American community in the Mediterranean looking for new opportunities in Latin America. Thomas Appleton himself recognized the trend when he wrote to William Shaler in 1820 about mutual acquaintances leaving for the Americas. In a single paragraph, he mentioned his nephew's relocation to "Rio Genaro," John Murray Forbes's appointment as chargé d'affaires in Buenos Aires and "your brother Sec'y Todd to the Venezuela." Forbes was a particularly ambitious merchant and consul to Hamburg from a prominent family who had long angled for a lucrative Mediterranean consulship. Todd most likely was Captain Robert Todd who later contracted with the Venezuelan government to run a mail service in the region.[14]

Other Americans followed, including Shaler himself, who left Algiers the next year and would soon relocate to the lucrative consulship in Havana. John Martin Baker, who wrote an important commercial manual on the Mediterranean based on his experience as consul to Minorca and Tarragona, Spain, wrote a similar manual for Brazil after being appointed consul to Rio de Janeiro in 1832. Charles Douglas of Alabama was appointed consul at Barcelona, but before he could head out, he received an appointment to Guazacualco, Mexico, which he took instead, a choice that no sane person would have made a decade or two earlier when Barcelona was a highly prized position. No doubt, many less prominent Americans – translators, commercial agents, secretaries, ship captains,

---

[13] "Act to Regulate the Diplomatic and Consular Systems of the US"; Lindsay Schakenbach Regele, *Manufacturing Advantage: War, the State, and the Origins of American Industry, 1776–1848* (Baltimore: Johns Hopkins University Press, 2019) 113.

[14] Thomas Appleton to William Shaler, Sept. 27, 1820, Shaler Papers; www.mostlyclassics .net/philatelic/StThomasEtcShipLocalStamps.pdf.

clerks, and others – made similar decisions at this time to leave the Mediterranean for Latin America and the Caribbean.[15]

In a sense, these New World consulships can be viewed as a continuation of their Old World predecessors. With so many of the same people as in the Mediterranean, the broader commercial networks would have had many familiar faces as well. Since consular posts remained unpaid until the 1850s, they would have continued to be attractive to ambitious merchants looking to set up shop with some official recognition. Certainly, that was the case for Robert Montgomery, hoping to move his business to Santa Marta. Similarly, in 1830, Thomas F. Knox of Fredericksburg, Virginia requested appointment to the consulship at Angostura, Colombia, where he was "making arrangements to establish himself" as a merchant. Following in the tradition of earlier Mediterranean merchants, Abraham Smith of New York had worked as a merchant and assistant to the American consul in Pará, Brazil for four years before requesting the consular post in 1830 when his predecessor resigned. Like many earlier applicants he emphasized he was "well versed in the language and customs" of the region.[16]

Yet, increasingly over time the American consular service in Latin America represented, and to an extent shaped, a very different community than in the Mediterranean. Particularly in the areas closest to the United States, consuls served as the entering wedge for an advancing cotton kingdom rather than as representatives of long-distance traders. Unlike in the Mediterranean, the vast majority of consular appointees to Latin America (94 percent) came directly from the United States. And in Mexico and the Louisiana territories – the region in the immediate path of cotton kingdom expansion – close to half were from slave states, many from the old Southwest including three from Kentucky, three from Missouri, and one each from Louisiana, Tennessee, and Mississippi. By contrast, those Americans appointed to the Mediterranean came almost exclusively from eastern ports.[17]

Appointees to Mexico, especially, appear to have been seeking sanctuary from debt and attempting to expand the footprint of the cotton kingdom. For example, General James Davis, born in Virginia in 1790, served in the War of 1812 and eventually moved to Alabama. In 1830 he asked to be appointed to a consulate in Texas, a Mexican province

[15] List of US Consular Officers; John M. Baker, *A View of the Commerce between the United Sates and Rio de Janeiro, Brazil* (DC: Democratic Review, 1838); John M. Baker, *A View of the Commerce of the Mediterranean* (Washington DC: Davis and Force, 1819).
[16] Files of Thomas F. Knox and Abraham R. Smith, Jackson Recs.
[17] Data compiled from Consular appointments.

notorious as a refuge for bankrupt cotton planters seeking to renege on their debts. He landed the consulate in Santa Fe and eventually became a leading Texas planter and political leader in the Republic and state of Texas. Similarly, Colonel Joseph Washington Wallace of Port Gibson, Mississippi, requested the Chihuahua, Mexico consulate, seeking, as one supporter wrote, to better "his situation and circumstances," suggesting he may have been hard hit by the fluctuations in the cotton market in the late 1820s. A Philadelphia native who served in the Seminole War, he was long on the front lines of southwestern expansion. Likewise, Missourian John Ward sought to relocate as consul to Chihuahua in 1829. Even his supporters alluded to "proceedings against him" and conceded that he had gambled (as one supporter noted, "who has not?"), all of which hinted that he, like others, was fleeing from debts being called in due to overextension in the cotton business.[18]

Given their origins and intentions, it is not surprising that these consuls emphasized territorial citizenship far more than the more cosmopolitan notion of citizenship as affinity for American interests and ideals so often held by Mediterranean consuls. With the great majority of Latin American consuls coming directly from the United States, American citizenship was generally assumed and therefore rarely an issue. The case of Sidney Mason, consul to San Juan, Puerto Rico was an exception that proved the rule. A Massachusetts native from an old Puritan family, no one questioned whether he had been a citizen. But a number of his critics claimed that during his long residence at Puerto Rico he had become a Spanish citizen, thereby disqualifying himself for the American consulship. Others argued that it was required that all foreigners, and particularly merchants doing business in Puerto Rico "take certain oaths to be faithful to the country during their residence." At least one other critic argued that the problem was less one of citizenship than that no actively trading merchant could represent the United States at that port without engaging in conflicts of interest. In all, the animus against noncitizens and merchants seems much stronger here than it had been in the Mediterranean, most likely because,

---

[18] Files for James Davis, Joseph Washington Wallace, and James Ward in Jackson Recs. "James Davis" and "Joseph Worthington Elliot Wallace" in Texas State Historical Association Handbook of Texas, www.tshaonline.org; "Joseph Worthington Elliot Wallace" in "Texas State Cemetery," www.cemetery.tspb.texas.gov. Note that Wallace was often referred to as Joseph Worthington rather than Joseph Washington. On cotton fluctuations, and particularly the 1825–26 crash and uncertainty of the late 1820s, see Calvin Schermerhorn, *The Business of Slavery and the Rise of American Capitalism, 1815–1860* (New Haven: Yale University Press, 2015) 95–102.

with so many nonmerchant US citizens nearby, it was less necessary and less customary to rely on noncitizen merchants for consular positions.[19]

The 1830s was also a period during which political allegiance became far more important than it had been a generation earlier. Now fealty to Andrew Jackson became more important than citizenship or faith in American ideals. Here, too, Mason came under suspicion, with one critic complaining, "He is strongly opposed to the present administration . . . ." Similarly, a supporter of Silas Everett for consul to Lima praised him as "a native American and one of the most [?] friends of Gen. Jackson during the last election for president." Opponents of John Jackson, consul to Martinique, complained that "during the canvas he was a most strident opposer of General Jackson's election" and that his brother-in-law was a "violent Adams man." Supporters of Abraham Smith for Pará, Brazil, noted that his father was "long an active and influential person in the ranks of the Republican Party." All of the politicking was a product of change over time as well as the shift to Latin America, reflecting the increasing importance of patronage during the Jacksonian era. Whatever the cause, though, it made consular life in Latin America in the 1830s much more akin to a patronage position than it had been in the Mediterranean in earlier decades.[20]

By the 1830s, some Latin American consuls, particularly in South America, were serving as the vanguard of what one historian has termed "industrial manifest destiny." As American manufacturing began to grow, a rising class of industrial capitalists began to look to South America as a new market for their products. New England textile producers were particularly aggressive in this regard, and they began to look at American consuls as akin to agents for their corporations. John Murray Forbes and Thomas Lloyd Halsey in Argentina, and William Tudor in Peru had particularly close relations to these firms. Some of their activities would have been familiar to their predecessors. They pushed for tariffs that would be favorable to American textiles, much as Montgomery had sought to reduce the Spanish fish tariff. But, unlike Montgomery, these consuls also acted as business agents on the payroll of New England textile firms. Tudor, in particular, worked tirelessly to promote sales of textiles produced by the Boston Manufacturing Company in Peru and to lobby for trade policies that would specifically favor that company.[21] Similarly, Silas

[19] Sidney Mason File, Jackson Recs; "Mason, Henry" Fitz Henry Lane Online (Cape Ann Museum) www.fitzhenrylaneonline.org.
[20] Sidney Mason, John Jackson, and Abraham Smith files, all in Jackson Recs.
[21] Schakenbach Regele, *Manufacturing Advantage*, 123–30.

Everett, consul to Panama, was selected specifically to act as the agent to an American company. Peter E. Burrows of New York wrote to Daniel Swartwout, the influential Collector of the Port, that he needed someone on the ground in Panama to assist with his proposed steamship line from New York to Lima and Bogota. "I must have an agent in Panama, and this agent I wish to be the United States consul," he insisted, explaining that, since the steamships would benefit the American trade, appointing Everett would be an easy, inexpensive way for the US government to support the endeavor. Swartwout agreed, writing to the president that Burrows "knows that his commercial agent, if clothed with consular dignity and authority, will be more respected in that country particularly than if he went there as a mere merchant." This argument succeeded, and Everett received the appointment.[22]

Thus, while the three consuls – Simpson, Montgomery, and Appleton – would have recognized the basic structure of the Latin American consular service and even recognized many of the names of Americans within it, ultimately they would have found much that was unfamiliar there. In the Mediterranean consuls represented a second- or third-rate power interacting with equally powerful or more powerful peers. There, the focus was primarily on keeping commerce moving unencumbered, and, only secondarily, negotiating the best terms for US shippers. It was a world in which a certain cosmopolitan ability to work with others from varying cultures was mandatory. Often citizenship was less important than affinity and ability. By contrast, Americans representing their country in Latin America were becoming functionaries within a government that was beginning to look very similar to other nineteenth-century imperial powers. They provided high-profit manufactured goods in exchange for raw materials, built transportation networks to facilitate trade, and, at least in the regions closer to the United States, worked to facilitate territorial domination and, finally, began to rely on threats of military coercion to force other government to comply with their demands.[23] This was a system of territorial imperialism and industrial capitalism that went far beyond the merchant capitalism of the cosmopolitan trading nation the three consuls helped to build within the Mediterranean, and it represented a fundamental change in the nature of the consular system and in American outlook generally.

---

[22] Peter E. Burrows to Daniel Swartwout Collector of the Port of NY, Aug. 14, 1829, Jackson Recs.
[23] On military coercion see Schakenbake-Regele, *Manufacturing* Advantage, 130–133.

Glossary

Adams Recs. National Archives and Records Administration, College Park, MD, General Records of the Department of State (Record Group 59), Letters of Application and Recommendation during the Administration of Johns Adams, 1797–1801, M406

Alicante Despatches National Archives and Records Administration, College Park, MD, General Records of the Department of State (Record Group 59), Despatches from US Consuls in Alicante, Spain, T357

Amsterdam Despatches National Archives and Records Administration, College Park, MD, General Records of the Department of State (Record Group 59), Despatches from US Consuls in Amsterdam, The Netherlands, M446.

Bristol Despatches National Archives and Records Administration, College Park, MD, General Records of the Department of State (Record Group 59), Despatches from US Consuls in Bristol, Great Britain, T185

B. & I. Records of Brown and Ives, 1796–1814, The John Carter Brown Library, Providence, RI

Consules Estranjeros, Estados Unidos Consules Estranjeros, Estados Unidos, Expedientes de la Junta de Dependencia de Extranjeros, Archivo Nacionales, Madrid

Despatches from US Ministers to Portugal Despatches from US Ministers to Portugal 1790–1906, M43 RG59, National Archives and Records Administration, College Park, MD

Humphreys-Marvin-Olmsted Yale University Sterling Memorial Library, New Haven, CT, Humphreys-Marvin-Olmsted Collection

Nantes Despatches National Archives and Records Administration, College Park, MD, General Records of the Department of State (Record Group 59), US Consuls in Nantes, France, T223

Eaton Papers Huntington Museum and Library, San Marino, CA, William Eaton Papers

Gibraltar Despatches National Archives and Records Administration, College Park, MD, General Records of the Department of State (Record Group 59), Despatches from US Consuls in Gibraltar, Spain, T206

Gibraltar Inhabitants, 1704–1914 Gibraltar National Archives, Gibraltar Inhabitants, 1704–1914, www.nationalarchives.gi/gna/Inha vitants.aspx

GL Gilder Lehrman Institute, New York: Appleton, Thomas, *Five Manuscript Letterbooks Compiled while Consul in Livorno, Italy*

Humphreys-Marvin-Olmsted Collection Yale University Sterling Memorial Library, New Haven, CT, Humphreys-Marvin-Olmsted Collection

Jackson Recs. National Archives and Records Administration, College Park, MD, General Records of the Department of State (Record Group 59), Letters of Application and Recommendation during the Administration of Andrew Jackson, 1829–37, M639

Jefferson Papers https://founders.archives.gov/?q=%20Author%3A%22 Jefferson%2C%20Thomas%22&s=1111211111&r=1

Jefferson Recs. National Archives and Records Administration, College Park, MD, General Records of the Department of State (Record Group 59), Letters of Application and Recommendation during the Administration of Thomas Jefferson, 1801–9, M418

Konsulatarkiv National Archives of Sweden, Arninge, Konsulatarkiv Marocko, Vol. 12: Konsulatets Journal, 1801–11

Leghorn Despatches National Archives and Records Administration, College Park, MD, General Records of the Department of State (Record Group 59), Despatches from US Consuls in Leghorn, Italy, T214

Lewis M. O'Brien File Consules Estranjeros, Estados Unidos, Expedientes de la Junta de Dependencia de Extranjeros, Archivo Nacionales, Madrid

McLean Letters National Library of New Zealand, Alexander Turnbull Collections McLean Papers, Inward Letters—Helen Ann Wilson

NARA National Archives and Records Administration, College Park, MD

New Harmony Working Men's Institute, New Harmony, IN (Archives Online), New Harmony Manuscripts, 1812–71

PARES Portal de Archivos Españoles, the online portal for the Archivos Nacionales, Madrid

PN Protocolo de Notariales Públicas, Provincial Archives, Alicante, Spain

Puerto Rico Despatches National Archives and Records Administration, College Park, MD, General Records of the Department of State (Record Group 59), Despatches from US Consuls in Puerto Rico, M76

Register of Events Records of the Foreign Service Posts of the Department of State (Record Group 84), "Register of Events (misc.) August 2, 1800 to Dec. 12, 1804," Leghorn Italy, Vol. 007

Rogers-Bridges Family Collection Arkansas History Commission, Little Rock, AR, Rogers-Bridges Family Collection (microfilm)

Shaler Papers Historical Society of Pennsylvania, Philadelphia, PA, William Shaler Papers

Simpson Letterbook Library of Congress, Washington DC, James Simpson Letterbook, 1793–97, Miscellaneous Manuscripts Collection

Simpson NARA James Simpson Letterbook, Consular Posts, Gibraltar, Spain, Vol. 027, RG84, Records of Foreign Service Posts, NARA

Tangier Despatches National Archives and Records Administration, College Park, MD, General Records of the Department of State (Record Group 59), Despatches from US Consuls in Tangier, Morocco, T61

Washington Papers Washington, George Papers, Series 7, Applications for Office, 1789–96, Library of Congress (www.loc.gov)

Washington Recs. Washington, George Papers, Series 7, Applications for Office, 1789–96, Library of Congress (www.loc.gov)

Bibliography

PRIMARY SOURCES

NOTE: When directly quoting despatches and other primary sources throughout this book I have, with few exceptions, modernized spelling and corrected spelling errors without use of *sic*.

Archival Materials

Archivo Nacionales, Madrid, Spain
    Expedientes de la Junta de Dependencia de Extranjeros
Arkansas History Commission, Little Rock, AR
    Rogers-Bridges Family Collection (microfilm)
Garrison Library, Gibraltar
    Gibraltar Chronicle
Gibraltar National Archives
    Consular Correspondence, 1780–1830
    Gibraltar Inhabitants, 1704–1914, www.nationalarchives.gi/gna/Inhavitants
        .aspx
    Governor's Letter Book, 1795–1801
Gilder Lehrman Institute, New York, NY
    Appleton, Thomas, *Five Manuscript Letterbooks Compiled while Consul in
        Livorno, Italy*
Historical Society of Pennsylvania, Philadelphia, PA
    William Shaler Papers
Huntington Museum and Library, San Marino, CA
    William Eaton Papers
John Carter Brown Library, Providence, RI

The Records of Brown and Ives, 1796–1814
Library of Congress, Washington DC
    James Simpson Letterbook, 1793–97, Miscellaneous Manuscripts Collection
Massachusetts Historical Society, Boston, MA
    Caleb Davis Papers
    Ralph Bennet Forbes Correspondence
    William Jarvis Papers
Municipal Archive, Alicante, Spain
    Giradora Libro 2
    Mesadas de Sanidad, Arm. 14
    Matriculó de Extranjeros, Legajo 96, Numero 94
National Archives and Records Administration (NARA), College Park, MD
General Records of the Department of State (Record Group 59)
    Despatches from US Consuls in Alicante, Spain, T357
    Despatches from US Consuls in Gibraltar, Spain, T206
    Despatches from US Consuls in Leghorn, Italy, T214
    Despatches from US Consuls in Tangier, Morocco, T61
    Despatches from US Consuls in Puerto Rico, M76
    Despatches of US Ministers to Portugal, M43
    Letters of Application and Recommendation during the Administration of
        Johns Adams, 1797–1801, M406
    Letters of Application and Recommendation during the Administration of
        Thomas Jefferson, 1801–9, M418
    Letters of Application and Recommendation during the Administration of
        Andrew Jackson, 1829–37, M639
    List of US Consular Officers, 1789–1939, M587
Records of the Foreign Service Posts of the Department of State (Record
    Group 84)
    Gibraltar Spain [should be Tangier], Vol. 027
    "Register of Events (misc.) August 2, 1800 to Dec. 12, 1804," Leghorn Italy,
        Vol. 007
National Archives of Sweden, Arninge
    Konsulatarkiv Marocko, Vol. 12: Konsulatets Journal, 1801–11
National Library of New Zealand
    Alexander Turnbull Collections McLean Papers, Inward Letters—Helen Ann
        Wilson
New York Public Library, New York, NY
    Cathcart Family Papers
Phillips-Peabody-Essex Institute, Salem, MA
    [Henry Prince], Log, *Astrea*, 1798–99
Provincial Archives, Alicante, Spain
    Protocolo de Notariales Públicas
Working Men's Institute, New Harmony, IN (Archives Online)
    New Harmony Manuscripts, 1812–71
Yale University Sterling Memorial Library, New Haven, CT
    Humphreys-Marvin-Olmsted Collection

Published Materials

Documentary Collections

Adams, John Quincy, Digital Diary, www.Masshist.org

Doskey, John S., ed., *The European Journals of William Maclure* (Philadelphia: American Philosophical Society Press, 1988)

Founders Online https://founders.archives.gov

Jay, John Papers of, www.app.cc.columbia.edu

Labaree, Leonard W., ed., *The Papers of Benjamin Franklin* (New Haven: Yale University Press, 1960)

Taylor, C. James, ed., *Founding Families: Digital Editions of the Papers of the Winthrops and the Adamses* (Boston: Massachusetts Historical Society, 2007)

Trent, William P. and George S. Hellman, eds., *The Journals of Washington Irving (hitherto unpublished)* (Boston: The Bibliophile Society, 1919), www.loc.gov

Washington, George Papers, Series 7, Applications for Office, 1789–96, www.loc.gov/collections/george-washington-papers/?fa=partof%3Ageorge+washington+papers%3A+series+7%2C+applications+for+office%2C+1789-1796

Books

Almanack Mercantil o Guía de Comerciantes Para el ano de 1797 (Madrid: Ramón Ruiz, 1797); *de 1800* (Madrid: D. Joaquín Ibarra); *de 1802* (Madrid: Vega y Compañia); *de 1803* (Madrid: Calle de Capellanes); *de 1808* (Madrid: Vega y Compañia)

Baker, John M., *A View of the Commerce between the United Sates and Rio de Janeiro, Brazil* (Washington DC: Democratic Review, 1838)

Baker, John M., *A View of the Commerce of the Mediterranean* (Washington DC: Davis and Force, 1819)

Buffa, John, MD, *Travels Through the Empire of Morocco* (London: J. J. Stockdale, 1810)

Caillé, Jacques, *La Mission du Capitaine Burel au Maroc en 1808* (Paris: Arts et Métiers Graphiques, 1953)

Cochelet, Charles, *Narrative of the Shipwreck of the Sophia on the 30th of May, 1819 . . .* (London: Richard Phillips, 1822)

Curtis, James, *A Journal of Travels in Barbary, in the Year 1801* (London: T. N. Longman and O. Rees, 1803)

Fort, G., *Coos-Coo-Soo: Letters from Tangier, in Africa* (Philadelphia: J. S. M'Calla, 1859)

Henshaw, J. Sidney, *A Manual for United States Consuls* (New York: J. C. Riker, 1849)

Irving, Washington, *Voyages and Discoveries of the Companions of Columbus* (Philadelphia: Carey, Lea and Blanchard, 1835

Jackson, James Grey, *An Account of the Empire of Morocco and the District of Suse* (London: W. Bulmer and Co., 1809)

Lemprière, William, *A Tour from Gibraltar to Tangier …* (London: J. Walter 1793)

Longfellow, Samuel, ed., *Life of Henry Wadsworth Longfellow With Extracts from His Journal and Correspondence* (Boston: Houghton Mifflin, 1891)

Montgomery, G. W., *Bernardo del Carpio* (Boston: Brainard and Col, 1843)

Montgomery, George Washington, *Narrative of a Journey to Guatemala in Central America in 1838* (New York: Wiley and Putnam, 1839)

NA [Maria Wilson], *Spain and Barbary: Letters to a Younger Sister, during a visit to Gibraltar, Seville, Cadiz, Tangier etc. etc.*(London: John Hatchard and Son, 1837)

Noah, Mordecai Manuel, *Travels in England, France, Spain, and the Barbary States in the Years 1813–1814 and 15* (New York: Kirk and Mercein, 1819)

Paddock, Judah, *A Narrative of the Shipwreck of the Oswego* (London, 1818)

Pitkin, Timothy, *A Statistical View of the Commerce of the United States of America* (Hartford: Charles Hosmer, 1816)

Riley, James, *An Authentic Narrative of the Loss of the American Brig Commerce* (Hartford: James Riley, 1817)

Riley, James, *Sequel to Riley's Narrative* (Columbus: George Brewster, 1851)

Robbins, Archibald, *A Journal Concerning an Account of the Loss of the Brig Comerce* (Hartford, 1849)

SECONDARY SOURCES

Abun-Nasr, J. M., *A History of the Maghrib* (Cambridge University Press, 1971)

Appleton, W. S., *A Rough Sketch of the Appleton Genealogy* (Boston: TR Marvin and Co., 1873)

Argiero, Maria and Algerina Neri, *Bostoniani a Livorno: il Console Thomas Appleton e I suoi conterranei* (Pisa University Press, 2012)

Brown, James A. O. C., *Crossing the Strait: Morocco, Gibraltar and Great Britain in the 18th and 19th Centuries* (Leiden: Brill, 2012)

Carlin, Colin, *William Kirkpatrick of Malaga* (Glasgow: Colin Carlin, 2011)

Carrasco-Gonzalez, Guadalupe, "La Delegacion Consular de Los Estados Unidas en España: La Oficina Consular de Cádiz a Principio del Siglo XIX," https://rodin.uca.es/bitstream/handle/10498/16397/LA%20DELEGACION%20CONSULAR%20DE%20CADIZ%5B1%5D.pdf?sequence=2

Castañada, Salvador García, "Acerca de George Washington Montgomery, Washington Irving y Otres Hispanistas Norteamericanos de la Época Fernandinas," in *Ideas en sus parsajes Homenaje al Profesor Russell P. Sebold* (Universidad de Alicante, 1999), 195–201

Codignola, Luca, *Blurred Nationalities Across the Atlantic: Traders, Priests, and Their Kin Travelling between North America and the Italian Peninsula, 1763–1846* (University of Toronto Press, 2019)

Conroy-Krutz, Emily, *Christian Imperialism: Converting the World in the Early American Republic* (Ithaca: Cornell University Press, 2015)

El Mansour, Mohamed, *Morocco in the Reign of Mawlay Sulayman* (Outwell: MENAS Press, 1990)

Korner, Axel, *America in Italy: The United States in the Political Thought and Imagination of the Risorgimento, 1763–1865* (Princeton University Press, 2017)

Fehl, Philipp, "The Account Book of Thomas Appleton of Livorno: A Document in the History of American Art, 1802–1825," *Winterthur Portfolio* 9 (1974)

Field, James A., *America and the Mediterranean World, 1776–1882* (Princeton University Press, 1969)

Frost, Alan, *The Precarious Life of James Mario Matra* (Melbourne University Press, 1995)

Galani, Katerina, "The Napoleonic Wars and the Disruption of Shipping and Trade: British, Greek, and American Merchants in Livorno," *Historical Review* VII (2010)

Giménez López, Enrique, *Alicante en el Siglo XVIII: Economice de una Cuidad Portuaria en el antiguo régimen* (Valencia: Institución Alfonso el Magnánimo, 1981)

Goey, Ferry de, *Consuls and the Institutions of Global Capitalism, 1783–1914* (London: Taylor and Francis, 2014)

Goodin, Brett, *From Captives to Consuls: Three Sailors in Barbary and Their Self-Making across the Early American Republic, 1770–1840* (Baltimore: Johns Hopkins University Press, 2020)

Hedges, James B., *The Browns of Providence Plantation: The Nineteenth Century* (Providence: Brown University, 1968)

Heyrman, Christine Leigh, *American Apostles: When Evangelicals Entered the World of Islam* (New York: Hill and Wang, 2015)

Humphreys, F. L., *Life and Times of David Humphreys* (New York: Putnam, 1917)

Kilbride, Daniel, *Being American in Europe, 1750–1860* (Baltimore: Johns Hopkins University Press, 2013)

Jaksić, Iván, *The Hispanic World and American Intellectual Life, 1820–1880* (New York: Palgrave McMillan, 2007)

Kagan, Richard L., ed., *Spain in the United States: The Origins of Hispanism in the United States* (Urbana: University of Illinois Press, 2002)

Kagan, Richard L., *The Spanish Craze: America's Fascination with the Hispanic World* (Lincoln: University of Nebraska Press, 2019)

Keene, Charles A., "American Shipping and Trade, 1798–1820: The Evidence from Leghorn," *Journal of Economic History* 38 (Sept. 1978) 681–700

Kennedy, Charles Stuart, *The American Consul: A History of the United States Consular Service, 1776–1914* (New York: Greenwood Press, 1990)

Lambert, Frank, *The Barbary Wars: American Independence in the Atlantic World* (New York: Hill and Wang, 2005)

Lydon, James G., *Fish and Flour for Gold, 1600–1800: Southern Europe in the Colonial Balance of Payments* (Philadelphia: Library Company of Philadelphia e-publication, 2008).

Mackintosh, Will B., *Selling the Sights: The Invention of the Tourist in American Culture* (New York University Press, 2019)

Marzagalli, Silvia, James R. Sofka, and John J. McCusker, *Rough Waters: American Involvement with the Mediterranean in the Eighteenth and Nineteenth Centuries*, Research in Maritime History No. 44 (Newfoundland: International Maritime Economic History Association, 2010)

Montgomery, Thomas Harrison, *A Genealogical History of the Family of Montgomery* (Philadelphia: Printed for Private Circulation, 1863)

North, Douglass C., *The Economic Growth of the United States 1790–1860* (New York: Norton, 1966)

Novales, Alberto Gil, "The Spain William Maclure Knew," *Indiana Magazine of History* 94 (June 1998) 99–109

Parker, Richard B., *Uncle Sam in Barbary: A Diplomatic History* (Gainesville: University Press of Florida, 2004)

Perl-Rosenthal, Nathan, *Citizen Sailors: Becoming American in the Age of Revolution* (Cambridge: Harvard University Press, 2015)

Peskin, Lawrence, *Captives and Countrymen: Barbary Slavery and the American Public, 1785–1816* (Baltimore: Johns Hopkins University Press, 2009)

Pinedo, Emiliano Fernández de, Alberto Gil Novales, and Albert Dérozier, *Historia de España* (Barcelona: Editorial Labor, 1987)

Raffety, Matthew Taylor, *The Republic Afloat: Law, Honor, and Citizenship in Maritime America* (University of Chicago Press, 2013)

Regele, Lindsay Schakenbach, *Manufacturing Advantage: War, the State, and the Origins of American Industry, 1776–1848* (Johns Hopkins University Press, 2019)

Roberts, Priscilla H. and Richard S., *Thomas Barclay (1728–1793): Consul in France, Diplomat in Barbary* (Bethlehem, PA: Lehigh University Press, 2008)

Rosenstock, Morton, "The House of Bacri and Busnach: A Chapter from Algeria's Commercial History," *Jewish Social Studies* 14 (Oct. 1952)

Rouleau, Brian. *With Sails Whitening Every Sea: Mariners and the Making of an American Maritime Empire* (Ithaca: Cornell University Press, 2015)

Sexton, Jay, *The Monroe Doctrine: Empire and Nation in Nineteenth-Century America* (New York: Hill and Wang, 2012)

Tucker, Norman Paul, "Obadiah Rich, 1783–1850: Early American Hispanist," PhD dissertation (Harvard University, 1973)

Walther, Karine V., *Sacred Interests: The United States and the Islamic World, 1821–1921* (Chapel Hill: University of North Carolina Press, 2015)

Whelan, Bernadette, *American Government in Ireland, 1790–1913: A History of the US Consular Service* (Manchester University Press, 2010)

Index